Disaster Risk Reduction

Methods, Approaches and Practices

Series Editor

Rajib Shaw, Keio University, Shonan Fujisawa Campus, Fujisawa, Japan

Disaster risk reduction is a process that leads to the safety of communities and nations. After the 2005 World Conference on Disaster Reduction, held in Kobe, Japan, the Hyogo Framework for Action (HFA) was adopted as a framework for risk reduction. The academic research and higher education in disaster risk reduction has made, and continues to make, a gradual shift from pure basic research to applied, implementation-oriented research. More emphasis is being given to multi-stakeholder collaboration and multi-disciplinary research. Emerging university networks in Asia, Europe, Africa, and the Americas have urged process-oriented research in the disaster risk reduction field. With this in mind, this new series will promote the output of action research on disaster risk reduction, which will be useful for a wide range of stakeholders including academicians, professionals, practitioners, and students and researchers in related fields. The series will focus on emerging needs in the risk reduction field, starting from climate change adaptation, urban ecosystem, coastal risk reduction, education for sustainable development, community-based practices, risk communication, and human security, among other areas. Through academic review, this series will encourage young researchers and practitioners to analyze field practices and link them to theory and policies with logic, data, and evidence. In this way, the series will emphasize evidence-based risk reduction methods, approaches, and practices.

More information about this series at http://www.springer.com/series/11575

Mihoko Sakurai · Rajib Shaw
Editors

Emerging Technologies for Disaster Resilience

Practical Cases and Theories

Springer

Editors
Mihoko Sakurai
Center for Global Communications
International University of Japan
Minato-ku, Tokyo, Japan

Rajib Shaw
Graduate School of Media and Governance
Keio University
Shonan Fujisawa Campus
Fujisawa, Kanagawa, Japan

ISSN 2196-4106 ISSN 2196-4114 (electronic)
Disaster Risk Reduction
ISBN 978-981-16-0359-4 ISBN 978-981-16-0360-0 (eBook)
https://doi.org/10.1007/978-981-16-0360-0

This Springer imprint is published by the registered company Springer Nature Singapore Pte Ltd.
The registered company address is: 152 Beach Road, #21-01/04 Gateway East, Singapore 189721, Singapore

Preface

Technologies become an enabler of strong and resilient local communities. The rapid development of technology has influenced everyday practice and people's behavior towards disaster preparedness and response. The socio-technological perspective tells us the importance of deep understanding of technologies, as well as human systems, that would be a user of certain technologies or a recipient of information generated by new technologies. We notice that disaster resilience is enhanced by the advancement of technology, however, there exist challenges in its use and management by people. The correct comprehension of a whole ecosystem is necessary.

This book has 13 chapters, which deal with various aspects of disaster resilience and addresses different types of technologies and their management. The first section discusses specific use of emerging technologies, issues, and a future prospect. The second section focuses on communication and information management through the use of technologies and their impact on disaster resilience. The third section deals with technologies that support decision-making in a field.

Covering significant aspects of emerging technologies and disaster resilience, this book is intended for students, researchers, academia, policymakers, and development practitioners in the fields of disaster resilience and technology implementation, especially in the Asia-Pacific region. It will help to better understand the role of technology and its use in local communities under a severe disaster. We will be happy if the readers find this book useful and relevant.

Minato Ward, Japan — Mihoko Sakurai
Fujisawa City, Japan — Rajib Shaw

About This Book

Technological advances have helped to enhance disaster resilience through better risk reduction, response, mitigation, rehabilitation, and reconstruction. In former times, it was local and traditional knowledge that was mainly relied upon for disaster risk reduction. Much of this local knowledge is still valid in today's world, even though possibly in different forms and contexts, and local knowledge remains a shared part of life within the communities. In contrast, with the advent of science and technology, scientists and engineers have become owners of advanced technologies, which have contributed significantly to reducing disaster risks across the globe.

This book analyzes emerging technologies and their effects in enhancing disaster resilience. It also evaluates the gaps, challenges, capacities required, and the way forward for future disaster management. A wide variety of technologies are addressed, focusing specifically on new technologies such as cyber physical systems, geotechnology, drone, and virtual reality (VR)/augmented reality (AR). Other sets of emerging advanced technologies including an early warning system and a decision support system are also reported on. Moreover, the book provides a variety of discussions regarding information management, communication, and community resilience at the time of a disaster. This book's coverage of different aspects of new technologies makes it a valuable resource for students, researchers, academics, policymakers, and development practitioners.

Contents

Editors and Contributors

About the Editors

Mihoko Sakurai is an associate professor at the International University of Japan, Center for Global Communications. Her academic background is in information systems and policy design. She has studied effective ways of using information communication technology in Japan's municipal governments. After the devastating Great East Japan Earthquake in 2011, she conducted field research and designed information systems to enhance the handling of future and unexpected disasters, especially for municipalities that have to deliver disaster relief to their residents. Her work related to the 2011 earthquake won the Best Paper Award at the International Telecommunication Union (ITU) Kaleidoscope Conference (2013) and the Hawaii International Conference on System Sciences (HICSS) (2016). Currently she is organising a research project discussing ICT use, disaster management and resilience with Japanese local councils and private enterprises. Her work has been published in the *International Journal of Disaster Risk Reduction, European Journal of Information Systems, IEEE Communications Magazine, International Journal of Information Systems for Crisis Response and Management, Communications of the Association for Information Systems, Sustainable Cities and Society* and in the proceedings of the leading international conferences.

Rajib Shaw is a professor in the Graduate School of Media and Governance of Keio University, Japan. He is also a senior fellow of the Institute of Global Environmental Strategies (IGES) Japan, and the chairperson of the Sustainable Environment and Ecological Development Society (SEEDS) Asia and the Church World Service (CWS) Japan, two Japanese NGOs. He is the co-founder of a Delhi-based social entrepreneur startup, Resilience Innovation Knowledge Academy (RIKA). Earlier, he was the executive director of Integrated Research on Disaster Risk (IRDR) and was a professor at Kyoto University. His expertise includes disaster governance, community-based disaster risk management, climate change adaptation, urban risk management, and disaster and environmental education. Professor Shaw is the chair of the United Nations Science Technology Advisory Group (STAG) for disaster risk reduction and the co-chair of the Asia Science Technology Academic Advisory Group (ASTAAG). He is also the coordinating lead author for the Asia chapter of IPCC's 6th Assessment Report. He is the editor-in-chief of the Elsevier journal *Progress in Disaster Science* and the series editor of the Springer book series on disaster risk reduction. Prof. Shaw has published more than 45 books and over 300 academic papers and book chapters.

Contributors

Ranit Chatterjee Resilience Innovation Knowledge Academy, New Delhi, India; Kyoto University, Kyoto, Japan

Ambika Dabral Resilience Innovation Knowledge Academy, New Delhi, India

Kashi Nath Datta National Institute of Technology Durgapur, Durgapur, India

Amjad Fayoumi Management Science, Lancaster University Management School, Lancaster, UK

Ryutaro Fujimoto Ad-sol Nissin Corporation, Osaka, Japan

Tomoyuki Furutani Faculty of Policy Management, Keio University, Tokyo, Japan

Tomoki Itamiya Department of Dental Education, School of Dentistry, Kanagawa Dental University, Yokosuka, Japan

Makoto Kitsuya Iwate Prefectural University, Iwate, Japan

Terukazu Makihara Ad-sol Nissin Corporation, Osaka, Japan

Andreas Mauthe University of Koblenz and Landau, Mainz, Germany

Masaki Minami Graduate School of Media and Governance, Keio University, Tokyo, Japan

Tamal Mondal National Institute of Technology Durgapur, Durgapur, India

Yoshifumi Murakami Ad-sol Nissin Corporation, Osaka, Japan

Yuko Murayama Institute for Mathematics and Computer Science, Tsuda University, Tokyo, Japan

Shun Nakayama Graduate School of Media and Governance, Keio University, Tokyo, Japan

Subrata Nandi National Institute of Technology Durgapur, Durgapur, India

Yamaimaiti Nizhamudong Challenge Co. Ltd., Sayama, Japan

Partha Sarathi Paul National Institute of Technology Durgapur, Durgapur, India

Prithviraj Pramanik National Institute of Technology Durgapur, Durgapur, India

Swaraj Pramanik National Institute of Technology Durgapur, Durgapur, India

Jaziar Radianti Centre for Integrated Emergency Management, Department of Information Systems, University of Agder, Kristiansand, Norway

Sujoy Saha National Institute of Technology Durgapur, Durgapur, India

Mihoko Sakurai Center for Global Communications, International University of Japan, Tokyo, Japan

Jun Sasaki Iwate Prefectural University, Iwate, Japan

Kazuo Sasaki Challenge Co. Ltd., Sayama, Japan

Rajib Shaw Graduate School of Media and Governance, Keio University, Fujisawa, Japan;
Resilience Innovation Knowledge Academy, New Delhi, India

Juliana Sutanto Management Science, Lancaster University Management School, Lancaster, UK

Yuko Tanaka Graduate School of Engineering, Nagoya Institute of Technology, Nagoya, Aichi, Japan

Yuichiro Usuda National Research Institute for Earth Science and Disaster Resilience, Tsukuba, Japan

Wanglin Yan Faculty of Environment and Information Studies, Keio University, Tokyo, Japan

Akinobu Yasuda Ad-sol Nissin Corporation, Osaka, Japan

Part I
Application of Emerging Technologies in Disaster Resilience

Chapter 1
Existing, New and Emerging Technologies for Disaster Resilience

Mihoko Sakurai and Rajib Shaw

Abstract Technologies have evolved over years in terms of their contents, usage, target groups and innovations. Over the last 30 years, different technologies at different phases of the disaster have been evolved, used and evaluated. We argue here that the technology includes both product and process and emphasizes the importance of the definition of (Kameda, Disaster management: global challenges and local solutions, University Press, Chennai, India, 2009). Technology needs an enabling environment, which needs governance support with techno-legal provision. There exist global and national mechanisms for enhancing governance. However, the key need is at the local level, where additional initiatives/efforts are required for technology-based decision-making, and as well as local ecosystem to promote technology and innovation in DRR. Innovation in technology development needs youth involvement, where multi-stakeholders, multi-disciplinary youth groups can interact, co-design and make co-delivery of the new innovations.

Keywords Innovation · Process and product technologies · New and emerging technologies · Co-design and co-delivery · Governance support

1.1 Introduction

Technologies have always been there for disaster risk reduction (DRR) and disaster resilience. However, its form, application, user groups have evolved over time. As we know that as of 2020, disaster risk reduction as a subject is now 30 years old (Shaw 2020), starting from 1990 as the United Nations International Decade for Natural Disaster Reduction (UN IDNDR). These 30 years have seen many major disasters in different parts of the world, and each disaster brought some unique lessons

M. Sakurai (✉)
Center for Global Communications, International University of Japan, Tokyo, Japan
e-mail: msakurai@glocom.ac.jp

R. Shaw
Graduate School of Media and Governance, Keio University, Fujisawa, Japan

M. Sakurai and R. Shaw (eds.), *Emerging Technologies for Disaster Resilience*, Disaster Risk Reduction,
https://doi.org/10.1007/978-981-16-0360-0_1

and new technologies emerged, applied and tested. The evolution of the terminologies is also important. Earlier, it was hazard reduction, which gradually changed to disaster reduction, risk reduction and resilience building. Similarly, natural disaster has been changed to natural hazards, cascading hazards and complex emergencies. At the global level, science technology advisory committee has played certain roles in advancing science and technology application at the national level. However, more important roles have been found by the national level science technology committee, which formulated strategies, policies and frameworks for applying science and technology in disaster risk reduction. The evolution from engineering-based solutions to social engineering multi-disciplinary solutions has also been prominent in recent years. Capacities to apply technological solutions at local levels have also been emphasized in different global, national and local forums. Thus, the traditional custodians of technologies have also evolved from scientists/academics to private sectors and non-government organizations.

The year 2020 was supposed to be a super year as the 5 years from major global frameworks: SDGs (sustainable development goals), Sendai Framework and Paris Agreement (Djlante et al. 2020). However, the global pandemic in terms of biological hazards has influenced the technological pathways for the last several months. Cascading disasters (natural hazards like flood or typhoon in the time of pandemic) have also posed new challenges of using technologies and prompted new innovations in linking different technologies.

This chapter provides a categorization of DRR-related technologies and argues that an enabling environment with a proper governance mechanism helps in generating new technologies as well as applying the existing technologies. The chapter also provides a brief background on the innovation of DRR technologies. Finally, the summaries of other chapters of the book are provided.

1.2 Categorization of Technologies for DRR

It is always challenging to categorize DRR-related technologies. There is hardly any specific definition or categorization. Kameda (2009) argued that "conventionally, technology meant just engineering products. But when we consider implementation strategies, technologies should involve not only products but processes as well. This requires innovation to move from 'product-focused research' to 'process-oriented' or 'product-process-linked research'. He also mentioned that there needs to be a paradigm shift in disaster risk reduction research and development.

Kameda (2009) argued for three types of technologies:

- Implementation-oriented technology (IOT): This relates to the outcomes that are practiced under clear implementation strategies.
- Process technology (PT): This contains knowhow for implementation and practice, capacity building and social development for knowledge ownership.

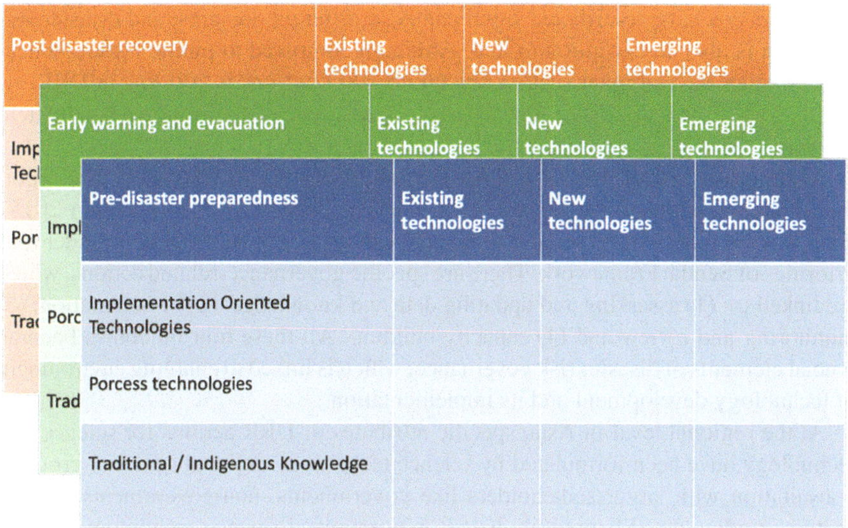

Fig. 1.1 Suggested matrix to categorize technologies

- Transferable indigenous knowledge (TIK): This refers to traditional art of disaster reduction that is indigenous to specific regions having potential to be applied to other.

The research program conducted by his group also developed a catalog for DRR technologies called DRH (Disaster Reduction Hyperbase), where the above three categorizations were used.

Over last decade, there has been tremendous progress in the technology domain, and there are many new and emerging technologies. Thus, we can possibly categorize the technologies in the following matrix (Fig. 1.1) with three types of technologies mentioned by Kameda (2009) and existing, new and emerging technologies. Needless to say that traditional knowledge of TIK would be under existing technologies; however, if this can be combined with new technologies, can also be considered as emerging technologies. This matrix can be used for disaster preparedness, early warning and evacuation as well as post-disaster recovery, thus can cover the full disaster cycle.

1.3 Enabling Environment

While technology generation is very important, it is equally important to develop an enabling ecosystem for technology and innovation. There, governance plays an important role, which needs resource support, legal support, capacities/human resource support, etc. for the generation and management of new technologies. These days, start-ups have contributed significantly in different domains, and disaster risk reduction is also no exception to that. Although compared to public health, education, or other development sectors, the number of start-ups is still low in DRR, its enabling environment or start-up ecosystem needs to be more promoted for the field of DRR.

At the global level, in 2019, a Science and Technology Roadmap to Support the Implementation of the Sendai Framework for Disaster Risk Reduction 2015–2030 was evolved, which includes four expected outcomes and 58 actions under four Priorities of Sendai Framework. There are specific governance-related actions, which are linked to: (1) assessing and updating data and knowledge, (2) dissemination, (3) monitoring and review and (4) capacity building. All these four outcomes become crucial elements of disaster risk governance, which is linked to enabling environment of technology development and its implementation.

At the regional level in Asia, specific attributes of DRR actions for science and technology have been formulated by science technology regional advisory group in consultation with larger stakeholders like governments, non-governments, private sectors, media, etc. (Shaw et al. 2016). A normalized science technology attribution score is developed for 11 countries with three specific attributes: (1) science and technology in decision making, (2) investment in science and technology and (3) link of science and technology to people. A survey of wider science technology partner groups in Asia mentioned that the key need for science and technology implementation is techno-legal regimes, where innovation, existing and new technologies can be applied pro-actively in different aspects of disaster risk reduction.

At the national level, different countries have taken different initiatives for linking technology and innovation at the national level. Some of them have formed the formalized structure for that, e.g., in case of Malaysia, there is a science technology group, which advises the national disaster management authority for science technology-based decision-making. In case of the Philippines, the partnership between government, science technology sector and private sectors has been formalized through national resilience platform. In case of Japan, a high-level multidisciplinary science technology advisory committee (*Chuo BousaiKaigi* in Japanese) provides critical advice to the cabinet office.

The real need of applying technology is at the local level. There still remains a gap in many countries. Involving local research and technical institutes to collaborate more proactively with the local governments is critical in this aspect. Local government may not have enough resources for this purpose. Certain resource sharing from national governments, new resource generation with private sectors and other entities is important. Co-design, co-delivery of solutions with both technical and social disciplines can make value addition to enhance enabling environment of applying science and technology at the local level.

1.4 Innovation in DRR Technologies

Innovation is a buzz word that has been used widely in recent years in different sectors, and DRR is not an exception to it. Aligning with Kameda (2009)'s argument of product and process, Izumi and Shaw (2020) developed "30 innovations" in disaster risk reduction with 14 products and 16 process innovation, which have changed the course of DRR over years. Each innovation was evaluated with six factors: (1) number of death/affected people, (2) reduction of economic losses, (3) cost of effectiveness, (4) level of application/penetration of innovation to the mass, (5) environmental friendliness and (6) behavioral changes. It was found that some innovations like GIS/remote sensing or drones have been used effectively for level of penetration/application, cost-effective as well as environmentally friendly, but not that effective to reduce the casualty. On the other hand, concrete/steel building materials were able to save many people lives, but are not environmentally effective. With a survey of more than 220 respondents from different stakeholders, disciplines and countries, it was observed that community-based disaster risk reduction and hazard mapping are the top two innovations over last 30 years or so which have impacted to save lives and properties in the case of disasters. This shows the importance of both process and product innovations in disaster risk reduction.

Recently, an innovative online hackathon by different universities in Japan and India has found interesting and innovative ideas to deal with SDGs, climate change and disaster risk reduction (SIOH 2020). University students, youth groups have immense potentials to generate innovations, provided they are properly guided and mentored for the social needs and market demands. Thus, the "last mile" becomes the "First mile" to start with underdamping community's needs and priorities. The concepts of "Living Labs" are getting popular where students and different other stakeholders can interact with communities to co-design and co-deliver the products and innovations. An enabling environment, as mentioned in the previous section, would be useful for generating an innovation ecosystem for young entrepreneurs in the field of DRR, and thus enhance disaster resilience.

Shaw (2020) described eight essential technologies (from original source of PWC), which have impacted significantly to the DRR. Society 5.0 concept of Japan promoted a human-centric yet technology-driven society where the technology benefit should get rid of digital divide and will reach the most vulnerable and needy people in the remote areas. Innovations in recent years should try to focus on this "inclusivity" aspects of DRR, and should benefit the "whole of society".

1.5 About the Book

This book is designed with 13 chapters. There are three parts of the book: the first part (with four chapters) discusses applications of emerging technologies in disaster risk reduction. A set of chapters provide specific use of emerging technologies and discuss issues and a future prospect. A framework or implementation of geospatial information technologies, an earthquake early warning system, drones and VR/AR are discussed. The second part (with five chapters) focuses on communication aspect. Chapters in this part reveal the issues of information management and its effects to disaster resilience. Variety of topics, information-sharing and delivery, community resilience, management of social media information, situation awareness and communication infrastructure are discussed. The third part (with three chapters) deals with technologies for decision support. Cases of a living lab-based emergency control center, a real-time mapping system for evacuation, and the Japanese national information sharing platform are introduced.

Chapter 2, "Developing the eXtended tangible user interface as an experimental platform for Geo CPS" by Yan et al., introduces the development of the eXtended tangible user interface for cyber–physical systems (CPS). After providing an overview of the tangible user interface concept, authors show a model of new Geo CPS platform. The given architecture bridges GIS content both in cyber and physical worlds. The chapter also shows a case trial in a Japanese city and discusses a potential use for future disaster reduction.

Chapter 3, "Innovation in earthquake early warning system: A case study of EQ Guard" by Dabral et al., discusses an earthquake early warning system (EEW). It proposes innovative early warning system developed in Japan after reviewing different EEWs in Mexico, the USA and Taiwan. Authors argue that the proposed system, named EQGuard, could be a better equipment for a community in making decisions under earthquake safety. Features of the proposed system and implementation are discussed.

Chapter 4, "Drones for disaster risk reduction and crisis response" by Furutani et al., provides empirical cases and discussions to understand how drones work for disaster prevention. The cases are illustrated under torrential rain in western Japan in 2018 and the typhoon Hagibis in 2019. Technological considerations, as well as training human resources, and a way of collaboration with local municipalities are discussed for future drone implementations.

Chapter 5, "VR/AR and its application to disaster risk reduction" by Itamiya, discusses evacuation drills and associated virtual reality (VR) and augmented reality (AR) technologies. The author developed a smartphone-based CG technology and collaborated with Japanese elementary and junior high schools in order to provide disaster preparedness seminars. Empirical demonstration reveals such technologies help people to understand flood or smoke situation and contribute to raise their awareness.

Chapter 6, "Communication structure, protocol and data model towards resilient cities in Japan" by Sakurai, discusses issues under communication and information sharing among municipal officials, first responders, relief agencies and citizens in Japan. The author introduces practical research project with Japanese local municipalities. The project illustrates structural problems under information collection, sharing and delivery among related stakeholders. The chapter proposes common data model and structure for information sharing and delivery for future disaster resilience.

Chapter 7, "A conceptual framework for designing an effective community resilience management system" by Fayoumi et al., provides a conceptual framework for community resilience management system (CRMS). The framework employs a holistic perspective for community resilience and is structured with data, information systems, communication technology networks, rules/regulations and various stakeholders. The authors extracted eight design requirements for a proposed system. The chapter also discusses an implementation scenario of the CRMS under a health pandemic situation.

Chapter 8, "Social media technologies and disaster management" by Tanaka, discusses benefit and issues through social media communication in an event of a disaster. Social media enables rapid information sharing among individuals, although it includes potential threat to information reliability. The chapter provides a framework of true and false information incorporating the definition of rumor. Various cases of social media communication in the world are discussed, and a way forward to controlling and managing rumor under a disaster is given, based on educational, technological and psychological perspectives.

Chapter 9, "Use of IT for situation awareness for disaster risk reduction" by Murayama, provides discussions of IT roles to increase situational awareness of people under a disaster. Discussions incorporate five phases of disaster management, which employs different expectations and requirements to IT in each phase. The author introduces the influence of information systems in immediate response, sustained response, recovery, mitigation and preparedness. Discussions show the process in which data are transformed into intelligence, being essential to disaster management and risk reduction.

Chapter 10, "Emergency communication and use of ICT in disaster management" by Mondal et al., illustrates communication infrastructure named Suraksh IT developed by authors. It employs deployment feasibility, infrastructural scalability and information management capabilities, which enables such communication infrastructure being resilient in the time of a disaster. The chapter reviews various emergency communication networks such as unmanned aerial vehicles and satellite phones, etc. The developed communication network infrastructure was tested in India and authors discuss its potential impact to disaster-resilient communication.

Chapter 11, "Experimental command and control center for crisis and disaster management: A Living-Lab Approach" by Radianti, introduces the innovative experimental control room for disaster management. Author applies a living-lab approach in implementing such a command and control center (C2C). The chapter discusses the benefit of C2C and a living-lab approach, so called a co-creation process, to disaster risk reduction. Essential technologies for C2C are also discussed. Insights into how to evaluate and what a requirement for a living-lab based C2C are drawn based on field experiments in Norway.

Chapter 12, "Real-time mapping system of shelters' condition for safety evacuation" by Kitsuya et al., introduces a real-time mapping system developed by authors, which visualizes condition of an evacuation shelter. The system crawls information online and provides the location of opened shelters and its capacity (the real-time data of the number of evacuees) using Web API and open source mapping library. It helps local residents see where to evacuate. The prototype system was implemented in a Japanese local municipality. The chapter discusses obstacles regarding data usability and data format for future system development and implementation.

Chapter 13, "Decision support system and new technologies" by Usuda, provides an overview of the national decision support system named SIP4D (Shared Information Platform for Disaster Management), which has been developed by National Research Institute for Earth Science and Disaster Resilience in Japan. The implementation of the system is helped by an information support team (ISUT) who is dispatched to a governmental office in disaster areas once a disaster happens. The development of the system is an ongoing process, however, due to the increased number of natural disasters in Japan, the system has been utilized since 2016 Kumamoto earthquake and has supported decision-making in the disaster management headquarters.

References

Djlante R, Shaw R, Dewitt A (2020) Building resilience against biological hazards and pandemics: COVID-19 and its implications for Sendai framework. Prog Disaster Sci. https://doi.org/10.1016/j.pdisas.2020.100080

Izumi T, Shaw R et al (2020) Disaster risk reduction and innovation. Prog Disaster Sci 2(2019):100033

Kameda H (2009) Implementation technology for disaster reduction. In: Shaw R, Krishnamurthy R (eds) Disaster management: global challenges and local solutions. University Press, Chennai, India, pp 206–219

Shaw R (2020) Thirty years of science and technology, and academia in disaster risk reduction and emerging responsibilities. Int J Disaster Risk Sci. https://doi.org/10.1007/s13753-020-00264-z

Shaw R, Izumi T, Shi P (2016) Perspectives of science and technology in disaster risk reduction of Asia. Int J Disaster Risk Sci 7:329–342

SIOH (2020) Social innovation online hackathon final report. https://www.kri.sfc.keio.ac.jp/en/wp/wp-content/uploads/2020/01/Final-report-SIOH.pdf. Accessed 10th Sept 2020

Chapter 2
Developing the eXtended Tangible User Interface as an Experimental Platform for Geo CPS

Wanglin Yan, Yoshifumi Murakami, Akinobu Yasuda, Terukazu Makihara, Ryutaro Fujimoto, and Shun Nakayama

Abstract Geotechnology, including GIS, remote sensing, and GNSS, is finding many applications in disaster risk reduction. Information flows in conventional systems tend to be one-way, however, from the physical world to cyber world, and their effectiveness often depends on professional training while support for participation is weak. This chapter overviews the history of the concept of the tangible user interface (TUI), which intuitively bridges GIS content in the cyber world onto a "tangible table," a mock-up of the physical world for intuitive communication. After examining the common features of TUIs, we extend the concepts to recent applications in cyber-physical systems (CPSs) in the geographic dimension. We show how a Geo CPS platform (a CPS spatialized in the geographic world) with eXtended TUI (XTUI) can enhance the integration of information within cyber, physical and social spaces as well as the interactions among them in the application context. The system architecture and functions of Geo CPS with XTUI are constructed to reflect intuitive interactions of sensing, process and actuation (iSPA). Finally, we present a community trial at the Urban Living Lab in Yokohama City and discuss the potential for the Geo CPS platform with XTUI for disaster risk reduction.

Keywords Tangible user interface · CPS · GIS · Participation · ISPA

W. Yan (✉)
Faculty of Environment and Information Studies, Keio University, Tokyo, Japan
e-mail: yan@sfc.keio.ac.jp

Y. Murakami · A. Yasuda · T. Makihara · R. Fujimoto
Ad-sol Nissin Corporation, Osaka, Japan

S. Nakayama
Graduate School of Media and Governance, Keio University, Tokyo, Japan

M. Sakurai and R. Shaw (eds.), *Emerging Technologies for Disaster Resilience*, Disaster Risk Reduction,
https://doi.org/10.1007/978-981-16-0360-0_2

2.1 Introduction

Geotechnology, a collective term that these days include geographic information systems (GIS), remote sensing (RS), and the Global Navigation and Service Systems (GNSS), is often applied in the area of disaster risk reduction. These three technologies all emerged in the 1960s, grew in the 1970s and 1980s, boomed in the 1990s, and developed further in the 2000s. For more than half a century, geotechnology has steadily evolved and established niches in various combinations in the spectrum of modern information technology. GNSS, started with the Global Positioning System (GPS) in the USA, has transformed positioning and become part of the infrastructure of human daily life and services; remote sensing gives us a periodic bird's eye view of the planet surface at low cost and with high performance; GIS can manage a huge amount of spatial data and is commonly used in various applications from daily life to business; participatory decision systems supported by GIS can engage communities in preparing for, organizing relief from, and managing reconstruction after disasters. The three technologies complement each other to form an informational chain for sensing in the physical world, processing in the computational cyber world, and visualizing by the user community in society. Geotechnology has been seen as one of the frontiers in the twenty-first century along with nanotechnology and biotechnology (Gewin 2004).

Disaster risk reduction (DRR) has benefited substantially from geotechnology in terms of sensing/monitoring, modeling/analyzing, and visualization/presentation (Ghapar et al. 2018). However, traditional geotechnology solutions were generally built on closed-system conditions with stand-alone or centralized computational architectures. Data transactions were siloed, requiring time to cooperate across sectors and sites. Sophisticated uses of geospatial systems often require intensive training for operation and data interpretation. User interfaces were typically confined to several input devices for operators and lacked the appeal needed to attract general users.

The proliferation of mobile devices and the Internet of Things (IoT) are bringing about change; however, location-aware devices can continuously track when, where, and how people and objects appear and move. From there it becomes possible to learn behaviors and extrapolate trends, to consider what was there previously, and to predict what might happen next (Bosch 2018). By integrating with IoT, geotechnology is enabled to not only collect geospatial data in the physical world and manage it in the cyber world but also to actuate tangible objects in real time. For instance, driverless vehicles can move around in the midst of complex road conditions. Drones can take off and land anytime, anyplace, and collect and process images in real time. These systems exemplify a new type of sensing and mapping technology—a cyber-physical system (CPS)—in which data and information interact across *cyber and physical worlds* quickly and seamlessly.

CPS along with IoT is considered one of the most promising technologies for Industry 4.0 and Society 5.0. It has been studied in engineering and applied in manufacturing, civil construction, and utility management, etc. and has emerged quickly in market applications, such as drone surveillance, driverless vehicles, robotic services, and so on. However, the term and concept of CPS have not yet been widely accepted in the geographic dimension. To have completely driverless vehicles operating on public roads, much intensive experimentation is needed. Communication gaps exist between developers, engineers, and users. The development of solutions has generally been a one-way process flowing from engineers to clients, which has less flexibility for user interaction and lacks methods for solving social issues in an open geographic environment. We know that "one size does not fit all" in open conditions, particularly in disaster risk reduction, which requires fine accuracy of data, high speed system responses in harsh natural conditions, and much cooperation with the public. Interactive platforms that bring together complex natural and social conditions are constantly being sought.

Regarding interaction and user communication, a unique approach has been explored by using a tangible user interface (TUI) (Ishii et al. 2004; Maquil et al. 2015; Petrasova et al. 2018; White and Ross 1984). TUI is a technique to mock up a physical space on a 2D, 2.5D, or 3D landscape table by using augmented reality. The key concept of TUI is to bridge the cyber and physical worlds in a tangible way for multiple users to participate simultaneously in discussions. The idea of TUI has been evolved with tangible bits (Ishii and Ullmer 1997), message bricks (Fitzmaurice et al. 1995), a dynamic terrain machine, and recently with "Tangible Landscapes" where a physical space can be mocked up by illuminating clay, plasticine, or sand (Petrasova et al. 2018) and GIS data in cyber space are projected onto the 3D mock-up by map projection. Modifications of the landscape in clay and sand can be captured with a gesture camera, processed, and projected back onto the landscape table.

Although TUI is powerful for use in presentation and communication, its applications are currently largely limited to demonstration and education. On the other hand, CPS and TUI share the idea of linking the cyber and physical worlds. CPS aims to work directly in the real world while TUI mocks up the physical space for social communications. This commonality shows the potential for us to combine their advantages by extending TUI for CPS, making the "black box" of the processing in CPS visible for user communication. We believe that linking CPS and TUI will help to explore a new style of system development and practice in information technology and social communication.

Therefore, this chapter proposes the eXtended Tangible User Interface (XTUI) for a CPS platform in the geographic dimension by connecting sensing, processing, actuation, and social interaction in cyber–physical–social worlds. Our idea is to extend TUI for co-designing CPS solutions in a participatory way by bridging cyber, physical, and social worlds in a physically shared space for group discussion. The system can be used as a platform for education in environmental and disaster management, or as a tool for technical training with GIS and CPS, or as a testbed for business solutions in a specific social context. In the following sections, we will first review the history of TUI and CPS trends. We will then introduce the concept of XTUI and system architecture for the Geo CPS platform. Finally, we will discuss the potential of XTUI for participatory disaster risk reduction.

2.2 History of TUI

TUI was originally an inspiration by Durrell Bishop in his graduate project at the Royal College of Art in 1992 (Petrasova 2015). Users could place a message ball at the designated points of a machine to receive and actuate messages. This could be considered the first experiment of IoT, making a physical space integrated with conceptual workings by a platform and a moveable device. Based on this idea, Ishii and Buxton introduced a concept of graspable user interfaces or "bricks" in 1995, an interface to control electronic or virtual objects on an ActiveDesk (Fitzmaurice et al. 1995). ActiveDesk is a large display surface on which the message "bricks" could be moved around and actuate responses. Since then, TUI has evolved continuously in terms of three issues: how to make the ActiveDesk tangible, how to enrich the contents of the table, and how to establish communications between the physical table and the cyber world.

In the early stage, efforts went toward the ActiveDesk. The first idea was the "tangible bits," which allow users to "grasp & manipulate" bits in the center of users' attention by coupling the bits with daily physical objects and architectural surfaces (Ishii and Ullmer 1997). It could be considered to be one of the origins of cyber–physical systems though the accuracy was limited to the size of bits. Underkoffler and Ishii (1999) set up a system dubbed "Urp" to cast light shadows on a physical architectural model for urban planning. This could be considered as one of the original examples of map projection.

A utopia of full interaction and communication between tangible table and cyber space was an experiment at Mitsubishi Electric Research Laboratories by the invention of the Diamond Touch Table (DTT) in 2001, and later under license to Circle Twelve Inc. in 2008. It is a multi-touch, interactive PC interface device that has the capability of allowing multiple persons to interact simultaneously while identifying which person is touching where. Profile recognition through radio frequency identification (RFID) is used in the system. Before the user approaches the system, the user information is gathered, stored in a database, and coupled to a RFID tag, which is part of the badge provided. When the user moves toward the model the person's profile is recognized and a selection of datasets will be automatically created based upon the profile information. This could be considered to be a pioneer of cyber–physical interactive communication systems with IoT in a laboratory setting for multiple users.

With ActiveDesk, a table can be equipped with a touchable 2D screen. A team in the Netherlands led by Alessandra Scotta developed a prototype multi-user touchable user interface (MUTI) in the form of a tangible table on which map layers and objects appear as buttons and icons. MUTI involves much more than touch-sensitive interface screens or whiteboards shaped like tables (Hofstra et al. 2008). In contrast to the DTT, this system does not "remember" what is drawn by whom. Participants did not see the flat screen table with buttons as being very inventive or attractive.

An ultimate trial of TUI is inFORM, a dynamic terrain model by Follmer et al. (2013). It is a 2.5D actuated shape display that supports object tracking, visualization via projection, and both direct and indirect physical manipulation. The shape display, the TerrainTable, is moved by a dense array of pins linked by connecting rods to a larger array of actuators below. Using an array of vertical pins beneath a silicone skin, the table can create virtually any curved surface within an area 52 by 40 inches, 6 inches high. When synchronized with a computer-controlled overhead projector, the TerrainTable makes a convincing topographical map. The table is equipped with an engine connected to a PC, which adjusts the height of the pins according to the raster values to be visualized in 3D on the table. When performing a change of location on the table, such a zoom or pan, pins are sent down, the user chooses the new location with movements of the hands and when the new extent of the raster to be displayed has been evaluated by the underlying GIS engine, the heights of the pins are recalculated according to the new input, and the silicon layer adapts again to produce the new 3D representation on the table. The advantage of the trials is the flexibility of terrain models. Users can manipulate the pins directly and model the terrain of a landscape quickly. However, the equipment is expensive, the system is heavy to move around, and its applicability is limited by the size of pins (Petrasova 2015).

TUI aims to combine the benefits of physical and digital models in the same representation. More generally, TUI gives physical form to digital information, seamlessly coupling the dual worlds of bits and atoms (Ratti et al. 2004b). People can make changes to the interface simply by using their hands. To take advantage of the capabilities, people using the interface must first have the idea that it is useful and that it brings added value. Second, the TUI must be easy to use (Scotta et al. 2006). However, the transportability of the ActiveDesk strategy was not always simple because of the amount, dimensions, and fragility of the components. The table interface, beamer, sensor, screens, and frame to hold components together needed to be moved from one location to another (Scotta et al. 2006).

Instead of the ActiveDesk, concern was also paid to the relationships that occur between different terrains, the physical parameters of terrains, and the landscape processes that occur in these terrains (Mitasova et al. 2006; Ratti et al. 2004a). Illumination of clay and sand was used as a low-cost alternative that also had high performance in terms of communication. Another prototype TUI was developed in 2002 by illuminating clay to model the physical space, using a scanner to capture the model on an ordinary table, and a projector to cast maps of GRASS GIS or a camera to receive infrared light under a transparent table (Piper et al. 2002; US007181362B2 2004) (Ratti et al. 2004a; Ishii et al. 2004). The University of California Davis developed the AR Sandbox to physically create topographic models that can be used as backgrounds for simulations (Kreylos 2020). The sand is overlaid by a digital projection of contour lines and a color elevation map. Data can be sent through a Microsoft Kinect 3D camera into either Ubuntu system or Grass GIS (Petrasova 2015), and into a software program that displays information onto the sand through the projector. Users can manipulate the sand table and observe changes in the elevation map, and the corresponding contour lines are projected back onto the sand. In other words, users shape the real sand which is then augmented in real time with contour lines, elevation color maps, and simulated water flows. By holding the hands under the

Kinect 3D camera, the user can add virtual water to the surface of the sand, flowing over the real surface of the sand with real-time water simulation (Kreylos 2020). The AR Sandbox can be used to teach many geographic concepts to users, such as reading and interpreting contour lines and topographic maps, flooding and formation of watersheds, and can also be used in field trip preparation and trail planning (Kreylos 2020).

TUIs combine the advantages of reality and virtuality by active desk, map projection, and interactive sensing–processing–actuation algorithms. They provide a means of visualization and interaction that attracts participants to the table and invites them to interact with each other, facilitating and assisting the conversation around the table. TUIs make interactions between humans and computers more natural and intuitive by giving digital data a physical form (Petrasova 2015).

Regarding the contents of the tangible table, one effective solution is to couple with GIS (Mitasova et al. 2006). Mitasova et al. have worked steadily with tangible GIS for decades (Maquil et al. 2015; Mitasova et al. 2006 2007). The latest development of TUI is the Tangible Landscape Project using GIS. GIS offers a set of ready-to-use tools for different types of geospatial analyses and simulations as well as an interface for visualization (Petrasova et al. 2014). However, because of the unintuitive nature of understanding and manipulating physical objects in the abstract, systems that work in the digital space via a graphical user interface (GUI) are often so challenging to learn and use that they restrict creativity (Petrasova 2015).

Tangible landscape is a tangible interface for GIS. It interactively couples physical and digital models of a landscape so that users can intuitively explore, model, and analyze geospatial data in a collaborative environment. Conceptually, tangible landscape gives users the feel of GIS in their hands as they can feel the shape of the topography, naturally sculpt new landforms, and interact with simulations like water flow. Since it only affords a bird's-eye view of the landscape, some attempts coupled it with an immersive virtual environment so that users can physically walk around the modeled landscape and visualize it at a human scale (Tabrizian et al. 2016; Harmon et al. 2016; Petrasova et al. 2018). Tangible landscape is a free, open source project with source code hosted on GitHub.

Nowadays, TUIs are increasingly accepted as an alternative paradigm to the more conventional GUIs (Ullmer and Ishii 2000). More than 150 facilities around the world have installed and are using AR Sandbox in various fields, mostly in education (Kreylos 2020). However, despite its popularity, its performance has not been evaluated objectively except in the recent research by Harmon et al. (2018). In their research, landscape architecture students, academics, and professionals were given a series of fundamental landscape design tasks—topographic modeling, cut-and-fill analysis, and water flow modeling. It turned out that the tangible modeling tool helped participants build more accurate models that better represented morphological features than with either digital or analog hand modeling. Participants were able to work in a rapid, iterative process informed by real-time geospatial analytics and simulations. With the aid of real-time simulations, they were able to quickly understand and then manipulate to see how complex topography controls the flow of water.

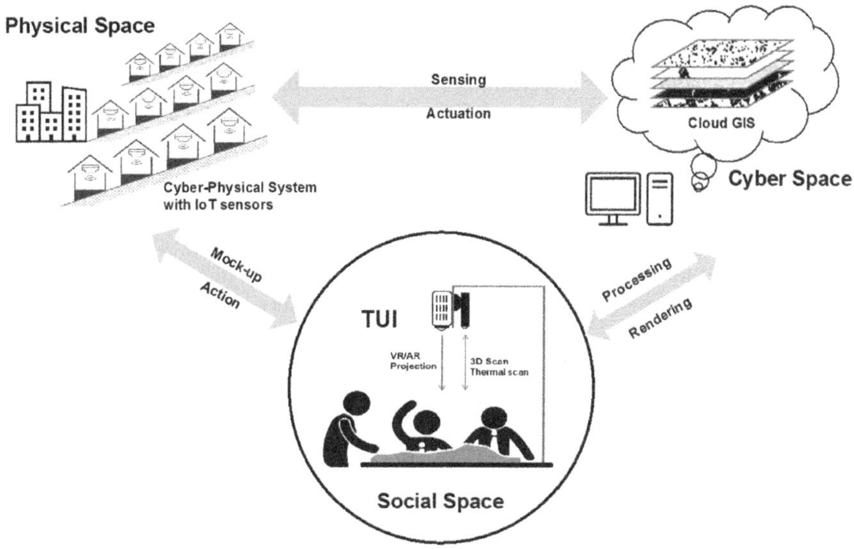

Fig. 2.1 A conceptual extension of TUI for the interaction of physical space, cyber space, and social space

We consider that the tangible user interface could be a bridge to connect physical space of real world, cyber space in computer world and users in social world, as illustrated in Fig. 2.1. The physical space is mocked up to the TUI table and monitored by IoT sensor to clous GIS in cyber spaces. The behaviors of users at the tangible table are scanned by 3D or thermal scanners and processed in GIS. The results shall be rendered and projected back on the tangible deck for user communications and actions to the real world. The detail of this novel idea is going to be discussed in the following sections.

2.3 CPS Platform in the Geographic Dimension

2.3.1 CPS, IoT, and Geo CPS

Yan and Sakairi (2019) have conducted an intensive review on the histories of key geographic technologies and then proposed the term Geo CPS.

CPS, proposed first Branicky et al. (2001), generally refers to physical and engineered systems whose operations are monitored, controlled, coordinated, and integrated by a computing and communicating core (Monostori et al. 2016; Hu et al. 2012; Lee and Seshia 2015; Liu et al. 2017). The functionality of CPS is built on the ability of sensing, cognition, and mapping of the physical space deployed in a geospatial context. "CPS requires the close interaction between the two distinct worlds. The interactions involve the discrete dynamics in the cyber space and the continuous dynamics in the physical space" (Shen 2015). The emergence of IoT has rapidly accelerated the integration of the two worlds, and precision of CPS has significantly improved. The commonality of CPS and IoT is the interaction between the cyber world and physical world.

CPS spatialized in the geographic world is referred to as "Geo CPS" (Yan and Sakairi 2019). Geo CPS is seen as a means of coming to grips with both the static and dynamic spatial relations between and among cyber and physical worlds. The physical world outside the laboratory is much more complex than indoor and comes with a high degree of uncertainty. They are often safety–critical, so the existing techniques focus on reducing latency to provide real-time performance. These open conditions call for advanced specifications in system design, power supply, and protocols for real-time communication. For example, driverless vehicles must simultaneously respond to traffic conditions, and healthcare robots must communicate with patients according to their conditions. The performance of Geo CPS will be determined by the ability of systems to process, analyze, and represent the vast amount of data that are gathered and stored.

Yan and Sakairi (2019) have proposed the basic framework of Geo CPS in which the bold horizontal line expresses the interactions between cyber and physical worlds. Sensing is the technology to recognize the static and dynamic situation of the physical world, cognition is applied to understand the ways in which the "world" works, and mapping is for rebuilding the physical "world" in cyber space. However, the interface between the cyber and physical worlds was not defined, the structure and function of the interface were not developed yet.

2.3.2 Geo CPS Platform

A key feature of Geo CPS is the integration of information within each space and the interaction between the pairs of spaces. Information integration within cyber space and physical space is characterized as Pseudo CPS and True-CPS, respectively (Yan and Sakairi 2019).

Pseudo CPS achieves information integration by using the position of IoT as a key to overlay real-time observations onto cyber space. This kind of pseudo CPS has been widely realized and applied. Doctors can provide telemedicine while they observe a monitor. Space centers can control a space station while watching monitors. Disaster response headquarters can make emergency response decisions while observing a large screen that combines information from multiple locations and departmental functions. Traffic management centers can monitor road conditions in real time. Conventional car navigation was also basically such an example. The GNSS system obtains the location, which is displayed on a digital map provided by DVD or internal HDD, and the user sees the current location. Road traffic information is sent with a delay of a few minutes via vehicle information and communication system (for instance, VICS in Japan) and that is displayed on the monitor. The information is in a separate layer, not incorporated into the map data. A similar technique is augmented reality (AR) (Khalid et al. 2015). GIS and computer-assisted design (CAD) are the same. Objects and systems in cyber space are not tactile and are too complex for non-professionals to understand. The dysconnectivity of closed systems with each other makes the feedback of information from cyber space to physical space difficult in real time. An operator plays a key role in the effectiveness of the system. There are other issues as well. For example, operator training takes time, systems may not be well suited to strategic decision-making, and systems might be partially optimized but not necessarily result in improved overall productivity.

On the other hand, a true CPS (TCPS) is a system that combines information from and to the physical world tightly in order to actuate objects. Sensors interact with object cross layers. Driverless vehicles are an example in the geographic dimension, using IoT online to obtain and monitor vehicle position, traffic conditions, and the peripheral environment in the physical world, process everything in real time, conduct integrated analysis for any layer, and actuate people and moving objects. Here, location-aware IoT in situ is the key to make the interaction possible. A TCPS places an emphasis on interactive functionality of systems. Sensing, processing, and actuation are installed, invisible, and work without human intervention. For a mature, complete system, this works well. However, problem-solving and system development often require intensive communications between developers and users. Solutions for social and environmental problems culminate from the participation of stakeholders. The interface between the cyber and physical worlds is critical in the installation of technologies.

As a solution to maximize the advantages and compensate for the disadvantages of PCPS and TCPS, we propose the Geo CPS platform with XTUI to accelerate the communication across spaces in specific social–physical contexts. The goal of the platform is to provide an intuitive tool for developers and stakeholders to understand how the physical environment evolves and how the interactions could be improved with cyber technologies. As functions, the tools actuate sensors in the physical space in real time and processors in cyber space and motivate people intuitively in the social space in order to co-design solutions to solve complex problems. As shown in Fig. 2.2, XTUI links physical, cyber, and social spaces with a common system architecture consisting of platform, network, apps, and users. The details of the concept and system architecture are discussed in the next section.

2.4 eXtended TUI for the Geo CPS Platform

The philosophy behind TUIs is to allow people to interact with computers via familiar tangible objects, therefore taking advantage of the richness of the tactile world combined with the power of numerical simulations (Ratti et al. 2004a). Informational flow in TUIs, from the acquisition of user input and the generation of GIS processing, to map projection and manipulation of the mock-up, forms a pseudo cycle of sensing,

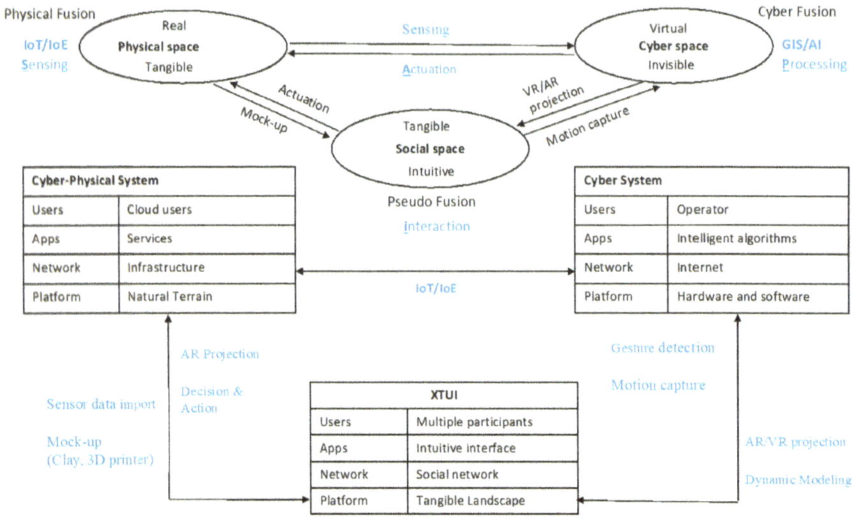

Fig. 2.2 The framework of XTUI and its system architecture, iSPA

processing and actuation in the laboratory. Our purpose is to create a TUI applicable for the development of CPS solutions in geographic and participatory conditions.

2.4.1 Conceptual Framework of eXtended TUI

The conceptual framework of eXtended Tangible User Interface (XTUI) is illustrated in Fig. 2.2. It is composed of physical, cyber, and social spaces, plus the interactions between each pair. Each space possesses its own structure of layers (platform, network, services, and users). XTUI is vital in the triangular relationships, which completes the link from the tangible table with the physical environment and cyber space. While maintaining interactivity for visualization, XTUI extends the functions in three ways.

First, XTUI considers TUI not only as an interface but also as a platform for participatory design of system solutions on social issues. TUI has indeed been a tool for human communications because from the beginning it has aimed to bridge gaps between cyber space and the physical environment, as well as the foreground and background of human activities (Ishii and Ullmer 1997). Compared with the cyber and physical spaces, however, the concept of TUI was generally limited to technical operation while other important factors (the social context and community of users) were hidden. Human factors did not receive much attention in applications so far. In XTUI, we introduce the user community (here referred to as the social space). Thus, the mission of XTUI is extended to the co-design of solutions for problem-solving, rather than mainly the demonstration of a pre-designed product.

This provides an innovative perspective for developing applications of TUI in disaster risk management.

Second, XTUI extends the target of TUI from the tangible desk to the real world through the IoT network and human network. Programs and algorithms can be tested by TUI with stakeholders so TUI is used as a participatory testbed. Human communication and decisions can be tested on the tangible table, reflected in cyber space, and actuated remotely with sensors and rovers. This extension connects the TUI tightly to the physical world while the mock-up becomes a living simulator in a specific context.

Third, XTUI is not only a visualization tool but also a platform for community and stakeholders to co-design solutions with a participatory approach, and it is used as a testbed in a living laboratory, rather than a manufacturing laboratory. XTUI establishes a third apex to cyber and physical systems by adding the interactive and intuitive human factor of social space, so that the system architecture of CPS becomes an *interaction of sensing, processing and actuation.* We call this structure *iSPA*, the featured system architecture of XTUI. This feature particularly suits to disaster risk communication in situ with support of scientific data.

In fact, CPS, GIS, and XTUI represent three ways of understanding, processing, and manipulating our world, in which each technology takes a unique position. CPS emphasizes direct interactions with the physical world; GIS manipulates those objects in the cyber world; XTUI fills the gap by brings the physical and virtual objects together into the social space for decision-making.

2.4.2 System Architecture of XTUI

Information integration in cyber–physical–social worlds has been studied substantially. As illustrated in Fig. 2.2, a computational cyber space is generally composed of hardware, operating system, applications, and users/clients. A physical space is constructed on physical terrain, social infrastructure including road and communication networks, institutions, and user services. The system architecture of CPS is often discussed with four layers: sensor/actuator, supervisory, control, and applications. The sensor/actuator layer contains various devices in the physical world. The latest TUIs use GIS, CAD, VR, and AR as applications to render geospatial content for map projections (Maquil et al. 2015, 2018). However, the interaction between all three spaces has not been discussed as much as bilateral mutual interactions between cyber, physical, and social spaces.

The key concept of the system architecture for XTUI is conceptually structured as iSPA, as shown in Fig. 2.2, where *S* expresses the part of sensing of cyber–physical system, *P* expresses algorithms of processing in cyber system, *i* expresses interaction of users with cyber and physical systems, and *A* expresses direct or indirect actuations between the cyber-physical systems through social systems.

We see that three spaces are considered similarly in the bottom-up operational structure by the layers of platform, network, apps, and users. A physical system works on physical terrain, infrastructure, private and public services, and cloud of users for data fusion while a cyber system is on computer hardware and software, the Internet, intelligent algorithms, and operators for virtual data fusion. XTUI is operated on tangible landscape, with a social network, intuitive interface, and multiple participants. While CPS is often considered to be interactive between cyber and physical systems only, the system built on iSPA is inclusive, including not only invisible communications in cyber–physical systems but also decisions and actions of the participation and discussion in the social space. The role of XTUI is to activate communication intuitively.

With iSPA, information is aggregated locally and delivered to the Internet in real time. The supervisory layer organizes data sources, conducts analysis and simulations, and provides the results to the application layer. IoT devices are monitored and controlled at the control layer. Eventually, we expect value to be created from connectivity based on a platform by integrated utilization of sensor data from different industries and sectors, as well as public data, and citizen data.

Therefore, iSPA provides a system structure to co-design the solutions of problems in the physical world, in a participatory fashion. Those solutions will be developed through communications with XTUI in a series of practices. By using iSPA, the functions and interactions between cyber, physical, and social spaces can be simulated at the community level. The performance of such systems will depend on the depth and breadth of interactions, as described in Fig. 2.1. A shallow level of interactions relays only data and messages. A deep loop will learn the causes and effects inside virtual content with real-time observation in the physical space and human operation in the social space. The experience of learning may start from the mock-up stage of XTUI, but more attention should be extended to multi-scales of cause and effect in the physical world.

2.4.3 Functions of Geo CPS Platform

Figure 2.3 presents the system functions of the Geo CPS platform. It is roughly categorized (on the left) in terms of iSPA, with *sensing* and *actuation* at the lower level and *processing* and *interaction* at the higher level. The column highlighted in gray expresses the classes of functions where sensor and actuation devices are grouped with network and communication protocol. Functions relevant to cyber space (data management, mining, and machine learning, etc.), are located near GIS, VR/AR, and map projection. XTUI brings various user services to the platform in tangible ways by using 2.5D, 3D mock-up, or illuminating clay in the physical world. Tangible landscape objects are enhanced with GIS projection or AR/VR simulation. Tangible objects could be a mock-up of buildings, facilities, or any other objects. Multiple users can touch the 2.5D or 3D objects to retrieve the deep layer of cyber spaces by using app interfaces like REST and SPARQL as well as any customized API. The potential of XTUI and the platform is demonstrated through a series of working scenarios.

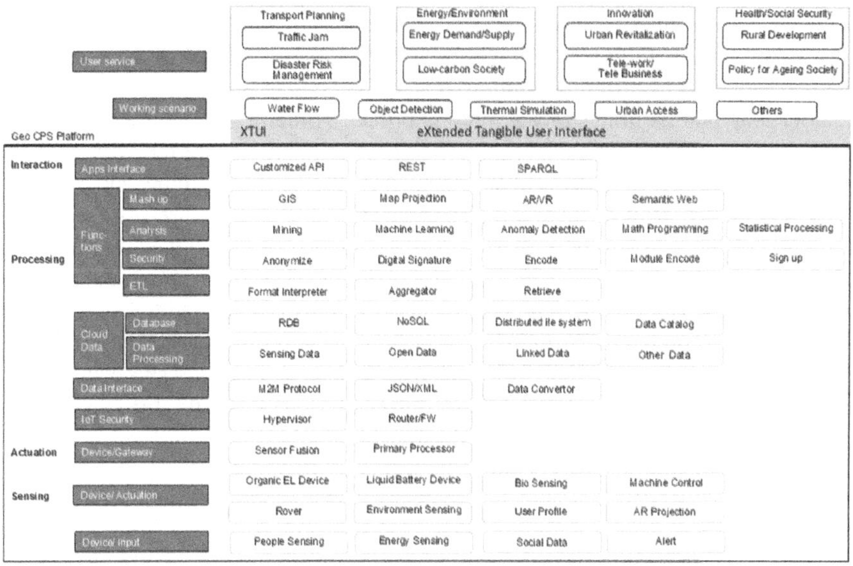

Fig. 2.3 System functions of Geo CPS Platform with XTUI

User services could be diverse, ranging from transportation planning, energy and environmental management, to innovation, social revitalization, and human health and security. Issues in each sector could be described as applied cases in the physical world by the integration of information from inside and interactions with the outside. Working scenarios, such as water flow, object detection, thermal simulation, and urban access assessment, provide several fundamental tools for the development of solutions. Meanwhile, ideas, feasibility, and applicability can be examined in a Geo CPS platform with XTUI.

2.4.4 *Working Scenarios*

The development of TUI has evolved since the early 1990s from (1) hand gestures and grasping to (2) interactive simulations of physical worlds, (3) working scenarios, and (4) commercial applications (Fitzmaurice et al. 1995). Although the tools have evolved from graspable bits and dynamic terrain models to AR Sandbox and Tangible Landscape, the fundamental issues have not changed significantly. To use TUIs, people need to realize that they can be useful and bring added value (Scotta et al. 2006). Systems that model elevation, contours, and water flow on an abstract landscape are limited in the scope of potential applications (Petrasova 2015), but the potential of the sandbox can be expanded by improving interactions in cyber space. Thus, our idea was to extend TUI with CPS and expand scenarios that link directly with the physical world.

To address the relative absence of TUI in urban-related applications, we proposed scenarios for a Geo CPS platform with XTUI using thermal cameras to simulate the thermal radiation of different building materials. The landscape model is made by contour map and buildings created by 3D printer. A thermal camera is installed to monitor radiation in the physical model. Solar radiation from materials with different albedo demonstrates the effects of anthropogenic surfaces on the living environment. By manipulating the material of the ground surface and building surfaces, the system simulates changes in real time and projects the results back onto the tangible table. Meanwhile, the system dynamically connects thermal sensors in situ to the tangible table and demonstrates the temporal change of observations. With this, environmental temperature can be simultaneously brought into discussion. By comparing reality and simulation in cyber–physical spaces, users in the social space are able to easily understand the effects of reactions. This can be very useful for discussions on mitigation of the urban heat island effect, for example.

Another scenario of XTUI is the accessibility to urban facilities. Urban access is largely influenced by topography and walkability. Many neighborhoods of cities in the world are built on hilly topographies, which results in extra effort required by people who are walking, and the extra burden could be more severe for the elderly and disabled persons. Having ways to assess walkability and visualize accessibility in different landscapes for people with different health conditions will help residents better understand the built environment and will assist urban planners and developers to better locate urban facilities. An algorithm using GIS was developed in Nakayama and Yan (2019) to evaluate "shop sheds." This algorithm was installed in an XTUI platform with topography mocked-up by contour map and buildings created by 3D printer in 2.5D. The "walkable shed" from a grocery shop or convenience store is then evaluated and projected onto the 3D model. Users can relocate a target object on the tangible environment and then update the accessibility via the shortest road network and consideration of "walk load" by age cohort. When the algorithm interacts with in situ weather conditions, the walkable paths and consumption of energy can be calibrated in real time.

The third scenario is application for risk communication in disaster management. Disaster management is one of the most targeted uses of TUIs. A popular working scenario in TUIs is for flood simulation in tangible landscape. While multiple users modify the landscape with sand, the elevation is scanned with an infrared camera and modeled in GIS. The contour map is generated and again projected on the TUI. Rainfall runoff, the effects of a reservoir, and the collapse of a dam can be simulated in real time. These intuitive education tools can help users understand the mechanisms of hydrology. Environmental and river sensors in the physical world bring information of water level to the social spaces and provide observations in real time for simulators in virtual space. Tangible landscape and projection of flooding simulators in XTUI give intuitive presentation of water level, flooding risk, and even evacuation routes. It can also easily simulate the impacts of collapses of dams and river banks and present the results on the tangible landscape.

2.5 Experiment and Potential of Geo CPS

2.5.1 Community Trial in Urban Living Lab

Map projection is often used in participatory urban planning and design. Those cases often consider TUI as a tool for visualization of cyber content only, without tight connections with the physical and social contexts at the local level. For instance, Maquil et al. (2015) introduce the concept of Geospatial Tangible User Interfaces (GTUI) and report on the design and implementation of such a GTUI to support stakeholder participation in collaborative urban planning. The proposed system uses physical objects to interact with large digital maps and geospatial data projected onto a tabletop. However, no researchers have mentioned how to set up the user community in a social context.

We brought the Geo CPS with XTUI to an Urban Living Lab for a community trial. An Urban Living Lab (ULL) is a geographical or institutional location or approach to have researchers, citizens, companies, and governments voluntarily cooperate in experimentation (McCormick and Hartmann 2017). A ULL provides a platform for governments, businesses, research institutions, communities, and citizens to plan, design, and test products and solutions cooperatively (Thinyane et al. 2012). The intrinsic properties of ULL are to learn from the real world, create knowledge in the real world, and produce solutions that can be applied in real life. Usually, companies and universities bring projects forward, conduct planning, design, application, and testing through co-creation, and receive social feedback. Early on, companies envisioned ULLs as having the purpose of developing, designing, and testing products from the user perspective (Kimbell 2011). This explains how in many cases ULLs were created and used as venues for co-creation or testbeds for product development by companies.

Yokohama has developed as a port town, with its city center near the waterfront playing a major role as a center of commerce in the Tokyo metropolitan region. Parts of Yokohama facing the mountains have large residential areas that serve as bedroom communities for Tokyo. Many of these residential areas were planned and constructed during Japan's postwar period of high economic growth, so their populations and infrastructure are aging, and the infrastructure is entering a period requiring renewal. To examine this situation, the Yokohama municipal government and Tokyu Corporation (a major private railway company) kicked off a joint project in April 2012 on the "Next-Generation Suburban Town Project" (NST, https://jisedaikogai.jp). Over the years, many study meetings and participatory workshops were organized with residents, resulting in an activity report entitled "2013 Basic Concept for NST: Community Development Vision for the Model District along the Tokyu Den-en-Toshi Line." Following the recommendations presented in the report, Tokyu Corporation established the WISE Living Lab (WLL) in 2017 and opened a facility at the property it owned in Tama-Plaza. WLL is an activity center for NST and has become a forum for residents, governments, businesses, and universities

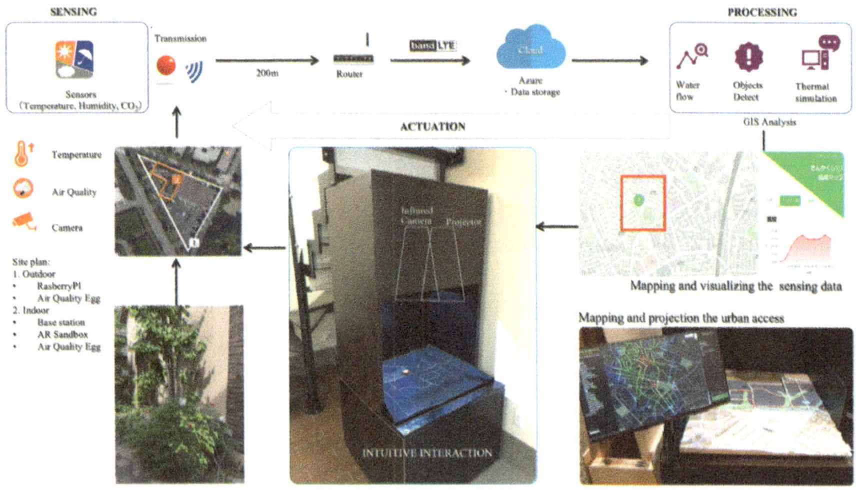

Fig. 2.4 System configuration of XTUI at WISE Living Lab

to communicate about local issues, think together about how to address them, co-create, and produce results. Under this scheme, we launched a project to cooperate with stakeholders, aiming to redesign the food life of the suburban town. A prototype of Geo CPS is installed at WLL. The site condition and system composition are shown in Fig. 2.4.

XTUI in this case is composed of a PC, a projector, an infrared camera to detect gestures and the designed frame. Sensors of temperature and air quality are installed at the living lab indoors and outdoors, and sensing data are transmitted to cloud data storage on the Internet. The data are processed in GIS for mapping and visualization. The processed data are presented by chart or map on the project website in virtual space. Meanwhile, the maps are projected onto a 3D model of the area. As a result, environmental conditions can be monitored in situ and the results can be reflected in the XTUI in real time. Participants can manipulate the land surface mocked up by clay or sand, or street blocks, buildings or road pavement by 3D printed objects. The participants' operations are captured by infrared camera and projected back as the thermal effect of modifications.

The walking accessibility of the area is calculated and displayed by monitor in a cyber system. It is projected onto the 3D model with the color red representing high accessibility along the road network. The user can move a tangible icon of a facility on the table to re-locate it. This interaction is in real time, so the result can be confirmed immediately. Overall, this XTUI helps users better understand their living conditions and consider ways to improve them.

2.5.2 Potential for Disaster Risk Reduction (DRR)

Disaster risk is the intersection of events, exposure, and vulnerability (IPCC 2012). Reducing the risk requires innovative techniques that can detect natural abnormalities quickly, alert early, and improve public awareness effectively. Geotechnology has attracted high expectations and found many applications due to its advanced use of technologies and potential for public participation.

For decades, many have advocated for public participation in disaster risk management, but in reality, it remains elusive (Ray et al. 2017). Samaddar et al. (2017) examined the process and identified outcome-based factors that account for successful participatory disaster risk management. The results unveiled that planners and practitioners are still struggling to find ways to meaningfully involve local communities in disaster management programs; so far, apparently successful projects and initiatives have seldom been scaled up or replicated. The reason for this is that no comprehensive framework for participatory disaster risk management exists, and no systematic evaluation has been made to assess the necessary elements and appropriate paths for meaningful public participation (Samaddar et al. 2017).

Some tools incorporate GIS and GPS and can be used by trained local communities to assess flood risk intensity at a local level and hence develop risk management plans (Singh 2014). Participatory GIS (PGIS) offers tools that can be used to help the public be meaningfully involved in decision-making processes affecting their communities (Jankowski 2009). PGIS usually involves communities in the production of spatial data and spatial decision-making (White and Ross 1984). Technologies utilized in PGIS have involved both commercially available and open-source GIS software, and more recently, free software. However, which PGIS tools should be used in a given participatory process depends largely on what level of participation is to be achieved (Jankowski 2009). Hazard inventories can also be produced using participatory mapping and PGIS. WebGIS was often used to enhance community resilience to flooding by identifying the Tangible and Intangible Local Flood Culture of the City of York (Chitty and Sprega 2017).

Cadag and Gaillard (2012) developed participatory three-dimensional modeling or mapping (P3DM) in the Philippines by building stand-alone scaled relief maps made of locally available materials (e.g., cardboard, paper) and thematic layers of geographical information. Guerin and Carrera (2010) used an interactive tangible 3D platform for the modeling and management of wildfires, with an interactive tangible 3D platform applied to conduct wildfire training, incident command and community outreach activities by allowing users to interactively visualize a variety of scenarios on sand tables, based on underlying wildfire, traffic, smoke, rain, and incident command models. "SandBox-FM" is a tool developed by Ottevanger et al. to combine either a Delft3D-Flexible Mesh (FM) or an XBeach model with Tangible Landscape (Ottevanger et al. 2017). Tonini et al. (2017) applied tangible landscape to the complex problem of managing an emerging infectious disease affecting trees in California, sudden oak death, and explored its potential to generate co-learning and collaborative management strategies among actors representing stakeholders with competing management aims.

IoT technology has also attracted interest for DRR (Park et al. 2018). A framework for how systems will come together for the purposes of DRR was proposed by (Baloyi and Telukdarie 2018; Ray et al. 2017). For instance, Baloyi and Telukdarie (2018) proposed a multi-layer structure of a cyber–physical system, but it lacks explicit consideration of the human interface. Zhang et al. (2018) reviewed advanced sensing, processing, and data fusion technology and described a framework for building an IoT-based geospatial sensor web focusing on service web capacity with four key methods, namely, integrated management, collaborative observation, scalable processing, and fusion. Some studies have also reviewed prototypes and applications for environmental, hydrological, and natural disaster analysis. Unfortunately, they mostly focus on sensing technology and pay less attention to integration and interaction with cyber and social factors, while interactions with user communities are generally outside their scope.

Geo CPS has significant potential for applications in disaster management at the community level by enhancing the integration and interaction of cyber–physical–social spaces. Figure 2.5 shows scenes in the community trial at WLL mentioned above, where GIS content is projected on the Tangible Table. In the photo on the left, the colored road network represents accessibility to a re-located convenience store, and the green coverage represents the landform of the neighborhood and low-lying areas prone to flooding. AR GIS and the Tangible Table bring together information in GIS and cyber space intuitively and interactively with participants.

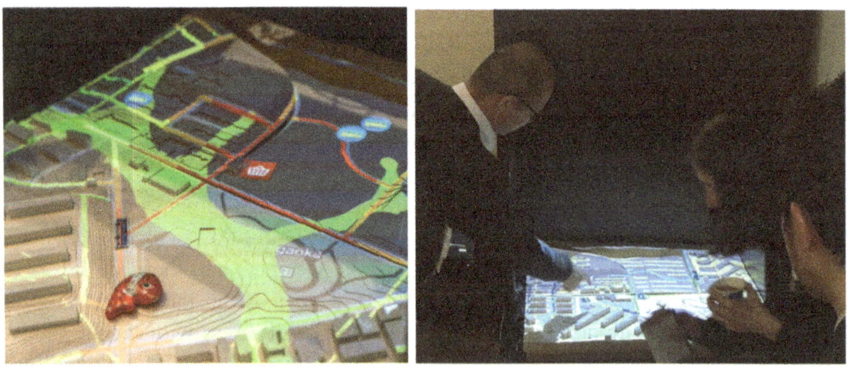

Fig. 2.5 Geo CPS experiment in the suburbs of Yokohama City. **a** Tangible Table with topographic information before development, accessibility after development. **b** Public participation with AR of map projection on XTUI

2.6 Conclusions

This chapter focused on the integration of geotechnology with IoT and TUI and presented an innovative picture of a Geo CPS platform with eXtended TUI (XTUI) for intuitive interaction in the cyber, physical, and social spaces.

Elemental technologies such as GIS, AR/VR, and GNSS have developed significantly and come into popular use in the mainstream of information society. Emerging technologies such as IoT and CPS are driving a new wave of industrial innovation, as in the example of Society 5.0. However, applications so far remain mostly in scientific and manufacturing laboratories and have not so easily found a place in light of the urgent demands of society. Geo CPS as a platform aims to bridge gaps that exist between cutting edge technologies, established geospatial industries, and practical issues of society. The platform, composed of CPS, GIS, and XTUI, takes the common advantages of the elemental technologies in the geospatial dimension and provides a new perspective to develop CPS solutions by focusing on integration and interaction in the physical, cyber, and social spaces. The platform requires developers to understand the location-specific context and pay attention to interactive processes with stakeholders and the synergistic effects of communications. The introduction of Geo CPS at the Urban Living Lab exemplified a model of implementation with community, which brings the physical environment visibly onto the XTUI table and intuitively drives interactive discussions. Interactions at the Living Lab create opportunities for system developers and community leaders to co-discover problems, co-design solutions, and co-deliver benefits to society.

Disaster management is mostly a social issue rather technological. Reducing disaster risks and improving resilience of communities require support of information and technology in a way of more real timely with finer datasets and seamless communications. The mission itself is completely location and context sensitive. The Geo CPS platform in this sense considers the importance of physical, cyber, and social spaces simultaneously with a system structure and functions in common structure. The working scenarios demonstrated the feasibility of implementation in community, such as the urban living labs.

The platform presented here is still in its infancy. Its functions have not been fully developed, the sensor network is still in the process of being installed, and scenarios need to be further developed. Nevertheless, we believe there is potential for the innovative ideas introduced here to make significant contributions in many geospatial applications, including disaster risk management.

Acknowledgements This paper is the result of research conducted jointly since 2017 by the SFC Institute of Keio University and Ad-sol Nissin Corporation. It was partially supported by Keio University Academic Development Funds for Individual Research in 2018 and 2019. During the project, the joint team co-designed the concepts and framework and co-developed the system. The prototype has been demonstrated annually at the SFC Open Research Forum. A community trial was conducted by the WISE Living Lab of Tokyu Co. Ltd., with support from the City of Yokohama. The research is also part of the M-NEX project (The Moveable Nexus: Design-led Approach for Urban Food-Energy-Water Management Innovations, Belmont Forum grant no. 11314551) in connection with the Sustainable Urbanization Global Initiative—Food-Water-Energy Nexus. We are also grateful for support from JPI Europe Urban as well as the Japan Science and Technology Agency.

References

Baloyi VT, Telukdarie A (2018) Internet of things: opportunity for disaster risk reduction. In: Proceedings of the international conference on industrial engineering and operations management, vol 2018(NOV), pp 2087–2096.

Branicky MS, Cenk MC, Liberatore V (2001) Multi-disciplinary challenges and directions in networked cyber-physical systems. IEEE Cont Syst Mag 21(1):84–99

Bosch (2018) 7 factors for getting the most value from your Geo IoT project. https://www.bosch-si.com/geo-iot/geo-iot/homepage-geo-iot.html. Accessed 03 Mar 2018

Cadag JRD, Gaillard JC (2012) Integrating knowledge and actions in disaster risk reduction: the contribution of participatory mapping. Area 44(1):100–109. https://doi.org/10.1111/j.1475-4762.2011.01065.x

Chitty G, Sprega A (2017) The use of WebGIS to enhance community resilience to flooding: discovering the tangible and intangible local flood cultture of the City of York. In: the use of webgis to enhance community resilience to flooding: discovering the Tangible and intangible local flood culture of the City of York. https://www.icomos.org/images/DOCUMENTS/General_Assemblies/19th_Delhi_2017/19th_GA_Outcomes/Scientific_Symposium_Final_Papers/ST3/26._ICOA_1091_Chitty_SM.pdf

Fitzmaurice G, Ishii H, Buxton W (1995) Bricks: laying the foundations for graspable user interfaces. In: Proceedings of the SIGCHI conference on human factors in computing systems, pp. 442–449. https://citeseerx.ist.psu.edu/viewdoc/download?doi=10.1.1.587.1729&rep=rep1&type=pdf

Follmer S, Leithinger D, Olwal A, Hogge A, Ishii H (2013) In: FORM: dynamic physical affordances and constraints through shape and object actuation. In: UIST '13 Proceedings of the 26th annual ACM symposium on User interface software and technology, vol 7, pp 417–426. https://doi.org/10.1080/03003938108432984

Gewin V (2004) Mapping opportunities. Nature 427(6972):376–377. https://doi.org/10.1038/nj6972-376a

Ghapar AA, Yussof S, Bakar AA (2018) Internet of things (IoT) architecture for flood data management. Int J Future Gen Commun Netw 11(1): 55–62. https://doi.org/10.14257/ijfgcn.2018.11.1.06

Guerin S, Carrera F (2010) Sand on fire: an interactive tangible 3D platform for the modeling and management of wildfires. WIT Trans Ecol Environ 137:57–68. https://doi.org/10.2495/FIVA100061

Harmon, B. A., Petrasova, A., Petras, V., Mitasova, H., & Meentemeyer, R. K. (2016). Tangible landscape: Cognitively grasping the flow of water. In: International archives of the photogrammetry, remote sensing and spatial information sciences—ISPRS archives, vol 41, pp 647–653. https://doi.org/10.5194/isprsarchives-XLI-B2-647-2016

Harmon BA, Petrasova A, Petras V, Mitasova H, Meentemeyer R (2018) Tangible topographic modeling for landscape architects. Int J Arch Comput 16(1):4–21. https://doi.org/10.1177/1478077117749959

Hofstra H, Scholten H, Zlatanova S, Scotta A (2008) Multi-user tangible interfaces for effective decision-making in disaster management. In: Nayak S, Zlatanova S (eds) Remote sensing and GIS technologies for monitoring and prediction of disasters. Springer, Berlin Heidelberg, pp 243–266

Hu L, Xie N, Kuang Z, Zhao K (2012) Review of cyber-physical system architecture. In: 2012 IEEE 15th international symposium on object/component/service-oriented real-time distributed computing workshops, pp 25–30. https://doi.org/10.1109/ISORCW.2012.15

IPCC (2012) Managing the risks of extreme events and disasters to advance climate change adaptation. In: Field CB, Barros V, Stocker TF, Dahe Q (eds). Cambridge University Press, Cambridge. https://doi.org/10.1017/CBO9781139177245

Ishii H, Ratti C, Piper B, Wang Y, Biderman A, Ben-Joseph E (2004) Bringing clay and sand into digital design—continous tangible user interfaces. BT Technol J 22(4):287–299. https://doi.org/10.1023/B:BTTJ.0000047607.16164.16

Ishii H, Ullmer B (1997) Tangible bits: towards seamless interfaces between people, bits and atoms. In: Proceedings of CHI '97, 22–27 March 1997. ACM Press, New York, USA, pp 234–241. https://doi.org/10.1166/jnn.2017.14175

Jankowski P (2009) Towards participatory geographic information systems for community-based environmental decision making. J Environ Manag 90(6):1966–1971. https://doi.org/10.1016/j.jenvman.2007.08.028

Khalid CML, Fathi MS, Mohamed Z (2015) Integration of cyber-physical systems technology with augmented reality in the pre-construction stage. In: Proceedings of 2014 2nd international conference on technology, informatics, management, engineering and environment, TIME-E 2014, 151–156. https://doi.org/10.1109/TIME-E.2014.7011609

Kimbell L (2011) Rethinking Design Thinking: Part I. Des Cult 3(3):285–306

Kreylos O (2020) Augmented reality sandbox [online]. https://web.cs.ucdavis.edu/~okreylos/. Accessed 13 May 2020

Lee EA, Seshia SA (2015) Introduction to embedded systems, a cyber-physical systems approach, 2nd edn. E A Lee and S A, Seshia, Berkley, USA

Liu Y, Peng Y, Wang B, Yao S, Liu Z, Concept A (2017) Review on cyber-physical systems. IEEE/CAA J Automatica SINICA 4(1):27–40

Maquil V, De Sousa L, Leopold U, Tobias E (2015) A geospatial tangible user interface to support stakeholder participation in urban planning. In GISTAM 2015—1st international conference on geographical information systems theory, applications and management, proceedings, pp 113–120. SCITEPRESS.

Maquil V, Leopold U, De Sousa LM, Schwartz L, Tobias E (2018) Towards a framework for geospatial tangible user interfaces in collaborative urban planning. J Geogr Syst 20(2):185–206. https://doi.org/10.1007/s10109-018-0265-6

McCormick K, Hartmann C (2017) The emerging landscape of urban living labs: characteristics, practices and examples. https://doi.org/10.1371/journal.pone.0099587

Mitasova H, Mitas L, Ratti C, Ishii H, Alonso J, Harmon RS (2006) Real-time landscape model interaction using a tangible geospatial modeling environment. IEEE Comput Graph Appl 26(4):55–63. https://doi.org/10.1109/MCG.2006.87

Mitasova H, Neteler M, Mitas L (2007) Environmental data management, analysis and modeling in GRASS6. In: Swayne DA, Hrebicek J (eds), 7th international symposium on environmental software systems (ISESS), 22–25 May 2007, Prague, Czech Republic. ENVIRONMEN, pp 60–78. https://doi.org/10.13140/2.1.3773.6001

Monostori L, Kádá B, Bauernhansl T, Kondoh S, Kumara S, Reinhart G, Kumara S (2016) Cyber-physical systems in manufacturing. CIRP Ann 65(2):621–641

Nakayama S, Yan W (2019) The package redelivery problem, convenience store solution, and the delivery desert: case study in Aoba Ward, Yokohama. J Urban Manag (May) 0–1. https://doi.org/10.1016/j.jum.2019.08.001

Ottevanger W, Haan R-J, den Baart F, Visser P, Jong J, de Pas B, van de ... Luijendijk A (2017) SandBox-FM : augmented reality CFD hydraulic engineering and education through collaborative modeling. https://hydro17.com/papers/PYwHMyoZruAfCsjQvOTbVgbwDL5u8EFvTSGafkyX.pdf

Park S, Park SH, Park LW, Park S, Lee S, Lee T, ... Park S (2018) Design and implementation of a Smart IoT based building and town disaster management system in Smart City Infrastructure. Appl Sci (Switzerland) 8(11). https://doi.org/10.3390/app8112239

Petrasova A (2015) Chapter 1 introduction. In: Petrasova A (ed), Tangible modeling with open source GIS, pp 1–15. https://doi.org/10.1007/978-3-319-25775-4

Petrasova A, Harmon B, Petras V, Mitasova H (2014) GIS-based environmental modeling with tangible interaction and dynamic visualization. In: Proceedings—7th international congress on environmental modelling and software: bold visions for environmental modeling, iEMSs 2014, vol 2, pp 758–765

Petrasova A, Harmon B, Petras V, Mitasova H (2018) Tangible modeling with open source. Springer

Piper B, Ratti C, Ishii H (2002) Illuminating clay: a tangible interface with potential GRASS applications. Proc SIGCHI Conf Hum Fact in Comput Syst 355–362. DOI: https://doi.org/10.1145/503376.503439

Ratti CF, Piper BTF, Ishii H, Wang Y, Biderman A (2004a). US007181362B2, US, pp 3–8

Ratti C, Ishii H, Frenchman D, Wang Y, Piper B (2004b) Tangible user interfaces (TUIs): a novel paradigm for GIS. Trans GIS 8(4):407–421. https://doi.org/10.1111/j.1467-9671.2004.00193.x

Ray PP, Mukherjee M, Shu L (2017) Internet of things for disaster management: state-of-the-art and prospects. IEEE Access 5(i):18818–18835. https://doi.org/10.1109/ACCESS.2017.2752174

Samaddar S, Okada N, Choi J, Tatano H (2017) What constitutes successful participatory disaster risk management? Insights from post-earthquake reconstruction work in rural Gujarat, India. Nat Hazards 85(1):111–138. https://doi.org/10.1007/s11069-016-2564-x

Scotta A, Scholten HJ, Pleizier ID (2006) Tangible user interfaces in order to improve collaborative interactions and decision making. In: Fendel E, Rumor R (eds), Proceedings of the 25th urban data management symposium, 15–17 May 2006. UDMS, Aalborg, Denmark

Shen B (2015) Overv Cloud-Relat Cyber-Phys Syst 1(2):8–13. https://doi.org/10.11648/j.ijdsa.20150102.11

Singh BK (2014) Flood hazard mapping with participatory GIS: the case of Gorakhpur. Environ Urban Asia 5(1):161–173. https://doi.org/10.1177/0975425314521546

Tabrizian P, Petrasova A, Harmon B, Petras V, Mitasova H, Meentemeyer R (2016) Immersive tangible geospatial modeling. In: GIS: proceedings of the ACM international symposium on advances in geographic information systems. https://doi.org/10.1145/2996913.2996950

Thinyane M, Terzoli A, Thinyane H, Hansen S, Gumbo S (2012) Living lab methodology as an approach to innovation in ICT4D: the Siyakhula living lab experience. IST-Africa 2012:1–9

Tonini F, Shoemaker D, Petrasova A, Harmon B, Petras V, Cobb RC, Meentemeyer RK (2017) Tangible geospatial modeling for collaborative solutions to invasive species management. Environ Model Softw 92:176–188. https://doi.org/10.1016/j.envsoft.2017.02.020

Ullmer B, Ishii H (2000) Emerging frameworks for tangible user interfaces. IBM Syst J 393(3):915–931

Underkoffler J, Ishii H (1999) Urp: A luminous-tangible workbench for urban planning and design. Conf Hum Fact Comput Syst—Proc 386–393. https://doi.org/10.1145/302979.303114

White J, Ross O (1984) Remote sensing and GIS for natural hazards assessment and disaster risk management. Public Relat Rev 10(3):66. https://doi.org/10.1016/S0363-8111(84)80101-0

Yan W, Sakairi T (2019) Geo CPS: Spatial challenges and opportunities for CPS in the geographic dimension. J Urban Manag 8(3):331–341. https://doi.org/10.1016/j.jum.2019.09.005

Zhang X, Chen N, Chen Z, Wu L, Li X, Zhang L, Li D (2018) Earth-science reviews geospatial sensor web : A cyber-physical infrastructure for geoscience research and application. Earth Sci Rev 185(July):684–703. https://doi.org/10.1016/j.earscirev.2018.07.006

Chapter 3
Innovation in Earthquake Early Warning System: A Case Study of EQ Guard

Ambika Dabral, Kazuo Sasaki, Yamaimaiti Nizhamudong, Ranit Chatterjee, and Rajib Shaw

Abstract Global frequency of disasters is following an upward trend. While the frequency of significant earthquake linked disasters is much less compared to hydrometeorological disasters, the causalities attributed to earthquakes considerably surpass those attributed to any other disasters. This makes earthquakes a low-frequency but high-impact hazard. Further, unlike other natural hazard warning mechanism, earthquake warning has a window of a few seconds to a minute, hence catching us mostly unaware and leading to more injuries and causalities. With the advancement in the field of earthquake research, and science and technology, many countries including Japan, Turkey, Mexico, and USA boast of having an earthquake warning system. Although it is not possible to reliably predict earthquakes, but the existing technologies create a window for decisive action by analyzing the P-wave, which provides advance information of the estimated seismic intensities and arrival time of strong tremors prior to their actual arrival. Ranging from a few seconds to a minute in hand, such a warning allows to take necessary safety measures including individual safety, evacuation, shutting down of critical/hazardous processes to mitigate impacts, stopping elevators, trains, initiating response, etc. This study discusses the innovation and advancement in earthquake early warning (EEW) systems in Japan. It explores the functioning of the existing product, namely, Earthquake Guard (EQG-III) developed by Challenge Co. Ltd., Japan which is being used for earthquake early warning.

A. Dabral (✉) · R. Chatterjee · R. Shaw
Resilience Innovation Knowledge Academy, New Delhi, India
e-mail: dabral.ambika@gmail.com

K. Sasaki · Y. Nizhamudong
Challenge Co. Ltd., Sayama, Japan

R. Chatterjee
Kyoto University, Kyoto, Japan

R. Shaw
Keio University, Tokyo, Japan

M. Sakurai and R. Shaw (eds.), *Emerging Technologies for Disaster Resilience*,
Disaster Risk Reduction,
https://doi.org/10.1007/978-981-16-0360-0_3

Keywords Earthquake safety · Early warning system · Dissemination · Decision-making · Evacuation

3.1 Introduction

Globally, in 2018, a total of 315 natural disaster events were recorded with 11,804 deaths, over 68 million people affected and US$131.7 billion of economic loss. Earthquakes were the deadliest type of disaster accounting for a whopping 45% of these deaths, though, in terms of a number of events, they constitute just 6.3% of the total 315 events (CRED 2019a). A similar trend is observed during 2000–2017 where the average death toll by earthquake (46,173) is 59.9% of the average deaths due to all disasters combined (77,144) (Annex 3.1). Thus, it can be inferred that while the frequency of significant earthquake-linked disasters is much less compared to climate-related and hydrometeorological disasters, the causalities attributed to earthquakes considerably surpass those attributed to any other disasters; making earthquakes a low-frequency but high-impact hazard.

Death toll in earthquake arises from three main causes: structural collapses, non-structural causes and cascading hazards like fire, tsunami, Natural Hazards Triggering Technological Disasters (NATECH) and others. Structural collapses are responsible for 75% of deaths in earthquakes (Cobum et al. 1992). Coupled with these, a possible reason for high earthquake-related mortality is the fact that unlike other natural hazards like cyclones, floods, tsunami, earthquakes mostly catch us unaware. In the 1989 Loma Prieta Earthquake in the San Francisco Bay Area and 1994 Northridge Earthquake in Southern California, more than 50% of injuries were linked to falls and non-structural falling hazards respectively; meaning that if everyone got a few seconds' warning of the coming shaking and dropped, took cover, and held on, the number of injuries in an earthquake could have been halved (Allen and Melgar 2019).

The Sendai Framework for Disaster Risk Reduction (SFDRR) 2015–2030 calls for strengthening of early warning system for the reduction in loss of life and economic assets. In the absence of any technology to accurately predict the occurrence of earthquakes, having in place an earthquake early warning system with even a few seconds of warning can help in reducing life loss, injuries, prevention of cascading damages in critical infrastructure and services by triggering automated or manual actions, etc. Earthquake Early Warning (EEW) has been part of the Japanese Shinkansen system since the 1960s and automatically slows and stops trains when earthquakes are detected. The high-speed trains in China are now also speeding up the development of EEW systems. In San Francisco, the Bay Area Rapid Transit (BART) train system began using EEW system for slowing and stopping the trains in response to strong ground shaking in 2012 (Given 2013). Elevators are another example of automated response application of EEW whereby they are prompted to go to the ground floor and open the doors, thus preventing hundreds of people from being trapped. A public survey in Japan in 2012 on the usefulness of EEW following the M9.1 East Japan earthquake and Tsunami (EJET) on March 11, 2011 shares that 82% of those surveyed in whole of Japan responded positively, and specifically in the Tohoku-Oki region, 90% responded positively (Allen and Melgar 2019). BART's success in maintaining continuous service directly after the 1989 Loma Prieta earthquake reconfirms the importance of EEW system as a transportation lifeline (BART).

While considerable progress has been made in recent decades in the field of early warning, these are generally less developed for geo-hazards and significant challenges remain in advancing their development for specific hazards, particularly for sudden-onset hazards such as earthquakes (UNESCO 2015). Even though the concept of EEW was proposed as early as 1868, there was hardly any progress made in the field till the advent of digital seismic instrumentation and digital communication technologies. The occurrence of some of the destructive earthquakes around the globe further underlined the dire need for EEWs and stimulated the pace of their development. Currently, these systems are operational in Japan, Taiwan, Mexico, etc. while in Turkey, Italy, Canada, Republic of Korea, China, USA (California), these are in development stages or under restricted applications. These systems mostly involve either development of a nationwide dense network of seismic sensors or smartphone-based applications for detecting and generating alerts. While the former is a long-term and costly affair, the latter is a non-stationary network and suffers from issues like potential background noise and hence a trade-off between false alarm probability and the detection delay.

This chapter briefly discusses earthquakes and different types of seismic waves. It then explores the innovation and advancement in earthquake early warning (EEW) systems, various algorithms and their limitations, the challenges or gaps in the functioning and usability of different EEW systems. Further, it presents the functioning of the existing product like Earthquake Guard (EQG-III) developed by Challenge Corporation Limited, Japan, which is being used for earthquake early warning by addressing some of the identified gaps in other existing EEWs, their limitations and way forward.

3.2 Literature Review

The lithosphere, comprising the Earth's crust and upper mantle, is fragmented into various major and minor rigid slabs called tectonic plates. Driven by internal forces of the Earth, these tectonic plates continuously move at rates of a few centimeters per year. Their movement relative to each other distorts the crust in the region of the boundaries creating systems of earthquake faults. Major faults and systems of faults also exist in the interiors of plates. As the plates move together, apart or past each other, tremendous stress is build up around the fault; however, due to the overlying rock strata, the friction locks these plates together (NCERT 2016). At some point of time, their tendency to move apart overcomes the friction resulting in abrupt slipping of the fault. This sudden release of accumulated strain energy causes series of vibrations (elastic waves) on the earth's surface, which is called an earthquake. The point where the energy is released is called the focus or hypocenter of an earthquake. The amount of energy released during an earthquake determines its magnitude (measured in Richter scale) and is dependent on the size (surface area) of the fault rupture. The energy waves travel from the focus in different directions and reach the surface. The point on the surface, nearest to the focus (directly above it), is called epicenter of the earthquake. It is the first one to experience the waves. Intensity of an earthquake is the level of shaking caused by seismic waves at a specific location. It depends on the magnitude of the earthquake, distance from the epicenter and local geology. For ruptures extending hundreds of kilometers along a fault, the shaking intensity at a location also depends on its distance to the fault rupture. Based on the causing factors, earthquakes can be broadly categorized as tectonic earthquakes (caused by rupture of earth crust due to geological forces), volcanic earthquakes (caused by tectonic forces in conjunction with volcanic activity), collapse earthquakes (small earthquakes in underground caves and mines caused by seismic waves produced from explosion of rock on the surface) and explosion earthquakes (caused due to detonation of a nuclear or chemical device).

Seismic waves, like all waves, transfer energy from one place to another without moving the material. Seismic waves are fundamental of two types, compressional longitudinal waves and shear transverse waves. Within the Earth's body, these are respectively called P-waves (primary because they are fastest) and S-waves (secondary since they are slower); together known as body waves. When the body waves reach the free surface of Earth, the two types of motion combine to form complex surface waves, which propagate along the Earth's surface. Surface waves have much higher amplitudes than the P-waves and S-waves and are destructive in nature. P-waves travel fastest and are the first to arrive at the earth's surface. They are generally smaller and have higher frequency than the subsequently reaching S-waves and surface waves and hence are not destructive. Two types of surface waves are L-waves (or love waves) and R-waves (or Rayleigh waves). Love waves exist because of the Earth's surface; they are largest at the surface and decrease in amplitude with depth. They are dispersive, that is, their wave velocity is dependent on frequency, with low frequencies normally propagating at higher velocity. Their depth of penetration is also dependent on frequency, with lower frequencies penetrating to greater depth. Rayleigh waves are also dispersive and their amplitudes generally decrease with depth in the Earth. Their appearance and particle motion are similar to that of water waves (British Geological Survey 2020).

The waves reaching the surface are recorded by an instrument called seismograph. Its recording is called seismogram and is based on the relative motion of pendulum and ground. The seismograph is equipped with the electromagnetic sensor that translates ground motions into electrical changes, which are processed and recorded by its analog or digital circuits (Britannica 2020). During an earthquake, the S-waves and the subsequent surface waves which cause strong ground shaking travel at about half the speed of the primary P-waves (Kumar et al. 2014), thus taking a few seconds or even minutes more to reach the surface. With the help of the time difference between the arrival of P-wave and S-wave, the distance between the earthquake and the seismograph is worked out. The waves arrive first at the closest station and last at the farthest one. By comparing the time difference from seismographs of atleast three recording stations, seismologists locate the epicenter of the earthquake.

The size of the earthquake or its magnitude depends on the size of the fault and the amount of slip on the fault. It is determined using the logarithm of the amplitude of the largest seismic wave calibrated to a scale by a seismograph. A short wiggly line that does not wiggle very much means a small earthquake, and a long wiggly line that wiggles a lot means a large earthquake. The length of the wiggle depends on the size of the fault, and the size of the wiggle depends on the amount of slip (USGS).

3.2.1 Earthquake Early Warning Systems

Early warning system is defined as an integrated system of hazard monitoring, forecasting and prediction, disaster risk assessment, communication and preparedness activities systems and processes that enable individuals, communities, governments, businesses and others to take timely action to reduce disaster risks in advance of hazardous events (UNDRR 2016).

Earthquake early warning (EEW) systems rapidly detect and characterize ongoing earthquakes in real time to provide advance warnings of impending ground motion. The concept of EEW has emanated from the understanding that radio waves travel about 100,000 times faster than the elastic waves that propagate strong shaking through the earth. Much before the required technology was available, the physics behind the EEW was highlighted by J. D. Cooper back in 1868 (Bakun et al. 1994). But, the implementation of EEW got stimulated only by the availability of digital seismic instrumentation and digital communication technologies. Further, over the years, the development of EEW has also been driven by major earthquakes across the globe. Some of these include the 1985 Mexico City earthquake (M 8.1), the 1995 Kobe earthquake (M 6.9) and the 2008 Wenchuan earthquake (M 7.9). The 1985 Mexico City earthquake even illustrated the possible time gap of at least 1 min between detection by seismic stations along the coast and the time when shaking was felt in the city (Allen and Melgar 2019); thereby highlighting the possibility of generating EEW.

The existing earthquake early warning (EEW) systems make use of the time difference in the arrival of P-wave and S-wave. EEWs rapidly detect the first sign of an earthquake, the P-wave and transmit the information to data center/servers for determination of location and intensity of earthquake, which is further disseminated to end users within seconds, before the arrival of the destructive S-wave and surface waves. This is possible because while seismic waves travel through the shallow earth at speeds ranging from 0.5 to 3 miles per second, information through communication systems can be sent instantaneously (Burkett et al. 2017). For local EEW installations, the P-wave is detected onsite (i.e. at the user location), and the difference between the P- and S-wave arrival times defines the maximum alert time. For regional networks, the P-waves are detected by sensors closest to the epicenter, and estimates are immediately relayed to earthquake alerting applications (TV, smartphones, radio, etc.) to the end users about the expected arrival and intensity of shaking at their location (Strauss et al. 2016).

Allen et al. (2019) put forth some of the key algorithms being used by different EEWs. Each of these algorithms offers some benefits and faces some limitations. Point source algorithm uses a few seconds of P-wave data from a few stations close to the epicenter for detecting an earthquake and finding its locations, time of origin and magnitude. Information of ground shaking can also be gathered from these using an appropriate ground motion prediction equation. While they are fastest and are able to provide alert as close as possible to the epicenter, thus providing the most warning time; they process information of only the first few seconds and also fail to provide the lateral extent of the rupture, thus their predictions typically saturate for M7 earthquakes. Finite fault algorithms can estimate the finite extent of the rupture and have limited or no issue of magnitude saturation. Thus, while being slower than point source algorithms, they are able to predict higher intensities of shaking, and over larger areas, for the largest earthquakes before the shaking is felt. Ground motion-driven algorithms are very different from the earlier two and do not characterize the earthquake source at all. Instead, they make use of observations of strong shaking to predict shaking at other locations. Thus, they are free from the challenges and uncertainties involved in detection of earthquakes, their locations and magnitude. However, their disadvantage is that the accuracy of ground shaking prediction decreases as a function of warning time, thus providing short lead time to act.

3.2.2 Importance of Earthquake Early Warning Systems

Unlike seismic retrofits, where a direct cost–benefit of damage reduction is tangible, early warning reduces many hidden costs that are difficult to monetarily delineate but are ultimately crucial for long-term resilience (Strauss et al. 2016). Even with a very short lead time of a few seconds to a minute, an advance warning can allow people and systems to take necessary safety measures including personal safety like drop, cover and hold or evacuation; automated controls like shutting down of critical/hazardous or production processes, stopping elevators, trains; or situational awareness like initiating response, rapid mobilization of response agencies, etc. EEW can reduce the number of injuries in earthquakes by more than 50% (ibid). Some of the benefits EEW provide for are:

1. Personal safety at home, school, offices from falling objects by practicing timely drop, cover or hold
2. Evacuating to safe assembly areas, if time permits
3. Planning for safety of vulnerable groups including differently-abled, old-aged persons, infants, children, sick persons, etc.

4. Protecting critical facilities or infrastructures through EEW-automated control facilities or applications including slowing and stopping trains, preventing planes from taxiing and landing, taking elevators to the ground floor and opening doors, automatically isolating hazardous chemicals, and stopping heavy and hazardous machinery
5. Preventing or mitigating NATECH and other catastrophic cascading impacts of earthquakes like fire, leakages, spillage involving chemicals, gas, radioactive material, etc.
6. Giving time to staff who work in more hazardous situations (construction sites, utility works, hazardous chemical plants, etc.) for stepping away from hazards, stopping machinery, putting down chemicals, securing safety harnesses and so on.
7. Even when the intensities are not high enough to cause damages, warnings followed by suitable actions by people allow them building a culture of seismic preparedness among the community.

3.2.3 Existing Earthquake Early Warning Systems

It is observed that the development and implementation of EEW have been accelerating with the advancement of communications technologies but have been limited to the regions with seismic networks (Allen et al. 2019). Broadly, the existing and developing EEWs across the globe can be categorized as those with alert distribution to nationwide or to public in large (as in Mexico, Japan, South Korea and Taiwan), those with limited alert distribution to only selected users (as in parts of India, Romania, Turkey and USA) and those which are still under the development or testing phase (as in Chile, China, Italy, Switzerland, etc.) (Allen and Melgar 2019).

Many countries are working toward establishing nationwide seismic observation system, which requires a good network of high-quality ground motion sensors with robust communication systems. Some of these include:

1. The Mexican Seismic Alert System (SASMEX) broadcasts EEWs to general population through a network of numerous monitoring stations, which are linked to control and distribution centers that receive, decode and broadcast the alerts by a redundant telecommunications network. The dissemination of EEW is done through low-cost radio receivers, subscribing television and radio stations and through system of municipal loudspeakers installed in the streets throughout the city (Suarez et al. 2018). In the case of the great Tehuantepec earthquake of 2017 (Mw 8.2), SASMEX gave almost 2 min of warning prior to the arrival of the strong-motion seismic waves in Mexico City (ibid).
2. Japan's public alert system for earthquake is operated by the Japan Meteorological Agency and is based on the point source algorithm to locate earthquakes based on arrival of P-wave. Alerts are broadcasted on cell phones, available commercial smartphone applications, TV, radios and various other dedicated communication channels. However, it faced many challenges during the 2011

M9.1 EJET. The earthquake caused significant shaking over a much larger area than predicted by the EEW algorithm, as the magnitude estimate saturated at M8.1. It also faced issues in generating quality of alerts due to intense aftershock sequence by not being able to distinguish seismic arrivals from separate simultaneous events. It has improved its algorithms ever since. Similarly, Taiwan also has a national seismic network that works on point source approach (Allen and Melgar 2019).

3. The demonstrative ShakeAlert system of United States Geological Survey (USGS) for West Coast of the USA is another example of nationwide seismic network. It has been in development since 2006 and began sending alerts to test users in California in 2012. It leverages a network of more than 400 high-quality ground motion sensors. The test users currently receive alerts through a computer application with both audible and visual alert features about the location of epicenter, time remaining until waves will reach the user's location and an estimated intensity. When fully operational, it will be able to distribute alerts through all available distribution channels, including those of FEMA, smartphone apps, social media providers and other electronic alert technologies as they develop (Burkett et al. 2017).
   While that system has demonstrated the feasibility of EEW in California, the system is not yet sufficiently tested or robust enough for public alerts, or, for institutional users to initiate potentially costly actions to mitigate the effects of strong ground shaking. Capital investment costs for a West Coast EEW system are projected to be \$38.3M, with additional annual maintenance and operations totaling \$16.1M—in addition to current expenditures for earthquake monitoring (Given et al. 2014). Though once functional, such a system would save lives, reduce injuries and damage, and improve community resilience by reducing longer term economic losses for both public and private entities; the system has two keys limitations: false and missed alerts are possible, and the area very near to an earthquake epicenter may receive little or no warning.

Apart from making use of nationwide network of seismic sensors, another set of EEW systems use smartphones for the purpose. Smartphones are equipped with accelerometers for sensing and detecting the movements. Further, making use of geolocation technology and internet connectivity, warnings are being sent and received. As they make use of existing smartphone infrastructure, they have been able to significantly address the cost concerns involved in developing a county-wide network. However, due to their constant mobility, a lot of background noise is generated, thus making it hard to differentiate and detect an earthquake using a single set of accelerometer data. Thus, data from a large number of smartphones in a specific geographical area are observed for a similar pattern of movement at roughly the same time (Finazzi 2016). Some of these systems include:

1. MyShake Platform is built on the existing smartphone technology to both detect earthquakes and issue warnings; thus having a potential to provide EEW wherever smartphones are available. It can also integrate other sources of alerts and deliver them to users and can also deliver its alerts through other channels as

needed. Its operations have shown that earthquakes can be detected, located, and the magnitude estimated in around 5–7 s after the origin time and alerts can be delivered to smartphones in around 1–5 s (Allen et al. 2019). It uses personal smartphones as sensors collecting earthquake data and delivering earthquake information to the user before, during and after earthquake, including EEW. Its uniqueness is that it involves no separate deployment or maintenance of sensors. Instead the sensing hardware is provided by smartphone owners and the deployment process is facilitated by the Google Pay and Apple iTunes stores. It attempts to distinguish seismic motions from other motions and records 5 min of accelerometer data when the motion is classified as an earthquake.

2. Earthquake Network is a crowdsourced smartphone-based EEW, which was started in 2012. The application collects data from the phone's accelerometer only when it is plugged in, charging and not being used. When movement of the smartphone exceeds a certain threshold, a signal is immediately sent to a central server where an algorithm decides, in real time, whether an earthquake is occurring. Based on many similar reports, if the occurrence of earthquake is determined, a warning is issued throughout the smartphone network (Finazzi 2016). Apart from warning, it automatically sends the coordinates of smartphones in the affected area to the trusted contacts before the internet gets compromised to aid in search and rescue operations, if needed. It also provides users to submit report after earthquake is felt, which helps in quick deployment of emergency team (Finazzi nd).
3. Mexico's SkyAlert and Grillo, run by private sector are other examples of smartphone-based alert applications.

Another set of EEWs are those based on onsite approach. Some of these use microelectromechanical system (MEMS) sensor to provide prompt onsite warnings to locations close to the epicenter. Some of these are:

1. P-alert system of Taiwan developed by the National Taiwan University. MEMS is a low-cost sensor and uses P-wave displacement thresholds to issue alerts within buildings that have installed P-alert devices.
2. National Centre for Research on Earthquake Engineering uses a few seconds of P-wave data for predicting the coming peak shaking but it uses six extracted features and a support model to decide when to alert.
3. Earthquake Guard (EQG-III) developed by Japan-based Challenge Co. Ltd. (discussed in detail in the subsequent section).

3.3 Gaps and Challenges

The development of a nationwide system for seismic observation and warning involves two key challenges. First, this is a long-term process involving at least a decade or two and second, this incurs a huge installation and maintenance cost. The huge cost does limit their scope for deployment in underdeveloped and developing countries and the long gestation period leaves the gap of not having any system in place to mitigate the losses due to earthquakes during this long development period.

Further, the 2011 M9.1 EJET earthquake highlighted a few limitations faced by an algorithm being used by one such network in Japan. While an alert was successfully issued, there was a problem of magnitude saturation experienced by the point source algorithm, which estimated the event at M8.1. Efforts are required for developing better approaches for more prompt and unsaturated estimation of large events including exploring approaches for using the evolving features of a waveform rather than fixed-length time windows.

In the backdrop of long gestation period and high cost incurred in installation and maintenance of nationwide network, smartphone-based EEWs do overcome these two concerns. As pointed out by Kong et al. (2019), smartphone-based EEWs do away with the need of deploying and maintaining separate sensors and can be easily scaled up to the regional and global level; thus reducing the financial costs involved in establishing nationwide sensor network. Besides, such systems can be used as a tool for generating public awareness and knowledge about earthquake. Further, with the growth of smartphones, the network of inbuilt sensors would inevitably grow; thus strengthening and improving the EEWs.

However, various gaps and limitations are also identified in the functioning of smartphone application-based EEW. First, due to their mobile nature, sensor network created by them is non-stationary and varies over time of the day and the region. As phones keep moving, the majority of the motions recorded by the accelerometer may not be seismic in nature. Thus, under this technology, there is a definite trade-off between false alarm probability and the detection delay, which needs to be balanced using appropriate statistical tools to ensure its efficacy. Second, users can join or leave the network by installing and uninstalling the application. To make such EEWs systems more acceptable and usable by end users, they are expected to consume minimal power so as to not adversely impact the normal functioning of the phone. Third, depending on the diversity of sensing hardware used in smartphones of different make and brands, they tend to differ in their detection sensitivities leading to potential inconsistency in timing of the ground motion recorded by them, which can significantly impact the quality and effectiveness of detection and generated EEWs (Kong et al. 2019). Besides, some of the smartphone-based EEW systems also face the challenge of real-time estimation of earthquake magnitude.

Minson et al. (2018) bring forth the concern that despite various existing EEW systems in various parts of the world, the question of how much warning time is physically possible for specified levels of ground motion has not been addressed. They further suggest that EEW systems have the greatest potential benefit for users willing to take action at relatively low ground motion thresholds, whereas users who set relatively high thresholds for taking action are less likely to receive timely and actionable information. This is so because strong ground motion only occurs near the rupture of a sufficiently large earthquake, where there is little wave propagation time between the earthquake source and the user location (ibid).

Unlike warnings of other natural hazards, EEWs cannot be based on real-time human oversight and approval before the issuance of alert to end users due to the very short time between rupture and propagation of ground motion. Besides the potential over or under estimation of ground shaking, an EEW is prone to technical glitches like false alerts[1] or missed alerts[2] (Minson 2019). Another related gap regarding the dissemination of the EEWs concerns lack of/inadequate understanding of risk perception and tolerance of end users to false and missed alerts. Having this understanding can help in making the EEW system more acceptable and usable to the end users.

Given the limitation of source parameter-based EEWs in providing timely and actionable warning of strong ground shaking, the information on false alert tolerance of users can be useful in undertaking cost–benefit analysis for different users and utilities for appropriate EEW systems and dissemination. False alert tolerant user can still be benefitted from the EEWs for low threshold of ground motions including the unnecessary alerts when these events do not go on to produce strong ground motions.

Further, with a generalized warning being currently sent out to all the users ranging from household, offices, schools, hospital staff and individuals engaged in more risky and hazardous sectors like construction sites, power utility, heavy plants, machineries, etc., the onus of taking appropriate mitigation and response action is rested with the end user. Thus, in the absence of awareness, specialized orientation and training of end users on how to respond to alerts, practical effectiveness of EEW system would remain very limited in saving lives and preventing injuries. This underscores the need for proper awareness and training of end users for appropriate response and effective utilization of the warnings received.

3.4 A Case Study of EQ Guard

As earthquakes can occur anytime and given that development of nationwide EEWs still require higher density coverage of seismic stations/sensors, further testing, enhanced technical and operational capacities, it may be useful to also explore other quick and low-cost solution, which can be effectively and quickly deployed and used even by developing countries. The need for such a technology and infrastructure is also being underscored in SFDRR, which calls for the application of simple and low-cost early warning equipment and facilities and broadening release channels for early warning information. A case in point is EQ Guard III (EQG-III).

EQG-III is an earthquake sensor alarm equipment. The accelerometer in EQG-III is a Micro-Electro-Mechanical Systems (MEMS) sensor, which is built to detect the initial small P-wave and issue an alarm before arrival of the big S-wave. The accelerometer issues the alarm immediately and the alarm through the server is issued after 1 s. The key technical specifications of the EQG-III are listed in Table 3.1.

---

[1] False alert is the alert generated when the actual ground motion falls short of the accepted threshold of the users.

[2] Missed alert is a lack of any alert by the system even when the actual ground motion exceeds the accepted threshold of the user.

Table 3.1 Technical specifications of EQG-III

Display: PC display
Noise level: 0.1 gal
ETA: PC display at −99 to 999 s per s display
Warning display: LED flash display
Audio/video output: Line output, Headphone output, Volume adjust
Warning output: Loop output 6 circuits
Transmit method: TIPv4, 100BASE-TX
Operational switches: Test switch*2, Reset switch, Setting-clearing switch
Power: DC5V
Exterior (mm): 188.7 × 160 × 50.5
Weight (g): Approx. 1 kg
Environment: Temp: −10 °C ~ +50 °C, no fogging
Facilities: Indoors, Power adaptor

Source (Authors)

Annex 3.1 Death toll by disaster type

Events	Average (2000–2017)
Drought	1,361
Earthquake	**46,173**
Extreme temperature	10,414
Flood	5,424
Landslide	929
Mass movement (dry)	20
Storm	12,722
Volcanic activity	31
Wildlife	71
Total	**77,144**

Source (CRED 2019b)

It is worth highlighting that EQG-III system works without the presence of any nationwide dense network of seismometer. It can work as a standalone device (Fig. 3.1) and multiple EQG-III devices can be used to develop a regional earthquake alarm system (Fig. 3.2). EQG-III is installed near the supposed epicenter and is connected to the server by internet. In case of an earthquake, EQG-III nearest to the epicenter detects the P-wave first and sends data to the data center. The data center processes such data and can calculate the location of epicenter and the magnitude of the earthquake. The shaking intensity is measured within 4 s from the arrival of P-wave. The information on location and expected intensity is sent to all EQG-III for issuing alarms.

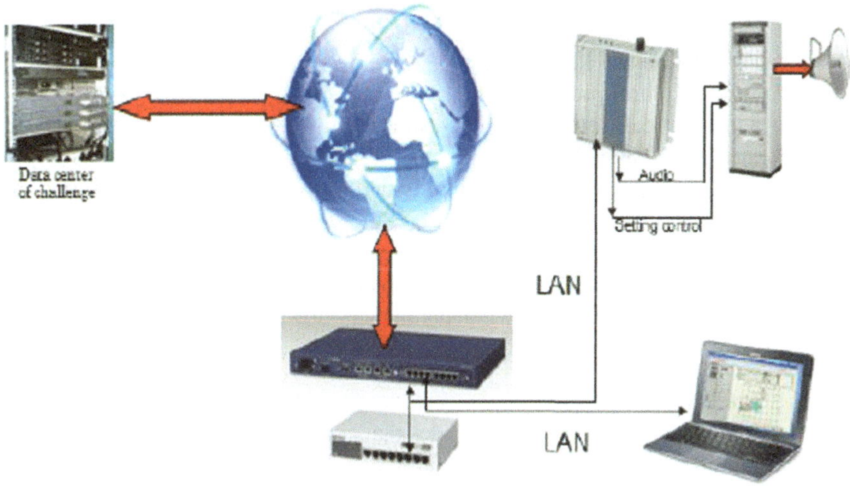

Fig. 3.1 System configuration of EQG-III. *Source* (Authors)

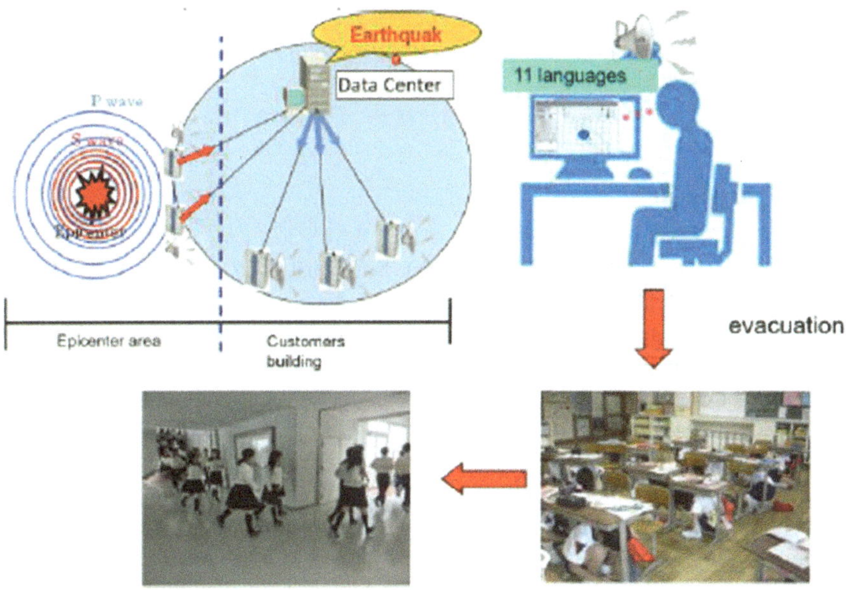

Fig. 3.2 Regional earthquake alarm system based on EQG-III; students conducting evacuation drill 'Drop, Cover, Hold on' triggered by alarm. *Source* (Authors)

Key features of EQG-III:

1. It can issue alarm in 11 languages.
2. It has pre-set alarm provision
3. It provides for real-time display of seismic intensity from each observation point indicated on the map.
4. Control signals from EQG-III can be issued to shut down critical facilities and services like chemical plants, nuclear facilities, gas or power installations, trains, etc. to mitigate any cascading impact of earthquake.
5. It makes use of a specialized software, which discerns an earthquake from noise generated near it. The following parameters are used to distinguish seismic waves from noise:
    a. Predominant frequency
    b. Time duration in peak amplitudes that exceeds a threshold level
    c. Number of zero crossings
    d. Seismic intensity in Japan Meteorological Agency (JMA) scale.

This system has been installed with varied end users and has been successfully functioning in various facilities including schools, companies, factories, hotels, residential apartments in Japan, Romania, Indonesia, South Korea, Turkey, Kazakhstan, Ghana, Papua New Guinea, etc.

3.5 Discussion

Many countries in the Indian Subcontinent, Southeast Asia, Central Asia, Middle East, Eastern Africa, Southeast Africa, Central America, South America and the Caribbean are located in the most seismically active regions of the world along the ring of fire or in areas with moderate seismicity but with high vulnerability and would strongly benefit from the development of an operational EEW system (UNESCO 2015). With an initial cost of 3000 US$ per device (sensor) and short installment period of 1 week for one unit, EQG-III can be a quick and low-cost solution for under-developed and developing countries, for their critical facilities. Further, it offers a potential of being developed into a regional earthquake alarm system for high risk areas in a very short duration (up to 3 months for constructing a regional alarm system with around 10 units) at a low cost by deployment of multiple units. Thus, EQG-III overcomes the two keys limitations of setting up a country-wide sensor system, namely, long gestation period and high cost.

EQG-III has also addressed the key challenge faced by most of the smartphone-based EEW system, i.e. generation of false alerts due to background noises. It does so by making use of a specialized software, which discerns an earthquake from noise generated near it. Most conventional seismic observations are made with a sampling frequency of 100 Hz or lower. Usually, most of the noise events have a frequency in a bandwidth centered at about 100 Hz. Therefore, it is difficult for data sampled at 100 Hz to accurately represent the special character of the noise. The sampling frequency of EQG-III is designed to be 500 Hz in order to: (a) accurately collect waveform data of the noise; (b) be assured of sufficient bandwidth for reliable analysis; and (c) discriminate seismic events from noise (Horiuchi et al. 2009). In addition to the software identification, since the data center collects each observation data in real time, EQG-III distinguishes between earthquake and noise through multiple detection method[3] to prevent false alarm.

While other sensors like Servo type strong seismograph with noise level less than 0.1 gal are available, they are expensive and are more suitable for the investigation of underground structure. EQG-III uses MEMS sensor with noise level 0.1 gal, which is quite sufficient for the purpose of EEW and for saving life of people without high financial implications.

As EQG-III is installed at the desired location and is stationary in nature, it also overcomes the challenge of non-stationary and varying sensor system faced by smartphone-based EEW systems. Besides, through its uniform and standard design across all EQG-III devices, the limitation of varying detection sensitivities faced by sensors of smartphones of different make is also overcome, thereby doing away with potential inconsistency in timing of ground motion.

By generating warning in terms of shaking intensity and not mere magnitude of the earthquake, EQG-III provides better understanding of the potential damage at a specific location to its end users for necessary and appropriate safety actions. However, as highlighted earlier, the efficacy of an EEW system lies in the right actions taken by end users on being triggered by the EEW. If people are trained well, given 5 s for evacuation, 80% of deaths can be prevented (Sasaki et al. 2019). Thus, along with the installation of EQG-III, the awareness generation about actions to be taken in case of earthquake is ensured through regular conduct of seminars and earthquake evacuation drills by using the test switch of the device. The test switch of EQG-III allows the end users to simulate the EEW for conducting mock drills to test and improve their evacuation planning and response actions. This aims to bridge the earlier highlighted gap of not effectively knowing what to do when a warning is received. Besides, it significantly increases the usability and efficacy of such a system.

With its ability to issue alarms in 11 languages, it aims to cater to end users in their local languages, so as to ensure easy comprehension and better impact of the disseminated warning on the end users and to trigger suitable actions at their end; thereby striving toward the principle of 'leaving no one behind'.

However, as the EQG-III is connected to its server through internet, the connectivity with the server is subject to potential disruption during a major earthquake. Though much before such a potential disruption, EQG-III would have passed the warning to its users, a gap in generating warnings for any aftershock is possible, in case of disruption of the internet due to the first shock. In the backdrop of this, redundancy in the system may further be explored and established to enhance the reliability

[3]Multiple detection method: If one EQG-III detects a P-wave but another EQG- III in nearby place does not detect the P-wave, so it is not an earthquake and no alarm is issued.

of such crucial systems. Besides, as EQG-III provides the warning to only the users who have installed the device, it can only be effective in alerting and reducing life loss and injuries of these limited users and not the masses in general. Thus, the level of risk perception of a community about earthquake and their level of risk tolerance to its potential impacts are very crucial for them to understand the importance of EEW and get it installed at an institutional or regional level.

Overall, the combined efforts are focusing on appropriate improvement and advancement in the existing EEW systems to overcome the highlighted gaps and challenges; enhanced use of such systems in earthquake-prone regions; and capacity building of the masses about various aspects of earthquakes and usability of EEW systems, would better equip the communities in making risk-informed choices and decisions toward earthquake safety.

3.6 Way Forward

Allen et al. discuss that it may not be desirable that detailed earthquake information (locations and magnitudes) is sent to all users who will then decide whether to react. To address this, they suggest that as most users will want to react when shaking is expected to be above some threshold, the information about the earthquake must be reduced into a map of shaking intensity and then an alert be issued to the appropriate region for different categories of users (ibid). Further, they also highlight that automated or other control applications with significant costs of implementation and/or significant costs/consequences of taking alert actions are unlikely to be implemented irrespective of high consequences of earthquake shaking. For example, nuclear power plants are unlikely to use EEW as the cost of implementing an emergency shutdown is significant because it shortens the lifetime of the reactor. In this regard, EQG-III and other existing EEWs can explore the possibility of sending users and infrastructure specific warnings by understanding their accepted threshold and seismic strength of the existing infrastructure.

The four elements of efficient, people-centered early warning systems are disaster risk knowledge based on the systematic collection of data and disaster risk assessments; detection, monitoring, analysis and forecasting of the hazards and possible consequences; dissemination and communication, by an official source, of authoritative, timely, accurate and actionable warnings and associated information on likelihood and impact; and preparedness at all levels to respond to the warnings received (International Network for Multi-hazard Early Warning Systems 2018). Thus, an EEW is only as effective as its users are in understanding and acting on the warnings. Large-scale awareness of the community in understanding various terminologies related to the warnings and the system must go hand in hand with the installation of such systems.

Further, EEWs can also explore the possibility of collecting feedback from the end users to better understand the gaps and challenges, if any, they face in using the EEW. The functional performance of EQG-III and other EEW systems during aftershock events may be assessed to understand its ability in distinguishing seismic waves from multiple simultaneous events and generating quality alerts. Accordingly, necessary modification can be made in the algorithm used. The feedback mechanism can also aid in assessing the tolerance of end users to false and missed alerts and can thereby help serve two-fold purposes. First, it can assist in designing contextualized/specialized alerts for different end users based on their tolerance and need. Second, the feedbacks from end users can provide field evidences on risk perception of local communities and can guide the local authorities in planning suitable capacity building and risk communication measures for respective communities.

Strategic installations of low cost and quick deployment systems like EQG-III across critical infrastructures and services, areas with high seismic exposure, etc. may be spurred to substantially mitigate life and other losses. EEWs may further be integrated with communication channels of response forces for raising prompt alert to the response force nearest to the area likely to be affected. This will aid in ensuring effective and timely response during the golden hour.

By ensuring its successful installations at strategic locations or at regional level, significant contributions toward achieving target A, B, C and D of the Sendai Framework for Disaster Risk Reduction (SFDRR), namely substantial reduction in global disaster mortality, number of affected people, direct disaster economic loss and disaster damage to critical infrastructure respectively can be made by working toward target G, which talks about substantial increase in the availability of and access to multi-hazard early warning systems and disaster risk information and assessments. It is noteworthy that one of the indicators for measuring target G of SFDRR includes 'percentage of population exposed to or at risk from disasters protected through pre-emptive evacuation following early warning' (UNDRR 2016).

References

Allen RM, Melgar D (2019) Earthquake early warning: advances, scientific challenges, and societal needs. Annu Rev Earth Planet Sci 47:361–388

Allen RM, Kong Q, Robert M-S (2019) The MyShake platform: a global vision for earthquake early warning. Pure Appl Geophys

Bakun WH et al (1994) Early warning system for aftershocks. Bulletin of the seismological society of America. https://pubs.geoscienceworld.org/ssa/bssa/article-abstract/84/2/359/119798

Britannica (2020) Seismograph. https://www.britannica.com/science/seismograph. Accessed 20 Jan 2020

British Geological Survey (2020) Discovering geology. https://www.bgs.ac.uk/discoveringGeology/hazards/earthquakes/seismicWaves.html. Accessed 27 Mar 2020

Burkett ER et al (2017) ShakeAlert-an earthquake early warning system for the US west coast. https://pubs.er.usgs.gov/publication/fs20143083. Accessed 20 Mar 2020

Cobum AW et al (1992) Factors determining human casualty levels in earthquakes: mortality prediction in building collapse. Earthq Eng Tenth World Conf 10:5989–5994

CRED (2019a) Natural disasters 2018. Centre for research on the epidemiology of disasters (CRED), Brussels. https://emdat.be/sies/default/files/adsr_2018.pdf. Accessed 15 Nov 2019

CRED (2019b) 2018 Review of disaster events: supplementary information. Centre for research on the epidemiology of disasters, Brussels. https://reliefweb.int/sites/reliefweb.int/files/resources/Review2018.pdf. Accessed 15 Nov 2019
Finazzi F (nd) Earthquake network project. https://sismo.app/. Accessed 20 Dec 2019
Finazzi F (2016) How a smartphone network detects earthquakes in real time. Significance 13. https://rss.onlinelibrary.wiley.com. https://doi.org/10.1111/j.1740-9713.2016.00974.x. Accessed 20 Dec 2019
Given DD (2013) Status of public earthquake early warning in the US American geophysical union. https://ui.adsabs.harvard.edu/abs/2013AGUFM.S43C..01G/abstract
Given DD et al (2014) Technical implementation plan for the ShakeAlert production system—an earthquake early warning system for the west coast of the United States: USGS open-file report 2014–1097. Department of the Interior, US Geological Survey, US. https://doi.org/10.3133/ofr20141097
Horiuchi S et al (2009) Home seismometer for earthquake early warning. Geophys Res Lett 36(5)
International Network for Multi-hazard Early Warning Systems (2018) Multi-hazard early warning systems: a checklist. cancun: world meteorological organization. https://reliefweb.int/sites/reliefweb.int/files/resources/Multi-hazard_Early_Warning_Systems_A_Checklist.pdf. Accessed 31 Mar 2020
Kazuo S et al (2019) How to save people from earthquake. In: 4th international conference on earthquake early warning
Kong Q et al (2019) Earthquake early warning and beyond: systems challenges in smartphone-based seismic network. https://www.researchgate.net/publication/330553304_Earthquake_Early_Warning_and_Beyond_Systems_Challenges_in_Smartphone-based_Seismic_Network. Accessed 2 July 2020
Kumar A et al (2014) Earthquake early warning system for Northern India. 15 SEE-2014, pp 231–238
Minson SE (2019) The limits of earthquake early warning accuracy and best alerting strategy. Sci Rep
Minson Sarah E et al (2018) The limits of earthquake early warning: Timeliness of ground motion estimates. Sci Adv 4(3
NCERT (2016) Interior of the earth. In: Fundamentals of physical geography. https://www.ncert.nic.in/ncerts/l/kegy203.pdf. Accessed 27 Mar 2020
Strauss JA et al (2016) Benefits and costs of earthquake early warning. Seismol Res Lett 87(3):765–772
Suarez G et al (2018) A dedicated seismic early warning network: the mexican seismic alert system (SASMEX). Seismol Rese Lett
Bay Area Rapid Transit (nd) Earthquake safety. https://www.bart.gov/guide/safety/earthquake. Accessed 28 June 2020
UNDRR (2016) Report of the open-ended intergovernmental expert working group on indicators and terminology relating to disaster risk reduction. United Nations
UNESCO (2015) International platform on earthquake early warning systems (IP-EEWS). UNESCO. https://www.unesco.org/new/en/natural-sciences/special-themes/disaster-risk-reduction/geohazard-risk-reduction/early-warning-systems/ip-eews/
USGS (nd) Earthquake hazards: earthquake early warning. https://www.usgs.gov/natural-hazards/earthquake-hazards/early-warning?qt-science_support_page_related_con=0#qt-science_support_page_related_con. Accessed 15 Dec 2019
USGS (nd) Earthquake hazards: the science of earthquakes. https://www.usgs.gov/natural-hazards/earthquake-hazards/science/science-earthquakes?qt-science_center_objects=0#qt-science_center_objects. Accessed 27 Mar 2020

Chapter 4
Drones for Disaster Risk Reduction and Crisis Response

Tomoyuki Furutani and Masaki Minami

Abstract This chapter aims to introduce how drones are employed for disaster prevention, disaster mitigation and crisis response, especially in Japan. The following threefolds are to be introduced; (1) needs of drones/UAVs for disaster risk reduction (DRR), (2) cases of drones/UAVs in Japan and (3) application technologies of drones for DRR. First, needs and sequential flow of drones/UAVs usage for immediate response, rescue and recovery after disaster are described. Processes and actions conducted to the devastated area, local administration and crisis response team are also explained. Second, drone DRR researches in Japan are to be introduced. Third, technologies operated for DRR with drones/UAVs are shown. Photogrammetry and SfM are essential techniques to build 3D model in the devastated areas. Finally, the authors would like to describe organizational activities/collaborations and preparedness for crisis responses as well as human resource education in Japan.

Keywords Drones · UAVs · DRR · Crisis response

4.1 Introduction

4.1.1 Backgrounds

Drones or unmanned aerial vehicles (UAVs) are emerging technology. They became popular among people since the beginning of 2010s; a French venture company Parrot launched a tinny "AR. Drone" in 2010 and a Chinese venture company DJI launched "Phantom" series from 2012. DJI now occupies almost 80% share of private drone market. Characteristics of these drones are like as "flying smart phones" in the

T. Furutani (✉)
Faculty of Policy Management, Keio University, Tokyo, Japan
e-mail: maunz@sfc.keio.ac.jp

M. Minami
Graduate School of Media and Governance, Keio University, Tokyo, Japan
e-mail: minami@sfc.keio.ac.jp

M. Sakurai and R. Shaw (eds.), *Emerging Technologies for Disaster Resilience*, Disaster Risk Reduction,
https://doi.org/10.1007/978-981-16-0360-0_4

meaning that they employ cameras and sensors, and that they can be manipulated by smart phones. Drones are now applied in the field of agriculture, construction, environment monitoring, entertainment and logistics.

It is also expected that drones play important roles in crisis response, disaster prevention and mitigation. Before private-use drones are deployed, helicopters had been used in this field. However, there are several limitations to employ helicopters for disaster management; (1) flight and maintenance costs are expensive in general, (2) flight altitude is over 150 m (in case of Japan) and (3) licensed pilots are necessary to fly helicopter. Instead, drones can be purchased for everyone in reasonable price, pilots can fly under 150 m and licenses can be obtained simply. Therefore, drones/UAVs are considered to play complementary roles to helicopters.

4.1.2 Everything Had Started on November 3, 2011

The authors' journey on disaster research and practices that employ drones/UAVs had started just after the East Japan Great Earthquake that had devastated a wide area of Eastern Japan on March 11, 2011. This great earthquake caused explosions of Fukushima Daiichi (No. 1) Nuclear Power Plant (F1) because of meltdown, to diffuse radioactive materials especially in Fukushima prefecture. Drones/UAVs had been employed to airborne surveys of air and soil radiation in the contaminated area of F1 accident. Before F1 accident, it had been general to conduct airborne surveys on radiation by employing helicopter that mounts high-spec scintillators. Ministry of Education, Culture, Sports, Science and Technology (MEXT) of Japan had also provided radiation maps by 1–2 km mesh scale that covers Eastern Japan by using the same methods. However, these data are not satisfiable for dwellings and farmers, because they would like to know about their local situation of contamination in detail. Therefore, airborne survey by UAV became a very powerful tool to provide contamination information, i.e. 5–100 m mesh scale on request.

In the winter of 2011, we started airborne survey by employing UAV (Robin PARS), usually used for pesticide spraying, with a small size scintillator and a camera, which was manipulated by professional UAV pilots (Furutani et al. 2012) (Fig. 4.1). The main purpose to use a UAV was not only to detect radiation by scintillator but also to build three-dimensional (3D) maps by structure from motion (SfM) so that the detected radiation can be modified according to elevation and ground surface. As shown in the right figure of Fig. 4.1, micro hot spots of radiation are detected in the midst of the forest. Here, detected data are calibrated by estimating the difference between aviation altitudes and surface elevation that is calculated elevation and the ground feature height by using digital surface model (DSM) so that air radiations at 1 m from the ground are estimated.

Airborne disaster surveys by helicopter and UAV could be complemented mutually. It cost about 1 million JP yen to fly a helicopter for 1 h to detect radiation. When scintillator failed to collect data, it costs higher than that. In 2011, airborne survey with UAV and SfM software was about 4 million JP yen in total, but it could be flown

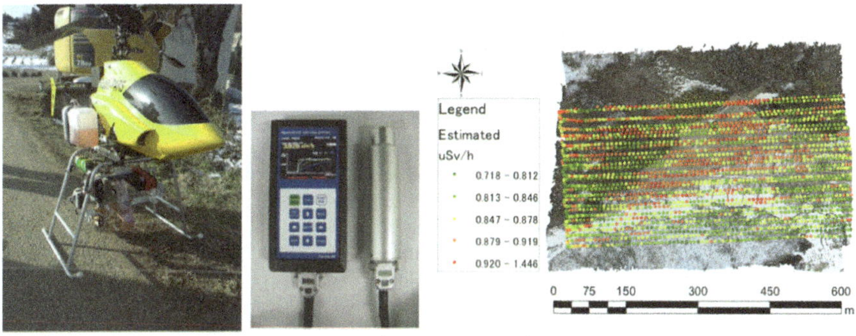

Fig. 4.1 A UAV, scintillator and radiation map employed for airborne survey in 2011

arbitrary as necessary. Helicopter can fly in vast area at high altitude, and UAV can fly in narrow area at low altitudes.

4.1.3 Outlines

This chapter aims to introduce how drones are employed for disaster prevention, disaster mitigation and crisis response, especially in Japan. The following threefolds are to be introduced; (1) needs of drones/UAVs for disaster risk reduction (DRR), (2) cases of drones/UAVs in Japan and (3) application technologies of drones for DRR. First, needs and sequential flow of drones/UAVs usage for immediate response, rescue and recovery after disaster are described. Processes and actions conducted to the devastated area, local administration and crisis response team are also explained. Secondary, several drone DRR researches conducted in Japan (in Hiroshima (landslide in 2018), Okayama (flood in 2018) and Kanagawa (flood and landslide in 2019)) are to be introduced. Third, technologies operated for DRR with drones/UAVs are shown. Photogrammetry and SfM are essential techniques to build 3D model in the devastated areas (Schumann et al. 2019; Gomez and Purdie 2016). Multi-spectrum cameras are also employed to detect wet and vegetation areas in order to understand the range of areas damaged by flood or typhoon. Hyper-zoom camera attached to drones is useful to shoot photos without approaching the devasted spots. Multi-weather type drones are developed to fly drones without considering weather conditions. Not only VTOL UAVs and multi-purpose usage drones but also autonomous vehicles (rovers) and water drones are also expected as next-generation drones/UAVs. A Robot test field in Fukushima is available for R&D on robotics including drones, especially for DRR. Finally, the authors would like to describe organizational activities/collaborations and preparedness for crisis responses as well as human resource education in Japan.

Table 4.1 Needs and Usage of UAVs/drones after disasters

Phase	Rescue, lifesaving and relief	Recover	Reconstruction
Expected usage	• Understanding situations of the devastated areas • Confirming rescuers • Transportation path • Guiding rescue workers • and conveying AED	• Collecting data of secondary disaster • Confirming route used for recovery • Confirming situation of devastated buildings • Supporting to publish damage certificates • Estimating devastated area and disaster garbage	• Support reconstructing life and industry in the devastated area

4.2 Why Drones in Disaster?

4.2.1 Needs and Usage of Drone

Drone is considered as one of the digital tools to solve social issues by utilizing air. Drones and UAVs are expected to provide new and interesting perspectives on the data gathering for disaster management (Tanzi et al. 2016). In the near future, the authors expect that drones and air mobilities are employed for conveying relief supplies, delivering victims and medicines and rescuing. In the Sendai Framework for DRR, drones are indicated as one of the innovative tools for DRR and crisis response (Izumi et al. 2019). In this chapter, unless noted otherwise, "disaster" means earthquake, tsunami, torrential rain/heavy rain, forest fire, landslide and flood.

Needs and usages of UAVs and drones are changing as shown in Table 4.1. Just after disasters happened, drones are used for rescue, lifesaving and relief. For example, they are employed for understanding the situations of the devastated areas, confirming rescuers required transportation path, guiding rescue workers, humanitarian supply chain (Rabta et al. 2018) and conveying AED. In the phase of recovery, they can be used for collecting data of secondary disaster, confirming route used for recovery, confirming situation of devastated buildings, supporting to publish damage certificates and estimating devastated area and disaster garbage. In the phase of reconstruction, drones can play roles to support reconstructing life and industry in the devastated areas.

4.2.2 Drone Specialists/Volunteers in the Devastated Area

In the devastated areas, it is considered that not only responsible persons for crisis response but also public servants, residences and volunteers need to understand risk of the sites and to make decisions by themselves. Local municipalities start to collect necessary information according to Disaster Countermeasures Basic Law; recommendations and orders to residents, disaster situation, protection of victims, reduction of disaster expansion factors, setting/elimination of dangerous areas, actions for recovery/reconstruction, requests for support, financial measures, etc. On the other hand, local residents require information to protect their and their family's life and safety of property; judgment of evacuation behavior, confirmation of safety, confirmation of property, securing of whereabouts, emergency rebuilding of life, grasp of damage situation, rehabilitation of life rebuilding, acceptance of support, cleaning up, response to evacuation life, etc. As mentioned in the previous section, it is considered that information about safety and risks could be provided by using drones so that local municipality, residents, volunteers and related organizations could share situations of the site.

Once a disaster happened, not a few people try to visit the site in order to support the devastated area as volunteers or specialists. Councils of social welfares (CSW) in each municipality become contact counter because authorities and budges are given by local municipalities so that volunteers could work. CSWs also confirm safety of the site when somebody tries to enter the devastated sites. Because suffered local municipalities are too busy to share risk information with residents, volunteers and organizations to accept volunteers. Therefore, they need to make decisions for recovery and reconstruction by understanding the risks of the sites.

4.3 Cases of Risk Surveys by Drones/UAVs

In this chapter, the authors introduce several case studies that we had conducted surveys by drones after disasters in Japan. Here, cases of heavy rain and landslides are to be introduced.

4.3.1 Torrential Rain in Western Japan (July 2018)

In July 2018, torrential rain had attacked Western Japan. Because of landslide and sediment disaster after heavy rain had collapsed many houses that caused 263 dead, 8 missing and 6783 houses destroyed (Wikipedia 2018). Especially in Hiroshima prefecture and Okayama prefecture, the number of dead and missing was 114 and 64, respectively (Fig. 4.2).

In August 2018, "UAV mapping project" had been launched in order to make 2D/3D map creation and to share created maps. Figure 4.3 shows a website and drone survey result in Hiroshima city. In this project, copyrights and downloads of aerial photos, photogrammetry maps and 3D maps are decided to be completely free.

In this case, the authors had conducted risk survey by configuring period, target and method as follows.

Fig. 4.2 Aerial photo by drone in Mabi town, Kurashiki city, Okayama prefecture in July 2018

Fig. 4.3 Website of UAV mapping project (left) and photogrammetry map by drone (right)

Period: 3 days after the disaster and later. Survival rate of the rescuers close to 0% after 72 h or 3 days after disasters and many residents start to recover their lives after that.

Targets: Landslides, mudstone dam and debris flow.

Methods: 3D map creation by software.

In Ninoshima Island, Hiroshima city, photogrammetry survey had been conducted to the entire island so that the local municipality could detect sediment disaster. In this case, pilots had operated Phantom 4 and Phantom 4 Pro at the altitude of 150 m so that ortho-tiles with 3 cm ground resolutions are created (Fig. 4.4). As a result of the survey, several landslide spots could be detected as shown in Fig. 4.5.

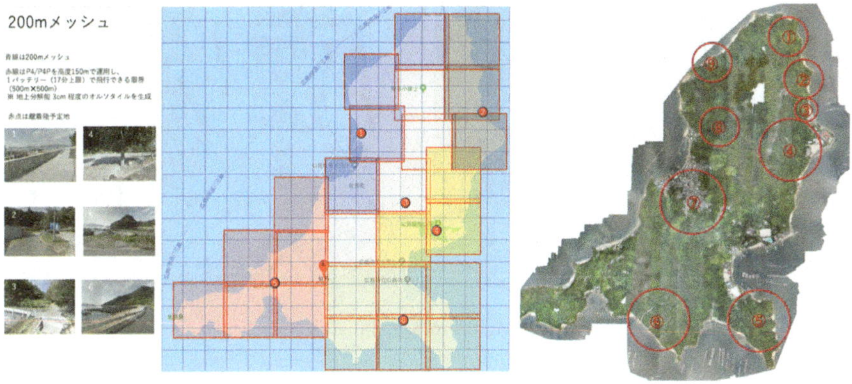

Fig. 4.4 Photogrammetry survey in Ninoshima Island

Fig. 4.5 Landslide spots detected by photogrammetry survey by drone in Ninoshima Island

4.3.2 Typhoon Hagibis (2019.10)

Typhoon Hagibis, also known as the Reiwa 1st East Japan Typhoon, had devastated Eastern Japan and caused widespread destruction in October 2019. In Japan, the number of dead and missing is 86 and 3, respectively in total. In this case, a collaborative team of Keio University and Aoyama Gakukin University had conducted photogrammetry mapping survey in Sagamihara city, Kanagawa prefecture just after the typhoon passed. Because Sagamihara city had a disaster prevention agreement with Prof. Furuhashi's laboratory of Aoyama Gakuin University before typhoon, the drone shooting team was able to act based on the agreement (Fig. 4.6).

Fig. 4.6 Landslide spots by Typhoon Hagibis in Sagamihara City

4.4 Collaboration with Local Municipalities

When conducting UAV surveys for disaster prevention and crisis response, it becomes a crucial point to collaborate with local municipalities. This is mainly because local municipalities need photogrammetry maps by UAV just after disaster attacked their sites. However, not a few residents accept to fly drones even for detecting the devastated areas. Therefore, the partnership between local government and drone specialists is necessary before disaster. In some cases, new technologies and human resources need to be developed according to the situations of target regions.

4.4.1 Provision of Data Collection and Analysis Results

Local municipalities request photogrammetry maps necessary to formulate a recovery plan after disaster. In this case, drone specialists are required to make 2D photogrammetry maps by using ortho-mosaic pictures and create 3D maps by using SfM (structure from motion) software. It is also crucial to provide mapping results so that officers in local administration could evaluate risks in the devastated areas. Therefore, in many cases, mapping results are provided as paper maps instead of digital maps on tablet PC or smart devices as ortho-photo pictures instead of videos.

On the other hand, residents in the devastated areas request bird's eye view pictures or videos on mapping applications in order to know situations of their surrounding area in detail via tablet PCs or smart devices. In case to provide photogrammetry maps to volunteers, the results are preferred to be provided as digital maps on Google Earth or simply as mapper maps, so that they could inform the residents of the situation easily.

4.4.2 Crisis Response Agreement

As indicated in the case of Sagamihara city (3.2), it becomes easier for drone pilots to fly drones after disasters when they have contracted some agreements with local municipalities for the purpose of disaster prevention and preparedness. In the agreements, it is clarified that drone pilots who belong to organizations certified by the local municipalities could fly drones under certain situations such that magnitude of earthquake excess M5, for example, occurred or breakwater due to heavy rain happened. Crisis mappers (Rabta et al. 2018), an NPO in Japan, is a well-known organization to create maps with UAVs for crisis responses.

This kind of agreement between UAV organization and local municipalities spreads after 2016 Kumamoto earthquake. When the 2016 Kumamoto earthquake happened, not a few drone pilots had thought to fly drone for the sake of rescuing and finding victims. As there was no rule between drone NPOs and local municipalities, pilots hesitated to fly drones by themselves. Several days after the earthquake, one dead male victim's body was found by drone. In case the drone survey had been conducted immediately after the disaster, the victim might be found earlier than that.

Once agreements are partnered and drone teams are deployed for crisis response after disaster, necessary expenses are borne by the drone teams and are claimed to the local municipalities. This is almost the same system between civil engineering companies and local municipalities for disaster recovery. It is also necessary for them to discuss how to protect privacy in the devastated areas.

4.4.3 Human Resource Development

In order to make it smooth to deploy drone pilots to the devastated areas after disaster, it is also crucial for local drone deploy team to understand who and where are able to cooperate as drone pilots after disaster. In many cases in Japan, they are licensed pilots and doing business such as drone shooting or drone engineering. It can be said that networking drone pilots in normal times can be useful in emergencies.

In Japan, emergency trainings are conducted in each local municipality every year or regularly. Recently in emergency trainings, drones are sometimes demonstrated to crisis response by fire brigades. As not a few fire stations introduce drones, training firemen as drone pilots are also an important issue (Fig. 4.7).

4.5 Technical Considerations

When conducting crisis response and disaster prevention by drones, photogrammetry is a pillar technology. 3D maps created by modeling techniques are very useful to understand the situation of the devastated sites and disaster prevention area. Structure

Fig. 4.7 Drone demonstrations in emergency training

from Motion (SfM) is one of the typical methods to create 3D maps from aerial photos. SfM is a modeling method for restoring the shape of a three-dimensional space from information that reflects the three-dimensional space contained in images captured by a camera attached at the bottom of drone. Drone teams are required to provide 3D maps to local municipalities or rescue teams immediately after survey. In order to produce precise maps for decision-making, the following threefolds are necessary to be considered; (1) to choose SfM processing method, (2) cleansing of data with errors and (3) survey method. Therefore, in this chapter, technical issues of photogrammetry that should be considered when 3D maps and aerial photos are utilized for crisis response and disaster preventions are indicated.

Regarding SfM, opensource software (i.e. OpenDroneMap) and commercial-based software (i.e. Pix4d and PhotoScan (Metashape)) are well known and well used in the world. How to choose the software is mainly because analysts would like to optimize disk I/O or to maximize GPU processing of their PCs. When motion pictures are used for SfM, Pix4D and PhotoScan are selected in many cases. 3D maps created by SfM and ortho-tile photos can be shared with OpenArealMap. When we consider to share the maps and photos on these kind of websites, it becomes necessary to describe the method of SfM by the analysts.

Because pictures taken by drone cameras sometimes have errors such as out of focus, it is necessary to eliminate these data with errors. Normally, photogrammetry measuring by UAVs has several reasons to include errors; (1) positioning errors by GPS/GNSS and location information errors caused because camera focus position (errors up to several meters) and (2) GPS receiver positions are out of alignment (error increases as altitude increases). In order to eliminate photos with out of focuses, two-dimensional FFT and/or machine learning is employed. When photos are taken by cameras, UAVs are operated in autopilot mode. In case that several drones are operated by many operators/pilots, it becomes necessary to make rules to operate drones in autopilot mode for homogeneous data quality.

The amount of aerial photo data is also one of the issues to be considered in order to operate drone crisis response. In case of photogrammetry survey conducted in Mabi town in Kurashiki city, Okayama prefecture, 3500 photos had been taken by using a fixed wing UAV. In Ninoshima Island in Hiroshima city, Hiroshima prefecture, 1900 photos were used to create 3D maps of the entire island by using rotate wing UAV. Ninoshima Island is a triangular island of about 4 km in the north–south direction and about 3 km in the east–west direction. Two teams (two to three staffs for one team) had taken about 2000 photos for an entire day with DJI Phantom 4 Pro. It also took about 4.5 h to create 3D map by Pix3D Cloud SfM processing. The key is how many aerial photographs can be taken by a limited number of operators using the autopilot.

4.6 Conclusions

In this chapter, how drones are employed in crisis response and disaster risk management in Japan is introduced. The authors would like to point out the following items in order to utilize UAVs/drones for crisis response and DRR in the future. (1) Human resource development is crucial because UAVs/drones cannot be used in the emergency in case that people do not use in the normal phase. It is important to deploy pilots and technicians to operate drones with basic skills. In order to fly drones smoothly and immediately after disaster, it is necessary to create a close relationship between the locals and drone organizations. Universities could play important roles to educate students with knowledge and skills on DRR, crisis response, GIS and robotics. It is the next challenge to make international core-curriculum in this field. (2) In many cases, offices of local municipalities are difficult to respond for requests of drone crisis responses immediately. Therefore, it is necessary for drone manipulators to clarify "needs of the disaster sites", "purposes" and "implementing entities" to fly drones and to cooperate with disaster response headquarters before disasters happen. (3) It is also a crucial point to operate UAVs/drones by multi-operators in order to maintain safety. This is mainly because operators are required to monitor the sky, drones and grounds at the same time.

References

Furutani T, Uehara K, Tanji K, Usami M, Asano T (2012) A study on micro-scale airborne radiation monitoring by unmanned aerial vehicle for rural area reform contaminated by radiation. In: Proceedings of the disaster management 2013, the 9th annual conference of international institute for infrastructure, renewal and reconstruction

Gomez C, Purdie H (2016) UAV-based photogrammetry and geocomputing for hazards and disaster risk monitoring—a review. Geoenviron Disasters 3: 23. https://doi.org/https://doi.org/10.1186/s40677-016-0060-y

Izumi T, Shaw R, Djalante R, Ishiwatari M, Kumoto T (2019) Disaster risk reduction and innovations. Prog Disaster Sci 2:100033. https://doi.org/https://doi.org/10.1016/j.pdisas.2019.100033

NPO Crisis mappers. https://crisismappers.jp/activity.html

Rabta B, Wankmuller C, Reiner G (2018) A drone fleet model for last-mile distribution in disaster relief operations. Int J Disaster Risk Reduct 28:107–112

Schumann G-P, Muhlhausen J, Andreadis KM (2019) Rapid mapping of small-scale river-floodplain environments using UAV SfM supports classical theory. Remote Sens 11:982

Tanzi TJ, Chandra M, Isnard J, Camara D, Sébastien O et al (2016) Towards "drone-borne" disaster management: future application scenarios. XXIII ISPRS congress, commission VIII (Volume III-8), Jul 2016, Prague, Czech Republic, pp 181–189. ff10.5194/isprs-annals-III-8–181–2016ff. ffhal-01516666f

Wikipedia (2018) 2018 Japan floods. https://en.wikipedia.org/wiki/2018_Japan_floods

Chapter 5
VR/AR and Its Application to Disaster Risk Reduction

Tomoki Itamiya

Abstract Evacuation drills are commonly conducted as traditional disaster education to reduce damage from natural disasters. However, participants are not always interested in or committed to such pieces of training. Many researchers are studying earthquakes and flood simulations, but there is a challenge for ordinary people to understand them, especially for young students entirely. Elementary and junior high schools and local governments host disaster preparedness seminars, using hazard maps and photos of past disaster areas to educate about potential risks. To understand the risk, participants select a house or school from the hazard map, read the depth of the floods, and using a numerical value, imagine the disaster scenario. These tasks are challenging to complete, especially for young students. Virtual reality (VR) and augmented reality (AR) technologies are beneficial for solving these issues.

Keywords Virtual reality · Augmented reality · Evacuation drills · Training · School

5.1 Virtual Reality

Virtual reality (VR) can provide an exceptional immersive experience for the experiencer. It has been used to train aircraft pilots and support design in manufacturing. However, traditional VR equipment has been so capable that only a few people can experience it. However, with the recent development of equipment, a realistic experience is now possible at a lower price. VR is the best way to experience the risk of a disaster that is rarely experienced but needs to understand.

T. Itamiya (✉)
Department of Dental Education, School of Dentistry, Kanagawa Dental University, Yokosuka, Japan
e-mail: itamiya@kdu.ac.jp

M. Sakurai and R. Shaw (eds.), *Emerging Technologies for Disaster Resilience*, Disaster Risk Reduction,
https://doi.org/10.1007/978-981-16-0360-0_5

5.1.1 Tsunami and Flash Floods when you are Driving a Car

It is necessary to evacuate as soon as possible when a tsunami occurs, but evacuation using a car is risky. However, many people do not realize the risk. Moreover, many people cannot correctly imagine a disaster situation only by looking at a paper map of hazard. We have developed a virtual tsunami disaster situation experience system called tsunami driving simulator utilizing Oculus Rift, a low-cost head-mounted display (HMD). Our system provides exclusive immersive experiences, such as a tsunami and flash floods attack while driving a car. A person wearing our system's HMD can visualize the disaster event in an actual representation of the area when it might happen, for instance, Tokyo or Nagoya. They can experience the interior of a car, and a tsunami flood that looks exactly like the real thing by 3D-CG using digital stereo images. A person can have the virtual experience of their car getting washed away and flooded by a horrible tsunami while looking at the situation from the driver. Three thousand people experienced this system at evacuation drills and disaster prevention exhibitions organized by local governments. Everyone who encountered our system feels the potential danger of the disaster. The experience is beneficial for disaster risk reduction education. It is an excellent way to help people become more aware of the dangerous risks of a tsunami. Figure 5.1 shows the appearance of the VR tsunami driving simulator. Figures 5.2 and 5.3 show the example of VR scene of tsunami driving simulator.

Fig. 5.1 The appearance of VR Tsunami driving simulator

Fig. 5.2 Example of VR scene of Tsunami driving simulator

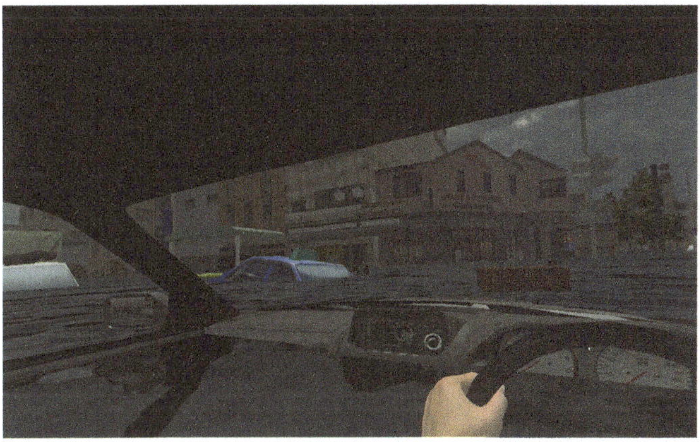

Fig. 5.3 Example of VR scene of Tsunami driving simulator

5.1.2 Evaluation of VR Tsunami Driving Simulator

We evaluated VR's usefulness. The same subjects experienced VR tsunami driving simulator, watched a movie of real flooded situation shoot inside a car, viewed a paper hazard map, and completed a five-point scale questionnaire after each experience. The survey was, "Did this experience make you want to do disaster preparedness?" The order of each experience was randomized to avoid the occurrence of bias. Figure 5.4 shows the comparison between VR and Movie, Map.

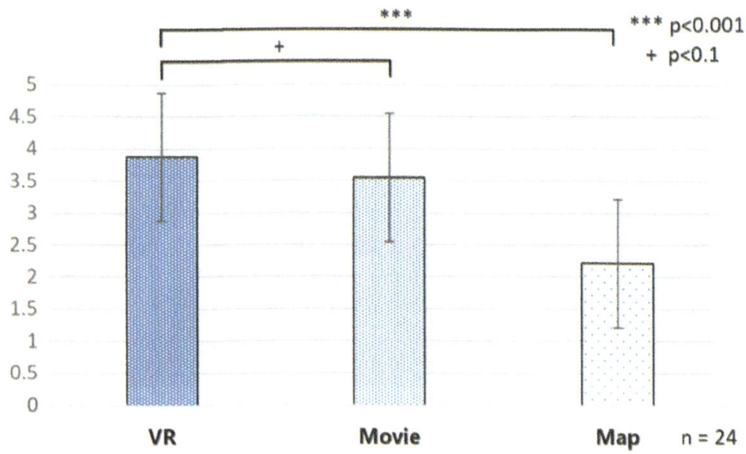

Fig. 5.4 The comparison between VR and Movie, Map

5.1.3 Earthquake

We developed the earthquake experience VR application software for citizens who have not yet experienced a significant earthquake to realize the risk of a substantial quake as their issue. The shaking of the VR earthquake is based on actual quake motion observation data published on the Japan Meteorological Agency website. Many people can experience the app simultaneously at low cost using stand-alone head-mounted display Oculus Go works without PC. It is effortless to use for evacuation drills and disaster prevention events. Users can experience each earthquake by launching this application and selecting the place where a massive earthquake occurred in the past from Japan's map displayed in the VR space with the controller. Various types of earthquake experiences, such as near-field earthquakes and long-period ground motions, can be performed in the same place so that users can understand the differences of shaking. The experience of this app will be a chance to reconsidering the way of thinking about evacuation and daily preparation, such as fixing furniture. We applied the app to disaster risk reduction education at Nasu junior high school at Nasu town, Tochigi prefecture, Japan. Thirty students were able to experience it simultaneously, and a total of 500 junior high school students had a very high educational effect. Figure 5.5 shows the scene of junior high school students experiencing earthquake VR. Figures 5.6 and 5.7 show the example scene of earthquake VR.

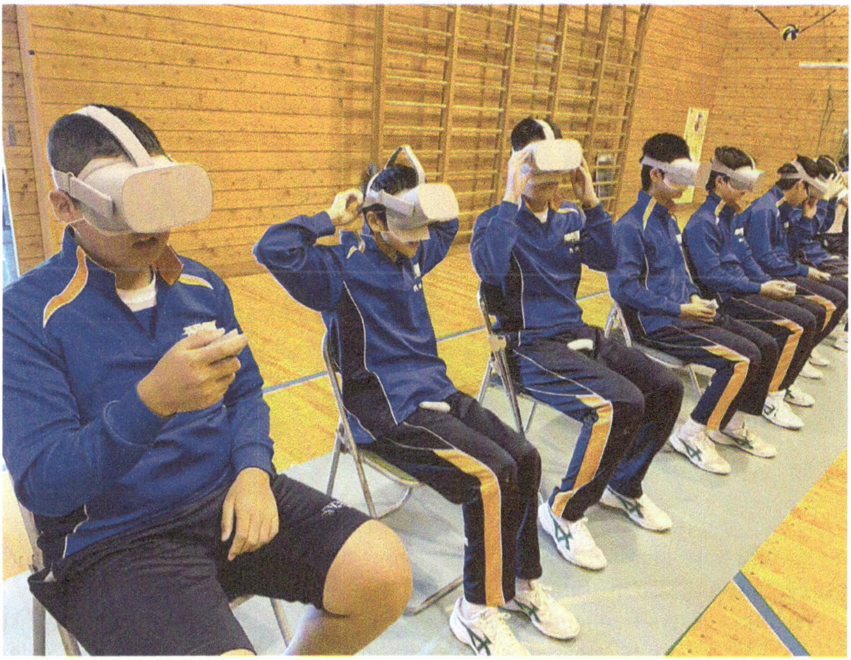

Fig. 5.5 Junior high school students experiencing earthquake VR

Fig. 5.6 Example scene of earthquake VR (Classroom)

5.2 Augmented Reality

Augmented reality (AR) is different from VR in that it can overlay computer graphics on a real-life landscape. With the rapid evolution of smartphones in recent years, AR

Fig. 5.7 Example scene of earthquake VR (Kitchen)

has become very familiar. While it is beginning to be used for directions and work instructions, it is also instrumental in disaster risk reduction education.

Natural disasters frequently occur in Japan. In the great east Japan earthquake in 2011 March and the massive rain disaster in western Japan in 2018 July, many people did not have the crisis consciousness enough to evacuate fast and safely. Numerous studies of flood simulation are performed (US Army 1992; National Research Council 2000), but it is not effortless to understand for ordinary people, especially young students. Elementary and junior high schools and local governments hold disaster preparedness seminars using hazard maps and photographs of past disaster areas and educate potential risks in each area. To understand the risk, they need to find a house from the hazard map, read the depth of the flood of people's home and school using the legend, imagine the disaster situation based on that numerical value. These tasks are challenging for a young student. There is a need for new teaching methods to improve the sense of disaster preparedness among young students in peacetime. We developed the augmented reality smartphone application called Disaster Scope. Users can recognize the danger of floods situation even at a low water level less than 1 m. Also, this application can experience how smoke fills the room when a fire occurs. This app needs only a smartphone and a low price paper headset; therefore, we can use it easily and can handle multiple at the same time.

5.2.1 Application of Tsunami and Flash Floods

The application Disaster Scope installed on a smartphone, CG flooding or fire smoke is displayed superimposed on the real scenery video shot by the camera of a smartphone. Users can experience immersions by wearing a paper headset on smartphones.

Many people can have a unique experience because the preparation is very easy. It is beneficial that many people can experience it at the same time.

After launching the application, the CG water surface is displayed at an arbitrary height, and the water height can be set every 10 cm. Real-time occlusion processing can be done without delay so that the water surface is not displayed behind the actual objects and above the set water height. It can also express the flooding stream and the drifting thing (debris) accompanying it. Furthermore, the collision detection of the real-world's objects and CG debris is also possible. CG debris bounces off when it strikes the actual wall and people. The flow speed can be set to three types (stable, 0.5, 1.5 m/s). Figure 5.8 shows the scene of elementary school students experiencing Tsunami and Flash Floods AR. Figures 5.9, 5.10 and 5.11 show the AR view of the tsunami situation with floating debris.

This app can connect to the Japanese Ministry of Land, Infrastructure, Transport, and Tourism server and get the estimated inundation depth at the current location. Users can view the flood level assumed by the government as augmented reality.

Users can change the color of the water surface. Users can choose transparent, which is easy to recognize as water, or brown as in actual floods. Figure 5.12 shows the AR view of transparent water. Figure 5.13 shows the interface buttons for changing water height and color, flow speed, debris, rainfall, wind speed, flying objects.

If the water height is higher than the height of the smartphone, the underwater expression is displayed. The view becomes brown and cloudy, and the user can see the bottom of the water surface when looking up overhead. By the AR depth meter

Fig. 5.8 Elementary school students experiencing Tsunami and flash floods AR

Fig. 5.9 The AR view of a Tsunami situation with floating debris

Fig. 5.10 The AR view of a Tsunami and flash floods situation

display and occlusion representation, it is easy to understand the height even above the overhead water height. Figure 5.14 shows the example AR view of an underwater expression.

Fig. 5.11 The AR view of a Tsunami and flash floods situation

Fig. 5.12 The AR view of a transparent water

5.2.2 Application of Heavy Rain and Storm

The Disaster Scope can express heavy rain and storms. The user can change the hourly rainfall and wind speed by tapping the button (shown in Fig. 5.13) on the smartphone screen. It can also represent flying objects caused by hurricanes or typhoons. Figures 5.15 and 5.16 show the AR view of heavy rain and storm.

Fig. 5.13 The display of interface buttons

Fig. 5.14 The AR view of an underwater expression

5.2.3 Application of Fire and Smoke

In the fire smoke experience application, a situation occurs where the fire occurs, and the smoke fills the room indoors. When wearing paper goggles and launching this application, the smoke expressed by CG is displayed superimposed on the image of the real landscape. Since the height position of the smartphone from the floor can be precisely sensed from the 3D depth sensor information or image processing (6DoF), in the state of standing up, the smoke expressed by CG is very dense. The surrounding visibility is inferior, but when taking a low crouching posture, even in the state, that smoke becomes thinner, and the real landscape becomes easier to see. Therefore, the user can feel the situation that there is little smoke near the floor. Users can realize

Fig. 5.15 The AR view of heavy rain and storm

Fig. 5.16 The AR view of heavy rain and storm with flying objects

the existence of the neutral zone, which is the boundary between smoke and fresh air. The place to use this application is assumed to be an accessible room with a ceiling height of about 2.8 m, the height of the eyes experiencing the application in a standing state is 1.4 m from the floor (1.4 m from the ceiling). The initial position of the neutral zone is 0.5 m from the floor (2.3 m from the ceiling). Smoke descent time generally depends on the amount of flammable material and the height of the ceiling. It should measure the distance from the ceiling to express smoke concentration. However, due to this application's development specification, the distance from the floor is also easier to obtain than the ceiling. Therefore, the placement position of the smoke is determined based on the height position from the floor. This setting can be arbitrarily changed. The ignition point can be set to any position from this application activation position. The appearance range of smoke can be set to a shape conforming to the actual building's internal structure. The representation of smoke of this application is based on the video taken by the author about the appearance of smoke generation, indoor filling, and diffusion in the actual fire training room of the Kyoto city firefighting activity general center (Minami-Ku, Kyoto city). The expression of smoke is under the guidance of firefighters. Figure 5.17 shows the scene of elementary school students experiencing Fire and Smoke AR. Figures 5.18, 5.19 and 5.20 show the example AR view of the fire and smoke app.

Fig. 5.17 Elementary school students experiencing fire and smoke AR

Fig. 5.18 The AR view of the fire and smoke app

Fig. 5.19 The AR view of the fire and smoke app

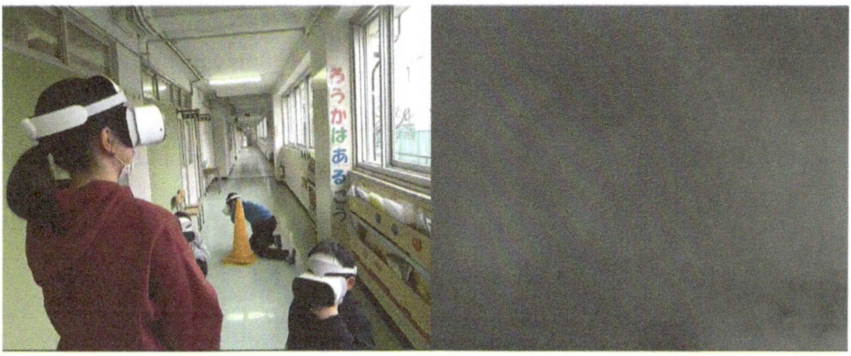

Fig. 5.20 The AR view of the fire and smoke app

5.2.4 Evaluation Scheme

As the first practical use in evacuation drills of elementary schools in this system, we used it on evacuation drills for 343 students in the 7th primary school in Mitaka city, Tokyo, Japan. All the students in that elementary school experienced it in one day. Five sets of smartphones and paper goggles for tsunami flash floods applications, five smartphones for smoke-experiencing applications were prepared, and five students in one group were under the management of teachers. First of all, students experienced a fire smoke situation experiencing an app in the corridor inside the school building, then moved to the schoolyard and experienced the tsunami floods situation experiencing application. Timekeeper staff was assigned, and the experience time was managed within 2 min by each session. After the experience, the children completed a survey and then attended a class with a disaster risk reduction specialist.

5.2.5 *Findings*

As a result of the free response in the questionnaire survey, students commented "In the smoke situation, it was full of smoke, I cannot see anything.", "Water came to my neck.", "I felt like I could understand the feelings of those who died in the tsunami." "This training was an excellent experience. I want to be able to act calm down even if I encounter a disaster." "I was more nervous than the usual evacuation drills." "I thought that evacuation drills are essential." "I thought that it is necessary to prepare for the disaster daily. "I got the impression." The elementary school principal commented: "There was an effect in trying to think about themselves, such as the way of evacuation so that they can be widely used not only at our school but also at other schools." In the questionnaire item, "Did you think about preparing for a disaster through floods and smoke experiences?" 70% of the fifth and sixth-grade 121 students in the 7th primary school in Mitaka city, Tokyo, Japan answered "Extremely well," and 26% answered, "Moderately well." Fig. 5.21 shows whether she/he thought about preparing for a disaster through floods and smoke AR experiences. Also, we practiced in the following schools in Japan, and 3,000 students experienced the AR application. Ibaraki Prefecture Tsuchiura Municipal Manabe Elementary School, Shizuoka Prefecture Kakegawa Municipal Chihama Elementary School, Aichi Prefecture Kota Municipal Southern Junior High School, Kanagawa Prefectural Kawasaki High School, Tochigi Prefecture Nasu junior high school.

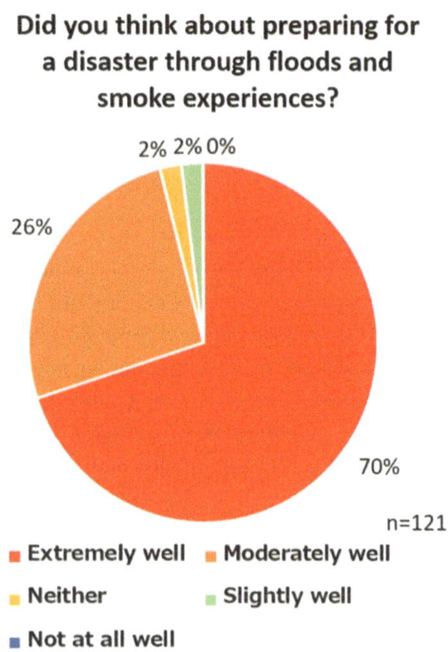

Fig. 5.21 The result of questionnaire survey of AR app

We also did a comparison survey between the tsunami and flash floods situation experience AR app and the tsunami hazard map made by paper. We did a questionnaire survey on 31 participants in evacuation drills and disaster prevention events held at Toyohashi city and Nishio city, Aichi prefecture, Japan. We set two conditions for this evaluation experiment. The first is to use two types of tsunami hazard maps published by Aichi prefecture Toyohashi city and Nishio city, Japan. The second is to indicate flood height using this AR app to 1.2 m above the ground. Similarly, a tsunami hazard map was designated with a circle marking one inundation point of 1.2 m above the ground and explained to the subjects. Table 5.1 shows the evaluation item of the AR app and the hazard map.

Figure 5.22 shows the comparison result between the tsunami and floods AR application and the tsunami hazard map.

In the fire smoke experience application, we compared the 6 DoF (Degrees of Freedom) application that can detect the height from the floor, and the 3 DoF application that can sense only the tilt of the smartphone, cannot detect the height. Table 5.2 shows the evaluation items of the Fire Smoke situation experience application and Fig. 5.23 shows fire smoke experience 6DoF and 3DoF application comparison.

The questionnaire survey suggested that using this AR application is useful for improving crisis awareness among young students and citizens.

Table 5.1 Evaluation item of the AR app and the Hazard map

	Contents of question	Evaluation
Q1	Can you accurately imagine the depth of the flood?	5 stages from 1 to 5
Q2	Did you feel a sense of crisis due to flood depth?	5 stages from 1 to 5
Q3	In the event of an earthquake or heavy rain, will you think about evacuating yourself by thinking of tsunamis and flooding?	5 stages from 1 to 5

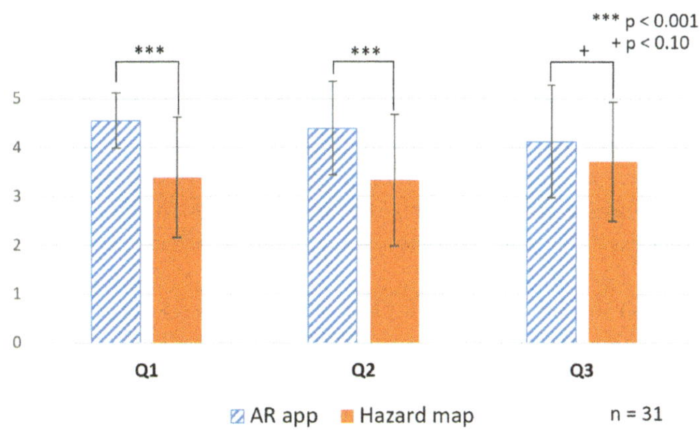

Fig. 5.22 Comparison result between the AR app and the Hazard map

Table 5.2 The evaluation items of fire smoke experience 6DoF and 3DoF application comparison

	Contents of question	Evaluation
Q1	Did you accurately imagine the occurrence of smoke caused by fire?	5 stages from 1 to 5
Q2	Did you feel the sense of crisis caused by smoke?	5 stages from 1 to 5
Q3	Did you think that you should evacuate by lowering your attitude so as not to get caught up in smoke?	5 stages from 1 to 5

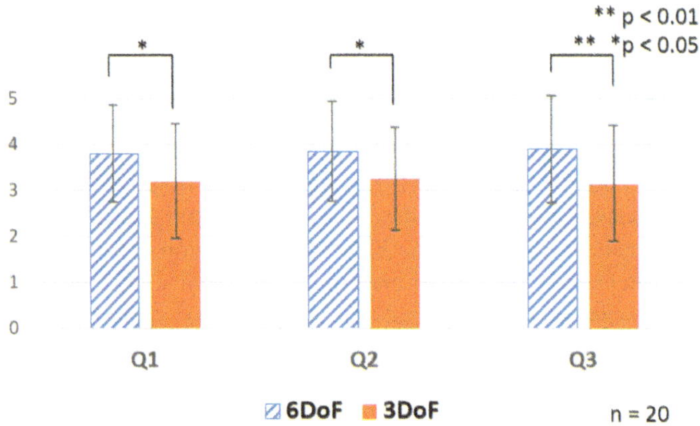

Fig. 5.23 Comparison result between the fire smoke app 6DoF and 3DoF

5.3 Discussion

Both VR and AR are useful for disaster risk reduction education, but each has its strengths and weaknesses. Users can perform interactive operations in VR and get a high-quality experience and immersion. However, VR needs to create CG of the experience place, and the production cost is high. Creating a new experience place desired by the user generally costs more than 10,000 USD. Since it takes about 3–5 min for each person to experience VR, it is difficult for everyone to experience a disaster prevention event involving many people. Also, there is a need for staff to support the experience, and operation requires cost. VR is uncomfortable for users when the HMD screen update speed is slower than 30 fps. When the 3D-CG model in the VR space is complicated, the frame rate tends to be slow, so developers need to take this into account.

Since AR can display CG on the place where users are, users do not need to create a 3D-CG model of the experience place like VR, and the cost is low. Recent improvements in smartphone performance have enabled high-quality AR expressions such as realistic floods and smoke. However, since the AR development environment is progressing rapidly, developers need to continually collect information and search for optimal methods at that time. In many cases, there is no precedent, so the skills of the developer are required.

5.4 Conclusion

We introduced that VR and AR are useful for disaster risk reduction education. Shortly, wearable devices, for instance, eyeglass-type devices, are likely to become mainstream as the next information devices after smartphones (Kelly 2017). With the spread of AR using eyeglass-type equipment and the next-generation communication network so-called 5G, it is possible to display real-time disaster prediction on each eyeglass. As a result, we can expect people to raise their awareness of the crisis and reduce the number of disaster victims due to early evacuation.

References

Kelly K (2017) The Inevitable: understanding the 12 technological forces that will shape our future. Penguin Books, New York

National Research Council (2000) Risk analysis and uncertainty in flood damage reduction studies. National Academy Press, Washington, DC

US Army Corps of Engineers Institute for Water resources, Guideline for Risk and Uncertainty Analysis in Water Resources Planning, Volume I: principles with technical appendices, IWR Report, 92-R-1, Mar 1992

Part II
Communication and Community Toward Disaster Resilience

Chapter 6
Communication Structure, Protocol and Data Model Toward Resilient Cities in Japan

Mihoko Sakurai

Abstract This chapter proposes a wider view of disaster risk reduction in local communities through structured communication and information exchange. Smart city planning shows that resilience toward disasters equates with confidence in efficient responses. Information collection, sharing and delivery are, therefore, the keys in local communities to providing effective disaster management operations and relief to citizens. Community members clearly demonstrate expectations in the organization of information and communication that would increase resilience. Multiple stakeholders such as local municipalities and communities, state and prefectural government, private industries, NPOs and civil volunteers should all be involved in disaster response. Required information at each organizational level varies in terms of information granularity and contents. Moreover, there is no prior understanding of who owns what information, a fact which hinders collecting and sharing it effectively in the event of a disaster. A standardized data model that can be shared by related organizations on an everyday basis is mandatory. In addition, a common structure must be in place for information delivery from a local municipality to its citizens. This chapter asks what the information needed in a disaster consists of and how we can structure it across different organizations and devise a communication protocol between local municipalities and their citizens.

Keywords Data model · Information sharing · Disaster management · Local municipalities · Communication protocol

6.1 Introduction

Natural disasters occur frequently in Japan and therefore require well thought-through responses premised on collaboration with various stakeholders. Many organizations, groups and individuals are involved in disaster response. At the forefront of coordination lie local municipalities, i.e., towns and villages. For them, the

---

M. Sakurai (✉)
Center for Global Communications, International University of Japan, Tokyo, Japan
e-mail: msakurai@glocom.ac.jp

M. Sakurai and R. Shaw (eds.), *Emerging Technologies for Disaster Resilience*, Disaster Risk Reduction,
https://doi.org/10.1007/978-981-16-0360-0_6

primary goal of disaster response is to save lives and ensure the safety of their citizens. Securing and operating evacuation shelters and managing relief supplies are on-going secondary missions (Sakurai et al. 2014). Local municipalities must also be prepared to respond to inquiries from citizens following a disaster. Information sharing with related organizations and communication with citizens are the keys to rapid disaster response operations. Specifically, effective communication is one of the major requirements of an organization aiming to bolster resilience (Horne and Orr 1998). Moreover, cross-sector collaboration is crucial in reducing disaster risks (Sakurai et al. 2017). Efficient communication strategies and coordinating activities in a disaster situation are found to enhance cross-sector and cross-organizational collaboration and consequently increase resilience.

According to a survey of mayors of the Japanese local government, which the author conducted in 2019, the following 10 items were listed as goals for disaster communication.

(1) Disaster mitigation
(2) Providing a sense of security to citizens and a safe environment
(3) Promptly grasping the situation, collecting accurate information and making appropriate decisions
(4) Fostering initiative and self-help, enabling citizens to act on their own accord
(5) Saving lives through community effort or individually
(6) Collaboration among citizens, local communities and city administration
(7) Rebuilding lives of victims
(8) Preventing secondary disasters
(9) Accurate transmission of support information to citizens
(10) Quick recovery and reconstruction

Although these goals sound general, emphasis is placed on encouraging self-help and mutual support on the basis of appropriate information from local communities.

The same survey enquired about important issues arising from adverse conditions negatively affecting the above goals. The following list was produced.

1. Lack of know-how of ICT tools in general
2. The need for a disaster response and information sharing tool that is standardized nationwide and actually in service (rather than kept for use-in-emergency)
3. Correct timing of evacuation advisories and instruction transmission
4. Dissemination of dangerous or vulnerable site information to citizens
5. Sharing knowledge and experience from lessons of past disasters
6. Spontaneously grasping a given situation in highly damaged areas
7. How to apply new technology to an already existing disaster prevention system
8. Information sharing with related organizations
9. Incompatibility of information systems among different stakeholders
10. Careful consideration of information-vulnerable people (e.g., the elderly)

While mayors recognized information sharing through IT platforms is critical, they alsonoted the lack of IT literacy within municipalities. Getting the big picture of a situation and transmitting risk information and appropriate evacuation instructions to citizens become top priority. Resilient cities or communities should sustain their functions even when a disaster or an emergency downgrades people's everyday life. The Rockefeller Foundation expressed this requirement in its definition of urban resilience as follows: "the capacity of individuals, communities, institutions, businesses, and systems within a city to survive, adapt, and grow no matter what kinds of chronic stresses and acute shocks they experience.[1]" This chapter focuses on disaster communication that helps a city to increase its capacity for resilience and calls for a common communication protocol for conducting smooth disaster relief operations. Disaster communication includes two types of activities: (1) information collection/sharing and (2) delivery. The former collects and shares information from related organizations, communities and citizens, aiming at smooth mutual collaboration. The latter primarily focuses on citizens by delivering risk and disaster information in order to reduce risks threatening the population at the time of a disaster.

The following section provides a systematic analysis to show how Japanese local municipalities collect and share information with other organizations and deliver information to citizens in a disaster response. The structure of the entire chapter relies on information system design theory stressing the following three characteristics (Markus et al. 2002): (1) working process, (2) work context and (3) information requirements. In addition, to get discussions to be grounded in social issues, this study employs design science methodology. First, a brief introduction of the methodology and data collection is given. Information requirements for disaster communication are specified followed by an illustration of a working process and context. Finally, a common communication protocol for information collection/sharing and delivery is discussed.

6.2 Methodology

Design science methodology aims to derive design requirements and systems features from practical observations. The design science approach begins with the notion of "the sciences of the artificial," advocated by Simon (1996). Design is defined as "the use of scientific principles, technical information and imagination in the definition of a structure, machine or system to perform pre-specified functions with the maximum economy and efficiency" (Walls et al. 1992). In an industry concerned with developing new products, the importance of careful observation is recognized as well. Direct observation and good understanding of people's needs and wants lead innovation activities following design principles to increase the value of a product (Brown 2008).

[1] https://100resilientcities.org/resources/#section-1, last accessed on May 25th, 2020.

The design science paradigm has its roots in engineering, and thus its aim is problem-solving (Hevner et al. 2004). Design science is concerned with creating artifacts to achieve certain goals while natural science is concerned with explaining how and why things are (Simon 1996). With regard to a product, then, its design refers to "a plan of something to be done," while the design process means "to plan the parts of the intended structure [so that] all requirements will be satisfied" (Walls et al. 1992). What this methodology aims to solve are particularly situated problems by providing new ways to develop or improve organizations through the design of artifacts. Design science methodology can produce concepts, constructs and models as well as artifact instantiations (March and Smith 1995). Previous research indicates that qualitative research methodologies are quite valuable when aiming to understand social settings (Myers 1997). In that sense, then, this study applies case study methodology to problem identification. Information requirements are derived from actual problems.

6.3 Data Collection

As part of this study, a series of workshops, motivated by the mayors' survey, were held with disaster management staff in a number of Japanese municipalities (Table 6.1). The overall objective was to get a handle on the issues involved in disaster communication, the processes of information collection/sharing and delivery. The participating towns and cities were: Muroran, Sendai, Joso, Chiba, Kamakura, Fujisawa, Higashishirakawa Village, Tanba, Kobe, Nishinomiya, Kochi, Genkai Town and Kumamoto.

In each workshop, a couple of municipalities shared their experiences and lessons learned from a past disaster. This was followed by discussions regarding communication, information sharing/delivery, the utilization of ICT and solutions applicable to future disasters. Specifically, our focus was on exploring the process of information collection/sharing and delivery as well as context, which would clarify the actors in that process.

Table 6.1 Workshop date and participants

Date of workshop	Number of participants
May 16, 2019	18
July 11, 2019	15
August 28, 2019	10
October 17, 2019	12
November 14, 2019	14
January 16, 2020	10

6.4 Process and Context Identification

6.4.1 Information Collection and Sharing

The Fig. 6.1 illustrates the process and context of information gathering before and during 72 h following a disaster. Local municipalities are located at the center. The figure shows what information is required by local municipalities and how to collect it. The asterisk refers to type of information, and italics denote tools that carry information.

Stakeholders, who are important when collecting information, are first infrastructure operators of utilities such as electricity and gas, which are indispensable for sustaining people's everyday life. At the same time, information on the operating status of railways and buses from transportation companies is also essential, especially in urban areas. Local municipalities exchange information on type and degree of damage and confirm the safety status of residents with fire departments and the police. Traditional communication tools such as phones and faxes are used to collect that information. Some municipalities have hotlines with infrastructure providers. For information such as weather warnings, local officials check the Japan Meteorological Agency (JMA) website or emergency bulletins. The officials also compile people's requirements of relief materials at an evacuation center. This is often done by analog means using pen and paper. In some cases, residents may send information about damage incurred directly through social media such as Twitter and other smartphone applications. Figure 6.1 shows that information which a municipal government should collect does not automatically collect at disaster management headquarters, but city officials take it there by themselves. It is indeed a labor-intensive operation.

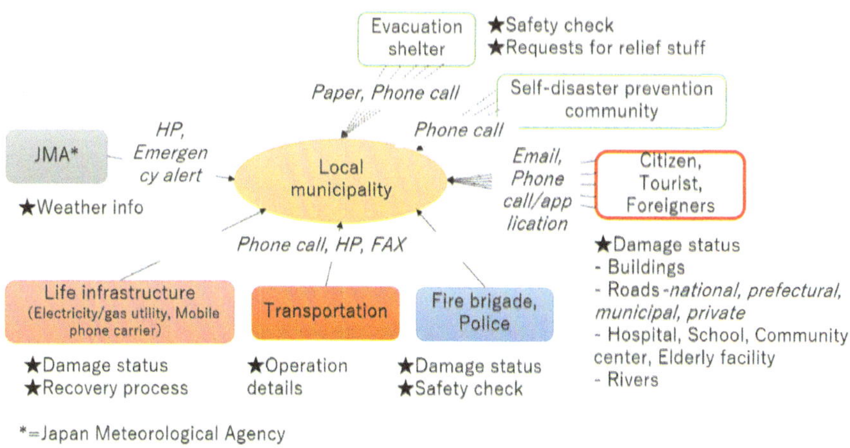

Fig. 6.1 Structure of information collection and sharing in Japanese municipality

6.4.2 Information Delivery

The Fig. 6.2 illustrates the structure of information delivery centered on local municipality. It shows that the ultimate purpose of information delivery for a local government is to deliver life support information to its citizens. As in Fig. 6.1, the asterisk and the italics refer to type of information and information delivery tools, respectively.

Compared with the process of information collection/sharing, that of information delivery is rather limited. Essential information is about evacuation centers, restoration status of lifeline infrastructure, emergency alerts and disaster support that helps people protect their own or their family's lives. Information delivery tools are diversifying with emails and smartphone applications. These days, even the development of disaster management applications for a smartphone has become quite popular. Also, AI speakers are now available as a means of information delivery to those who do not possess or are unable to use a smartphone or disaster radio.

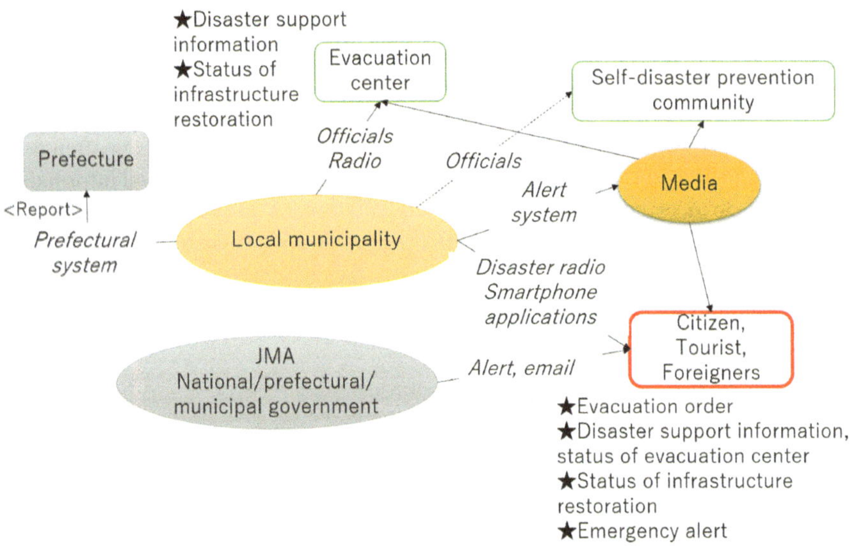

Fig. 6.2 Structure of information delivery in Japanese municipality

6.5 Issues and Requirements

This section identifies problems in information sharing and delivery and guides us to consider what is required for future disaster communication.

6.5.1 Information Collection and Sharing

The workshop pointed to the following seven issues in information collection and sharing, which were shared in all participating localities. Quotations made at the workshop are in italics.

(1) Townships collect information in a labor-intensive manner using phone call, FAX, media sources and scrolling websites. Although there is no difference among municipalities in the types of information gathered at the time of a disaster, there is no common system or guideline to effectively collect them. As an official says: *(Looking back on the past earthquake), the sources of information from which to grasp the situation were TV, Yahoo, and aerial Google photographs. From these sources, we learned about gas supply interruption and water pipe rupture. Safety confirmation is the responsibility of self-help disaster prevention communities and residents' associations. However, systematic methods of collecting information from these groups have not been established.*

(2) Local municipalities receive various information from citizens through a number of tools and channels including phone call, email, SNS, fax and so on. However, a method of organized use within municipal governments has not been established.

(3) Inadequate information collaboration with a prefectural government. An official comments: *When the gas supply was restored, our city received no advance information and we suddenly got a phone call from a utility company asking us to specify the location for a recovery unit. (Prefectural government might have known the supply resumption in advance, but) no information was passed between prefectural and municipal governments.*

(4) Since the granularity of information that a municipality needs to collect differs from that of prefectures, information sharing becomes complicated and duplicated in some cases. An official says: *The city needs an individual's name to confirm its safety, but a prefectural government requires information on where and how many people are affected.*

(5) Each stakeholder has a different information management system. Information is not shared on daily basis. An official says: *The fire department has one information system for managing daily emergency work. Construction and civil engineering departments have another to record daily malfunctions such as water leaks in gutters.*

(6) It is difficult to correctly interpret collected information and grasp the full picture which would guide mayors to make appropriate decisions.
An official says: *Unable to get any information, a staff member took a tablet and patrolled the site in the middle of the night. Photos and videos convey the situation, but I could not see exactly how bad the situation really was. It was difficult to judge.*
Another official says: *For storm and flood damage, the information we can check in advance is the weather forecast and the webcam. Since live cameras were not installed along all rivers, it was difficult to know the place where the water level was rising. It is hard to grasp the situation from information coming in by telephone from nearby citizens.*
(7) There are many residents who require support when evacuating. But there are not enough people to support them and confirm their safety.
These issues can be broadly divided into three categories: (a) how to collect information, (b) how to organize and share collected information and (c) how to use collected information for decision-making.

Based on these findings, fundamental requirements for information collection and sharing are:

(1) A common information structure or data model for organizing collected and/or required information and
(2) The managing and sharing of such information with stakeholders on a daily basis.

In addition to gathering information on the big picture of a disaster, municipal government officials are busy in responding to inquiries from residents. Human resources are not necessarily sufficient when organizing inquiries. Inquiries are often duplicated. For example, the most frequently asked questions are "where are evacuation shelters," "is my house subject to evacuation instructions," "what should I do now that my house is heavily damaged," including also complaints about gas/water leaks, and a washed away road or collapsed bridge, and queries such as "when will relief goods arrive," "when are roadblocks removed," "when are electricity, gas and water restored," "when will a disaster victim certificate be issued," "what happened to city hall," and so on. Citizens need a status update on the situation, while officials move about trying to collect that information on foot.

This was the case in Kamakura, where city officials received 1,153 inquiries when Typhoon Faxai hit the area in September 2019. There were also 924 enquiries when Typhoon Hagibis struck Japan a month later. The city appointed 20 officials to answer the phone. However, it became impossible to catch up with all inquiries as their number increased rapidly. Consequently, the city organized an information team with six officials. The team members recorded inquiry information onto a PC, eliminated duplication and organized content. While there was an enormous increase of information and tasks, which are mandatory following a disaster, the number of officials that could handle it remained about the same as it was before the disaster.

This points to the need for more efficient organization of incoming information, rather than the need for adding personnel in an ad hoc fashion.

6.5.2 Information Delivery

Issues in information delivery are also common to local communities. (Statements made at the workshop are again in italics.)

(1) How to deliver information to tourists, foreigners and business travelers who are temporarily staying in an affected area.
One official says: *We need to consider what people are looking for when they move beyond the (geographical) boundary of the local area.*
Another official says: *Information required for individual travelers and business travelers should be differentiated. We also need to prepare different types of information in different locations, i.e., at a tourist information site and at a general information center in the municipal office.*

(2) How to promote multilingual support and how to transmit multilingual information to those who do not understand Japanese.

(3) How should information be personalized and customized? It is necessary to consider the status of the recipient in terms of age, family composition and mental or physical challenges, before contacting those who need to evacuate immediately or require support in evacuation.
An official comments: *In heavy rain, city officials made a phone call to elderly people living alone in the evacuation areas and requiring evacuation support, and [merely] informed them that an evacuation advisory had been issued.*
Another official says: *It is important to have an arrangement and a system for sharing information among local welfare officers and care workers who will provide necessary support to those who need it.*

(4) What are desirable tools and what is the best timing for the delivery of information facilitating evacuation?
An official says: *In some cases, the mayor himself urged people to evacuate via disaster prevention radio, and the residents started to feel a sense of great urgency.*

(5) How to balance information delivery in normal times and during a crisis.
An official comments: *A tool that is not used during normal times cannot be used during a disaster.*
Another official says: *If we oversupply information during normal times, citizens will hesitate to look at essential information during a disaster.*

The workshops summarized the requirements in information delivery into proper timing of dissemination, personalized information delivery, multilingualization and appropriate balance between normal and critical times of information delivery. It was also pointed out that while delivery tools were diversifying, consideration would have to be given to people who are not readily familiar with digital technology.

Basic requirements for information delivery are:

(1) Organization of collected information allowing efficient access and
(2) Personalized information delivery to those who need immediate action for saving their lives.

6.5.3 Bottlenecks of Information Systems

Somewhat different issues also arose from the workshop discussions and revealed a bottleneck due to the differentiation of information systems. One example is the daily use of incompatible information systems by different organizations. Police, fire departments and other related agencies use different systems for disaster management. Differentiation of daily use systems hinders interoperability of information integration which results in additional trouble in information sharing. City officials are forced to extract data from their own disaster management system in CSV format and input them into another system, which is used for sending emergency alerts to citizens' cellphones and smartphones. The same thing happens when a local government reports its damage status to a prefectural government. Duplication emerges due to different systems of data management.

Another example comes from Kumamoto city. The city drew up a disaster information triage form on paper, instead of employing an information system when responding to phone calls from citizens. Officials filled out the triage form based on what they heard on the phone and faxed it to the related department within local government. Such information collection/sharing is performed by human resources. It means officials may not necessarily be familiar with aspects of information technology. In the event of a disaster, they tend to use what they already know and are familiar with. Disaster risk reduction is, therefore, not only always achieved with high-tech solutions but also with methods people are comfortable with.

6.6 Discussion: Solution Proposition

As mentioned previously, a single shared structure for organizing information collection and delivery can contribute to disaster risk reduction effectively. The fundamental issue of current disaster communication in local municipalities is that information is not shared among stakeholders on an everyday basis. The inefficiency of information gathering by human trial and error is due to the fact that municipal officials have no advance knowledge of the stakeholders who have the required information. In addition, in the event of a disaster, various industries and civil organizations will begin to support the affected area. Because information sharing by newly joined organizations is done ad-hoc, a relief organization will not know when a disaster-affected municipality is in trouble and what their needs may be, and vice versa. An official in municipal government cannot tell what a relief organization can do to support them. Indeed, there exists a gap in communication between different stakeholders. Therefore, it is necessary to establish a common data model that enables continuous information sharing beyond any particular municipal government office. It is also important to share a common communication protocol for smooth and quick information delivery to citizens.

6.6.1 Common Structure for Information Collection and Sharing

Chen et al. (2013) developed an emergency data model for a fire department in the USA based on the activity theory. Chen et al. (2013) produced an ununified information-sharing format for all the different regions the fire department belongs to. They developed an emergency data model for smooth information sharing among the different fire departments. It categorizes necessary information for emergency response into threat assessment and incident command.

Following the Great East Japan Earthquake in 2011, the Ministry of Internal Affairs and Communications in Japan classified the information required at the time of a disaster into the specific information categories (Ministry of Internal Affairs and Communications 2013).

They include information and instructions on evacuation, evacuee safety, victims and injuries, fire, earthquake, tsunami, evacuation center locations, missing person notifications, temporary accommodation, transportation, roads, electricity and gas restoration, medical institutions, administrative service, school and public facilities, financial institutions, shops, volunteers, relief supplies, volunteer application and recruitment, temporary housing, disaster victim certificates, subsidies donations and house reconstruction.

Based on discussions in our series of workshops and on an earlier study of disaster information categories and appropriate data model, this chapter proposes the following model for information collection and sharing (Fig. 6.3).

The model consists of three categories: (1) threat assessment, (2) service restoration and (3) response command. The first category specifies the event. It includes hazard risk information that gives detailed information on different types of crises; earthquake, tsunami, flooding and so on. Threat information for property, population and environment needs to be collected under this category. The second category shows the restoration status of public/private services, which are necessary to recover people's everyday lives. Major items under this category are transportation, lifeline infrastructure and public/private facilities such as hospitals and schools. The final category aims to organize internal command operations. This includes the details of response teams, available resources and organizations/individuals who are involved in relief activities. The status of relief operations also needs to be recorded. The most complicated and critical operations might be the opening of evacuation

Fig. 6.3 Common data model for information collection and sharing in a disaster (*data source* Chen et al. 2013; Ministry of Internal Affairs and Communications 2013 and our workshops)

centers, counting the number of evacuees and other related tasks. Therefore, careful information collection and sharing are important.

Each category requires different stakeholders to collaborate with. There are a small number of cases where a local government itself acts as an information source. For instance, the first category requires weather and risk information from JMA, casualty and damage information from police and a fire department, and hazard information from an expert in the area. It might be possible to extract sensor information through IoT devices throughout a city, which could show the real-time water level of a river. The second category obviously needs collaboration with transportation and utility companies. Stakeholders managing schools, hospitals, retail shops are also essential partners. Sharing such information in every day, year-round operations can strengthen the immediate response after a disaster and thus contribute to disaster risk reduction. The third category is focusing on internal operations and administrative information. When compared to the other categories, far fewer stakeholders are involved.

However, internal information sharing and collaboration with volunteers and NPOs, who participate in relief operations, become crucial.

The proposed data model covers most of the frequently asked questions from citizens. If a local municipality stored information according to that structure, they would be able to respond smoothly to inquiries. Suitable information technology is readily available to develop data storage supporting comprehensive information collection and sharing for everyday use.

6.6.2 Common Structure for Information Delivery

In order to effect the quick organization of collected information as well as personalized and multilingual information delivery, having a common communication protocol is required. As shown previously, information from municipal governments to citizens is delivered through various IT tools. While delivery tools are differentiated, there is no standardized form of information delivery except emergency alert and evacuation advisory.

Based on the workshop sessions discussed above and the report by the Ministry of Internal Affairs and Communications (2013), this chapter proposes the following structure for information delivery (Fig. 6.4). Items in italics indicate information that can be personalized according to the condition of citizens or residential location. For instance, weather forecast and hazard prediction can be delivered to groups or

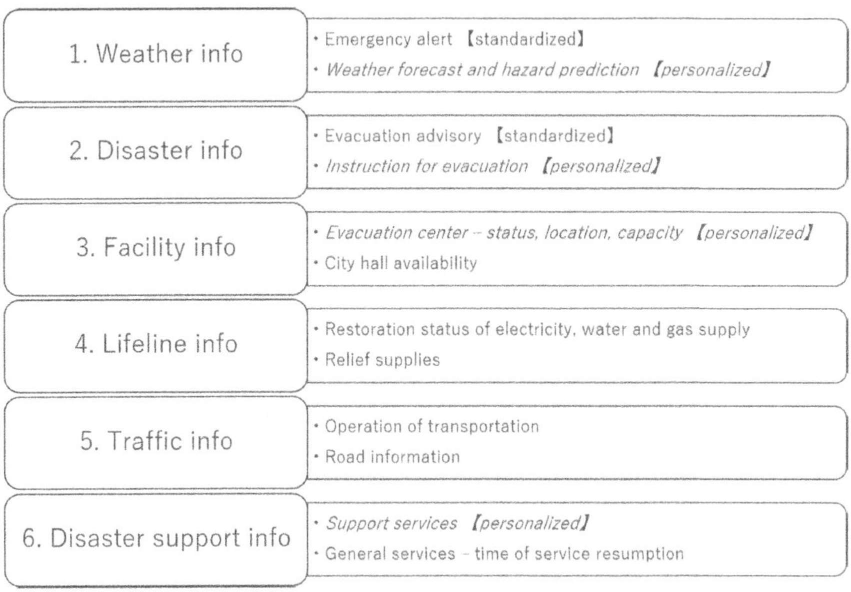

Fig. 6.4 Common information structure for information delivery in a disaster

individuals who live in disaster vulnerable areas. It promotes situation awareness of those groups and enhances immediate actions to save their lives. Instruction for evacuation is also demanded by foreign tourists who are not familiar with Japanese evacuation practices, and people who need special support for evacuation. Location of the evacuation center, its opening status and capacity are also necessary to those who are living nearby. Finally, disaster support information can be customized according to the level of damage and household composition.

Preferably, just as for emergency alerts and evacuation advisories that possess a standardized format of alert level and message, other items are also supposed to follow a standardized protocol when delivered to citizens. Information technology can support multilingualization much more conveniently if each information item follows a common communication protocol. It enables the coding of information data such that it is smoothly and quickly transacted throughout the technological platform.

6.6.3 Policy Implications at the National Level

The Japanese National Government has developed various programs for enhancing resilience of municipal government. Most of them aim to create a shared platform between itself and local municipalities, private companies, universities and national ministries. This platform provides for appropriate and stream-lined matching between needs and solutions in the shape of a hub-and-spokes network. Special interest groups are organized under such a program and platform in order to provide space for coordinated discussions on specific topics. A municipality submits its needs to be resolved, and the shared platform enhances public–private collaboration. Stakeholders who are interested in accessing and providing topics or problems can contact and collaborate with the local government. As of early 2020, collaboration platforms around smart city, SDGs and green infrastructure are active and each of them appeals to hundreds of members from government, enterprise and research sectors.

This chapter's proposition on communication structure might fit well into these initiatives. First, the present study started with identifying problems in disaster communication. There is a commonality in taking the problem-oriented approach. Second, as stated previously, disaster communication requires collaboration with various stakeholders. Common communication structure can help such collaboration in the field. Third, even though recognizing that the proposed structure cannot be entirely fixed, but will be changing in association with future disaster situations, a public–private collaboration platform will be useful.

While noticing similarities and the fit of this study into national government initiatives, there are some policy implications, which should be acknowledged.

(1) A research organization or other-related institutions that can identify problems based on what happened in past events ought to play an essential role on the given platform.

Local government possesses lessons from past disasters, though without always being aware of all problems and their interconnectedness. So, when a local municipality submits its aspirations to a given national platform they are commonly translated into an idealized strategy such as "protect people's safety and save lives" rather than being oriented toward the actual problems encountered at disaster sites. Specific desires or needs that came up in those lessons learned from past emergencies are not taken into account. It is in this area that a research organization can help clarify and organize what is necessary for future submissions.

(2) Practical implications based on empirical research should be reflected in national policy-making.
A process of national policy-making involves various external experts or experts committee. These experts provide their domain knowledge. If a policy theme relates to local municipalities, such as disasters, a few representative officials from a municipality may be invited to provide insights from their experiences. However, local perspectives are hardly considered when discussing a national policy. This generates a gap between a municipal and national policy. Evidence-based policy-making should be more encouraged in order to reflect critical requirements in the field.

(3) Horizontal learning platform for local municipality can enhance a city's resilience.
This study organized a series of workshops to identify information requirements in disaster communication. Participants were officials from local governments. Research activities can record lessons learned from a past event, but it would be better to have a national repository, which cares to store past disaster lessons such as to allow communication and information exchange laterally among all local communities. However, any given national collaboration platform aims to connect a municipality and other stakeholders hierarchically, top to bottom, therefore horizontal connections between municipalities are lost in such initiatives. In general, even though prefectural government takes a role in organizing its municipalities, it too creates mostly vertical connections. Based on this chapter's empirical research, we could benefit from sharing knowledge beyond the prefectural boundary, resulting in a strong horizontally spaced structure between municipalities.

6.7 Conclusion

Almost every year in recent Japan, we experience a disaster usually referred to as "once every few decades." Those disasters are quite large-scale and require the dispatch of self-defense forces to act as a disaster relief agency. Despite our experience and knowledge accumulated over time, we have not yet developed the best practice for efficient communication among a local municipality, stakeholders and citizens in such times. On the other hand, with the widespread of IT tools, disaster support at the individual level is also being actively mobilized, and more players are joining disaster response sites.

Resilient cities require the ability to survive, adapt and grow in any unexpected calamity. A municipal government stands at the forefront of disaster response and it requires to have the ability to rapidly coordinate with various organizations and individuals up to the national level. Information and communication are the keys in the process of gaining such ability, as decisions by mayors are made on information collected through communication activities. Whereas the amount of information exchanged online is increasing year by year, the progress of developing the ability to select and organize information is still open to debate. Standardized, structured management of information will help us strengthen such ability. We note that there are obvious limitations on human resources at the local level when responding to a disaster. Appropriate communal support must be developed for the management of future disasters. The timely provision of information to citizens is essential for enhancing mutual support among individuals and civil communities.

This chapter tries to sublimate lessons and knowledge gained from past disasters into solutions. Specifically, this chapter focuses on a common, shared structure for comprehensive disaster communication in Japanese local governments. The proposed solution includes a standardized communication protocol, which will enable information sharing both in everyday use and in times of crisis across various stakeholders. It will enable personalized information delivery to all citizens in a form of society benefiting from emerging technologies characteristic of Industry 4.0. This, in turn, will strengthen individual capacity for self-help, raise the maturity level of personal resilience and thereby contribute to future disaster risk reduction.

References

Brown T (2008) Design thinking. Harv Bus Rev 86(6):84–92. https://search.ebscohost.com/login.aspx%3Fdirect%3Dtrue%26db%3Dbuh%26AN%3D32108052%26lang%3Dja%26site%3Dehost-live

Chen R, Sharman R, Rao HR, Upadhyaya SJ (2013) Data model development for fire related extreme events: an activity theory approach. MIS Quart 37(1):125–147. https://search.ebscohost.com/login.aspx%3Fdirect%3Dtrue%26db%3Dbuh%26AN%3D32108052%26lang%3Dja%26site%3Dehost-live

Hevner AR, March ST, Park J, Ram S (2004) Design science in information systems research. MIS Quart 28:75–105

Horne JF, Orr JE (1998) Assessing behaviors that create resilient organizations. Employ Relat Today 24(4):29–39. https://doi.org/10.1002/ert.3910240405

March ST, Smith GF (1995) Design and natural science research on information technology. Decis Supp Syst 15(4):251–266. https://doi.org/10.1016/0167-9236(94)00041-2

Markus ML, Majchrzak A, Gasser L (2002) A design theory for systems that support emergent knowledge processes. MIS Quart 26:179–212

Ministry of Internal Affairs and Communications (2013) *災害に強い電子自治体に関する研究会ICT利活用WG報告書*.

Myers MD (1997) Qualitative research in information systems. MIS Quart 21(2):241–242. https://search.ebscohost.com/login.aspx%3Fdirect%3Dtrue%26db%3Dbuh%26AN%3D9708156184%26lang%3Dja%26site%3Dehost-live

Sakurai M, Majchrzak TA, Latinos V (2017) Towards a framework for cross-sector collaboration: implementing a resilience information portal. In: Dokas I, Bellamine-Ben Saoud N, Dugdale J, Díaz P (eds) Information systems for crisis response and management in mediterranean countries. ISCRAM-med 2017. Lecture notes in business information processing, vol 301. Springer, Cham, pp 177–192

Sakurai M, Watson R, Abraham C, Kokuryo J (2014) Sustaining life during the early stages of disaster relief with a frugal information system: learning from the great east Japan earthquake. Commun Mag IEEE 52(1):176–185. https://doi.org/10.1109/MCOM.2014.6710081

Simon HA (1996) The sciences of the artificial, 3rd edn. MIT Press, MA

Walls J, Widmeyer GR, El Sawy OA (1992) Building an information system design theory for vigilant EIS. Inf Syst Res 3:36–59. https://doi.org/10.1287/isre.3.1.36

Chapter 7
A Conceptual Framework for Designing an Effective Community Resilience Management System

Amjad Fayoumi, Juliana Sutanto, and Andreas Mauthe

Abstract This chapter presents a conceptual framework for designing community resilience management system (CRMS). We review and discuss the current frameworks on community resilience from different disciplines. We then deep dive into the data, information systems, and communication technology networks in community resilience, which are important elements of community resilience but often neglected by the current community resilience frameworks. Following this, we conceptualize the CRMS with the data, infrastructure, rules and regulations, and stakeholders as interrelated key elements in improving community resilience that should be holistically viewed and improved. We explain how the CRMS should operate, inheriting concepts from operations management and systems analysis and design, and present the design requirements for CRMS. An implementation scenario of the CRMS in a temporary community of a large event during health pandemic is illustrated.

Keywords Community resilience · Data and information and communication technology resilience · Network resilience · Community resilience management systems (CRMS) · CRMS requirements

7.1 Introduction

The world is witnessing major global climate change that is having a drastic impact on the environment. According to a 2017's report by the United Nations Office for Disaster Risk Reduction (UNISDR), between 1998 and 2017, climate-related

A. Fayoumi (✉) · J. Sutanto
Management Science, Lancaster University Management School, Bailrigg, Lancaster L1 4YX, UK
e-mail: a.fayoumi@lancaster.ac.uk

J. Sutanto
e-mail: j.sutanto@lancaster.ac.uk

A. Mauthe
University of Koblenz and Landau, Rhabanusstraße 3, 55118 Mainz, Germany
e-mail: mauthe@uni-koblenz.de

M. Sakurai and R. Shaw (eds.), *Emerging Technologies for Disaster Resilience*, Disaster Risk Reduction,
https://doi.org/10.1007/978-981-16-0360-0_7

disasters account for 91% of the major recorded disaster events; the two most frequently occurring disasters are floods (43.4%) and storms (28.2%). During this period, 1.3 million people lost their lives, 4.4 billion people were injured, displaced, or in need of emergency assistance, and the disaster-hit countries reported direct economic losses of US$2,245 billion from climate-related disasters (Wallemacq and House 2018). Recently, researchers from Cambridge University predicted that climate change could add around 20% to the global cost of extreme weather events. Besides natural disasters, man-made disasters, such as intentional forest fires and illegal logging, add to the significant economic loss and loss of lives (CCRS 2020) . In 2013, the Guardian reported that the Sumatran (Indonesia) rainforest would mostly disappear within 20 years (Vidal 2013). Seven years on, the end seems to be in sight for many forests in Sumatra. In early 2019, the Amazon rainforest suffered from fires burning down an area of 906,000 ha. Equally, Australia was suffering from a dreadful bushfire in late 2019 and early 2020.

The recent years have seen many local councils, governments, and non-governmental organizations declaring that the world is in a state of "climate emergency". They are continuously putting effort and resources into developing preventive or at least mitigating solutions. For example, in 2018, following severe floods and landslides that affected up to 5.4 million people in Kerala (India), the World Bank announced that it is supporting the government of Kerala with up to US$500 million to build more resilient institutions, systems, and infrastructure to better deal with future environmental shocks. As risks and urban population are dramatically increasing, the United Nations Habitat is collaborating with several cities, such as Asuncion in Paraguay, Barcelona in Spain, Dakar in Senegal, Maputo in Mozambique, Port Vila in Vanuatu, and Yakutsk in Russia, in implementing and enforcing resilience. In the United Nations' Resilient Communities and Cities Partnership Program, a resilient community is defined as a city, town, or neighborhood that reduces its vulnerability to dramatic change or extreme events and responds creatively to economic, social, and environmental change in order to increase its long-term sustainability. Accordingly, we see community resilience as the ability and the capacity of a given community to sustain to a certain extent their pre-crisis situation immediately after an emergency situation while minimizing the risk of long-term economic, societal, and environmental impacts.

Alongside the efforts of the local councils, governments, and non-governmental organizations to build resilient communities, over the years, there have been plenty of frameworks proposed for community resilience. Some frameworks are socially oriented, e.g. Saja et al. (2018)'s framework focuses on the elements of social structure, social capital, engagement, aspiration, safety, institutions, processes, education, equality, equity, culture, belief, and competent. Other frameworks combine the physical environment, social, economy, and governance elements (e.g. Cimellaro et al. 2016; Joerin et al. 2012). Although extremely useful, these frameworks do not have in-depth discussion on information and communication technologies (ICT) as an important element of community resilience. ICT is part of the increasingly digitalized communities where the individuals interact, coordinate, self-organize, work, and learn using technologies, and where decisions are increasingly made with technology support such as the decision support system. A few frameworks highlighted that the quality of decisions depends on data availability and data quality (e.g. Zautra et al. 2008; Roberts et al. 2015). However, the data element as well as the corresponding ICT infrastructure element is not discussed in depth. The UNISDR's PEOPLES resilience framework, which also does neither embed the ICT nor its corresponding data element, highlights the integration possibility with Geographical Information Systems, statistical services, satellite/aerial imagery, and other data; hence they are acknowledging (indirectly) the importance of data and ICT.

The objective of this chapter is to introduce a conceptual framework for designing a Community Resilience Management System (CRMS) considering the crises as well as nominal situation. We will focus on the data and ICT elements as the key enabling elements of the framework. This chapter is organized as follows: Sect. 2 presents the concept of community resilience and discusses the relevant frameworks. In Sect. 3, we discuss and elaborate on the core elements of our framework, i.e., data, information systems, and telecommunication networks. Then, we present our proposed CRMS framework, and the set of requirements to design a CRMS, followed by an illustrative implementation scenario of the CRMS in a temporary community of a large event during health pandemic in Sect. 4. We conclude the chapter in Sect. 5.

7.2 Frameworks and Approaches for Community Resilience

The resilience concept was introduced a long time ago in ecological system literature (Koliou et al. 2017). According to Patel et al. (2017), there are 57 unique definitions of community resilience in the literature, defining it as a process, outcome or absence of adverse effect, or attributes. Some of the exemplary community resilience frameworks in the literature that we will discuss below are classified based on whether community resilience is viewed as a process, outcome or absence of adverse effect, or attributes.

A number of frameworks view community resilience as a process. Cutter et al. (2008) view resilience as a dynamic process that links between the emergence, severity, and frequency of hazards, and the community's ability to adapt to the impacts of the crisis event. The framework highlights about the changes in the environment, which might cause a hazard to a certain community that has a certain level of vulnerability. This vulnerability is dealt with by the community's adaptive capacity, which determines the community's resilience level. In the event of a crisis, the communities are impelled to respond in the most possible, effective way to minimize the impact of the crisis event. If the required response does not exceed the adaptive capacity of the community, then the recovery from the crisis will be quick and its impact is minimal. If the required response exceeds the adaptive capacity of the community, the community will either learn how to cope with the crisis and adapt, or fail to adapt and cope. In this case, the recovery from the crisis will take a long time and have long-lasting impact (Cutter et al. 2008). Zautra et al. (2008) suggested that there are dynamic interactions and feedbacks among resources, processes, and outcomes and these should be measured to understand the impact of either crises or development which in return stimulates the development of a resilient community that has the right governance, strong leadership, services, connections, and well-being. The framework necessitates good data and high-quality feedback; however, the enabling information and communication infrastructure are not discussed. Another framework discusses community resilience to natural hazards called the emBRACE framework (Kruse et al. 2017). The emBRACE framework is an iterative process with intertwined components in three layers of what is called intra-community: (1) resources and capacities, (2) actions, and (3) learning to create resilience in response to what they call "extra-community" that entails disaster risk governance, the context of hazard, socio-ecological change, and disturbances.

The second strand of the literature views community resilience as an outcome of adverse effects. Norris et al. (2018) reviewed a number of NGOs and public standard frameworks such as SENDAI, GOAL, PEOPLES, and CCRAM, investigated the role of e-health in increasing community resilience and presented a disaster e-health framework for community resilience. In their framework, they call for universal health and care for all community members and more cooperation among stakeholders (responders, decision-makers, and government) to make sure that the health system is resilient in the long term particularly under disaster events. Norris et al. (2008) mentioned about the importance of information and communication in enabling networked adaptive capacities for community resilience (Norris et al. 2008). While Norris et al. (2008) discussed community resilience from a health system perspective, Dückers (2017) focused on the social and psychosocial aspects, looking at the impact on the individuals, community and society levels. Taking a wider perspective, Magis (2010) views community resilience as an indicator of sustainability and several dimensions need to be considered to achieve this ultimate goal (resilience), such as resources availability, resources development, resources engagement, active agents, collective and strategic actions, and equity.

The final strand of the literature views community resilience as attributes and hence focuses on assessing and measuring community resilience. There are many frameworks in this strand. The framework presented by Cutter et al. (2014) suggests that community resilience is determined by a combination of social, cultural, ecological, economic, and political factors. Shortly afterward, a holistic review of 36 frameworks and tools for assessing community resilience was conducted by Sharifi (2016). Sharifi (2016) then grouped the assessment criteria into five different dimensions that contain 124 unique criteria to assess resilience of the modern societies. Cimellaro et al. (2016) considered further assessment details that are relevant to the functionality, objective, and required timeframe of recovery in the community. Another holistic community resilience assessment metrics was proposed by Johansen et al. (2017), focusing on sectoral measures, sociological measures, and community-level measures. Revell and Henderson (2019) proposed a tool with indicators for assessing resilience maturity with three levels: Breakdown, Breakeven, and Breakthrough for each of the resilience dimensions suggested in their model: social, culture, economy, and cross-communities links. Similarly, Berkes and Ross (2013, 2016) consider resilience as a characteristic that the communities continuously develop. They describe the function of strengths or characteristics of individual and community resilience, which entail positive outlook, community infrastructure, diverse and innovative economy, people–place relationship, leadership, knowledge, skills and learning, values and beliefs, social networks, and engaged governance. Socially oriented, Saja et al. (2018) developed social resilience measure that includes inclusion, safety, skills, connections, and support. Finally, departing from strong social inclination, Roberts et al. (2015) suggested that new digital technologies should also be assessed through their contribution to both individual and community resiliencies. As part of their proposed framework, they include assessment of broadband access, digital literacy, and skills.

As aforementioned, we see community resilience as the ability and the capacity of a given community to sustain to a certain extent their pre-crisis situation immediately after an emergency situation while minimizing the risk of long-term economic, societal, and environmental impacts. Our view of community resilience is, therefore, a process view; accordingly, our proposed framework is a process-based framework. Moreover, we believe that in the increasingly digitalized communities, ICT and data should be important elements of a community resilience framework. While the current frameworks provide significant contributions, only a few mention about data quality, digital technologies and systems, and broadband access (Zautra et al. 2008; Norris et al. 2018; Roberts et al. 2015). Moreover, ICT and data are not embedded as integral elements of the proposed community resilience process.

In the next section, we deep dive into data and ICT (information systems and information communication networks) as important and integral elements of community resilience. Following this, we present our proposed framework of Community Resilience Management System (CRMS) and identify the key requirements that should be incorporated in the implementation of a CRMS.

7.3 The Role of Data and Information and Communication Technology Resilience

We view data as a central component that enables community resilience. In the following sections, we discuss the resilience of data, information systems, and information communication networks as without the resilience of these three elements, community resilience will be difficult to achieve from both the operational and structural sides.

7.3.1 Data Resilience

The seminal early literature on information systems stressed the need for quality data management that contributes to its resilience. Gorry and Scott Morton (1971) described how the three levels of decision-making in an organization (strategic, tactical, and operational levels) have different data requirements. People who are working in each of the mentioned levels will deal with different sorts of data. Data are central components that lead to augmented decisions: decisions that are taking by human with the help of artificial intelligence (AI) and analytics (e.g. decision support system and expert system), and automated decisions: decisions made by AI algorithms and acted upon by actuators and robotics. These types of decisions can either be (1) real-time: decisions made on the local processors or edge, or (2) close real-time: with a delay and typically processed on the local processor or the edge, or (3) deferred decisions: decisions based on big data in the data lake that is processed on the cloud (e.g. strategic decisions).

To make a good decision, the data have to be precise and dependable. Data quality is determined by the correctness, currency, completeness, and confidence in the data. While internal data can be to a greater extent under control and resilience is achievable by performing data quality management, the quality of external data is rather questionable since data sometimes acquired from unknown, untrustworthy, or speculative sources. Dealing with external data requires extreme caution to minimize the impact on decision quality. Also, data resilience is determined by the ability to absorb and store the wide varieties of data types, i.e., structured, semi-structured, and unstructured data, by both manual data entry and automated capturing. The ability of people and systems to navigate consistent data granularity from the instance, set, class, and backward is a crucial determinant of data analytics resilience. Decision-makers must be able to analyze and aggregate data across granularity levels following a sophisticated analysis methodology, mechanism, algorithms, and visualization approaches to perform descriptive, diagnostic, predictive, and prescriptive analytics. Redman (2008) suggests that data quality positioned between ICT infrastructure and exploitation can be augmented. Data quality can be split into four different categories according to Strong et al. (1997), which are (a) intrinsic quality (accuracy, objectivity, believability, and reputation); (b) accessibility quality (accessibility, access security); (c) contextual quality (relevancy, value-added, timeliness, completeness, amount of data); and (d) representational quality (interpretability, ease of understanding, concise representation, consistent representation).

All data should be processed according to regulations, ethical, and legal considerations. After the data are presented, visualized, and analyzed through a structured data pipeline process, an analytic task is applied that is either, descriptive, diagnostic, predictive, or prescriptive. Vidgen et al. (2017) studied the challenges that organizations face in creating value from data analytics where managing data quality is identified as the biggest challenge. Data lifecycle stages are handled either fully or partly by information systems (IS), data collection technologies, e.g. sensors and IoTs, data storages, e.g. DBMS and NoSQL, and functions that are embedded in the

IS to process the data, e.g. algorithmic codes and workflows and data output and distribution mediums. These must all be secured to ensure data integrity and availability. Recent studies suggest using emergent trends such as blockchain to ensure distributed data assurance and resilience (Liang et al. 2017). In the following section, we discuss data as part of the IS requirements for resilience.

7.3.2 *Information Systems Resilience*

A recent literature review on IS and resilience (Heeks and Ospina 2019) claimed that most studies from 2003 until 2017 are examining resilience as the property of IS. These studies are focusing on the IS itself and its resilience to withstand external stressors or to "bounce back" after damage by external stressors (Heeks and Ospina 2019). Few studies examine resilience as the property of IS input system, which is typically a human system inputting data to IS during its development and/or operation, or resilience as the property of IS outcome system, which is the impact of the IS on the resilience of other systems such as organizations and communities (Heeks and Ospina 2019). Following this review, we searched for the literature on IS and resilience until March 2020. We found more studies examining resilience as either the property of IS input system, e.g. the provision of extensive, real-time information from the citizens and the provision of information from municipal authorities (Cohen et al. 2017), or the property of IS outcome system, e.g. improving supply chain resilience by improving the resilience of the information sharing (Macdonald et al. 2018).

Although there are three different positions on IS and resilience research, most studies are examining the IS resilience for supporting daily operations such as supply chain management system and hospital information system. Few studies examine IS for crisis situations such as disaster management system, or IS for both nominal and crisis situations such as the social media applications. The previous study showed that when the IS is only used during severe crisis situation, its cost overshadow its value because severe crisis such as a tsunami and a pandemic disease are highly unlikely events (Fedorowicz and Gogan 2010). Moreover, when the IS is only designed for use during the crisis situation, it may not actually be utilized when the crisis happens because the turbulence period at the start of a crisis may create panic and during the moment of panic, users may unconsciously use the IS that they frequently use such as the use of the off-the-shelf messaging application instead of the official disaster response application. By extending the system's coverage from the less frequent—more damaging crisis to the more frequent—less damaging crisis that complements daily operations, the value of the system and its utilization increase (Allenby and Fink 2005; Bharosa et al. 2010; Fedorowicz and Gogan 2010). There is a need for dual-use IS that is embedded in daily work and offers societal benefits even if the anticipated disasters never occur (Allenby and Fink 2005) to maintain community resilience in nominal and crisis situations. Ipe et al. (2010) examined public health emergency preparedness system in Arizona after the September 11 attacks. They found that the stakeholders' commitment is enhanced and their friction is minimized when the systems are embedded in the everyday operations to extend organizational capabilities for information sharing and exchange. IS for disaster management has to support daily operations so that the use of such system becomes a norm rather than an exception. The usage patterns should remain the same. The only difference is the change from nominal to crisis situation.

7.3.2.1 Resilience as the Property of IS Input System

From the literature, it seems that the benefits of having dual-use IS disappear when the crisis situation involves responders from multiple agencies, local, and international agencies. Van de Walle and Dugdale (2012) investigated the use of information management during the 2010 Haiti earthquake. They identified three prominent systems that were used to support the inter-agency humanitarian relief in Haiti, i.e. an inter-agency website to enhance coordination and support the exchange of information, a web-based system to manage coordination and map everything that was happening in Haiti, and an open source web application for information collection, visualization, and interactive mapping. In the first weeks during the turbulent period of the crisis situation, there were chaos with the inter-agency responders claiming that the systems did not function as well as they would have liked. Moreover, the responders remarked that the most important is not the existence of a crisis information platform; instead, it is the existence of a crisis information repository with a common data standard as there were data overload in different languages, some lack geospatial data, etc. Hence it seems that when multiple agencies are responding to a crisis, resilience is not the IS itself but the property of the IS input system which is a human system inputting data to IS during the crisis response. It is important to enforce data standards in the input fields of the IS. Nevertheless, such restriction may demotivate the inter-agency responders from inputting data. To avoid such restriction from demotivating the responders during emergency situation, the system must play a vital role in every emergency response drill (Lee et al. 2011; Raman et al. 2006). Moreover, the system must support and not hinder the existing emergency response protocol, (Raman et al. 2006).

Yates and Paquette (2011) also examined the 2010 Haiti's earthquake, focusing on how the government agencies used social media. They asserted that social media facilitated knowledge sharing in two ways, i.e. by increasing knowledge reuse and by eliminating the reliance on formal liaison structures in terms of both personnel and systems. However, the lack of structure of the shared knowledge makes it difficult to use social media as knowledge resource when there is a time constraint to respond to the disaster (Yates and Paquette 2011). This is in line with the aforementioned issue of data overload when there is no common data standard. Moreover, social media data add complexities in terms of coordination as most of them are untruth information, which are difficult to check properly during a disaster (Bharosa et al. 2010). Even though social media can empower the community during crisis by allowing them to have a voice and to help in disaster response (Leong et al. 2015; Palen and Anderson

2016), rumormongering is a key issue when the human system inputting data to IS during crisis response not only consists of the responders but also include members of the public. Oh et al. (2013) analyzed Twitter messages of the Mumbai terrorist attack in 2008 and Seattle café's shooting incident in 2012 and Toyota recalls in 2010. They found that while content ambiguity did not contribute to rumormongering, source ambiguity did so very significantly. Content ambiguity was mainly composed of questions seeking information on the crisis situation or doubts expressing suspicion on Twitter posts, whereas source ambiguity frequently resembled third-person situation reports without sources being attached (Oh et al. 2013). Lu and Yang (2011) surveyed members of a web forum for students after a massive earthquake struck Wenchuan at Sichuan province in China in 2008 and investigated the forum activity data. They found that social interaction ties increase information quantity, whereas trust, reciprocity, shared language, and shared vision increase information quality. Data reliability during crisis, especially during the turbulent period of the crisis, is crucial yet extremely difficult to achieve when the information is from the social media as the people may not be able to readily recall the sources of the different pieces of information. The extensive literature on rumors and fake news detection on social media were conducted after the fact. How the emergency responders can distinguish inaccurate information from the truth when responding to crisis is an important question to address yet it has not been adequately investigated.

7.3.2.2 Resilience as the Property of IS Output System

Beyond the IS itself and the property of IS input system, resilience is also related to the property of the IS output system, which is the IS impact on the resilience of other systems such as organizations and communities (Heeks and Ospina 2019). IS can promote resilience by informing a broad range of actors of a stressing situation and, potentially, empower these actors to become informed decision-makers (Comes et al. 2019). Investigating the Fukushima Daiichi's nuclear power disaster in 2011, Thatcher et al. (2015) highlighted the impact of information behaviors on information failure. Even though some people working in Fukushima Daiichi's nuclear power were aware of the potential disaster when they began to see some warning signs, the interweaving between the information behavior and their decisions to not escalate the warning signs led to the disaster (Thatcher et al. 2015). The IS impact on the resilience of other systems heavily depends on the information behavior. There are critical, distinctions between human behaviors that result from endogenous hazards that can be captured such as the Fukushima nuclear power disaster versus exogenous hazards that cannot be captured such as the natural disasters (Palen and Anderson 2016). Moreover, compared to business crisis, community crises such as terrorist attacks or natural disasters involve high levels of anxiety when the community became aware of the stressing situation (Oh et al. 2013), which may lead to social discrimination, looting, and other socially harmful behavior. For example, the anxiety of the recent coronavirus pandemic led to some communities discriminating members of the community who are of Chinese descendant. As the community gains most of their information from the social media that represent the opinions of some people, leadership is a central element of community resilience (Cohen et al. 2017; Palen and Anderson 2016). During emergencies, the municipal authorities should provide information that meets the population's needs and reduce their anxiety (Cohen et al. 2017). Chou et al. (2014) assessed the utility of 50 US states' natural disaster management websites and found that all US states still had a long way to go toward building comprehensive websites for managing natural disasters. The websites lack information about the general preparation, preparation for a predicted disaster, disaster in progress, recovery, and mitigation (Chou et al. 2014). It is also appalling that a number of websites and mobile applications emerge during disaster such as those that aim to mobilize the neighborhood to help the senior citizens in times of crisis. Without clear direction and message from the municipal authorities, the impact of such IS on the resilience of the communities is in doubt, as some of them may in fact be harmful to the communities. It is important to carefully assess the balance between the authority and community-based IS toward increasing community resilience.

7.3.3 ICT Networks Resilience

Another infrastructure that is core to the community resilience is the ICT network. Resilience is a characteristic of communication networks, which has been associated with telecommunication systems since they emerged as a vital element for the interaction between humans. Originally resilience defines the ability of networks to resist the loss of capacity due to failures or foreseen overload (Vlacheas et al. 2011). As such the focus has been on fault management and recovery methods after an incident (Cholda et al. 2007). In recent years, resilience in communication and telecommunication networks has got into further focus due to the prominence of the Internet. The computer and telecommunication networks are now part of the critical national infrastructure (CNI). Due to this, they have also become a target for attacks (physical as well as cyber-attacks). Hence, in order to ensure that the networks remain operational, they have to be resilience against all kinds of adverse events.

A general definition of communication resilience specifies that networks have to have the ability to "maintain acceptable levels of operation in the face of challenges, including malicious attacks, operational overload, misconfiguration, and equipment failures", which encompasses structural and operational as well as wider context related considerations (Dobson et al. 2019, p. 819). Mauthe et al. (2016, p. 2) define resilience of a communication network in more details as "a quantitative property of a network that occurs on each level of its hierarchy, and is related to the ability to maintain the same level of functionality in the face of internal changes and external disturbances as a result of large-scale natural disasters and corresponding failures, weather-based disruptions, technology-related disasters, and malicious human activities; to withstand all these without losing the capacity to allocate resources efficiently; to maintain acceptable level of service in the face of various faults, challenges to normal operation, fluctuating environment, and human use; and to absorb recurrent disturbances so as to retain essential infrastructures and processes, with sufficient cost-efficiency and flexibility over the long term".

In Sterbenz et al. (2010), a resilience strategy is described that captures the main components of the resilience process and can be used to consider resilience in the design as well as the operation of communication networks. The main components are captured within an online and an off-line control loop expressed through D^2R^2 + DR. The inner, real-time control loop D^2R^2 expresses concepts that help ***d***efending from attacks, ***d***etect anomalies, ***r***emediate against them, and ***r***ecover from an incident. These also cover active, operational defenses and methods to observe and mitigate in case something is going wrong. The outer loop, DR, stands for ***d***iagnose and ***r***efinement and represents a non-real-time control loop through which the resilience-related infrastructure aspects as well as the operational strategies are analyzed and improved, reflecting the longer term experiences and developments within the environment. The D^2R^2 + DR conceptual resilience model provides design guidance but is not an architectural blueprint; it addresses different aspects as part of an overall resilience architecture.

From a higher level perspective, network resilience can be divided into structural and operational viewpoints. The former is concerned with structural arrangements. These are specifically related to the recovery of different connections, for instance, self-healing networks that restore a cut fiber in an optical mesh network through a distributed algorithm that allows dynamically routing. Operational resilience specifies the level of active resilience management within network that provides mechanisms to actively defend, detect, and mitigate against threats. It uses, for example, challenge analysis in conjunction with a resilience estimator that determines if specified resilience targets are being met. If this is not the case, appropriate resilience mechanisms have to be invoked to counter or adapt to challenges in order to maintain a high level of resilience (Dobson et al. 2019).

7.3.3.1 Structural Network Resilience

In the area of structural network resilience, the communication infrastructure has to be assessed toward its ability to continue providing an acceptable level of service even in the face of challenges. A higher level of resilience can be achieved through providing redundancy of key components such as routers and also links. Through the concept of diversity, an infrastructure can be made more resilient since a failure of hardware, software, a geographic link, etc. will in the case diversity, not fail in the same way (Sterbenz et al. 2010). This is due to the fact that vulnerabilities in one system element will not be the same in another that provides the same service but in structurally and operationally different ways.

The level of resilience of a network or network infrastructures has to be analyzed with respect to their ability to withstand and structurally compensate for challenges and failures. The analysis considers a number of factors and metrics that indicate if and to what extent this is the case. For instance, the replication degree and inbuilt redundancy are used as indicators alongside diversity. If this analysis is done within one system context, it can provide a good indicator about the challenges and the severity of their impact on a specific system in the case of disruptions, e.g. due to local incidences or more widespread disasters. The assessment can be horizontally, i.e. across a number of (sub-)systems of the same kind. An example here is interconnected communication networks belonging to different domains. It can also be carried out vertically where the resilience metrics are assessed at different levels or layers of the communication network with the goal to establish the overall system resilience (Sterbenz et al. 2014). The indicators that are used here are (again) considering the levels of redundancy and diversity, alongside connectivity and association. For example at the:

- *physical level*, they look at link quality, availability, reliability, and potential component failure;
- *topology level*, they consider topological data by using graph metrics such as clustering coefficient, target component size, etc.;
- *path-routing level*, they look at routing delays, path dependability, and overhead;
- *inter-realm level*, (i.e. intersection between different network providers), they specifically look at inter-domain connectivity and transit;
- *end-to-end transport level*, they are considering path latency, goodput, and packet-delivery ratio;
- *application level*, they look at latency, throughput, and quality of experience.

Resilience analysis carried out considering these factors can, for instance, help to uncover structural vulnerabilities, and in the design phase of a network can be used to evaluate alternatives. Using metrics such as topology diversity and connectivity, path routing diversity and connectivity, etc. can be analyzed to demonstrate the effect failures of individual components or links have on the overall network resilience. The analysis of resilience metrics across independent (sub-)networks and across the different levels of the infrastructure can be done for interconnected networks from different providers across all layers and that way identifies weakness in the wider network infrastructure for instance on a national a supra-national level.

Another way of assessing network vulnerabilities is the use of simulations and off-line network data analysis. Simulation can help to evaluate different network resilience strategies, also considering the behavior of the network in the nominal case compared to a crisis situation, e.g. in the case of a large-scale disaster (Schaeffer-Filho et al. 2013). Off-line network data analysis uses network data, which is processed in a non-parametric way to identify unprecedented events in uncertain environments (Angelov 2014). In this approach, autonomous learning systems allow a new way of learning from streaming data without the need for large scale data retention (i.e. it uses rule-based information created on the fly). The case studies of the algorithm have found application in various cyber physical and network infrastructure and can detect, classify, and analyze massive machine data prior captured prior and during a disaster.

7.3.3.2 Operational Network Resilience

Operational resilience specifies the level of active resilience management capabilities within networks to actively defend, detect, and mitigate against threats (Dobson et al. 2019). In order to provide resilience during network operations, network management functions and operational resilience functions have to work in conjunction. The resilience functions are divided into two parts, i.e. challenge detection and mitigation (i.e. remediation and recovery from failure). To detect challenges, the network state has to be assessed continuously by anomaly detection components. These should be distributed throughout an interconnected network infrastructure and can sit alongside the routing infrastructure or be part of it (Mauthe et al. 2016). Additionally, challenge detection of an interconnected network has to be done in a coordinated manner and can also consider additional situational data (Marnerides et al. 2016). To realize this, an approach that makes use of policies, in conjunction with remediation mechanisms that can be progressively refined, has been proposed (Schaeffer-Filho et al. 2012). Here detection and mitigation are interleaved, i.e. an initial indication of an anomaly triggers a staged network management and resilience process in which the diagnosis is refined in order to gain more certainty about the challenge. The more is known about the anomaly, the better the mitigation actions are refined, in order to become more targeted.

A number of anomaly detection techniques exist, based on statistical methods, information theory, entropy distributions, data density, EEMD, machine learning technology, etc. (c.f. Marnerides et al. 2015; Shirazi et al. 2016; Fernandes et al. 2019; Garg et al. 2019). Further, methods used for the structural assessment of networks (e.g. Angelov 2014) can also be deployed in the context of operational resilience as long as the analysis can be carried out in or close to real-time.

7.3.3.3 Emergency Communication

While there has been a lot of consideration and effort gone into making communication networks resilient (after all, even the Internet's original design has been done with having resilience in mind), in the case of major incidences (e.g. natural disaster, technology-related failures, or malicious attacks) communication infrastructures might be destroyed or be insufficient considering the higher demand and changed use (Mauthe et al. 2016). In these situations, alternative and additional networks (i.e. emergency networks) can be set up, for instance using ad-hoc or mesh technology, or other means to provide basic communication in case normal communication networks are disrupted. Self-organizing Mobile Ad-hoc Networks (MANETs) based on Delay Tolerant Networking (DTN) have been proposed for a while as powerful tools for maintaining or reestablishing telecommunications following disasters and infrastructure disrupting events. The issue here is that these networks have usually only limited bandwidth compared with infrastructure-based networks. This has the effect that they cannot satisfy every demand placed upon them. Thus, if the most critical traffic is to be delivered in a timely manner some form of filtering or prioritization is needed as described in Lieser et al. (2017). Another way of dealing with this is to integrate the emergency network with the still existing parts of the infrastructure-based network. For instance, unmanned aerial vehicles (UAVs) have been proposed as a solution to extend coverage for disaster-resilient communication networks and to increase the capacity of the normal network. In this case, the UAV provides communication and has to ensure that the base station is not overloaded so that communication can be maintained (Yang et al. 2019). Others propose a combination of wireless networks based, for instance, on long-term evolution (LTE) technology and handheld terminals, drones, data acquisition terminals, etc. to provide cluster coverage. This should result in a secure communication between users and ideally provides reliable, robust and flexible power emergency communication networks (Zhang et al. 2019). Due to the emergence of Internet of Things (IoT) networks, these are also considered as a backup infrastructure in the case of emergencies (Álvarez et al. 2019). An issue here, as for many wireless based emergency networks are link quality. Early on there has been research to improve channel sensing, noise detection, the use of white spaces, etc., (e.g. Gorcin et al. 2011; Sun and Chowdhury 2014). Whilst there is still ongoing research in this area, due to the integration of emergency networks with infrastructure-based networks, attention has shifted to higher level resilience concerns within emergency communication.

Recently, the role of adaption and transition to provide resilient communication in crisis situation is being investigated to make best use of the existing or remaining infrastructure (Kalle et al. 2019). This means that more and more of the (still) existing network infrastructure is considered as valuable resource in crisis situation. It has further been recognized that the resilience (in the nominal as well as crisis case) of emerging digital cities can be enhanced through ICT but only if the communication technology itself is resilient. In order to achieve this, self-organization is proposed since in combination with resilience they offer the prospect of combating threats and allowing essential services that run on networked systems to continue operating satisfactorily even during an emergency (Dobson et al. 2019). This is helped when the network infrastructure transitions toward a self-configuring, self-healing, self-optimizing, and self-protecting way of operation. This should also be even the case outside the original design envelope. Further, it is stated that human interaction needs to be considered too (Engels et al. 2019). Hence, the structural and operational network resilience of these regular communication infrastructures as well as emergency networks are key to support community resilience through communication in nominal as well as crisis situations. In the following section, we will explain our proposed community resilience framework.

7.4 Proposed Framework for Designing a Community Resilience Management System (CRMS)

The review in Sect. 2 was conducted to identify the gaps in the currently available frameworks of community resilience in the literature. Upon identifying the important yet often neglected elements of community resilience, which are data and ICT elements, in Sect. 3, we explained in-depth the resilience of data, information systems, and information communication networks. In this section, we further identified the key constituent elements of community resilience and their interrelationships as presented in various frameworks and presented our proposed framework for designing an effective Community Resilience Management System (CRMS). In developing the proposed framework, we have adopted the relevant concepts and tools from Total Quality Management (TQM) (Du et al. 2008) and Systems Analysis (Siau and Rossi 2011).

Figure 7.1 shows the proposed conceptual framework while Fig. 7.2 shows a fragment of Ishikawa diagram for cause and effect analysis. In this diagram the primary contributing elements, e.g. data, rules and regulations, and infrastructure, to the improvement of community resilience are identified. The resilience of the infrastructure per se is one of the key determinants of the overall community resilience. This is because critical community needs, i.e. mobility, power supply, water supply, can be effectively fulfilled only when the infrastructure needed for their delivery is resilient and can perform their intendent functions. In addition, certain elements of the infrastructure such as power supply, and information and communication network may affect data acquisition and communication. Data are core elements of a CRMS. The availability of reliable, accurate, and current data along with appropriate models are key determinants of the quality of the resilience management decisions. In a crisis situation when the infrastructure is seriously damaged, data-driven decision-making will be compromised. Nevertheless, even when the infrastructure is solid and reliable at any time, the rules and regulations may constrain data collection, processing, analysis, presentation, and use. For instance, the institutional policies may constrain certain stakeholders from accessing the data. Beyond the formal institutional policies, the social system may further define how the stakeholders should interact with each other, their roles and responsibilities, and how they should coordinate with each other. Hence, we view the data, infrastructure, rules and regulations, and stakeholders as interrelated key elements in improving community resilience that should be holistically viewed and improved.

The proposed framework also emphasizes that community resilience should be ensured under both nominal and crisis situations, and as such, resilience should be built into all sub-systems and components that determine the performance of community resilience. This approach views resilience as a process rather than as an outcome. This means that in order to improve community resilience, one needs to control the process that generates a given level of performance as opposed of checking only its outcome. In addition, our approach recognizes the dynamic character of community resilience and introduces the idea of continuous resilience improvement. This

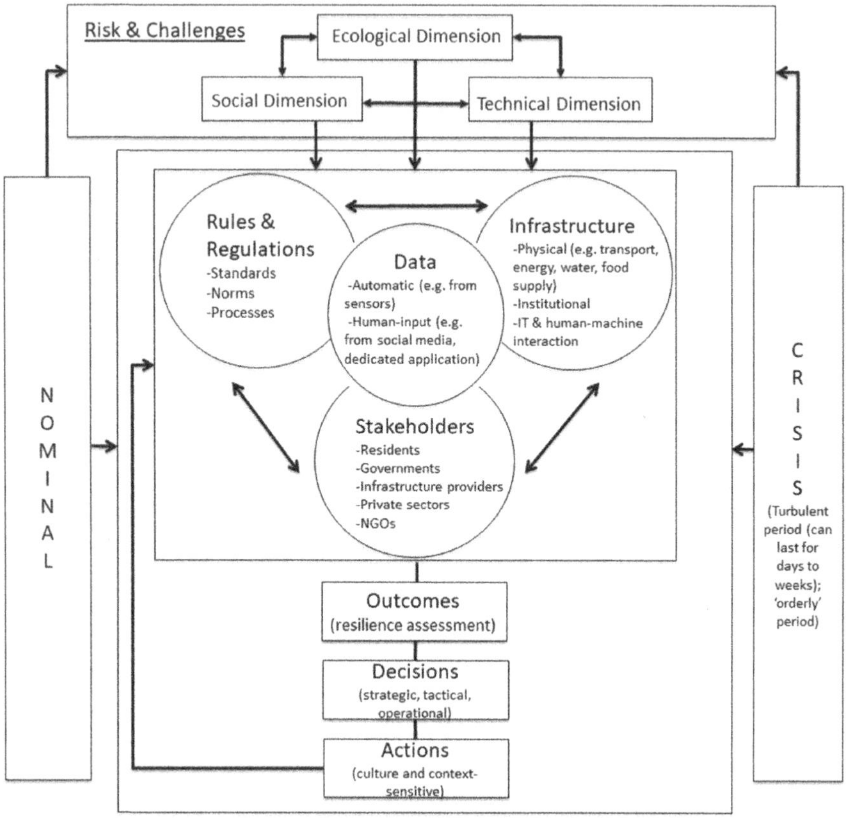

Fig. 7.1 Proposed conceptual framework for designing a community resilience management system (CRMS)

approach requires the dynamic implementation of the Plan-Do-Check-Act (PDCA) cycle for improving the resilience level of the community through the consideration of the emerging risks and challenges. Figure 7.3 illustrates the concept of the continuous resilience improvement, which is a key concept of the proposed framework.

The emerging risks and challenges (due to crisis situations) are influencing the social and technical dimensions of community resilience. The technical dimension of community resilience involves the community infrastructure networks, i.e. energy generation and supply, water supply, sewage, transportation, information systems and ICT networks, the infrastructure design, and operational standards and rules. The social dimension of community resilience includes the stakeholders involved in and affected by the resilience management system, along with the institutional and regulatory arrangements defining the interactions among the infrastructural elements. The state of the key determinants of community resilience, i.e. data, rules and regulations, infrastructure, and social system, and their interaction determines the current state of community resilience outcome (Ri) in time (ti). The CRMS should

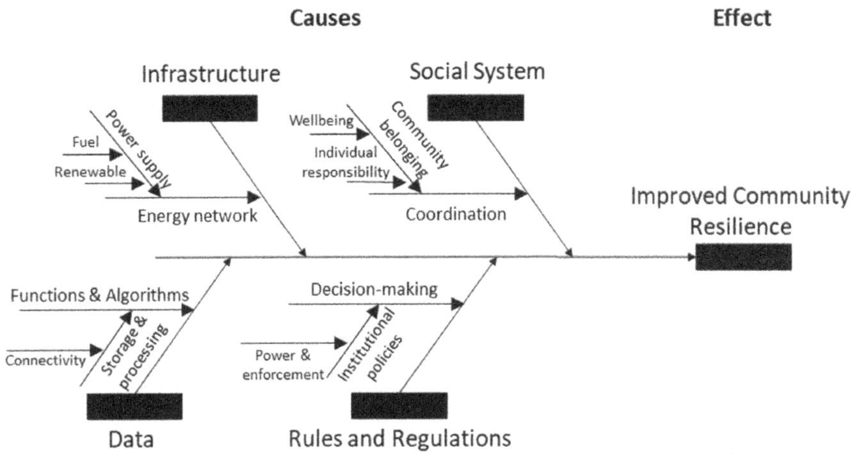

Fig. 7.2 A fragment of Ishikawa diagram for identifying factors contributing to community resilience

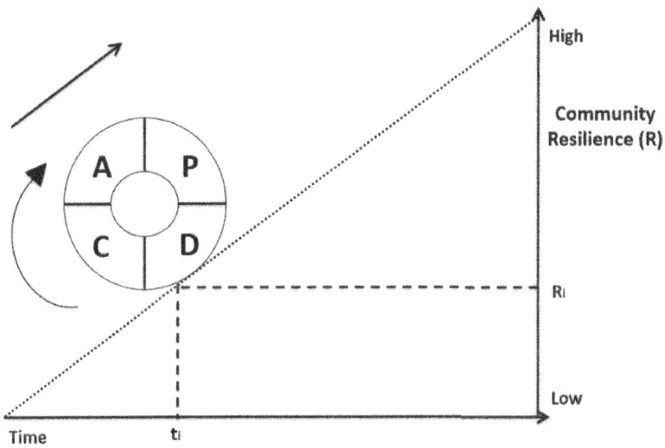

Fig. 7.3 The PDCA cycle leading to continuous community resilience improvement

be capable of addressing strategic, tactical, and operational decisions. The implementation of these decisions will lead to community resilience improvements. The Plan-Do-Check-Act cycle can be used as the mechanism for developing community resilience plans, implementing them, checking their performance, and identifying potential improvements.

7.4.1 Synthesis and Design Requirements for CRMS

Overall, to enable communities to anticipate challenges, being proactive to the anticipated situations and agile enough to respond in the way that is needed and when it is needed, the availability of quality inputs and outputs data should be ensured all the time. The infrastructure, including information systems and ICT network should be dynamically adjusted and continually improved for its dual use (in nominal and crisis situation). Moreover, the distinction between standard communication and emergency communication is slowly disappearing since it is recognized that communication has to be possible under all circumstances (nominal and crisis) and that existing infrastructures should be used and probably enhanced even in crisis situations. Altogether within this space, the solutions are adaptive and have often already adopted self-organization principles within their design in order to enable the required real-time response to all situations. As a result of the previous discussion and the centrality of data in community resilience, the approach presented in this chapter suggests that a CRMS should fulfill the following requirements in Table 7.1.

Table 7.1 Requirements for designing a community resilience management systems

Requirement 1	The CRMS should consider both nominal and emergency situations
Requirement 2	The CRMS should be proactive and embedded in all elements that determine the overall community resilience
Requirement 3	Its performance should be ensured through process improvements taking into consideration the efficiency and effectiveness of the processes
Requirement 4	The CRMS should be dynamically adjusted and continually improved to reconfigure and orchestrate resources and capabilities to navigate different circumstances
Requirement 5	The CRMS should be managed/governed based on evidence: therefore, each phase of the management cycle should be data and observation driven
Requirement 6	The quality of data should be ensured in all time (e.g. current, accurate, easily accessible, etc.) for all systems and sub-systems to ensure both a) robust interoperability and b) decisions quality
Requirement 7	The CRMS should address the entire resilience management cycle, i.e. Plan, Do, Check, Act
Requirement 8	Its performance indicators should satisfy the S.M.A.R.T[1] (Doran 1981) criteria (Specific, Measurable, Attainable, Relevant, Time-Bound)

[1]https://assets.publishing.service.gov.uk/government/uploads/system/uploads/attachment_data/file/835527/KPI-4-number-people-resilience-improved1.pdf

7.4.2 An Implementation Scenario in Temporary Large Events During Health Pandemic

A large event such as music concert or sport event constitutes a temporary community. During the preparation of large events, the main stakeholder, i.e. the organizing committees will develop a robust multi-level plan for risk planning and emergency intervention. These levels can be mapped to strategic planning, tactical practices, and operational routines. The typical comprehensive plan for nominal and crisis situations covers a wide range of disturbances including weather, earthquakes, typhoons, traffic, spectators' congestions, riots, and man-made destructions. Each has challenges and risks to at least one of the social, ecological, and technical aspects. While the strategy for each disturbance that covers the PDCA cycle is developed, the planning for health pandemic is not typically envisioned as its occurrence is extremely rare. Such unexpected disturbance requires reconfiguration of the structure and capabilities of the CRMS, for instance, the strategic planning may not fully eliminate the impact of the pandemic; however, it could provide alternative options of minimizing the cost and rethinking the way that the collective capabilities are configured such as balancing between autonomous systems and manpower in doing routine tasks. The CRMS should be dynamically adjusted and continually improved to reconfigure and orchestrate resources and capabilities to navigate the circumstances. New priorities emerge during the crisis, safety and public health become superior to commercial and profit gain. Reconfiguring capabilities posed by stakeholders, reutilizing infrastructure, and changing regulations and policies are triggered by the crisis event vs the nominal planned situation. Each of the framework main components will be affected by the pandemic differently, for instance:

Rules and regulations: Policies of social distancing, mask-wearing in public places and within the event facilities, guidelines for hygiene, regulations for temperature check on the spot, self-declaration policy and procedures for handling symptoms or quarantine spectators and visitors with symptoms.

Infrastructures: While most infrastructures are affected by other types of disturbances, managing these infrastructures is a challenge when social distancing is a necessity, and part of the workforces is quarantined or ill. Moreover, the ICT infrastructure is under intense demand during the pandemic due to people working from home, spending more time on the internet, using warning and tracking apps, homeschooling, and others. Considering partial utilization of the physical space, providing more automated self-services and relaying more on robotic services to adhere with regulations. Nevertheless, the increasing reliance on technologies means that network redundancy should be in place to ensure uninterrupted automated self-services and robotic services.

Stakeholders: As the government recommends to change the way of doing daily working activities (more electronic and distanced working), the multiple stakeholders involved in running the events might not be able to communicate in the same traditional manner. Their responsibilities continue to change and more tasks are required, e.g. NGOs to provide wellbeing and health support to spectators and visitors, and provide more logistic support to healthcare providers. Healthcare providers need to cope with the demand due to the large number of tests required, a restructuring of their units and workforces. Manufacturers to reconfigure their manufacturing capabilities to reduce the nominal productions and increase the crisis-related productions, e.g. recyclable beds created for the spectators can be used for temporary hospitals that are constructed to deal with the pandemic. Spectators to self-organize themselves to support the more vulnerable people, adhere to new rules and regulations, use tracing app on their phones, and adjust to the new way of event attending.

Data: With the increasing reliance on technology-supported operations while maintaining social distancing during the event coordination, the stakeholders will heavily rely on data for strategic and operational decisions. Data related to the new policies, regulations, and numbers and locations of infected people; data related to tracing app (people locations and their close contacts), places visited, and the time of visits; data about an individual's health and well-being (e.g. any chronic disease); data about testing centers, nearest healthcare providers, emergency units, and their capacities and availabilities; data about transportation, food, water supply, and private sectors, e.g. shops and services including the availability of PPE, sanitizers, and masks. The quality of data should be ensured in all time (e.g. current, accurate, easily accessible, etc.) to ensure robust interoperability and decisions quality.

For implementation, a hybrid centralized data storage to enable collective intelligence and complex data processing and decentralized data storages to enable initiatives and new application integrations are recommended. Both onshore and offshore storages are needed to mitigate any ecological distribution to the physical location. Role-based access control will be offered to focal users from government and emergency planning and handling organizations. Implementing Internet of Things (IoTs) from wired and wireless sensors, GPS, and CCTVs all to be aggregated and stored in data lake on the cloud. Actuators to be designed for fully or semi-automatic endogenous decision-making based on algorithms of AI, machine learning, and deep learning. All to constitute a large-scale digital twin that represents the event's structural, behavioral, and functional aspects within its environment in real time. Information systems for collaboration, reporting, simulation, and distributed intelligence should be offered in multiple forms (e.g. smartwatches, mobile phones app, or web app) with multi-level privileges for the different stakeholders. Suitable dashboards and visualization are also to be implemented for different targeted user groups. Targeted and viral alerts, notifications and tips to be communicated by speakers and mobile phones SMS. ICT infrastructure will be implanted in a hybrid approach of fiber cables, wireless (e.g. 5G network), and satellite to mitigate any disruptions in communication as the network load increases. The disaster recovery plan, intelligent routing, load balancing for maximum resource utilization are de-facto practices in the contemporary ICT design approaches. On-demand elasticity of ICT services is crucial for the continuity of services during a sharp spike in demand. Further, the implementation must consider sustainable (i.e. CO_2, energy, and waste footprints) and ethical (i.e. digital footprints) practices. For operational aspects, practices of

TQM, agile management, process improvement, modeling and simulation should be used (Fayoumi and Loucopoulos 2016). The CRMS performance will be ensured through process improvements by taking into consideration the efficiency and effectiveness of the process as resilience is a continuous process of planning, implementing, monitoring, and acting that evolves as the temporary community, in this case, the large event evolves.

7.5 Conclusion

Challenges and disasters either natural or man-made have brought numerous concerns to attention from their impacts on community resilience. The cost of dealing with climate change, which is partly caused by human activities (structural and behavioral), is ever increasing. Despite the disagreement on the causes of disasters, the understanding and planning for mitigating large-scale disasters are crucial for protecting human lives, and reducing negative environmental, economic, and societal impacts. We adopted the concept of community resilience as a process, which is the ability of any community in predicting, mitigating, and recovering from a large-scale disaster and sustaining their pre-disaster activities with minimal impact.

Using three key elements of the community resilience ecosystem (i.e. data, information system (IS), and communication network), we demonstrate how community resilience is supported and relied on the resilience of these three elements. We emphasize on data as a central component that enables community resilience. Data quality partly defines the resilience of the IS. Resilient network provides the backbone to all operations within networked systems. Closely related to these are the systems at the periphery or edge of the network such as clouds or sensors that form major elements of Internet of Things (IoT) and smart infrastructures (e.g. Smart City infrastructures). For communication and network resilience, it is a key that data about the network state are available and can be analyzed in a timely manner in order to manage the related resilience aspects within the context of the network management cycle. All the actions have to be based on measurable, current, and relevant data and criteria. While a detailed discussion of data resilience, information system resilience, and networked systems resilience is beyond the scope of this chapter, the proposed framework contributes to the multi-analysis of the socio-technical and institutional systems that take into account the ecological sustainability and threats.

We proposed a proactive holistic CRMS, which embeds resilience into the design of all constituent elements defining the overall community resilience. The proposed framework considers community resilience under nominal and disaster conditions and views resilience as a continuous process of planning, implementing, monitoring, and acting that evolves as the communities evolve and challenges mountain. Our holistic and dynamic framework considers the interaction among physical and technological infrastructure elements, organizational and procedural norms, institutional arrangements, and human behavior. The proposed framework is data-centric, which can utilize intelligent technologies as complementary enablers for mitigating the impact of disasters. The requirements for CRMS provide guidance to the practitioners.

Acknowledgements An earlier version of the framework was developed in the Southeast Asia-Lancaster Springboard Event in Sunway University, Malaysia on 2–4 November 2017. We acknowledge the input of the following individuals: Adam Fish (Lancaster University), Ayu Abdullah (ENACT), Azman Ali (Telekom Malaysia), Chamoreun Sok (Cambodian Institute Urban Studies), Fatma Lestari (Universitas Indonesia), Kian Meng Yap (Sunway University), Konstantinos Zografos (Lancaster Univesity), Marc Goerigk (University of Siegen), Michelle Lee Chin Chin (Sunway University), Ruslan Rainis (Universiti Sains Malaysia), Sian Lun Lau (Sunway University), and Yau Kok Lim (Sunway University). We also acknowledge the funding from Lancaster University for the event and subsequent workshop.

References

Allenby B, Fink J (2005) Toward inherently secure and resilient societies. Science 309:1034–1036

Álvarez F, Almon L, Radtki H, Hollick M (2019) Bluemergency: mediating post-disaster communication systems using the internet of things and bluetooth mesh. In: 2019 IEEE global humanitarian technology conference (GHTC). IEEE, pp 1–8

Angelov P (2014) Outside the box: an alternative data analytics framework. J Autom Mob Robot Intell Syst 8:29–35

Berkes F, Ross H (2013) Community resilience: toward an integrated approach. Soc Nat Resour 26:5–20

Berkes F, Ross H (2016) Panarchy and community resilience: sustainability science and policy implications. Environ Sci Polic 61:185–193

Bharosa N, Lee J, Janssen M (2010) Challenges and obstacles in sharing and coordinating information during multi-agency disaster response: propositions from field exercises. Inf Syst Front 12:49–65

Cambridge Centre for Risk Studies (CCRS) (2020) Global Risk Index 2020 research news, Cambridge Centre for Risk Studies, University of Cambridge. https://www.cam.ac.uk/research/news/new-approaches-to-help-businesses-tackle-climate-change

Cholda P, Mykkeltveit A, Helvik BE, Wittner OJ, Jajszczyk A (2007) A survey of resilience differentiation frameworks in communication networks. IEEE Commun Surv Tutor 9:32–55

Chou C-H, Zahedi FM, Zhao H (2014) Ontology-Based evaluation of natural disaster management websites. Mis Quart 38:997–1016

Cimellaro GP, Renschler C, Reinhorn AM, Arendt L (2016) PEOPLES: a framework for evaluating resilience. J Struct Eng 142:04016063

Cohen O, Goldberg A, Lahad M, Aharonson-Daniel L (2017) Building resilience: the relationship between information provided by municipal authorities during emergency situations and community resilience. Technol Forecast Soc Chang 121:119–125

Comes T, Meesters K, Torjesen S (2019) Making sense of crises: the implications of information asymmetries for resilience and social justice in disaster-ridden communities. Sustain Resilient Infrastruct 4:124–136

Cutter SL, Barnes L, Berry M, Burton C, Evans E, Tate E, Webb J (2008) A place-based model for understanding community resilience to natural disasters. Global Environ Change 18:598–606

Cutter SL, Ash KD, Emrich, CT (2014) The geographies of community disaster resilience. Global Environ Change 29:65–77

Dobson S, Hutchison D, Mauthe A, Schaeffer-Filho A, Smith P, Sterbenz JP (2019) Self-organization and resilience for networked systems: design principles and open research issues. Proc IEEE 107:819–834
Doran GT (1981) There's a SMART Way to write management's goals and objectives. Manag Rev 70:35–36
Du Q-L, Cao S-M, Ba L-L, Cheng J-M (2008) Application of PDCA cycle in the performance management system. In: 2008 4th international conference on wireless communications, networking and mobile computing. IEEE, pp 1–4
Dückers ML (2017) A multilayered psychosocial resilience framework and its implications for community-focused crisis management. J Contingencies Crisis Manag 25:182–187
Engels JI, Hollick M, Knodt M, Rudolph-Cleff A (2019) The emergency responsive digital city. Singapore, pp 136–139
Fayoumi A, Loucopoulos P (2016) Conceptual modeling for the design of intelligent and emergent information systems. Expert Syst Appl 59:174–194
Fedorowicz J, Gogan JL (2010) Reinvention of interorganizational systems: a case analysis of the diffusion of a bio-terror surveillance system. Inf Syst Front 12:81–95
Fernandes G, Rodrigues JJ, Carvalho LF, AL-Muhtadi JF, Proença ML (2019) A comprehensive survey on network anomaly detection. Telecommun Syst 70:447–489
Garg S, Kaur K, Kumar N, Kaddoum G, Zomaya AY, Ranjan R (2019) A hybrid deep learning-based model for anomaly detection in cloud datacenter networks. IEEE Trans Netw Serv Manage 16:924–935
Gorcin A, Celebi H, Qaraqe KA, Arslan H (2011) A framework on wideband sensing and direction finding for location aware public safety cognitive radio. In: WAMICON 2011 conference proceedings. IEEE, pp 1–5
Gorry GA, Scott Morton MS (1971) A framework for management information systems. Sloan Manag Rev
Heeks R, Ospina AV (2019) Conceptualising the link between information systems and resilience: a developing country field study. Inf Syst J 29:70–96
Ipe M, Raghu T, Vinze A (2010) Information intermediaries for emergency preparedness and response: a case study from public health. Inf Syst Front 12:67–79
Joerin J, Shaw R, Takeuchi Y, Krishnamurthy R (2012) Assessing community resilience to climate-related disasters in Chennai, India. Int J Disaster Risk Reduct 1:44–54
Johansen C, Horney J, Tien I (2017) Metrics for evaluating and improving community resilience. J Infrastruct Syst 23:04016032
Kalle T, Kaufhold M-A, Kuntke F, Reuter C, Rizk A, Steinmetz R (2019) Resilience in security and crises through adaptions and transitions. INFORMATIK 2019: 50 Jahre Gesellschaft für Informatik–Informatik für Gesellschaft (Workshop-Beiträge), 2019. Gesellschaft für Informatik eV
Koliou M, Van de Lindt JW, Mcallister TP, Ellingwood BR, Dillard M, Cutler H (2017) State of the research in community resilience: progress and challenges. Sustain Resil Infrastruct 1–21
Kruse S, Abeling T, Deeming H, Fordham M, Forrester J, Jülich S, Karanci AN, Kuhlicke C, Pelling M, Pedoth L (2017) Conceptualizing community resilience to natural hazards–the emBRACE framework. Nat Hazards Earth Syst Sci 17:2321–2333
Lee J, Bharosa N, Yang J, Janssen M, Rao HR (2011) Group value and intention to use—a study of multi-agency disaster management information systems for public safety. Decis Support Syst 50:404–414
Leong CML, Pan SL, Ractham P, Kaewkitipong L (2015) ICT-enabled community empowerment in crisis response: social media in Thailand flooding 2011. J Assoc Inf Syst 16:1
Liang X, Zhao J, Shetty S, Li D (2017) Towards data assurance and resilience in IoT using blockchain. In: MILCOM 2017–2017 IEEE military communications conference (MILCOM). IEEE, pp 261–266

Lieser P, Alvarez F, Gardner-Stephen P, Hollick M, Oehnstedt D (2017) Architecture for responsive emergency communications networks. In: 2017 IEEE global humanitarian technology conference (GHTC). IEEE, pp 1–9
Lu Y, Yang D (2011) Information exchange in virtual communities under extreme disaster conditions. Decis Support Syst 50:529–538
Macdonald JR, Zobel CW, Melnyk SA, Griffis SE (2018) Supply chain risk and resilience: theory building through structured experiments and simulation. Int J Prod Res 56:4337–4355
Magis K (2010) Community resilience: an indicator of social sustainability. Soc Nat Resour 23:401–416
Marnerides AK, Pezaros DP, Jose J, Mauthe AU, Hutchison D (2016) A situation aware information infrastructure framework. In: International conference on smart objects and technologies for social good, 2016. Springer, pp 186–194
Marnerides AK, Spachos P, Chatzimisios P, Mauthe AU (2015) Malware detection in the cloud under ensemble empirical mode decomposition. 2015 international conference on computing, networking and communications (iCNC). IEEE, pp 82–88
Mauthe A, Hutchison D, Cetinkaya EK, Ganchev I, Rak J, Sterbenz JP, Gunkelk M, Smith P, Gomes T (2016) Disaster-resilient communication networks: principles and best practices. In: 2016 8th international workshop on resilient networks design and modeling (RNDM). IEEE, pp 1–10
Norris A, Gonzalez J, Martinez S, Parry D (2018) Disaster e-Health framework for community resilience. Hawaii international conference on system sciences (HICSS), pp 35–44
Norris FH, Stevens SP, Pfefferbaum B, Wyche KF, Pfefferbaum RL (2008) Community resilience as a metaphor, theory, set of capacities, and strategy for disaster readiness. Am J Community Psychol 41:127–150
Oh O, Agrawal M, Rao HR (2013) Community intelligence and social media services: a rumor theoretic analysis of tweets during social crises. MIS Quart 407–426
Palen L, Anderson KM (2016) Crisis informatics—new data for extraordinary times. Science 353:224–225
Patel SS, Rogers MB, Amlôt R, Rubin GJ (2017) What do we mean by'community resilience'? A systematic literature review of how it is defined in the literature. PLoS Currents 9
Raman M, Ryan T, Olfman L (2006) Knowledge management systems for emergency preparedness: the Claremont University Consortium experience. Int J Knowl Manag (IJKM) 2:33–50
Redman TC (2008) Data driven: profiting from your most important business asset. Harvard Business Press
Revell P, Henderson C (2019) Operationalising a framework for understanding community resilience in Europe. Reg Environ Change 19:967–979
Roberts E, Farrington J, Skerratt S (2015) Evaluating new digital technologies through a framework of resilience. Scott Geograph J 131:253–264
Saja AA, Teo M, Goonetilleke A, Ziyath AM (2018) An inclusive and adaptive framework for measuring social resilience to disasters. Int J Disaster Risk Reduct 28:862–873
Schaeffer-Filho A, Mauthe A, Hutchison D, Smith P, Yu Y, Fry M (2013) PReSET: a toolset for the evaluation of network resilience strategies. In: 2013 IFIP/IEEE international symposium on integrated network management (IM 2013). IEEE, pp 202–209
Schaeffer-Filho A, Smith P, Mauthe A, Hutchison D, Yu Y, Fry M (2012) A framework for the design and evaluation of network resilience management. In: 2012 IEEE network operations and management symposium. IEEE, 401–408
Sharifi A (2016) A critical review of selected tools for assessing community resilience. Ecol Ind 69:629–647
Shirazi SN, Simpson S, Gouglidis A, Mauthe A, Hutchison D (2016) Anomaly detection in the cloud using data density. In: 2016 IEEE 9th international conference on cloud computing (CLOUD), 2016. IEEE, pp 616–623
Siau K, Rossi M (2011) Evaluation techniques for systems analysis and design modelling methods–a review and comparative analysis. Inf Syst J 21:249–268

Sterbenz JP, Hutchison D, Çetinkaya EK, Jabbar A, Rohrer JP, Schöller M, Smith P (2010) Resilience and survivability in communication networks: Strategies, principles, and survey of disciplines. Comput Netw 54:1245–1265

Sterbenz JP, Hutchison D, Çetinkaya EK, Jabbar A, Rohrer JP, Schöller M, Smith P (2014) Redundancy, diversity, and connectivity to achieve multilevel network resilience, survivability, and disruption tolerance invited paper. Telecommun Syst 56:17–31

Strong DM, Lee YW, Wang RY (1997) Data quality in context. Commun ACM 40:103–110

Sun Y, Chowdhury KR (2014) Enabling emergency communication through a cognitive radio vehicular network. IEEE Commun Mag 52:68–75

Thatcher A, Vasconcelos AC, Ellis D (2015) An investigation into the impact of information behaviour on information failure: The Fukushima Daiichi nuclear power disaster. Int J Inf Manage 35:57–63

van de Walle B, Dugdale J (2012) Information management and humanitarian relief coordination: findings from the Haiti earthquake response. Int J Bus Cont Risk Manag 3:278–305

Vidal J (2013) The sumatran rainforest will mostly disappear within 20 years. The Guardian News Report. https://www.theguardian.com/world/2013/may/26/sumatra-borneo-deforestation-tigers-palm-oil. Accessed 03 July 2020

Vidgen R, Shaw S, Grant DB (2017) Management challenges in creating value from business analytics. Eur J Oper Res 261:626–639

Vlacheas P, Stavroulaki V, Demestichas P, Cadzow S, Gorniak S, Ikonomou D (2011) Ontology and taxonomies of resilience. European Network and Information Security Agency (ENISA)

Wallemacq P, House R (2018) Economic losses, poverty & disasters: 1998–2017. Centre for Research on the Epidemiology of Disasters

United Nations Office for Disaster Risk Reduction, UNDRR & UNISDR REPORT. https://www.undrr.org/publication/economic-losses-poverty-disasters-1998-2017

Yang M-H, Chen W-P, Tsai A-H, Cheng S-H (2019) Coverage extension with UAV based on constrained uplink and downlink phases for disaster-resilient communication networks. In: 2019 IEEE VTS Asia pacific wireless communications symposium (APWCS). IEEE, pp 1–5

Yates D, Paquette S (2011) Emergency knowledge management and social media technologies: A case study of the 2010 Haitian earthquake. Int J Inf Manage 31:6–13

Zautra A, Hall J, Murray K (2008) Community development and community resilience: an integrative approach. Community Dev 39:130–147

Zhang X, Liu D, Yuan P, Wang W, Cheng X, Jia W, Qiu Y (2019) Architecture design of electric power emergency communication based on 4G LTE network. In: 2019 IEEE 4th international conference on cloud computing and big data analysis (ICCCBDA). IEEE, pp 600–603

Chapter 8
Social Media Technologies and Disaster Management

Yuko Tanaka

Abstract The social–technological developments of the past decade have changed how we communicate during disasters. Given the wide reach of social media, when a disaster occurs in the digital era, people check social media platforms such as Twitter and Facebook immediately to explore and to share disaster-related information. These help us to understand the extent of the serious damage it would cause, where and whether to evacuate, and what kind of support victims might need. Although social media has just recently emerged as a social–technological tool, past research has shown that it is human nature to share information during disasters. This chapter provides an overview of how the characteristics of social media platforms influence our information-sharing behavior during disasters. In addition, it focuses on not only the advantages but also the potential threat of using social technology based on recent empirical research. While social media makes it possible to share information more rapidly, widely, and easily than ever before, their technological characteristics could benefit us only if we share reliable information; however, social problems could be caused if false information is spread. By reviewing the psychological aspects behind false information spreading through social media, anticipated challenges in using social technology during disasters will be discussed.

Keywords Social media · Disaster · Psychological perspective · False rumor · Information management

8.1 Introduction

The latest social media technologies allow individuals to share information more rapidly and extensively anywhere and anytime, even in the middle of a disaster situation. In January 2020, there were 3.8 billion active users of social media platforms such as Facebook and Twitter (Hootsuite and We Are Social 2020). The number has

Y. Tanaka (✉)
Graduate School of Engineering, Nagoya Institute of Technology, Gokiso-Cho, Showa-Ku, Nagoya, Aichi 466-8555, Japan
e-mail: tanaka.yuko@nitech.ac.jp

M. Sakurai and R. Shaw (eds.), *Emerging Technologies for Disaster Resilience*, Disaster Risk Reduction,
https://doi.org/10.1007/978-981-16-0360-0_8

increased by one billion in only 3 years and amounts to almost half of the world population. People use mobile devices daily for an average of 3.7 h, and approximately 50% of this time is spent on social platforms and communication applications. This chapter provides an overview of how the characteristics of social media platforms influence information-sharing behaviors during disasters. The primary focus of this chapter is natural disasters (e.g., earthquake and hurricane), although a disaster is a usually complex phenomenon and some natural disasters are followed by human-made crises (e.g., nuclear accidents) that can result in secondary damage. Social media has evolved into an important communication tool to help people prepare for, respond to, and recover from natural disasters. According to the White Paper on Disaster Management (Cabinet Office, Government of Japan 2018), people in their 20 s and 30 s particularly tend to emphasize the importance of social media as a source of disaster-related information. However, with the rapidly growing number of social media users worldwide, both the benefits and repercussions of using social media during disasters have been magnified.

8.2 Roles of Social Media During a Disaster

When an earthquake occurs, the shaking makes a person realize that something unusual is suddenly happening. Many questions come to mind in a few seconds. Is this shaking caused by an earthquake or just road construction? How long will it last? Was this just a foreshock? Is the mainshock coming? Should I evacuate immediately? Where is the epicenter? Is my family safe? Attempts are made to find information that could explain the situational change. These are only examples of information needs that arise in the early phases of a disaster. Then, information needs to change continually. As Mikami (2004) described, different information needs emerge as the phases progress: In the early phase, which starts immediately after a disaster, people need information such as early warnings, cause of the disaster, and location and severity of the damages. In the next phase, people need security and safety information as they would be concerned about the risks of crimes such as looting, and of losing contact with their family and friends, or finding the missing. In the post-event phase, people need living information to recover and rebuild from the disaster.

Gathering and sharing information quickly and appropriately is the foundation of efficient disaster management. However, during a catastrophic disaster, some information channels might not be available. For instance, before the era of the Internet and social media, evacuees needed to depend on mass media (e.g., printed newspapers, TV, radio) to acquire disaster-related information. The traditional media essentially provides one-way communication and does not fulfill individual information needs. The emergence of social media has changed the process of dissemination of information during disasters by allowing two-way communication that connects victims directly with family, friends, governments, on-site and off-site volunteers, mass media, and international aid. In addition, social media has the advantage of being accessible during a disaster. For instance, while the 2011 Japan earthquake disabled a large number of fixed communication networks and mobile communications using cellular phones owing to the damage to their base stations (Ichiguchi 2011), people could still communicate through social media by accessing the Internet.

There has been widespread use of social media during disasters since the mid-2000s. People started communicating through social media during the 2005 suicide bombing attack in UK and 2007 wildfires in the USA (Peary et al. 2012). During the 2010 Haiti earthquake, the Ushahidi crisis map, which collects disaster information from Twitter and Facebook, was widely used (Norheim-Hagtun and Meier 2010). In the case of the severe flood that began from the northern region of Thailand in July 2011, the number of messages via Twitter increased by 52% by the time the flood reached the Bangkok Metropolitan area in October (Kongthon et al. 2012). People shared the following information: situational announcements and alerts, support announcements, requests for assistance, and requests for information. The 2012 Yilian earthquake in China is another instance where social media was used for information sharing. Disaster-related information transmitted via Sina Weibo, a Chinese microblogging platform, included personal posts, caution and advice, actualities and damage, donation of money, goods or services, and appeals for help (Li et al. 2018).

Social media plays an important role in both emergency management (sharing emergency information and coordinating community response) and community development (increasing and improving social networks through social media). With respect to emergency management, one of the primary concerns people have during a catastrophic disaster is safety information. People are anxious to know whether their family, friends, and relatives are safe. Social media has been used as a platform to exchange information about missing, injured, and isolated people (Imran et al. 2015; Subba and Bui 2017). The following is an outstanding example of how social media helps information sharing and rescue. On the night of the 2011 Japan earthquake, the then Tokyo Governor found an SOS message on Twitter. The tweet was posted by a Japanese man living in London, UK, and asking for help. His mother, who was the head of a kindergarten, and a dozen kindergarten children were isolated on the third floor of a shelter which nobody could approach from the ground because the lower floors were flooded due to a tsunami. The Governor immediately contacted a fire-rescue helicopter dispatched by Tokyo Metropolitan Government and succeeded in rescuing them. A person in charge of the Tokyo Fire Department later said "we sometimes receive 119 calls by people based on Twitter information. Although not always checking (Twitter), but we would like to respond to the information as much as possible." (Mainichi Shimbun 2011). This case clearly shows how emergency information was transmitted via social media and resulted in saving lives. Moreover, there are numerous studies examining the utilization of social media for emergency information sharing such as early disaster detection and warning (Chatfield et al. 2013; Bui 2019), visualizing affected and secure locations, and mapping the locations and the types of help needed (Gao et al. 2011; Reuter et al. 2015; Slamet et al. 2018).

In accordance with community development, Taylor et al. (2012) discussed the role of social media from a psychological perspective. During Cyclone Yasi, which was a destructive tropical cyclone that hit Australia in January 2011, a Facebook page named "Cyclone Yasi Update" was created 5 days after the disaster hit the area. Organized and coordinated by several administrators and content managers living in scattered locations, the page functioned as a disaster management hub. Taylor et al. (2012) illustrated the two roles of maintaining a Facebook page during a disaster. One is for timely information gathering and dissemination from both official and informal sources (e.g., sharing images, the details of the affected area, links by official sources, and warnings). The other is to create connections among, and provide psychological support to, people who are anxious about the disaster (e.g., users made comments such as "glad everyone is ok," "don't worry, they're safe and well," and "Great job by all involved, kept me sane throughout the time, knowing what was going on for my loved ones"). The number of messages posted on the Facebook page and direct page views surged to 3,576 and 509,743, respectively, in the first 3 days. An advantage of social media for community development is that it engenders mutual support. During a disaster, the significance of mutual help is emphasized as public assistance (e.g., supports by the local government) but has its limitations (Cabinet Office, Government of Japan 2015). In addition, there are gaps between citizens and public organizations in cases where citizens in the areas that are affected to a lesser extent are more concerned about their daily necessities, such as food supplies in local stores, while the local government needs to prioritize life-saving efforts in the severely damaged areas (Hong et al. 2018). In this regard, social media would be appropriate to fill this gap by promoting mutual assistance among people within the local community.

8.3 Risks of Using Social Media During a Disaster

In contrast with the cases that shed light on the benefits or promising aspects of the use of social media platforms for disaster management, a number of recent studies have also explored the repercussions of the same (Castillo et al. 2011; Oh et al. 2013; Starbird et al. 2016; Vosoughi et al. 2018; Zubiaga et al. 2018). The biggest threat is "information pollution." Social media platforms allow users to share information rapidly and widely without any regard to its reliability. As reliable information is imperative for disaster management, the repercussions of false rumor propagation could have negative impacts on our society and result in recovery delay.

The earthquakes that hit Haiti in January 2010 and Chile in February 2010 are the first disaster situations where rumors were spread through social media (Mendoza et al. 2010; Oh et al. 2010; Gao et al. 2011; Castillo et al. 2013). In the case of the 2010 Chile earthquake of magnitude 8.8, which was one of the largest recorded earthquakes in the world, more than 500 people died, and there was extensive damage to infrastructure. Mendoza et al. (2010) analyzed the disaster-related information shared through social media 4 days after the earthquake had occurred. There were nearly 5 million tweets by more than 700 thousand different users. The result revealed that several types of false rumors were posted and retweeted. The following are some examples: "Tsunami warning in Valparaiso," "Death of artist Ricardo Arjona," "Looting in some districts in Santiago." After a year, another devastating earthquake hits the northern part of Japan in March 2011, triggering tsunami waves and the Fukushima Daiichi nuclear accident. The catastrophic disaster that resulted in the deaths of more than 15,000 people, with 2,000 people missing, and hundreds of thousands of victims forced to evacuate across several prefectures, was also a case where many false rumors were spread.

One serious repercussion of rumors during a disaster is the wastage of limited human resources for disaster management. For instance, the following false rumor spread through Twitter after the 2011 Japan earthquake: in summary, "I was in a server room at the office when the earthquake occurred. A rack collapsed. My abdomen is crushed and I am bleeding. I can't breathe. I can't call for help by myself." This message was retweeted by many users who were worried about the person, asking help by providing the address information of his company and trying to reassure the person (Tachiiri 2011). However, an acquaintance soon tweeted that the original tweet was false. Another such case emerged after a large earthquake hit Kumamoto, the western part of Japan, in 2016. The following text message was posted: "The earthquake caused a lion to escape from a neighboring zoo," along with a picture of a lion walking across a street in a town. This tweet was posted on Twitter just after the earthquake hit Kumamoto prefecture and retweeted more than 20,000 times, resulting in the officials at a zoo in the disaster area being compelled to answer repeated telephone calls more than 100 times. The person who posted the tweet was a 20-year-old man living in Kanagawa prefecture, which is located roughly 1,000 km away from the epicenter, and was ultimately arrested on the suspicion of forcibly obstructing business (Shimbun 2016). This was the first case in Japan of an arrest being made for posting a false rumor on social media. The culprit accepted the charges and confessed that he was playing a practical joke. Both tweets were posted less than 30 min after the earthquakes and were originated outside the perimeter of the disaster. Although the intention of posting the tweets was to play a joke, many users took the tweets seriously and genuinely attempted to take appropriate actions. As seen in these examples, it is challenging during disasters to distinguish serious warnings and rescue requests from false ones, resulting in wastage of resources. The characteristics of social media platforms, that allow anyone from anywhere to post messages, enable malicious users to take pleasure in other people's reactions to their pretense of being the victims of a disaster.

It is to be noted that while there are malicious rumor spreaders, some users post and spread false rumors without confirming their reliability. They believe that the information is true and thus try to share it with others. In addition, in certain instances, information that used to be true could become false in a different context. For instance, imagine that an evacuee posted the following message: "There was a shortage of relief supplies at our shelter. We need your help. Please send supplies!!" This was true at that moment and was shared by many people through social media. Shortly after, sufficient relief supplies arrived at the shelter, and the evacuee posted another message: "Thank you for your great help! The shortage has been solved." However, the first message was still circulating among users who were unaware of the second message.

Because of their redundant requests, excessive relief supplies were dispatched to the specific shelter and, as a result, were not appropriately distributed to the other shelters. Although everyone who was involved in this information-sharing process did so with good intentions, it ended up hindering disaster recovery. Such proliferation of unreliable information during disasters not only causes wastage of limited human resources but also unnecessary anxiety, confusion, and distrust among people in the society.

8.4 Frameworks for Understanding Rumor Propagation

Although circulation of rumors through social media is a recent social problem in the digital era, rumors during disasters have been recognized as problematic social phenomena as early as the beginning of the nineteenth century. As a framework to better understanding rumor propagation through social media, this section will briefly review the findings of social science research on rumors.

8.4.1 Defining a Rumor

The history of research into rumors in social sciences goes back to a study into rumors spread during a specific disaster. A catastrophic earthquake hits the northern part of India on January 15, 1934, causing widespread damage to bridges, railway lines, and roads. Prasad (1935) observed and classified numerous rumors in the aftermath of the disaster such as "the earthquake was a punishment for our sin," "a large house has disappeared in the cracks of the earth," and "January 23 will be a fatal day. Unforeseeable calamities will arise." These were false or fabricated information. In later research, Prasad (1950) illustrated that rumors spread during earthquakes that occurred in different locations in the past 1000 years had similar characteristics. Since then, research has shown that similar types of disaster-related rumors were repeatedly propagated, such as reporting unlikely natural phenomena (e.g., rain of blood, disappearance of rivers) (Prasad 1950), warnings of human-induced threats (e.g., looting, rape) (Ogiue 2011), and fabricating the death of famous people (Castillo et al. 2013). Shibutani (1966, p. 17) defined rumor as "a recurrent form of communication through which men caught together in an ambiguous situation attempt to construct a meaningful interpretation of it by pooling their intellectual resources." Rumor spreads as a means of filling a discrepancy between information needs and supply. Note that the definition of a rumor does not determine the authenticity of information and includes unverified information to support its authenticity. This frequently happens especially in disaster situations as identifying true or false information is time-consuming during the chaos after a disaster.

Recently, "fake news," a term that is similar to "rumor," has been used frequently. As indicated, the term is used in myriad ways, and accordingly, Wardle and

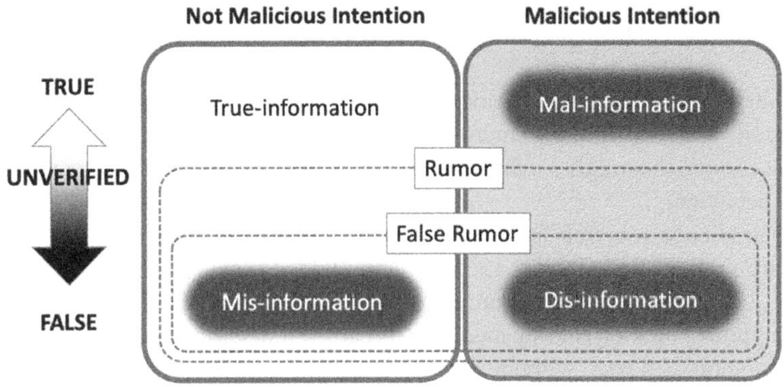

Fig. 8.1 Categorization of false information based on falsehood and maliciousness (modified Wardle and Derakhshan (2017)'s three components by incorporating with the definition of rumor)

Derakhshan (2017) proposed a conceptual framework to adequately describe information pollution. The framework consists of three components (i.e., mis-information, dis-information, and mal-information) based on two criteria: falsehood and existence of harmful intention. False information is categorized into either mis-information or dis-information. The latter is generated intentionally to cause harm to others, but the former is not. Mal-information is also generated with a harmful intention, but it is not false. For example, accusing a politician based on a leaked e-mail corresponds to mal-information. To clarify the terminology of rumor, false rumor, mis-information, dis-information, and mal-information, a conceptual framework (Wardle and Derakhshan 2017) was modified by incorporating the definition of rumors (Fig. 8.1). Considering that the intention of posting rumors during a disaster is not necessarily to harm someone, but rather it is to enjoy watching the confusion of people or to take undue advantage of the chaos after a disaster, the wording "harmful" of intention was replaced by the contextually appropriate word "malicious." The figure also added a spectrum of falsehood shown as a vertical arrow on the left. The middle of the spectrum refers to information that is not verified as true or false. Once a rumor has been identified as being untrue, the rumor is called a false rumor. As was illustrated in the aforementioned example of rumors during disasters, social media users shared outdated information and it resulted in the dispatch of excessive relief supplies to a shelter. As they were involved in information sharing with the good intention of helping evacuees, this is categorized into mis-information in false rumors. On the other hand, the previously mentioned rumor that included the picture of a lion walking in a town corresponds to dis-information in false rumor. The picture itself was originally taken in Africa for a film shooting and thus not fabricated, but it became a rumor when it was used in a false context (i.e., false location of "Kumamoto," and inappropriate timing such as after an earthquake). However, other users would immediately misunderstand the picture as a lion escaping from a zoo after the damage from an earthquake. This false rumor corresponds to an example of dis-information.

8.4.2 Psychological Factors

The observations of recurrent rumor spreading in disaster situations inevitably raised a question: Why do rumors emerge in most disaster situations? Why do people transmit rumors that might be false? What types of psychological factors are behind human behavior?

Social science research has established that rumors emerge when information needs are not satisfied (Prasad 1935; Knapp 1944; Shibutani 1966). DiFonzo and Bordia (2007, p. 14) analyzed rumor communication as a means of understanding an ambiguous situation and managing a threat. In a disaster situation, information supply cannot keep pace with the sharply rising information needs. The unsatisfied needs for information trigger peoples' attempts to compensate for this discrepancy by sharing unreliable information (Hong et al. 2018).

Allport and Postman (1946) proposed a basic formula to comprehend the intensity of a rumor as follows: $R \sim i \times a$. Analyzing rumors spread during WWII, they found that two conditions were essential to explain the phenomena: the importance (i) of the message and the ambiguity (a) of the situation. The formula envisions that the number of rumors increases by multiplying i and a. They emphasized that the relationship between these two conditions is not additive but multiplicative, that is, if either condition is not met, no rumor emerges. In addition, as carefully noted by Allport and Postman (1947), not every individual spreads the rumor when these two conditions are met. Therefore, extending the basic formula of rumormongering, Chorus (1953) inserted individual critical sense (c) into the formula as follows: $R \sim i \times a \times I/c$. Here, c refers to the individual characteristic to reflect, consider, and morally criticize a rumor. I stands for the general average of c. He states rumor dissemination reduces or stopped if c increases and that the influence of individual characteristic can be negligible if c equals to I. Further studies have empirically demonstrated that along with importance and ambiguity, anxiety and accuracy are also associated with rumor propagation (Anthony 1973; Rosnow 1980; Walker and Beckerle 1987).

8.4.3 Roles and Networks

In the collective process of rumor circulation by a crowd, there are different levels of involvement by individuals. For example, Shibutani (1966) distinguished them into a *messenger* who brings related information to a group, an *interpreter* who evaluates the information, a *skeptic* who doubts it, a *protagonist/agitato*r who supports one side over the others when several interpretations are possible, an *auditor* who is a bystander, and a *decision-maker* who assesses the information and decides further actions. The emerging social–technological environments highlight another role: a *transmitter*. A *transmitter* is a person who is involved in the transmission of rumors but not in the direct generation, evaluation, or modification of the content of the rumor. This person just receives information from someone and reposts or forwards it to others.

Normally, the social media environment is different in three perspectives from the traditional environment in which rumors spread from person to person: speed, impact, and anonymity. First, rumors spread digitally through social–technological environment and can be instantaneously circulated worldwide. Second, rumors can be transmitted from one person to thousands of others by just a single click. This impact is further magnified when the person is a social media influencer, who has access to, and is persuasive to a large number of followers. The third characteristic is anonymity. Some users interact on social media networks with their real names, but others do so anonymously by using nicknames or false names. Even if a person uses his/her real name, other attributes such as age and location are often implicit. Third, social media allows a person to have several social media accounts or usernames for different purposes. These characteristics create further complexity in understanding the social influence of a rumor.

In addition, social media technologies have made it easier than before to analyze to a greater extent the manner of propagation of a rumor, that is, metadata allow us to identify where the rumor originated, how many times the rumor was transmitted, and by how many users to how many other users. These phenomena are called a *cascade*, which is the successive transmission of information (Sunstein 2009). A recent study, which analyzed approximately 126,000 rumor cascades tweeted or retweeted more than 4.5 million times, demonstrated that false rumors spread significantly further (i.e., more hops from the original message), faster, and are more widespread (i.e., rapidly reach more people) than true information (Vosoughi et al. 2018). False rumor propagation can cause *group polarization*, which induces social group members to take a wrong course of action. Another network analysis of false rumors supports this possibility. Choi et al. (2020) demonstrated that false rumors tended to propagate in an *echo chamber network*. In echo chambers that were operationally defined in the study as a cluster in which members share at least two common false rumors, the transmission of false rumors was faster when compared to transmission by non-members of an echo chamber. However, we note that these analyses were performed using Twitter meta-information, and it is questionable how generalizable the results are with respect to other social media environments and to specific rumors spreading during disaster situations. Recent advances in network analysis are beneficial for a general understanding of rumor propagation and eventually could facilitate better rumor control.

8.5 Rumor Control as Disaster Management

Anyone who uses social media is at risk of being affected by false rumors and being involved in their propagation. Rumors spread through social media have become a matter of public concern due to their influence on the community, especially during a disaster, and consequently have become an interdisciplinary research topic. This section will consider three approaches to mitigate the negative impacts of rumors: educational, technological, and psychological approaches. These three approaches have different backgrounds with varying methodologies. However, given the wide-ranging implications of rumors on society, it is important to consider these approaches as mutually complementary and to identify methods to integrate them so as to assist in rumor management, especially during a disaster.

8.5.1 Educational Approach

Chorus (1953) focused on the critical thinking abilities of individuals and assumed that as critical thinking grows, rumor propagation would weaken. A widely accepted definition of critical thinking is "*reasonable reflective thinking focused on deciding what to believe or do*" (Ennis 1996). Critical thinking consists of two components: ability (e.g., to analyze arguments, ask and answer clarification questions, judge the credibility of a source, understand and use graphs and mathematics, and deal with fallacy labels) and disposition (e.g., to seek and offer clear reasons, be alert for alternatives, withhold judgment when the evidence and reasons are insufficient) (Ennis 2015). These components are indispensable for differentiating reliable information from false information. In the current information society, anyone can take the role of information gatekeeper. Given the fact that even children can be involved in rumor transmission through social media, teaching critical thinking to students should be an essential component of the curriculum at all educational levels. Numerous education-related studies have proposed enhancements to teaching methods (Marin and Halpern 2011; Hitchcock 2015), assessments of ability and disposition (Watson and Glaser 1980; Facione et al. 2001), and explanations for developmental and cognitive mechanisms of critical thinking (Brabeck 1983; Marin and Halpern 2011). In the case of disaster, it is also helpful to have metacognitive knowledge in advance, such as "rumors tend to emerge during a disaster" or "people tend to share false rumors without confirming their reliability." Understanding the human tendency of trying to understand an "ambiguous situation" will help children to prepare for a disaster situation, and encourage them to use their best thinking skills and disposition especially during such crises.

8.5.2 Technological Approach

Perhaps, the ultimate goal should be that every user is able to critically assess any information on social media at all times. However, in reality, human cognitive resources (e.g., memory, time, mental effort) are limited to consciously examine each piece of information. Particularly, as critical thinking is an effortful cognitive process (Halpern 2014), people who are victims of a disaster cannot afford to check the veracity of every scrap of information. Instead, certain forms of support that counterbalance the limited individual cognitive resources are required. Further in-depth studies regarding rumor detection are one way to contribute to this issue (Han and Ciravegna 2019). If it is possible to computationally detect rumors on social media, especially in disastrous situations, that are highly likely to be false, it would help reduce wastage, and more efficiently allocate human resources.

There are two main approaches to research with regard to rumor detection. One approach focuses on the contents of messages. Based on an assumption that a rumor tends to be followed by countering-posts, it utilizes countering messages as an indicator to detect rumors. For instance, a potentially false rumor is traced back using countering-posts that are identified with specific expressions (e.g., "is (that | this | it) true," "real? | really? | unconfirmed," "(that | this | it) is not true," "see the list of the earthquake related false rumors http://...") as signals (Miyabe et al. 2014; Zhao et al. 2015). However, social media messages include fluctuations in text (e.g., abbreviations, emoticons, slang expressions) and multimodal contents (e.g., text, video, photo, image, URL). Moreover, not all false rumors evoke countering messages. A rumor may be followed by only supportive comments at a certain point in time, that is, the rumor will spread as if it was true until countering messages appear. This period is crucial for rumor control during disasters because disaster management requires rapid decision making. Thus, taking into consideration these possibilities, the other approach focuses on the context of messages, instead of the contents. Recent studies have developed computational models to detect rumors and revealed specific network patterns of false information diffusion on social media (Mondal et al. 2018; Rosenfeld et al. 2020). When the above-mentioned systems are implemented, they will mitigate the negative impacts of false rumors during disasters on society during any future disasters.

8.5.3 Psychological Approach

Numerous psychological studies have endeavored to understand the psychological mechanisms behind rumor spreading behavior and to develop strategies of minimizing its negative impacts on society. The experimental results have demonstrated consistently the effectiveness of exposure to countering-messaging that denies, refutes, corrects, inquires, or criticizes the rumor: Exposure to countering-message reduced both beliefs in the rumor (Jaeger et al. 1980; Iyer and Debevec 1991; Einwiller and Kamins 2008; Garrett 2011), as well as the anxiety created by the rumor (Bordia et al. 2005; Tanaka et al. 2014). In a real-life disaster situation, numerous attempts to combat false rumors by showing countering-messages have been demonstrated. As an illustration, here are some false rumors and the corresponding countering-messages that were posted on social media during the 2011 Japan earthquake: "Tokyo Electric Power Co.'s workers ran and left. They were drinking in another city." (false rumor) and "Tokyo Electric Power Co. announced that the workers were found dead" (countering-message); "Chubu, Kansai, and Kyusyu Electric Power companies are beginning to transfer electricity to Kanto. Please cooperate!" (false rumor) and "Transfer is impossible because of the differences in frequencies" (countering-message). The attempt to mitigate a false rumor by correction is usually done by authorized organizations officially (e.g., government offices, public institutions, mass media). For instance, the Federal Emergency Management Agency (FEMA) implemented rumor control by creating a web page that shows a list of rumors and the corresponding corrections during Hurricane Michael (FEMA 2018). Additionally, attempts are also made by social media users collectively and voluntarily (Arif et al. 2017). Empirically, an experimental study was conducted after the 2011 Japan earthquake, utilizing the rumors and countering-messages spread during the disaster as stimuli. The results demonstrated that exposure to countering-messages about the rumors increased the proportion of users who intended to stop transmitting it to others from 32.1 to 49.3%, with subjective decrease in the anxiety, accuracy, and importance of the rumor (Tanaka et al. 2014). Furthermore, a meta-analysis revealed that detailed countering-messages had stronger effects on weakening belief in rumors (Chan et al. 2017). For this purpose, effective strategies were proposed to influence individuals at the cognitive and emotional process level to curb the propagation of mis-information (Lewandowsky et al. 2012).

8.5.4 Outstanding Issues

Ultimately, from the perspective of efficient disaster information management, we envisage a society that promotes long-term critical thinking education and builds the foundation of citizens who examine information deliberately and take decisive action in preparation for future disasters. When a disaster occurs, the computational technologies would screen rapidly and comprehensively for potential false information on social media and prioritize the falsehood. Then, experts would examine the high priority potential false information and its negative implications on society in detail. If the information is confirmed to be false and having negative implications, official organizations (e.g., governments, ministries) make an announcement with corrections, to citizens through widely spreading information channels (e.g., websites, social media, mass media), mitigating unnecessary anxiety and false belief.

However, even if the society became cognizant, some outstanding issues that need to be addressed remain. First, although the countering strategy is effective at weakening psychological reactions to false rumors, in general, a question remains about the extent to which the strategy is effective in combating false rumors. For example, as the above-mentioned result showed (Tanaka et al. 2014), 50.7% of people still intended to transmit false rumors even after exposure to countering-messages. This was on account of their unchanged high anxiety about, and belief in, the false rumors. Another past study consistently demonstrated that countering strategy decreased pre-belief in a false rumor by 30% on average, although the post-belief was positive, if anything, against the rumor (Bordia et al. 2005). Chan et al. (2017) named this tendency as "misinformation-persistence effect" and argued that countering-message exposure tends to be less effective unless it provides new and detailed information.

In reality, human behavior that supports the results of these laboratory experiments can be observed. For example, a false rumor "toilet paper will run out due to coronavirus" spread at the end of February 2020, causing people to stockpile it across Japan. A paper manufacturing company immediately denied it by explaining that abundant stock was available. Mass media and experts repeatedly stated that it was a false rumor and called for deliberative behavior by consumers. However, people kept lining up before a store opened. In an interview, a housewife who was waiting in the line stated that though she knew that the rumor was false, the possibility of short supply made her anxious (Shimbun 2020).

As this case clearly shows, human behavior is not so straightforward, as people can be easily persuaded by simple exposure to countering information. In a natural disaster, though a government calls on residents in potentially affected areas to evacuate early, some residents remain at home for many reasons and fail to get out in time. In an epidemic, despite being asked to stay self-isolated when exhibiting symptoms of being positive for a serious virus, people still go out to restaurants, gyms, or concerts and end up spreading the virus to others. Such human behaviors could cause negative impacts on the society and hinder disaster recovery, however, this is not due to the unavailability of appropriate information. In reality, of late, social media and mass media tend to provide early warning messages ahead of disasters, so that important information reaches the smartphone in our hand. Nonetheless, such important information is as good as being nonexistent unless end users process and integrate it into their consciousness. In this process, there are many factors that mediate human behavior such as the information source, personal interest, quality (Bordia et al. 2005; Einwiller and Kamins 2008), backfire effect of countering-message (Lewandowsky et al. 2012), and cognitive biases and heuristics (e.g., confirmation bias) that can influence the interaction of the user based on the design of the communicating technology (Metzger and Flanagin 2013).

8.6 Concluding Remarks

Information is important for efficient disaster management. Reliable information is needed not only for experts but also citizens to cope together with severe disasters. The present chapter has tried to summarize the potential role of social media in information sharing during disasters. Social media is promising for sharing disaster-related information rapidly and widely and enabling mutual help among citizens. On the other hand, this chapter also emphasized the repercussion of social media when it is used as a rumor mill. However, the negative impacts of social media during the past disasters might have contributed to clarifying the issue of rumor propagation because social media platforms allow users to reflect later whether or not, and how, they were involved in rumor transmission. The digital platforms enable researchers to demonstrate rumor propagation and to raise an alarm at disaster-related human behavior based on empirical evidences. Rumor will emerge again in the next disaster.

We still have much to learn from interdisciplinary research into utilizing social media during disasters.

References

Allport GW, Postman L (1946) An analysis of rumor. Public Opin Q 10:501–517. https://doi.org/10.1093/poq/10.4.501

Allport GW, Postman L (1947) The psychology of rumor. Henry Holt and Company, New York, NY

Anthony S (1973) Anxiety and rumor. J Soc Psychol 89:91–98. https://doi.org/10.1080/00224545.1973.9922572

Arif A, Robinson JJ, Stanek SA et al (2017) A closer look at the self-correcting crowd: examining corrections in online rumors. In: Proceedings of the 2017 ACM conference on computer supported cooperative work and social computing association for computing machinery. New York, NY, pp 155–168

Bordia P, DiFonzo N, Haines R, Chaseling E (2005) Rumors denials as persuasive messages: effects of personal relevance, source, and message characteristics. J Appl Soc Psychol 35:1301–1331. https://doi.org/10.1111/j.1559-1816.2005.tb02172.x

Brabeck MM (1983) Critical thinking skills and reflective judgment development: redefining the aims of higher education. J Appl Dev Psychol 4:23–34. https://doi.org/10.1016/0193-3973(83)90056-4

Bui L (2019) Social media, rumors, and hurricane warning systems in Puerto Rico. In: Proceedings of the 52nd Hawaii international conference on system sciences. Hawaii, HI, pp 2667–2676

Cabinet Office, Government of Japan (2015) White paper on disaster management. http://www.bousai.go.jp/kyoiku/panf/pdf/WP2015_DM_Full_Version.pdf. Accessed 20 June 2020

Cabinet Office, Government of Japan (2018) White paper on disaster management. http://www.bousai.go.jp/kaigirep/hakusho/pdf/H30_hakusho_english.pdf. Accessed 20 June 2020

Castillo C, Mendoza M, Poblete B (2011) Information credibility on Twitter. In: Proceedings of the 20th international conference companion on world wide web, WWW 2011. ACM Press, New York, NY, pp 675–684

Castillo C, Mendoza M, Poblete B (2013) Predicting information credibility in time-sensitive social media. Internet Res 23:560–588. https://doi.org/10.1108/IntR-05-2012-0095

Chan MS, Jones CR, Hall Jamieson K, Albarracín D (2017) Debunking: a meta-analysis of the psychological efficacy of messages countering misinformation. Psychol Sci 28:1531–1546. https://doi.org/10.1177/0956797617714579

Chatfield AT, Scholl HJ, Brajawidagda U (2013) Tsunami early warnings via Twitter in government: Net-savvy citizens' co-production of time-critical public information services. Gov Inf Quartely 30:377–386. https://doi.org/10.1016/j.giq.2013.05.021

Choi D, Chun S, Oh H et al (2020) Rumor propagation is amplified by echo chambers in social media. Sci Rep 10:310. https://doi.org/10.1038/s41598-019-57272-3

Chorus A (1953) The basic law of rumor. J Abnorm Psychol 48:313–314. https://doi.org/10.1037/h0060600

Hootsuite and We Are Social (2020) Digital 2020 global digital overview. https://datareportal.com/reports/digital-2020-global-digital-yearbook. Accessed 10 Feb 2020

DiFonzo N, Bordia P (2007) Rumor psychology: social and organizational approaches American Psychological Association, Washington, DC

Einwiller SA, Kamins MA (2008) Rumor has it: the moderating effect of identification on rumor impact and the effectiveness of rumor refutation. J Appl Soc Psychol 38:2248–2272. https://doi.org/10.1111/j.1559-1816.2008.00390.x

Ennis RH (1996) Critical thinking dispositions: their nature and assessability. Informal Log 18:165–182. https://doi.org/10.1353/jge.2007.0011
Ennis RH (2015) Critical thinking: a streamlined conception. In: Davies M, Barnett D (eds) The Palgrave handbook of critical thinking in higher education. Palgrave Macmillan, New York, NY, pp 31–47
Facione P, Facione N, Giancarlo C (2001) California critical thinking disposition inventory: CCTDI inventory manual. California Academic Press, Millbrae, CA
FEMA (2018) Hurricane Michael rumor control. https://www.fema.gov/hurricane-michael-rumor-control. Accessed 2 Mar 2020
Gao H, Barbier G, Goolsby R (2011) Harnessing the crowdsourcing power of social media for disaster relief. IEEE Intell Syst 26:10–14. https://doi.org/10.1109/MIS.2011.52
Garrett RK (2011) Troubling consequences of online political rumoring. Hum Commun Res 37:255–274. https://doi.org/10.1111/j.1468-2958.2010.01401.x
Halpern DF (2014) Thought and knowledge: an introduction to critical thinking, 5th Ed. Psychology Press, New York, NY
Han S, Ciravegna F (2019) Rumour detection on social media for crisis management. In: Proceedings of the 16th international ISCRAM conference. Valencia, pp 660–673
Hitchcock D (2015) The effectiveness of instruction in critical thinking. In: Davies M, Barnett D (eds) The Palgrave handbook of critical thinking in higher education. Palgrave Macmillan, New York, NY, pp 283–294
Hong L, Fu C, Wu J, Frias-Martinez V (2018) Information needs and communication gaps between citizens and local governments online during natural disasters. Inf Syst Front 20:1027–1039. https://doi.org/10.1007/s10796-018-9832-0
Ichiguchi T (2011) Robust and usable media for communication in a disaster. Q Rev 4(41):44–55
Imran M, Castillo C, Diaz F, Vieweg S (2015) Processing social media messages in mass emergency: a survey. ACM Comput Surv 47:1–38. https://doi.org/10.1145/2771588
Iyer ES, Debevec K (1991) Origin of rumor and tone of message in rumor quelling strategies. Psychol Mark 8:161–175. https://doi.org/10.1002/mar.4220080303
Jaeger ME, Anthony S, Rosnow RL (1980) Who hears what from whom and with what effect: a study of rumor. Personal Soc Psychol Bull 6:473–478. https://doi.org/10.1177/014616728063024
Knapp RH (1944) A psychology of rumor. Public Opin Q 8:22–37. https://doi.org/10.1086/265665
Kongthon A, Haruechaiyasak C, Pailai J, Kongyoung S (2012) The role of Twitter during a natural disaster: case study of 2011 Thai Flood. In: Proceedings of the Portland international center for management of engineering and technology. Voncouver, pp 2227–2232
Lewandowsky S, Ecker UKH, Seifert CM et al (2012) Misinformation and its correction: continued influence and successful debiasing. Psychol Sci Public Interest 13:106–131. https://doi.org/10.1177/1529100612451018
Li L, Zhang Q, Tian J, Wang H (2018) Characterizing information propagation patterns in emergencies: a case study with Yiliang Earthquake. Int J Inf Manag 38:34–41. https://doi.org/10.1016/j.ijinfomgt.2017.08.008
Marin LM, Halpern DF (2011) Pedagogy for developing critical thinking in adolescents: explicit instruction produces greatest gains. Think Ski Creat 6:1–13. https://doi.org/10.1016/j.tsc.2010.08.002
Mendoza M, Poblete B, Castillo C (2010) Twitter under crisis: can we trust what we RT? In: Proceedings of the 1st workshop on social media analytics. Washington D. C., pp 71–79
Metzger MJ, Flanagin AJ (2013) Credibility and trust of information in online environments: the use of cognitive heuristics. J Pragmat 59:210–220. https://doi.org/10.1016/j.pragma.2013.07.012
Mikami S (2004) 災害情報と流言 [Disaster information and rumor]. In: Hiroi O (Ed) 災害情報と社会心理 [Disaster Information and Social Psychology]. 北樹出版, pp 35–53
Miyabe M, Nadamoto A, Aramaki E (2014) Development of service for prevention of spreading of false rumors based on rumor-correction information. J Inf Process 55:563–573
Mondal T, Pramanik P, Bhattacharya I et al (2018) Analysis and early detection of rumors in a post disaster scenario. Inf Syst Front 20:961–979. https://doi.org/10.1007/s10796-018-9837-8

Mainichi Shimbun (2011) 大震災と報道: 未曾有の事態, どう報じたか [The great earthquake and media: How it was reported during the unprecedented disaster]. Mainichi Shimbun Morning Ed

Norheim-Hagtun I, Meier P (2010) Crowdsourcing for crisis mapping in Haiti. Innov Technol Gov Global 5:81–89. https://doi.org/10.1162/INOV_a_00046

Ogiue C (2011) 検証 東日本大震災の流言・デマ [An examination of rumors and false rumors during the great east Japan earthquake]. Kobunsha Tokyo

Oh O, Agrawal M, Rao HR (2013) Community intelligence and social media services: a rumor theoretic analysis of tweets during social crises. MIS Q 37:407–426. https://doi.org/10.25300/MISQ/2013/37.2.05

Oh O, Kwon KH, Rao HR (2010) An exploration of social media in extreme events: rumor theory and Twitter during the Haiti earthquake 2010. In: Thirty-First international conference on information systems, pp 1–13

Peary BDM, Shaw R, Takeuchi Y (2012) Utilization of social media in the east Japan earthquake and tsunami and its effectiveness. J Nat Disaster Sci 34:3–18. https://doi.org/10.2328/jnds.34.3

Prasad J (1935) The psychology of rumour: a study relating to the great Indian earthquake of 1934. Br J Psychol Gen Sect 26:1–15

Prasad J (1950) A comparative study of rumours and reports in earthquakes. Br J Psychol Gen Sect 41:129–144. https://doi.org/10.1111/j.2044-8295.1950.tb00271.x

Reuter C, Ludwig T, Kaufhold MA, Pipek V (2015) XHELP: Design of a cross-platform social-media application to support volunteer moderators in disasters. In: Proceedings of the 33rd annual ACM conference on human factors in computing systems, Seoul, pp 4093–4102

Rosenfeld N, Szanto A, Parkes DC (2020) A kernel of truth: determining rumor veracity on Twitter by diffusion pattern alone. In: Huang Y, King I, Liu TY et al (eds) Proceedings of the 29th world wide web conference (WWW 2020), Taipei, pp 1018–1028. https://doi.org/10.1145/3366423.3380180

Rosnow RL (1980) Psychology of rumor reconsidered. Psychol Bull 87:578–591. https://doi.org/10.1037/0033-2909.87.3.578

Shimbun S (2016) 「ライオン脱走」とデマ 業務妨害容疑 20歳男逮捕 [False rumor"lion escape" 20-year-old man arrested on suspicion of disrupting business]. Sankei Shimbun Morning Ed

Shibutani T (1966) Improvised news: A sociological study of rumor the Bobbs-Merrill Company Inc. Indianapolis, IN

Slamet C, Rahman A, Sutedi A et al (2018) Social media-based identifier for natural disaster. In: IOP conference series: materials science and engineering 288

Starbird K, Spiro E, Edwards I et al (2016) Could this be true?: I think so! Expressed uncertainty in online rumoring. In: Proceedings of the 2016 CHI conference on human factors in computing systems. San Jose, CA, pp 360–371

Subba R, Bui T (2017) Online convergence behavior, social media communications and crisis response: an empirical study of the 2015 Nepal earthquake police Twitter project. In: Proceedings of the 50th Hawaii international conference on System Sciences. Hawaii, HI, pp 284–293

Sunstein CR (2009) republic.com 2.0. Princeton University Press, Princeton, NJ

Tachiiri K (2011) 検証 東日本大震災 そのときソーシャルメディアは何を伝えたか? [An examination of the great east Japan earthquake: What did social media report during the disaster?]. Discover 21 Tokyo

Tanaka Y, Sakamoto Y, Honda H (2014) The impact of posting URLs in disaster-related tweets on rumor spreading behavior. In: Proceedings of the 47th Hawaii international conference on System Sciences. Hawaii, HI, pp 520–529

Taylor BM, Wells G, Howell G, Raphael B (2012) The role of social media as psychological first aid as a support to community resilience building. Aust J Emerg Manag 27:20–26

Vosoughi S, Roy D, Aral S (2018) The spread of true and false news online. Science 359:1146–1151. https://doi.org/10.1126/science.aap9559

Walker CJ, Beckerle CA (1987) The effect of state anxiety on rumor transmission. J Soc Behav Personal 2:353–360

Wardle C, Derakhshan H (2017) Information disorder: toward an interdisciplinary framework for research and policy making. Council of Europe, Strasbourg Cedex http://tverezo.info/wp-content/uploads/2017/11/PREMS-162317-GBR-2018-Report-desinformation-A4-BAT.pdf.. Accessed 20 June 2020

Watson G, Glaser EM (1980) Watson-Glaser critical thinking appraisal manual. Psychological Corporation, San Antonio, TX

Shimbun Y (2020) デマ影響紙製品品薄 新型肺炎 在庫十分 物流追いつかず=静岡 [Impact of false rumor: Paper shortages COVID-19, sufficient stocks, logistics cannot keep up = Shizuoka]. Yomiuri Shimbun Tokyo Morning Ed

Zhao Z, Resnick P, Mei Q (2015) Enquiring minds: early detection of rumors in social media from enquiry posts. In: Proceedings of the 24th international conference world wide web. Florence, pp 1395–1405. https://doi.org/10.1145/2736277.2741637

Zubiaga A, Aker A, Bontcheva K et al (2018) Detection and resolution of rumours in social media: a survey. ACM Comput Surv 51:1–36. https://doi.org/10.1145/3161603

Chapter 9
Use of IT for Situation Awareness for Disaster Risk Reduction

Yuko Murayama

Abstract Situation awareness is one of the key issues for first responders and relief agencies. Communication is important to raise situation awareness and share common pictures between relevant stakeholders. This chapter describes IT roles to increase situation awareness for disaster risk reduction. We look at situation awareness in each phase of the disaster management cycle. For instance, the first responders need to know what has happened and where they should have priority to go and rescue victims. During and before a disaster, people in the disaster area need to know what situations are to decide whether and how to evacuate. A command control office needs to know the size of disaster to locate resources to deal with rescue as well as with damages. Shelters need to be set up accordingly and local government may well need to manage those shelters in terms of providing goods and foods keeping track of the number of victims in the shelters as well as the statistics of the people vulnerable in disaster such as people with disabilities, elderly, children, and pregnant women. In the recovery phase, one may well need to keep informing people outside the disaster area about the recovery process so that they can share the disaster recovery together with the victims to keep providing helps. We look into how those requirements of situation awareness could be supported by the use of IT and ICT.

Keywords Situation awareness · Team situation awareness · IT use in disaster risk reduction

9.1 Introduction

In this chapter, we present the use of information technologies for situation awareness at disaster. Research on situation awareness started originally in aviation as a pilot needs to know the situations (Endsley 1998). It has been applied to many other areas in other dynamic and complex situations which require human control such as driving, nuclear plant operation, medical treatment, and firefighting. It is important

Y. Murayama (✉)
Institute for Mathematics and Computer Science, Tsuda University, Tokyo, Japan
e-mail: murayama@tsuda.ac.jp

M. Sakurai and R. Shaw (eds.), *Emerging Technologies for Disaster Resilience*, Disaster Risk Reduction,
https://doi.org/10.1007/978-981-16-0360-0_9

for disaster management as well and we discuss the issues in situation awareness taking examples of applications in each phase of disaster management.

This chapter is composed as follows. We present original work on situation awareness in the next section. Section 9.3 describes disaster management cycle and situation awareness in this context. Section 9.4 reports the IT use for situation awareness at disaster with some case studies. Section 9.5 discusses the situation awareness at disaster. Section 9.6 gives some conclusions.

9.2 Research Domain of Situation Awareness

The term, situation awareness (SA) came originally from the aviation area for aerial warfare (Endsley 1988, 1995, 1998; Endsley and Selcon 1997). It was recognized as important for military aircraft crews in the First World War and its importance has been increasing since then (Endsley 1988). SA is defined by Endsley as follows (Endsley 1998):

> Situational awareness or situation awareness (SA) is the perception of environmental elements within a volume of time and space, the comprehension of their meaning, and the projection of their status in the near future.

Endsley introduced the three hierarchical phases of the above definition (Endsley 1988):

Level 1. Perception of the Elements in the Environment
Level 2. Comprehension of the Situation
Level 3. Projection of Future Status.

At Level 1 above, one needs to perceive the status, attributes, and dynamics of the relevant elements. At Level 2, based on Level 1, one needs to understand the significance of those elements and events to form a holistic view of the environment. Based on the knowledge from Levels 1 and 2, one can project future actions in the near future. In this way, SA is not only the perception of the status of the environment but also includes more activities. SA is also applicable in other domains than serial warfare, such as air traffic control, large system operations such as nuclear power plant, and tactical and strategic systems such as firefighters and police.

Harrald and Jefferson (2007) summarized the above such that SA has an information component, a perception component, and a meaning component. They described more about the information component as follows:

> To provide the information component required for situational awareness, the system must be capable of collecting, filtering, analyzing, structuring, and transmitting data. Situational awareness is not only the correct perception of reality, it the correct perception of the relevant elements of the current reality necessary for correct, protective, tactical, and strategic response.

According to Sapateiro and Antunes (2009) and Salmon et al. (2008), Dominguez defines individual SA as follows:

> the continuous extraction of environmental information and integration with previous knowledge to form a coherent mental picture and using that picture to directing and anticipating future events. (Sapateiro and Antunes 2009)

Endsley (1995) described another type of situation awareness (SA) within a group of people as team SA. It requires team members to share a mental model at level 2 to comprehend the situations, whereas they need to share the level 1 situation awareness information. Endsley presented the needs for some overlap between each team member's SA requirements. Moreover, a shared mental model is important for each team member to achieve the same higher level SA.

According to Endsley and Jones (Endsley and Robertson 2015), team SA requires both that team members have a high level of individual SA and that shared SA be developed between the team members as follows:

(1) Team SA requirements: an examination of what constitutes SA requirements in team settings. These requirements consist of information at each of the three levels of SA: Perception (basic data), comprehension, and projection.
(2) Team SA devices: for information transmission and communication.
(3) Team SA mechanism: it is important to develop internal mechanisms for shared mental models for achieving high levels of shared SA.
(4) Team SA processes for teams to use for effective group decision-making and performance.

They also introduce inter-team SA in which the issues in achieving shared SA between teams are similar to those in achieving shared SA between the individuals within a team (Endsley and Robertson 2015) as follows:

(1) *Inter-Team SA Requirements: shared SA requirements between teams will be less than that within a team as usually the goals between teams will be more independent than within teams.*
(2) *Inter-Team SA Devices: the devices available for achieving shared SA will be essentially the same as those available within the team, bearing in mind that these teams will almost always be distributed.*
(3) *Inter-Team SA Mechanisms: Significant issues exist regarding the degree to which multiple teams will share a common mental model with which to interpret shared data. One needs to get over the differences in organizational/team culture, jargon, and perspectives for communications for the development of a shared mental model.*
(4) *Inter-Team SA Processes: it may not be necessarily true the more information to be shared, the better mutual understanding between different teams for effective decision-making and performance. Sub-optimal decisions may well be better with less information to share compared to a good decision with a lot of information to share.*

According to Salas et al. (1995), coordination and sharing information are required specifically for team SA. They provided a framework for conceptualizing team SA and presented issues on measurement and training of team SA. The compatibility of the mental models among team members could be measured for a shared mental model.

Kanno et al. (2013) proposed a cognition model based on a mutual belief for team SA. The model is composed of three layers, viz. the first layer for individual cognition, the second layer for the individual's belief about the partner's cognition, and the third layer for the individual's beliefs about the partner's belief (Mahardhika et al. 2016).

Moreover, Endsley described organizational SA (Endsley and Robertson 2015) with team SA in a hierarchical way. On the other hand, disaster management has a heterogeneous nature in terms of stakeholders from different backgrounds (Murayama et al. 2013) and one needs to deal with this heterogeneity for SA so that inter-organizational SA or inter-team SA (Endsley and Jones 2001) may well be expected for disaster management.

9.3 Situation Awareness in the Disaster Management

In this section, we describe the needs for situation awareness in disaster management. The disaster management cycle identifies the flow of management at disaster in terms of the phases such as response, recovery, mitigation, and preparedness (Hiltz et al. 2010). We look into situation awareness in each phase. Figure 9.1 shows the cycle based on the integrated disaster management cycle originally produced by Guy Weets (Fig. 1.1 of (Hiltz et al. 2010)).

Just before and after a disaster, immediate response is required. The purpose of this phase is to save lives as many as possible as well as property losses. Alert should be issued timely so that people are aware of the situation and evacuate early enough

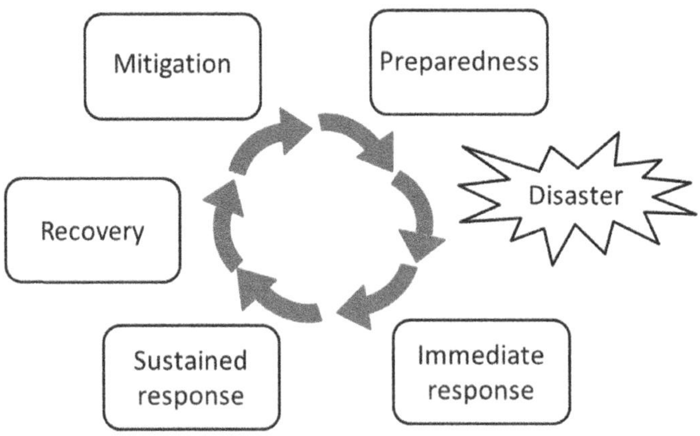

Fig. 9.1 Disaster management cycle

so that they are not attacked. Rescue is required as the first response. Meanwhile, one needs to set up shelters and manage them for evacuated people. Lifeline recovery is required here such as water supply as well as energy provision such as electricity, petrol, gas, and all that.

At a few months after the disaster, the recovery phase starts when victims are moving from shelters to temporary housing and then to more concrete housing in a few or more years. Social infrastructures such as public transportation services, roads, governmental services including health and education, and many other services required for daily life would be recovered.

At the mitigation phase, one would need to identify risks and providing countermeasures to those risks by modifying the current status of infrastructures, policies, and rules to mitigate the risks. A hazard turns into two responses, viz. risk and danger. For those who will try and mitigate the effect of hazard, it will turn to be a risk, while for those without such a challenge, it will be a danger which will cause anxiety and fear to people. Anxiety and fear are the feelings of insecure and unsafe. Experts accept a hazard as a risk, whereas people without knowledge about the hazard could remain in anxiety. Comprehensive risk communications would be important to the public at this phase. IT could be used by those experts to find out risks and countermeasures.

At the preparedness phase, one might provide training to disaster responders as well as evacuation exercise for people.

Situation awareness has been researched in emergency management. Johnson et al. (2011) combine the data available from various sources with human expertise to build customized models for situation awareness at an emergency. Sophronides et al. (2017) discuss the need for a centric network for sharing the common view at situation awareness.

9.4 IT in Disaster Risk Reduction for Situation Awareness

The use of Information Technology (IT) in Disaster Risk Reduction has been researched in terms of information systems for emergency management (Hiltz et al. 2010).

Turoff introduced the historical background of emergency management information systems (Turoff 2002).

Vieweg et al. (2010) analyzed the use of twitter for enhancing situation awareness at Spring 2009 Red River Floods and Oklahoma grass fires and anticipated the use by emergency responders. White et al. looked into the use of Social Network Services (SNS) for emergency management (White et al. 2009; Hiltz et al. 2014). Trustworthiness was one of the factors that causes risk managers in the U.S. not to use social media (Hiltz et al. 2014). Tanaka, Sakamoto et al. tried to deal with false rumor with SNS and presented the need for critical thinking (Tanaka et al. 2014). We identified how people would decide to spread rumor over SNS (Abdullah et al. 2017). On the other hand, it might be quite difficult to judge precisely whether a piece of information is true or not. One may well need to go on with uncertainty in such a chaotic situation as emergency response. There appear to be individual preferences on how to deal with the information collected using SNS.

IT could support situation awareness in each phase of the disaster management cycle introduced in the previous section. In this section, we introduce some example cases of IT use in disaster management and examine them particularly in terms of individual SA as well as team SA.

Most cases, those tools, and systems support individual SA Level 1. On the other hand, it needs the expertise of an individual for Levels 2 and 3. When we only had a limited number of emergency management experts, we would need to use intelligent system making use of Artificial Intelligence (AI) and learning systems based on a big amount of data in future.

Sapateiro and Antunes (2009) looked into team SA, based on which they proposed their emergency-response model (Sapateiro and Antunes 2009) based on the work by Bolstad and Endsley (2000) on the following four crucial factors of team SA: "

(1) *Shared SA—the degree each team member understands what information is needed by the other team members);*
(2) *Shared SA devices—supporting communication and information sharing;*
(3) *Shared SA mechanisms—supporting shared mental models; and*
(4) *Shared SA processes—supporting effective team processes."*

We shall look at the use of IT for individual and team SA as the above in disaster management in the following sections.

9.4.1 Information Systems for Immediate Response

We had interviews with several people coping with disaster management at the Great East Japan Earthquake and Tsunami in March 2011 in Iwate Prefecture located in the northern part of the main Island, Japan (Murayama et al. 2016). We introduce the two systems which we came to know of after interviews; an integrated disaster management information system (DIS) (Cabinet Office 2011; Cabinet Office, Government of Japan 2015) and the emergency medical information system (EMIS) (Ministry of Health, Labour and Welfare of Japan 2020).

DIS is developed by the Cabinet Office of the Japanese Government based on the experience from the Great Hanshin-Awaji Earthquake in Japan on 17 January 1995. The main features of the system include the functions for early assessment of damage from earthquakes based on the information received from Japan Meteorological Agency (JMA) as well as from satellite images and for information sharing with the use of a map. The system is to be activated by a big earthquake with an intensity level 4 according to the seismic intensity scale defined by the Japan Meteorological Agency (JMA) or greater and estimate the number of deaths.

According to one of the interviewees, a medical doctor who used to work in the emergency response team in Iwate, DIS underestimated the number of deaths in Iwate as the cause of the death was mainly by tsunami and not earthquake. Consequently, the government overlooked the situation and the Disaster Medical Assistance Team (DMAT) did not respond promptly. Moreover, the past earthquake along the coast of Miyagi and Iwate was named after Miyagi prefecture, south of Iwate, and Iwate Prefecture looked presumably fine.

In terms of Endsley's three SA levels for individual SA, DIS gives the information at level 1 while it may well depend on the information receiver's knowledge or experience to comprehend the situation at level 2. If the receiver presumed the threats from tsunami related to the earthquake, one might have gone and checked for its possibility. In terms of team SA or team SA, there was a lack of shared mental model (shares SA mechanisms) in the view of possibility of multiple disasters—i.e. tsunami after the earthquake.

The nation-wide EMIS is an information-sharing system operated by the Ministry of Health, Labour and Welfare of Japan. It collects and provides information on disaster medical care and relief, such as the situations of hospitals, shelters, and first-aid stations in the disaster area. EMIS was not working on 11 March 2011 due to the destruction of telecommunication links so that no information was available from northern Japan.

According to three individual SA levels, again it depended on the information receivers to comprehend the outcomes at level 2 that no information might indicate the possibility of the telecommunication destruction. Alternatively, at level 1, the system could have provided the receivers with the current status of the communication links.

In terms of team SA, EMIS operators or users need to have another channel for "devices for shared SA" to communicate with organizations in disaster area to figure out the possibility of the distraction. Moreover, the EMIS users might have needed to improve "the mechanisms for shared SA" so that their mental models could be updated enough to presume the possibilities of multiple disasters as well as consequent communication link distractions.

According to the interviewed doctor, SNS was not used because there was too much information available for him to process and some were inaccurate. On the other hand, another doctor who was a member of the emergency response team at Iwate Prefecture told us that he would prefer to get all the information including incorrect ones so that he could decide whether to trust the information or not by himself. That would raise the issue of how to deal with a big amount of information and to deduce which was trustworthy as discussed in Sect. 9.3.

Indeed, the trustworthiness problem of information from SNS at disaster was resolved by the Disaster-information Analyzer (DISAANA) (Mizuno 2016). DISAANA analyzes the messages (tweets) on Twitter real time, deduces automatically problems at disaster, and shows any related tweets as a reply to a question. It deals with bogus tweets with presenting all the related tweets together with an attention mark so that the user is aware of the contradictions; it leaves the user to decide which one is trustworthy (Otake 2015). The system would be of help for the information receiver to understand the situations at SA level 2.

This issue is also related to the use of SNS or any other ICT tools for citizens to report emergency. Emergency call using SNS has been researched. The identification of a reporter such as location with GIS information and telephone number of the reporter would be the major factors to make the message trustworthy (Torieda 2014). Such authentication helps individual SA at level 2. In terms of team SA incorporating SNS as an input for such first responders could be regarded as unreliable information from "devices for shared SA" so that the receivers need to justify whether to take the information or not. The "mechanisms for shared SA" need to take account of the authentication information of reporters such as GIS and the telephone numbers for decision making. Moreover, the first responder team needs to update their shared mental models.

For fire emergency, a web service, The Net119 emergency reporting system was introduced recently in Japan for people with disabilities to report fire or call an ambulance (Fire and Disaster Management Agency 2019). This service provides individual situation awareness at level 1.

McManus et al. (2007), Milis and Van de Walle (2007), and Kanno and Futura (2006) looked into organizational resilience at emergency in terms of situation awareness.

9.4.2 *Information Systems for Sustained Response*

Throughout our experience of IT support to provide personal computers and internet connections in disaster area at the Great East Japan Earthquake and Tsunami in March 2011, we could not find any information system available at hand in Japan for emergency response (Murayama et al. 2013, 2016). In the middle of April 2011, we were asked by our prefectural governmental emergency management officers to implement an information system for shelter management in 3 days so that the distribution of goods to shelters from the capital of Iwate Prefecture could be performed timely and effectively. That was impossible but we asked industrial volunteers to implement such system based on Sahana (Currion et al. 2007).

Sahana, an information-sharing system for relief operations at disaster, was developed originally by programmers in Sri Lanka just after the 2004 Indian Ocean earthquake and tsunami which hit Indonesia, Thailand, Sri Lanka, India, and many other countries in December, 2004 (Currion et al. 2007; Careem et al. 2006), and was used for disaster response such as the 2008 Chengdu-Sitzuan Earthquake in China and the 2010 Earthquake in Haiti (Sahana Software Foundation 2020). The system was implemented as a free and open-source software application and has been supported by a developers' community (Sahana Software Foundation 2020).

Sahana came into the Japanese open source community in 2010 and was started operating with Sahana Eden which is based on Python (Yoshino 2012). Just after the Great East Japan Earthquake and Tsunami, Sahana was introduced to Iwate Prefecture and expected to be used for shelter management.

The system was developed by the industrial volunteers developed with the support Sahana Japan Team (SJT). It was ready at the end of May, but too late. Shelters were supposed to accommodate the victims only for a few months and then those victims were expected to move to temporary housing in July. The earlier the system had been provided, the more it would have been of help. Nevertheless, the system was used to a certain extent in some cities (Yoshino 2012). The system was used to collect the requests for daily necessities as well as the statistics such as the total number of people in a shelter as well as the number of vulnerable people (Murayama et al. 2016; Yoshino 2012).

The system provides individual situation awareness of shelters at levels 1 and 2. With the past requests, one may estimate the future requests so that it could have served for individual situation awareness at level 3. We could see the users of the system as an inter team with shelter managers from the local government, responders including governmental officers, doctors, and first responders for Iwate prefectural governmental emergency management headquarters, who would make decisions on goods distribution to shelters as well as collecting statistics of the people in shelters. The system was used to provide shelters for goods and statistical information, indeed so that requirements and devices for shared SA are provided. On the other hand, the system could not pass the perspectives of the requirements—i.e., why people need those good items. Therefore, "Shared SA mechanisms" to support shared mental models might have been missing. Nine years ago, local government officers were victims in the way that many of them lost their family members, and under those stress, they had to work for shelter management and other work in the disaster area. Several years later, one of the officers who used to work at the prefectural governmental emergency management headquarter had a chance to visit and work for one of the local governments in the disaster area, told me that he was not aware of how the local officers felt when communicating with those in the headquarters. There was a gap between those in different teams—a team in the disaster area and a term outside the disaster area. Sharing SA mechanisms between shelters and the emergency management headquarter are important and missing in such an information-sharing system for disaster management.

While there was a desperate need for the information system for disaster response such as shelter management at the 2011 disaster in northern Japan, Sahana was not used immediately. We presume the following two reasons (Murayama et al. 2016). One was a language problem. The SJT made the system eventually workable in the Japanese language environment in April 2011, whereas the disaster came in March 2011; accordingly, the introduction of the system was a bit late. The other reason would be the programing language, Python used in Sahana. We only had a limited number of programmers who knew Python in Japan at that time. On the other hand, one had to adapt the system according to the needs in Iwate (Murayama et al. 2016).

9.4.3 Information Systems for Recovery

We introduce a system we developed, Recovery Watcher, for situation awareness for people outside the disaster area to know the recovery pace by sending camera images periodically from the disaster area (Saito et al. 2012; Murayama and Yamamoto 2017; Murayama et al. 2019). Recovery from disaster takes long; meanwhile, people outside the disaster area may well lose their interest in how the recovery goes the disaster as time goes by. How can we let those people to keep their interests? This is our original motivation to develop the Recovery Watcher system. Presumably, the system could be used for situation awareness at the earlier stage of disaster management than recovery, such as for emergency response as well as rescue (Murayama and Yamamoto 2017; Murayama et al. 2019).

The first version of our system used the streaming service, U-stream. The live camera was set up at the town hall of Yamada, Iwate, Japan. As video took much bandwidth of the town hall network, a still image-based system was implemented (Saito et al. 2012). The system accumulates images as an archive and presents them to a user to look back to the past. The system was operated for a few years in other two cities in Iwate and then had to stop the operation due to administration changes (Murayama and Yamamoto 2017; Murayama et al. 2019).

We have been implementing a newer version of the system using smartphones as cameras instead of a web camera attached to personal computers so that it is easier to set up the observation site in the disaster area (Murayama and Yamamoto 2017; Murayama et al. 2019). The server receives images from smartphones periodically and locates them on each camera's Web page.

Camera locations are to be presented on a map using Open Street Map (OSM) and a user looks up the images specifying the camera on the map. Images are presented in a calendar through which the user can specify the month and date to get the images on a specific day (Murayama and Yamamoto 2017; Murayama et al. 2019).

The system for watching recovery provides individual users outside the disaster area with situation awareness possibly at levels 1 and 2 in a way that seeing is believing. Our first version of the system made use of Ustream which provides users with live-streaming of the disaster area with a chat function so that users can watch the disaster area and talk with others to share the feelings. Later we changed to provide images rather than video-streaming without chat so that users lost a chance to communicate with others. The chat function worked as a social media and might have provided users with an opportunity to share individual mental models at level 2 to understand more in a subjective way on the video information they saw. Such subjective and emotional aspects were not discussed in individual SA as the research domain of SA started with more military and professional perspectives. It needs further study to investigate how such emotional aspects of information receivers could influence mental models to comprehend the situation with individual SA.

Moreover, it may well be possible for the system to help the users to project future status at level 3. If the system would be used for the emergency response phase, the emergency responders may take the information from the system in a similar way as the one from social media. It may well depend on how much trustworthy those responders feel about the system providers, the system itself and the provided information. That is the trust is required for "shared SA devices" for those responders to use the information. That would be a part of "shared SA mechanism" how much mental models are shared between the system providers and the responders as a user. The authenticity of the images and camera locations in the disaster area may well be presented. Another information source could be used by responders to authenticate the images such as the communications with local government officers or any others whom those responders trust.

We use android smartphones for implementation and operate for an experimental use for barrier-free information support at a university environment. The idea is to help people with disabilities and their supporters to be aware of the situations of the university campus before they come. Through our work on Recovery Watcher, we came to know that the system could be used for situation awareness not only for disaster but also for inclusive support (Murayama and Yamamoto 2020).

9.4.4 Information Systems for Mitigation

At the mitigation phase, IT could be of use for those experts to find out risks and the countermeasures. Based on simulation, environmental scientists use it for identifying risks. Simulation is used for disaster response (Imamura 1995; Imamura et al. 2006). Simulation has been used extensively for evacuation as well (Makinoshima et al. 2018). Dangdale et al. look into building evacuation using simulation and use of recent Internet of Things (IoT) technologies (Dugdale et al. 2019). Simulation would help individual SA at all three levels. We can look at those responsible for building management as a team and they may well need such information to produce an evacuation plan for emergency, which could be considered as team SA. Simulation is a "shared SA device" and team members need to have the mechanism to share mental models to understand the implications of the simulation results.

Recent technologies, such as artificial intelligence (AI) and big data mining technologies could be used. Barakbah provided information on risk about earthquake in a region in Indonesia by use of big data analysis (Barakbah 2017).

9.4.5 Information Systems for Preparedness

One of the active uses of IT in the preparedness phase of the disaster management cycle is an evacuation map which could be a good indication for people how to evacuate when facing a disaster. In the northern coast of the main island in Japan, there used to be an old wisdom, "Tendenko": scatter away and evacuate first without trying to save your family (Kahoku Shimpo Online NEWS 2015). The region has been attacked by tsunami every 30 or 40 years, so the wisdom is important for people to remember. However, people felt guilty to evacuate by themselves without taking care of family and the other people they know when facing tsunami. Yamori (2012) suggests that it is important to have the mental preparedness to save oneself first, trusting that the other people shall make best effort by themselves to evacuate.

Evacuation mapping has been conducted from the viewpoint of urban planning (Yamamoto et al. 2015; Yamamoto 2015). Yamamoto and industrial members provide workshops to produce evacuation maps with residents in several towns including those hit by disaster in Japan (Noigechizu Web 2020). As a result of the workshop, they produce the evacuation map on a sheet of paper, in which roads and paths on an evacuation route are presented in different colors according to how long it would take from the evacuation goal with a walking speed of the elderly for instance; e.g., green indicates a 3-minute distance, lawn green for 3–6 min, yellow for 6–9 min, and so on. Participants to the workshop discussed and colored the map as well as inputting more information on a map. While the map could be digitalized and more information would be input on the map, the process to create a map is paper-based.

Through the course of producing an evacuation map in a workshop, the participants would be aware of the situation in their residential area and the final map would inform the other residents with the situations as well. IT could be used to support to production and presentation of the map. The workshop would help the participants to understand the meaning of the information they collected so that individual SA levels 1 and 2 are achieved. Also, at the workshop or after the workshop, one may well find future risks so that level 3 could be achieved.

We can also view the workshop as a community activity, so that it provides team SA. Participants share "requirements," and "shared SA devices and mechanisms" throughout the course of the workshop. As a result, effective decision-making and performance are possible based on the map and interactive communications to share mental models.

Yoshino and his team have been working on an information system for disaster prevention and support for people at disaster, Akari map which would motivate users to try and use regularly before the disaster (Yoshino 2017; Hamamura et al. 2014). Users would download the disaster information before the disaster so that they could make use of it offline even there is no network connections after disaster.

More recently, Yoshino and his research group developed another disaster information system, Agara map to support participants of the evacuation map workshop (Enokida et al. 2018a, b). With the Agara map system, users would take a walk with a smartphone in a town and collect information. After that they attend the workshop and based on the collected information on a map, one can produce an evacuation map which would be presented to stakeholders so that the workshop participants would get more feedback. The Agara map system would help team SA as a useful device to collect the information for producing a map at the workshop. Within the workshop participants share "requirements," "mechanisms" to share mental models with stakeholders and teammates which would produce a better map for future decision making and effective performance at disaster.

9.5 Discussion

In the disaster communications which is the communications between stakeholders in disaster management (Koshino 2015), we looked into a specific aspect, situation awareness.

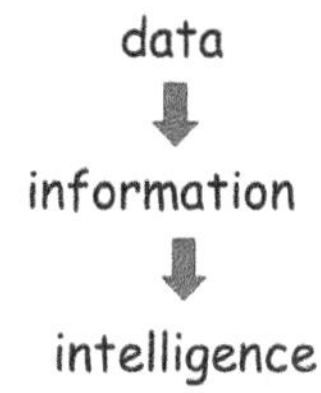

Fig. 9.2 Information processing in disaster management

Information processing in disaster management is to create intelligence as in Fig. 9.2 whereas traditional information processing in information science and technology is to create information. In a specific IT research domain, Artificial Intelligence, information processing is to produce Fig. 9.2. Information Processing in Disaster Management intelligence and knowledge out of data.

In situation awareness at disaster management, with the same data and information, each one of the information receivers would take it differently depending on their knowledge, experience, and mental model. From the viewpoint of distributed name management, Sollins (1985) described that it is necessary for the sender and the receiver to share the context in order to have a common understanding of a piece of information.

For sharing situation awareness in disaster management, we need to exchange this context for understanding the situation in the same way. On the other hand, when the context is based on experience and knowledge, only a limited number of experts have them in disaster management, since disasters including recent disasters, COVID-19, differ completely from one another. Previous knowledge may well be not useful or even harmful for a new disaster. AI and machine learning may well help us to produce such a context based on the previous data so that even novice could have a common comprehension with the experts. On the other hand, "unlearning" (Grisold et al. 2017) would be required for experts to deal with a new type of disaster where knowledge and experience would be harmful.

9.6 Conclusions

In this chapter, we looked at some exemplar IT uses for disaster management in the viewpoint of situation awareness. Related work on situation awareness suggested that it requires to share information as well as its comprehension. One needs to have enough intelligence, knowledge, and experience to understand situations. We need to share such intelligence, knowledge, and experience to share situation awareness. Recent technologies such as AI and learning methods may well be of help.

References

Abdullah NA, Nishioka D, Tanaka Y, Murayama Y (2017) Why I Retweet? Exploring user's perspective on decision-making of information spreading during disasters. Proceedings of the 50th Hawaii international conference on system sciences (HICSS-50). Waikoloa, HI, USA, pp 432–441

Barakbah AR et al (2017) big data analysis for spatio-temporal earthquake risk-mapping system in Indonesia with automatic clustering. In Proceedingd of the 2017 International conference on big data research (ICBDR 2017). ACM, Osaka, Japan, pp 33–37

Bolstad CA, Endsley MR (2000) The effect of task load and shared displays on team situation awareness. In Proceedings of the Human factors and ergonomics society annual meeting, vol 44, no 1. San Diego, California, USA, pp 189–192. https://doi.org/10.1177/154193120004400150

Cabinet Office (2011) Government of Japan: disaster management in Japan. http://www.bousai.go.jp/kyoiku/pdf/saigaipanf_e.pdf. Accessed 15 Mar 2020)

Cabinet Office, Government of Japan (2015) Disaster management in Japan. http://www.bousai.go.jp/1info/pdf/saigaipamphlet_je.pdf. Accessed 15 Mar 2020

Careem M, De Silva C, De Silva R, Raschid L, Weerawarana S (2006) Sahana: overview of a disaster management system. 2006 International Conference on Information and Automation. Shandong, pp361–366. https://doi.org/10.1109/icinfa.2006.374152

Currion P, Silva C, Van de Walle B (2007) Open source software for disaster management. Comm ACM 50(3), 61–65

Dugdale J, Moghaddam MT, Muccini H (2019) Agent-based simulation for IoT facilitated building evacuation. In Proceedings of the International conference on information and communication technologies for disaster (ICT-DM). Paris, France, pp 1–8

Endsley MR (1988) Situation awareness global assessment technique (SAGAT), In Proceedings of the IEEE 1988 National Aerospace and Electronics Conference, vol 3. IEEE, Dayton, OH, USA, pp 789–795. http://ieeexplore.ieee.org/stamp/stamp.jsp?tp=&arnumber=195097&isnumber=5021

Endsley MR (1995) Toward a theory of situation awareness in dynamic systems. Hum Factors J 37(1):32–64

Endsley MR (1998) Design and evaluation for situation awareness enhancement. In: Proceedings of the human factors and ergonomics society 32nd annual meeting, pp 97–101

Endsley MR, Jones WM (2001)A model of inter- and intra-team situation awareness: implications for design, training and measurement, In McNeese M, Salas E, Endsley M (eds) New trends in cooperative activities: understanding system dynamics in complex environments. Human Factors and Ergonomics Society, Santa Monica, CA

Endsley MR, Robertson MM (2015) A model of organizational situation awareness: macro-ergonomic factors impacting SA in organizations, Proc. 19th Triennial Congress of the IEA

Endsley MR, Selcon SJ (1997) Designing to aid decisions through situation awareness enhancement, the 2nd Symposium on situation awareness in tactical aircraft

Enokida S, Yoshino T, Fukushima T, Sugimoto K, Egusa N (2018a) An integrated support system for disaster prevention map making through town-walk type of gathering information. On Proceedings of the 10th International Conference CollabTech 2018, LNCS11000. Springer, pp 19–34

Enokida S, Fukushima T, Yoshino T, Sugimoto K, Egusa N (2018b) Proposal of an integrated support system for disaster-preparedness map making through town-walk type of gathering information. IPSJ J 59(3), 992–1004. Information Processing Society of Japan (2018). In Japanese

Fire and Disaster Management Agency (2019) Ministry of Internal Affairs and Communications of Japan: Net119 emergency report system. https://www.fdma.go.jp/mission/prepare/transmission/net119.html

Grisold T, Kaiser A, Hafner J (2017) Unlearning before creating new knowledge: a cognitive process. Proceedings of the 50th Hawaii international conference on system sciences (HICSS-50), pp 4614–4623

Hamamura A, Fukushima T, Yoshino T, Egusa N (2014) Evacuation support system for everyday use in the aftermath of a natural disaster. In: Proceedings of the 16th international conference on human-computer interaction (HCII 2014), LNCS 8529. Heraklion, Crete, Greece, pp 600–611
Harrald J, Jefferson T (2007) Shared situational awareness in emergency management mitigation and response. In Proc. HICSS-40. IEEE, Waikoloa, HI, USA, pp 23–23
Hiltz SR, Van de Walle B, Turoff M (2010) The domain of emergency management information, chapter 1. In: Van de Walle B, Turoff M, Hiltz SR (eds) Information systems for emergency management. M.E. Sharpe, pp 3–22
Hiltz SR, Kushma J, Plotnick L (2014) Use of social media by U.S. public sector emergency managers: barriers and wish lists. Proceedings of the 11th international conference on information systems for crisis response and management (ISCRAM), ID11, University Park, PA, USA
Imamura F (1995) Review of tsunami simulation with a finite difference method. Long-Wave runup models. World Scientific, pp 25–42
Imamura F, Yalciner AC, Ozyurt G (2006) Tsunami modelling manual (TUNAMI model). http://www.tsunami.civil.tohoku.ac.jp/hokusai3/J/projects/manual-ver-3.1.pdf. Accessed 15 Mar 2020
Johnson D et al (2011) Improved situational awareness in emergency management through automated data analysis and modeling. J Homel Sec Emerg Manag 8(1). https://doi.org/10.2202/1547-7355.1873
Kahoku Shimpo Online NEWS (2015) Part 8: Teachings (2) Tsunami Tendenko (to each his/her own)/Evacuation and Rescue, Haunting Indecision, (10 March 2015). https://www.kahoku.co.jp/special/spe1151/20150309_02.html. Accessed 15 Mar 2020
Kanno T, Futura K (2006) Resilience of emergency response systems. In Proceedings of the 2nd Symposium on Resilience Engineering. Antibes-Juan-les-Pins, France, pp 149–156
Kanno T, Furuta K, Kitahara Y (2013) A model of team cognition based on mutual beliefs. Theor Issues in Ergon Sci 14(1):38–52. https://doi.org/10.1080/1464536X.2011.573010
Koshino S (2015) The text material of the course for disaster managers. Iwate University (2015). In Japanese
Mahardhika D, Kanno T, Furuta K (2016) Team cognition model based on mutual beliefs and mental subgrouping. J Interact Sci 4:1. https://doi.org/10.1186/s40166-016-0014-6
Makinoshima F, Imamura F, Abe Y (2018) Enhancing a tsunami evacuation simulation for a multi-scenario analysis using parallel computing. Simulation modelling practice and theory, vol 83. Elsevier, pp 36–50
McManus S, Seville E, Brunsdon D, Vargo J (2007) Resilience management: a framework for assessing and improving the resilience of organisations
Milis K, Van de Walle B (2007) IT for corporate crisis management: findings from a survey in 6 different industries on management attention, intention and actual use. In Proc. HICSS-40. IEEE, Waikoloa, HI, USA, pp 24–24
Ministry of Health,Labour and Welfare of Japan (2020) Damages and response to Great East Japan Earthquake. https://www.mhlw.go.jp/file/06-Seisakujouhou-10800000-Iseikyoku/0000103405.pdf. Accessed 15 Mar 2020
Mizuno J et al (2016) WISDOM X, DISAANA and D-SUMM: Large-scale NLP systems for analyzing textual big data. Proceedings of the 26th international conference on computational linguistics (COLING 2016) (Demo Track)
Murayama Y, Yamamoto K (2017) Research on disaster communications. In: Murayama Y, Velev D, Zlateva P (eds) ITDRR 2017, IFIP AICT, vol 516. Springer, Sofia, Bulgaria, pp 1–11
Murayama Y, Yamamoto K (2020) Issues in the use of the recovery watcher for situation awareness in disaster and inclusive communications. In: Murayama Y, Velev D, Zlateva P (eds) Information technology in disaster risk reduction. ITDRR 2019. IFIP advances in information and communication technology, vol 575. Springer, Cham. https://doi.org/10.1007/978-3-030-48939-7_1
Murayama Y, Saito Y, Nishioka D (2013) Trust issues in disaster communication. Proceedings of the 46th Hawaiian International Conference on System Sciences (HICSS-46), pp 335–342

Murayama Y, Sasaki J, Nishioka D (2016) Experiences in emergency response at the great east Japan earthquake and tsunami. In: Proc. HICSS-49. IEEE, Koloa, HI, USA, pp 146–151
Murayama Y, Yamamoto K, Sasaki J (2019) Recovery watcher: a disaster communication system for situation awareness and its use for barrier-free information provision. In: Murayama Y, Velev D, Zlateva P (eds) ITDRR 2018, IFIP AICT, vol 550. Springer, Poznan, Poland, pp 1–11
Noigechizu Web (2020) http://nigechizu.com/. Accessed 15 Mar 2020
Otake K et al (2015) The disaster SNS information analyzing system, DISAANA, NICT News, no. 452, pp 8–9. National Institute of Information and Communications Technology, in Japanese. http://www.nict.go.jp/data/nict-news/NICT_NEWS_1506_J.pdf. Accessed 15 Mar 2020
Sahana Software Foundation (2020) https://sahanafoundation.org/. Accessed 5 Oct 2020
Saito Y, Fujihara Y, Murayama Y (2012) A study of reconstruction watcher in disaster area, In Proc. CHI2012 Extended Abstracts. ACM, Austin Texas USA, pp 811–814
Salas E, Prince C, Baker PD, Shrestha L (1995) Situation awareness in team performance: implications for measurement and training. Hum Factors 37(1):123–126
Salmon PM, Staton NA et al (2008) What really is going on? A review of situation awareness models for individuals and teams. Theor Issues Ergon Sci 9(4):297–323
Sapateiro C, Antunes P (2009) An emergency response model toward situational awareness improvement. In: Proceedings of the 6th International ISCRAM Conference, Gothenburg, Sweden. http://idl.iscram.org/files/sapateiro/2009/913_Sapateiro+Antunes2009.pdf. Resent Accessed 15 Mar 2020
Sollins K (1985) Distributed name management, Ph.D. Thesis, MIT/LCS/TR-331, MIT. https://apps.dtic.mil/dtic/tr/fulltext/u2/a154785.pdf. Accessed 15 Mar 2020
Sophronides P, Papadopoulou CA, Giaoutzi M, Scholten H (2017) A common operational picture in support of situational awareness for efficient emergency response operations. J Future Internet 2(1):10–35. https://doi.org/10.18488/journal.102.2017.21.10.35
Tanaka Y, Sakamoto Y, Honda H (2014) The impact of posting URLs in disaster-related tweets on rumor spreading behavior. In: Proceedings of the 47th Hawaii international conference on system sciences (HICCS-47). Waikoloa, HI, USA, pp 520–529
Torieda H (2014) Possibility of the use of SNS for 119 reporting at disaster, studies of broadcasting and media, no 11, pp 180–199. https://www.nhk.or.jp/bunken/book/media/pdf/2014_23.pdf. Accessed 15 Mar 2020
Turoff M (2002) Past and future emergency response information systems, Comm. of the ACM vol 45, no 4, pp 29–32
Vieweg S et al (2010) Microblogging during two natural hazards events: what twitter may contribute to situational awareness. In: Proc. CHI2010. ACM, pp 1079–1088, Atlanta, GA, USA. https://doi.org/10.1145/1753326.1753486. Accessed 20 March 2020
White C, Plotnick L, Kushma J, Hiltz SR, Turoff M (2009) An online social network for emergency management. Int J Emerg Manage 6(3–4):369–382
Yamamoto T et al (2015) 7172 Setting method of evacuation condition on Nigechizu making workshop: Study on tsunami disaster mitigation using evacuation map #4, Urban Planning, pp 351–352. In Japanese
Yamamoto T (2015) Tsunami disaster prevention education using Nigechizu, The Forum "disaster prevention education for children" of the Third United Nations World Conference on Disaster Risk Reduction. Sendai
Yamori K (2012) Revisiting the concept of "tsunamitendenko". Nat Disaster Sci 31(1), 35–46. Japan Society for Natural Disaster Science (JSNDS)
Yoshino T (2012) Fuga Operation and evaluation of a disaster relief information sharing system, Sahana at the Great East Japan Earthquake. J Digital Pract, IPSJ, 3(3), 177–183 in Japanese
Yoshino T et al (2017) Making of disaster-prevention maps by local residents using the akarimap evacuation support system. IPSJ J 58(1), 215–224. Information Processing Society of Japan. In Japanese

Chapter 10
Emergency Communication and Use of ICT in Disaster Management

Tamal Mondal, Swaraj Pramanik, Prithviraj Pramanik, Kashi Nath Datta, Partha Sarathi Paul, Sujoy Saha, and Subrata Nandi

Abstract The resilience of communication is of utmost importance at the time of any disaster. Unfortunately, disaster can occur at any time without any prior warning. The recent escalation in the number of natural and/or human-made disasters has ravaged millions of lives and caused billions of dollars in property damage without any discrimination between the developing and the developed countries. Minimizing the effect of such disasters becomes the primary objective. The impact can be mitigated by maintaining a consistent flow of information among locals affected by the disaster. The disaster management organizations are responsible for maintaining situational awareness to assess the damages and needs. Such insights become difficult to source when the communication systems fail, as often seen, in the immediate aftermath of a disaster. The catastrophic collapse of conventional network infrastructure and the failure in establishing real-time emergency communication paradigms restrict disaster salvage (/rescue) efforts, thereby increasing casualty count in a post-disaster scenario. Every region, from any spectrum of development, faces such challenges in the wake of a disaster. These issues beg for the creation of resilient and

T. Mondal · S. Pramanik · P. Pramanik (✉) · K. N. Datta · P. S. Paul · S. Saha · S. Nandi
National Institute of Technology Durgapur, Durgapur, India
e-mail: prithvirajpramanik@yahoo.co.in

T. Mondal
e-mail: tamalkalyanigov@gmail.com

S. Pramanik
e-mail: swarajpramanik97@gmail.com

K. N. Datta
e-mail: kashi.re2014@gmail.com

P. S. Paul
e-mail: mtc0113@gmail.com

S. Saha
e-mail: sujoy.ju@gmail.com

S. Nandi
e-mail: subrata.nandi@gmail.com

M. Sakurai and R. Shaw (eds.), *Emerging Technologies for Disaster Resilience*, Disaster Risk Reduction,
https://doi.org/10.1007/978-981-16-0360-0_10

swiftly deployable communication infrastructure. Furthermore, such an infrastructure should address the data management issues to stave off congestion, optimize bandwidth utilization, and maximize throughput in the network. Here, we survey state of the art in emergency communication technologies for disaster management. Then, we present how these solutions can be applied to create a rapidly deployable network infrastructure for moving toward disaster resilience, further augmented by Information and Communication Technology (ICT). In this scope, we further discuss such infrastructures keeping in mind the deployment conditions like deployment feasibility, infrastructural scalability, and information management capabilities. Consequently, we discuss *SurakshIT*, a new network infrastructure, which incorporates hybrid communication technologies and protocol stacks to create a resilient framework for emergency communication while providing multiple application interfaces.

Keywords Disaster communication · Challenged networks · Crisis mapping · Data-Driven disaster management

10.1 Disaster Aftermath and Fate of Traditional Communication Services

Communication refers to the exchange of views and information subject to a set of predefined rules or protocols. In this digital age, a proper, reliable communication system has become an integral part of human life for our daily activities. Internet-based distributed communication systems are sufficient to cater to the needs of our day-to-day requirements. In this age of the Internet, social media-based crisis-combat tools like Facebook Crisis Response, and Google Person Finder, have been proven to be effective during large-scale disasters in extremely challenging environments like Disaster Response Scenarios due to the critical nature of transmission for time-sensitive information. However, in the aftermath of any natural disaster, traditional digital communication services and protocols like *GSM, PSTN, Internet, and others* are disrupted in affected regions. Such communication disruption poses significant challenges for the citizens to disseminate exigent post-disaster situational information. More often than not, a catastrophic breakdown of connectivity often restricts them from sharing real-time situational data with the outside world. Consequently, the dearth of real-time data flow produces difficulties for *various public–private stakeholders, including the first responders, policymakers, among others* to analyze the disaster response situation. Such limitation, in turn, escalates the delay in relief and response efforts, which may lead to increased loss of lives, the spread of epidemics, and expansion of injuries (EL Khaled and Mcheick 2019).

Communication blackouts after large-scale disasters are rare in conventional digital and communication channels; such incidents take place for multiple reasons. In fact, from the past studies (Kabra and Ramesh 2015; Menon et al. 2016), it is evident in the aftermath of a disaster, digital and analog communication system failures are caused for the following reasons,

1. Vulnerability of transmission towers and base stations due to their deployment regions and structures.
2. Disruption of supporting elements, i.e., power, electricity supply, transportation, and other auxiliary amenities that assist the usual functioning of digital communication systems.
3. Communication network overload due to the participation of a large number of simultaneously active users, which in turn affects the available bandwidth.

Irrespective of the reason, such a situation adversely impacts the communication systems by restricting the affected community from communicating with the outside world, thus isolating them and often leads to unintended causality due to the lack of vital information propagation through any real-time medium, even if the disaster managers are in close proximity. The affected population is stranded on a metaphorical island with no way of communication to the outside world. This isolation leads to a feeling of disassociation from the mainstream, which leads the population to a feeling of apprehension, leading to mass frenzy toward the disaster managers, the responsible authorities, and the rest of the world, eventually jeopardizing the disaster response as a whole, which further leads to outrage, mistrust, and starts a blame game between the different authorities. Even the disaster managers become susceptible to the catastrophic effects of the disaster if they are unable to communicate properly with each other at the ground level and with the headquarter. An integrated crisis data management system to collect, process, and disseminate the situational data is required at large for "*enhancing disaster preparedness for effective response and to Build Back Better in recovery, rehabilitation and reconstruction*" (UNISDR 2015).

In the recent past, the number of disasters and their intensity has been on the rise. In Table 10.1, several disaster response scenarios from the recent past and the relevant information in correspondence with the severity of the incidents in terms of the *number of fatalities, economic losses, the restoration of electricity, and conventional digital network connectivity* are highlighted. For instance, the lack of proper communication infrastructure and the ensuing communication breakdown in various regions raised the death toll during the Indian Ocean tsunami in 2004 (Townsend and Moss 2005). After 2004, when the tsunami struck the coasts of Thailand, cell phone networks were congested, rendering only Short Messaging Service (SMS) operational (Townsend and Moss 2005). The Cyclone Aila, which stuck the eastern coast of the Indian subcontinent in 2009, totally disrupted communication services for 3–4 days (Table 10.1). The after-effects of the Nepal Earthquake in 2015 resulted in the loss of cellular connectivity for a couple of weeks as a majority of the base stations went down.[1] In recent times, the tropical Cyclone Fani in 2019 stuck the coastline of India and Bangladesh, resulting in communication failure for 9–10 days.

Besides causing devastation in the developing countries, the traditional digital communication services in developed regions are also brought to their knees in front

[1] https://bit.ly/2Wel8Hl.

Table 10.1 Few Large-Scale natural disasters from last decade and information of their severities

Disaster event	Aila	Hurricane Sandy	Fukushima Daiichi Nuclear Disaster	Gorkha earthquake	Hurricane Harvey	Hurricane Maria	Japan floods
Disaster type	Cyclone flood	Tropical cyclone	Earthquake, Tsunami, Nuclear disaster	Earthquake	Category 4 Hurricane	Category 5 Hurricane	Heavy downpours
Year	2009	2012	2011	2015	2017	2017	2018
Country	Bangladesh, India. Myanmar	USA. Canada	Japan	Nepal	USA, Barbados	Dominica, St Croix, and Puerto Rico	Japan
Affected population	2.3 million (Cyclone Aila 2009)	60 million (Hurricane Sandy 2012)	0.4 to 1.0 million (Japan-366 days after the Quake 2011)	5.6 million (Earthquake in Nepal 2015)	13 million (Hurricane Harvey has affected 13 2017)	3.4 million (Hurricane Maria 2017)	8 million (Japan flood 2018)
Time to restore electricity	More than 24 hours (Impact of Cyclone Aila 2009)	More than 7 days (Hurricane sandy power outage map 2017)	One week (Tohoku earthquake and tsunami event recap report 2011)	Couple of weeks (Restoring the internet in Nepal 2016)	One to two days after the flooding (Hurricane Harvey has affected 13 2017)	328 days (It took 11 months to restore power to Puerto Rico after Hurricane Maria. A similar crisis could happen again 2018)	2 weeks (Slug causes power outage 2019)

(continued)

Table 10.1 (continued)

Time to restore connectivity	3–4 days	4–7 days in some regions (Sandy created a Black Hole of communication 2013)	7 days (PDF 2013)	Few days, 38% of 2G and 4% of 3G network sites went down after the quake (Restoring the internet in Nepal 2016)	Networks remained Stable mostly (Harvey shows progress on emergency 2017)	More than 3 months (Trying to communicate 2017)	Not known
Alternative network used	Amateur radio (Ham radio helps combat Cyclone Aila 2009)	Not known	Portable satellite equipment, IPSTAR. UAV (Available 2020)	A radar detector, known as Finder by NASA, 35 satellite phones, 10 BGAN terminals with 10 laptops for these terminals, 25 solar chargers for SAT phones and batteries for them (Nepal earthquake 2015)	Zello A walkie talkie app used (Harvey shows progress on emergency 2017)	Google loon[a], ham radio[b], cellular over Wi-Fi, satellite phones, VSAT Systems[c]	Not known

[a]https://bit.ly/3kbloRk
[b]https://bit.ly/2BP6z5r
[c]https://bit.ly/3hRTRIG

of the wrath of natural disasters. In 2012, Hurricane Sandy struck the eastern coast of the USA and Canada and resulted in a communication outage spanning for 4–7 days in some regions (Table 10.1). The reason behind such catastrophic loss of communication was the power loss in 300 central wireline stations and damage to several data centers.[2] In 2011, the Fukushima Nuclear disaster resulted in a power outage for one week in different parts of Japan. Due to such a failure, the telecommunication services were totally disrupted (Shaw et al. 2012). A devastating "Category 5" Hurricane Maria stuck at Puerto Rico Island in 2017. The devastation resulted in the damage of power sources and communication infrastructures, and it took around three months to restore connectivity.[3] As observed from Table 10.1, the problem of Internet outages after large-scale, level 3 (L3) kind of natural disasters like cyclones, flash floods, and earthquakes is a severe problem in the backward areas of the low- and middle-economy countries (Utani et al. 2011); nevertheless, the high-economy countries are not very far behind (Internet Impacts of Hurricanes Harvey, Irma, and Maria 2019). It can be seen that the duration of such obtrusion varied from a couple of days to a couple of weeks. A multitude of solutions are present if the Internet is intact, but when down, these solutions would become non-functional.

In addition, the prolonged power outages were also a serious concern for the victims and other stakeholders alike, for example, even if the telecommunication network backbone were not affected, mobile phones would not work if it runs out of power. These insights help us illustrate the interrelation between the status of the traditional communication systems and services in the aftermath of a disaster. Based on such resourceful cognizance, we can draw some conclusive remarks which hold to be universally true in the aftermath of any natural disaster.

- After a large-scale disaster, cellular connectivity (GSM and Internet) becomes intermittent; sometimes it goes off completely even for days.
- Power crisis is a big issue that restricts the continual usage of devices like smartphones, radio, and TV for information transmission to disaster response personnel.
- During the golden hour, alternate sophisticated digital communication services can be used to manage disaster response situations, but deploying them at ground zero may prove to be a challenge in the post-disaster scenario.

10.2 Requirement of Emergency Communication Services

Communication systems like GSM and Broadband have become a ubiquitous and integral part of modern human society in providing services through the Internet. Although, in the aftermath of the majority of the natural crises, such communication systems are often out of order, and it leads to the services being disrupted or congested or purely absent in varying degrees in the affected regions. From most of the historical

[2] https://bit.ly/2A2iQlI.

[3] https://bit.ly/35GWrGj.

data from different crises, it is evident that communication failure is a pertinent side effect and may stretch for a prolonged duration even after the disaster has occurred. These after-effects mentioned above clearly indicate the vulnerability of conventional communication services and the requirement of other communication services for real-time information exchange among the community in post-disaster situations.

In any critical scenario, the community requires a temporary communication service to be set up for real-time damage and need assessment, and effective response and recovery operations until the conventional infrastructure becomes operational (Ali et al. 2015). Several emergency communication strategies have been followed in the recent past (Ali et al. 2015) through utilizing (a) handheld, movable or immovable devices and components, *i.e., Smartphones, laptops, PDAs, mobile towers, UAVs or other vehicles, uninterrupted base stations, wireless balloons, Satellites among others*, (b) Various communication links, *i.e., short-range Wi-Fi and Bluetooth, WiMAX, short-range AM or FM, satellite links, cellular communication with modified frequency bands among others,* and (c) the application layer services *like I am Alive, Person Finder, Twimight, and other offline crowd sensing tools* for generation, processing, and exchange of multidimensional information (i.e., text, image, audio, video, and map data) among the community. Any subset of such devices, communication links, and applications can be utilized in collaboration among the victims, local residents, and the different disaster management organizations for establishing a resilient emergency network infrastructure. It is quite evident from analyzing various disaster cases that such communication infrastructures had been made accessible for carrying out effective post-disaster management operations and services during the absence of conventional networks. As an illustration, during the tropical Cyclone Aila (2009), *HAM radio* with varying modulations had been activated as a backup communication service at remote locations. Several voice messages regarding situation assessments, official reports on relief disbursement, and public health information were exchanged among the volunteers using this service.[4] In the aftermath of the Nepal earthquake (2015), various rapidly deployable communication services like *radar-based finder, UAVs, and satellite phones* were used to locate trapped persons, aid delivery, provide disaster intent information to NGO workers.[5] In the aftermath of the Great Earthquake and Tsunami in Japan (2011), several *mobile base stations* were set up for providing voice message services to the people of affected regions. Besides that, the *satellite communication services* also played a critical role in providing emergency communication to the rescue personnel and government officials (Rajib Shaw et al. 2012). During the disaster response operations after the massive Hurricane Harvey (2017), the rescue workers and victims had used *push to talk application, i.e., walkie talkie* as an emergency communication tool.[6] In the case study of recent tropical Cyclone Fani (2019), it has been

[4]https://bit.ly/3b9yaK9.

[5]https://bit.ly/2ziAod1.

[6]https://bit.ly/3dsXaxK.

observed that mobile base stations like *cell on wheels*[7] were deployed for establishing cellular connectivity. Besides, the number of *UAVs and satellite phones* are also utilized for real-time damage and need assessment. These insights indicate the utility of emergency communication services in any disaster aftermath. Although, in establishing emergency communication, there are still significant issues which need to be addressed,

- The communication equipment used should be interoperable across all types of disaster management organizations.
- The perception and participation of the affected people should be utilized through designing solutions that can connect them to the rest of the world through some mode of communication.
- Due to budgetary constraints and other issues, in most of the developing and underdeveloped regions, satellite antennas, mobile towers, high output power generators, among others, are difficult to import and thus use. Further, these types of equipment cannot be deployed at ground zero in a short time duration.

Considering such key facts regarding emergency communication services, we have studied state-of-the-art emergency communication infrastructures in this work. We have also discussed issues with their deployment, along with *organizational scalability and information management capabilities* in context to disaster response situations. Besides, we discuss the case study of our proposed network infrastructure, i.e., *SurakshIT*, which utilizes a rapidly deployable communication system to create a resilient emergency mode of communication in the aftermath of a disaster.

The rest of the chapter has been organized as follows: In Sect. 10.3, the overview of devices commonly used during the post-disaster communication setup and the underlying wireless technologies are discussed. Then, we delve into a rigorous discussion about the post-disaster communication architectures in Sect. 10.4. A detailed description of each of these network infrastructures has been carried out along with their utility in resilient communication establishment in a disaster response situation. After that, in Sect. 10.5, we present the case study of a new disaster communication system, *SurakshIT*, leveraging the power of Delay Tolerant Network, and Android Phones to reach out and communicate with the mass population. The discussion encompasses:

1. The utility *SurakshIT* in contrast to the state-of-the-art technologies.
2. The proposed architecture of *SurakshIT*.
3. The modular description of each of the devices, components, communication technologies, and protocol stacks.
4. Field trials of the proposed architecture.

Finally, we conclude the chapter in Sect. 10.6.

[7]http://www.jrdcup.com/products-cells-on-wheel.

10.3 Wireless Communication Technologies in Disaster Management: An Overview

In this section, we provide an overview of the different types of wireless networks that can be used to establish an emergency network in post-disaster scenarios. Accordingly, we have also discussed the devices deployed, applications used, and supportive architectures utilized to enable these networking solutions and provide communication services in disaster relief scenarios.

10.3.1 Classification of Communication Networks in Emergency

Emergency communication networks can be classified based on different perspectives (Legendre et al. 2011), which include but are not limited to *protocol stacks at which it operates, local or global communication, infrastructure, or infrastructure-less topology, communication coverage among others*. Here, we have chosen the classification of communication networks in terms of mobile networks (i.e., cellular networks), wireless ad hoc networks, and satellite communication networks. The descriptions of each of these communication networks are discussed as follows:

Cellular Networks: When the users span around a large geographical area, these networks provide a wide range of networking services to them. By design, network coverage, and Quality of Service (QoS) provided by cellular networks surpasses that of wireless ad hoc networks. There are different generations of cellular communication that have evolved to improve connectivity and communication coverage. The 2G standard of GSM cellular protocol has been developed, which offers a data rate of 40 Kbit/s.[8] UMTS[9] which is a third-generation of GSM standard offers a data rate of 42 Mbit/s. Followed by the fourth-generation LTE[10] standard that achieves data rate approximately 1 Gb/s. Seamless network coverage of Cellular networks, which is the USP of these networks, is an outcome of a sophisticated interconnection of high-power base stations that are spatially distributed over the covered region. However, the need for significant infrastructure and high deployment and maintenance cost restricts usability in rapid-deployment scenarios. Nevertheless, cellular networks are highly preferred for disaster relief networking, since mobile cellular phones in the affected region can be then used for efficient communication establishment.

Wireless Ad Hoc Networks: The Ad hoc network concept aims to bring about an end-to-end connection between two devices, which is done by some multi-hop routing over a constantly changing topology. The end-to-end connection is the main

---

[8]https://www.etsi.org/technologies/mobile/2g.

[9]https://www.electronics-notes.com/articles/connectivity/3g-umts/whatis-umts-wcdma-tutorial.php.

[10]https://www.4g.co.uk/what-is-4g/.

assumption in the ad hoc network, which is not realistic. So, delay-tolerant network (Meissner et al. 2002) is a class of ad hoc networks where the store and forward strategies are used for data sending as an end-to-end connection is unpredictable (Meissner et al. 2002). Mobile Ad hoc Network (MANET) is a class of ad hoc networks where nodes in ad hoc networks are mobile, and nodes continuously change their location, configure themselves on the fly, and change the network topology. Here, the communicating nodes act as hosts and routers at the same time. This network can be extended to Vehicular Ad hoc Network (Ku et al. 2014), where nodes have high mobility and link between nodes connect and disconnect rapidly, which leads to the dynamic change of the network topology. This network has the potential to include large-scale participant nodes. All types of ad hoc networks use short-range communication devices like smartphones, tablets, and laptops, using different interfaces like Wi-Fi, Bluetooth, and others to continue the information exchange. All ad hoc communication uses multi-hop communication to transmit data. Device to device communication is a subset of the multi-hop communication system without a central control system. It uses short-range communication systems to improve spectral efficiency (Du et al. 2012; Zhou et al. 2013). All the ad hoc wireless communication techniques help to build an emergency communication system.

Satellite Communication Network This mode of communication consists of portable satellite phones and terminals. These can be mounted on vehicles or can be carried by individuals. The satellite phone (Sat Phone) service provided by satellites is termed as the Mobile Satellite Services (MSS), which uses two types of frequency bands; L-band (1-2 GHz) and the S-band (2–4 GHz). The data rate varies from 2.4 kbps (fax/data) and 4.8 kbps (voice) for the Inmarsat Sat Phone to 64 kbps for the Inmarsat BGAN mobile ISDN. The propagation delay also plays an integral part in message transfer in the case of Sat Phones. The cost of a typical Sat Phone handset can extend to about 1000 USD, although a used handset could be obtained at around 200 USD. Making voice calls may vary from 0.15–2 USD per minute, while the cost of data transfer is more costly. It can range up to 3.87 USD per MB. Connecting with other networks includes extra charges. Based on the countries, there are significant issues in acquiring such devices, and hence it is not widely available to the general public.

10.3.2 Devices Applications and Supporting Network Architecture

In section, we shall discuss different technologies, i.e., systems, applications, and network infrastructure, which have been designed to deal with disaster relief scenarios. These technologies generally use the notion of any of these abovementioned communication networks and different kinds of communication interfaces, i.e., Wi-Fi, WiMAX, Bluetooth, GSM, among others.

Communication System based on Cellular Technology: In the disaster aftermath, it might be possible that a few base stations are still operational and in a state of providing connectivity. In such circumstances, these remaining base stations can be utilized for establishing cellular connectivity with a different frequency band and an increase in transmission power for larger area coverage (Devi Pradeep and Anil Kumar 2015; Kishorbhai and Vasantbhai 2017). Besides, one can also utilize portable and easily transportable mobile base stations (e.g., Cell of Wheels) in remote regions and regions where few or none of the base stations are left (Devi Pradeep and Anil Kumar 2015; Kishorbhai and Vasantbhai 2017). The inclusion of such mobile base stations would restore the cellular connectivity, further augmenting the rescue and relief activities in a post-disaster situation. In past literature, various cellular communication systems are proposed for emergency management. The prime objective of such systems is to establish or improve the cellular connectivity in rural areas and disaster-affected regions by utilizing state-of-the-art devices, technologies, and organizational frameworks. For instance, the concept of Village Base Station (VBTS) (Heimerl and Brewer 2010) has been proposed to provide GSM-based communication locally in terms of *local calls, SMSs, voice messages, and more.* Using an outdoor PC and a software-defined radio implements a low-power and cost-effective GSM base station. An SMS-based technology has been proposed in (Meyer 2013) for establishing real-time communication between first responders and emergency operation centers. Such communications are backed up either by indigenous mobile phone service providers or network service obtained through deploying cell-on-wheels, UAVs, and rapidly deployable towers. Once such a network is set up, the end users, using his/her cell phones and a native SMS application can communicate with each other via phone's IMEI number or any other access control method. A small scale, robust, and easily deployable cellular communication framework named *Emergenet* has been proposed in (Iland and Belding 2014). It is an open-source platform that utilizes software-defined radio transceiver for enabling GSM communication. "*Emergenet*" incorporates the features like *calling and messaging facilities over "voice over internet protocol",*[11] *automatic configuration of base stations for maximizing area coverage.* In (Cheng et al. 2015), the authors discussed the concept of low-power and low-cost small cell emergency base stations for establishing communication in disaster-affected regions. With the aid of developed applications (App) on the phone, emergency base stations could automatically collect information from the attached mobile phones. Through such an emergency communication network, the victims, relief authorities, and rescue workers can communicate among themselves in the form of *voice call or SMSs.*

Advanced Cellular Communication - 5G: is the fifth generation cellular networks with greater bandwidth, higher download speed, and the recommended data rate for every user is around 10 Gbit/s. This new generation of communication is used not only to serve cell phones but also as an Internet service provider for laptops, PCs, UAVs, and other portable IoT devices. Due to the high capacity, reliability,

[11]https://www.3cx.com/pbx/voice-over-ip/.

and spectrum efficiency of 5G, it is also useful in the mission-critical requirements of public safety communication (Sakano et al. 2016). The utilization of the 5G framework for resilient disaster management communication has been reflected in a few studies in past literature. For instance, a 5G-based communication framework named *FINDER* (Thomas and Raja 2019) has been designed for minimizing the loss of life in a disaster. Due to the self-healing, offloading, coverage extension, and potential in disaster recovery using drone-based communication, it has the scope to be integrated into the 5G standard. In (Selim and Kamal 2018), authors formulate an optimization problem to minimize the energy consumption of drones in the 5G communication framework. The emergence of 5G communication technologies and protocols for benefiting disaster management communication has been addressed in (Rawat et al. 2015). Here, the authors have specified the usage of potential emerging wireless communication technologies such as 5G, D2D (Device to Device), 4G/LTE, and software-defined radio for disaster response situations.

Communication in Ad Hoc Mode: In case all the base stations are completely disrupted, or the transportation of mobile base stations may not be feasible in disaster-affected regions, then we can utilize the notion of Ad hoc network architecture. Here, mobile phones, laptops, PDAs, and other equipment can be set up to communicate with each other using short-range communication interfaces like *Wi-Fi, WiMAX, and Bluetooth*. For extension of the ad hoc connectivity, the equipment should be configured in such a way that they can communicate with other satellite-enabled phones available nearby. Various communication systems and applications are proposed under this mode of communication. *WORKPAD* (Mecella et al. 2006) is designed as an adaptive peer-to-peer software infrastructure (software, models, and services) for coordinating rescue-relief operators in disaster scenarios. The proposed two-level framework in WORKPAD consists of a peer-to-peer community built by *static traditional computers in the backend*—provides advanced black haul connectivity and *relief workers, who are equipped with mobile devices*—forms an ad hoc network at the front end. An open-source Wi-Fi-based ad hoc networking software platform, i.e., LifeNet[12] has been proposed and designed by Mehendale et al. (2011) to run on consumer devices *like laptops, smartphones, and wireless routers*. The multi-path ad hoc routing protocol present at the core of the software design enables *LifeNet* platform to grow incrementally as per requirement, to become robust to node failures, to provide large area coverage, and to share the Internet across nodes in the network. A delay-tolerant application Twimight (Hossmann et al. 2011), which is introduced by *Hossmann* et al. *is* implemented as a disaster mode extension for an open-source Twitter client for smartphones, as a case study. Twimight has two modes of operations, viz. Normal Mode and Disaster mode. The application could access the corresponding user's data if the user grants access to her user account by providing her Twitter credentials to the application when connected to the Internet. A multi-hop Bluetooth Low Energy (BLE) based mesh networking for public safety communications aspect of Proximity Services is presented in (Zhang et al. 2018). The work also

[12]http://www.thelifenetwork.org/about/.

provided a Proximity Services development framework titled *BLE Mesh.* The *BLE Mesh* development kit can be used to build a public safety communications application for smartphones that distribute emergency information in nearby areas without the Internet. *Hochst* et al. (Ho¨chst et al. 2020) came up with a chat-based application for mobile devices backed by long-range radio (LoRa) technology for communication. The authors used a custom firmware for Arduino-SDK compatible boards, called *rf95modem* to upgrade *Smartphones, Laptops, and other mobile devices* for long-range wireless communication. The authors have field-tested the prototype both in urban and rural environment scenarios. *Sciullo* et al. (Sciullo et al. 2018) proposed a LoRa-based technology Emergency Communication System titled *LOCATE* using which the smartphone users could convey minimal yet vital data during an emergency over multi-hop LoRa links. The proof-of-concept, as mentioned earlier system, was built using an Android smartphone connected to an Adafruit Feather M0 RFM96 LoRa Radio (433 MHz) System-on-Chip (SoC) via a USB cable. The *LOCATE* system extended further in (Sciullo et al. 2020) into a wearable IoT system where an Android smartphone connects a LoRa transceiver via "Bluetooth Low Energy (BLE)" interface. They have devised a wearable LOCATE prototype, including the mobile application, and the IoT device composed of *Adafruit RFM96W LoRa* radio transceiver module and *HM-10 BLE* modules. Buyukakkaslar et al. (2017) studied the application of the *LoRaWAN* technology for e-Health IoT applications (or applications like sending critical health data in disaster environments). The authors developed *LoRaWAN* nodes using LoRa supported *RFM95* chipset on top of an Arduino Uno device, which they used for an indoor application scenario specialized for e-Health services.

Communication Systems Based on Satellite: Apart from the utilization of ad hoc communication infrastructure, *the survivors, local residents, and first responders* can also use satellite communication services in case the base stations are completely disrupted or absent in disaster-affected regions. In such a scheme, the handheld devices should be able to communicate with the satellite with some modifications to *communication channels, hardware, or software configurations and add extendable antennas for long-range communication coverage* (Devi Pradeep and Anil Kumar 2015; Kishorbhai and Vasantbhai 2017). Several modes of satellite communications are available and can be used in post-disaster response and recovery operations. *Satellite Mobile Phones* (Shaw et al. 2012) provide voice and data communication facilities from remote areas where terrestrial communication is absent. The voice and data communication mostly use *VSAT*[13] satellite broadband service, which has a data rate of 4 Kbit/s up to 16 Mbit/s. Mobile sat-phones with such a communication interface can provide connections to different disaster management organizations and stakeholders for a rapid response in post-disaster situations. Besides, some other modes of satellite communications like *Portable and truck-mounted satellite earth stations and Marine earth stations* (Shaw et al. 2012) are also available, which

[13]https://www.vsat-systems.com/.

can provide situational data of disaster-affected regions through image and video transmission.

Apart from these communication systems, some other communication equipment is also available for post-disaster emergency communication. These types of communications are primarily utilized *P2P connectivity mode, and radio frequency spectrum* for exchanging emergency messages. Such emergency communication systems are discussed as follows:

Walkie-Talkie Based Communication: Walkie-Talkie is a handheld portable communication system that has been built upon P2P communication technology. P2P network is a temporary group communication system for the transmission of emergency voice messages to one or more members of the group. There are two types of communication modes in the P2P network that mainly supports the communication using Walkie-Talkie (Lien et al. 2009): (a) *Uncontrolled Single Hop Communication:* Here, each node broadcast messages to others in the single-hop distance. No authorization is required. Short-range Walkie-Talkie uses such mode of communication and (b) *Uncontrolled K-Hop Communication Network:* Here, each node broadcast messages to others using K-hop distance. Here also, no authorization will be enforced. Long-range Walkie-Talkie uses such a mode of communication. Availability of Walkie-Talkie-based mobile applications like *Zello, Voxer, and goTenna,*[14] which can be installed as smartphone applications, are utilized for emergency voice communication over the radio interface.

Amateur Radio for Emergency Communication: Amateur radio, known as HAM, supports emergency voice communication primarily while other modes of digital communication services are completely disrupted. It is currently becoming a crucial mode of communication, as it does not rely upon any centralized infrastructure. It only requires *transceivers, portable batteries, and antennas* for establishing regional and long-distance communication in a disaster response scenario. HAM radio operators (also known as HAM volunteers) use high-frequency bands (HF) for communication, which is regulated by International Telecommunication Union (ITU) (Shingate et al. 2015; Gill 2019). The high-frequency band includes different modes of transmission, out of which the HAM uses the frequency modulation (FM) and single sideband (SSB) for qualitative and long-distance voice communication up to 300–500 km. Figure 10.1 summarizes the existing emergency communication networks with their associated communication technologies, devices, and applications.

So far, we have discussed the notion of various wireless communication technologies that can be utilized to establish a post-disaster emergency communication infrastructure. The supporting devices, applications, and architectures used for resilient communication building adhering to any of these communication techniques are also described in detail. However, in context to emergency communication in a disaster response scenario, the communication coverage and quality of service should be the most important features for systematic analysis and response in disaster aftermath. Besides, the communication should be interoperable across

[14]https://www.digitaltrends.com/mobile/best-walkie-talkie-apps/.

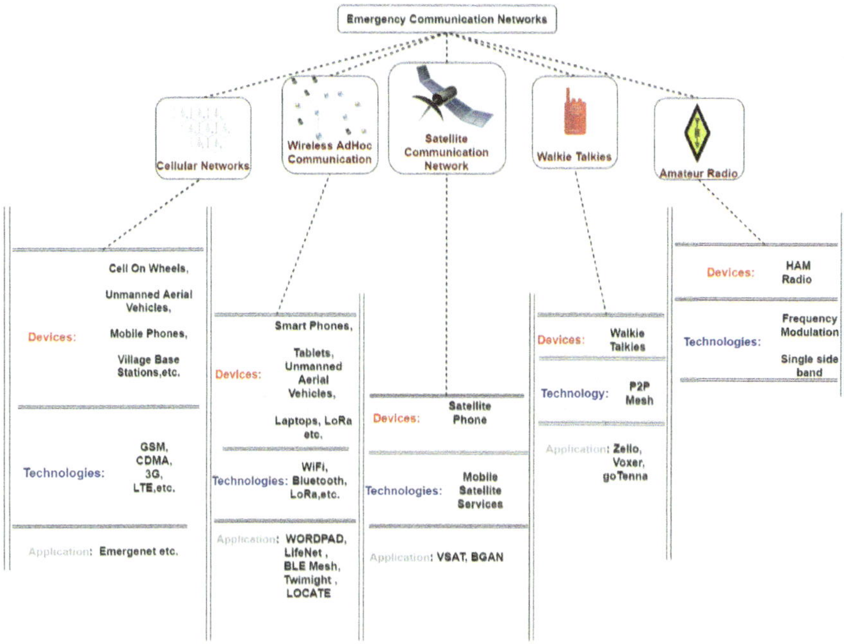

Fig. 10.1 Existing emergency communication networks

different organizations, cost-effective, and should have the capability to connect the common people of disaster-affected regions. Such issues entail the requirement of extreme network architecture through bridging the gaps of existing communication technologies in terms of *limited coverage, incompatibility, limited outreach, and budgetary constraints*. Through combining the network topology, supporting devices and applications found in existing communication technologies can introduce a communication architecture (namely hybrid communication) (Legendre et al. 2011) that can make up the individual limitations. In the next section, we have studied such communication architecture in greater detail.

10.4 Wireless Hybrid Communication Networks

In this section, the study on possible communication architectures formed through the amalgamation of *existing communication technologies, devices, and applications* has been performed in detail. In a disaster response situation, it might be possible that cellular base stations are completely disrupted or absent in the affected regions. The mobilization of mobile base stations to those regions incurs time. In such circumstances, a temporary ad hoc communication infrastructure can be established through utilizing *the users' smartphones, data mules, i.e., UAVs, cars, boats, and other modes of transports; portable communication devices, i.e., single board computers, portable towers, and LoRa modules; and short-range communication interfaces, i.e., Bluetooth, Wi-Fi, WiMAX among others.* However, such a networking solution alone provides a limited range and can mostly communicate in a few kilometers. In another vein, devices like heavy-duty power generators and satellite antennas are costly and very difficult to carry to the disaster site. Further, satellite phones, VSAT, and BGAN broadband services are sensitive pieces of equipment that often carry the threat to be misused if they go in the wrong hands. Only the senior government officials and a few selected rescue-relief personnel are given access to these devices to prevent potential wrongdoings. As a result, the broad population from the affected site eventually remains deprived of the communication access. A similar scenario also exists in the case of HAM radio communication. There are several issues while getting a license for using HAM services, and it is beyond the reach of most common citizens. These key problems of existing stand-alone communication technologies lead to the requirement of hybrid communication architectures which can ensure end-to-end connectivity among all types of operational nodes and devices in disaster response situations. The primary goal of such a network is to secure necessary communications to support proper situation analysis and relief management in damaged regions. A generic representation of hybrid communication infrastructure has been depicted in Fig. 10.2. Here, we discuss a few modern communication infrastructures. A description of each of these network infrastructures has been provided along with their deployment feasibility.

Integrating stand-alone ad hoc networks with mobile infrastructure has more potential than stand-alone ad hoc networks in a hostile environment. The key architectural principles (Naghian and Tervonen 2003) and elements of the ad hoc mesh networks together form the semi-structured ad hoc infrastructure. This semi-structured network consists of three parts: (*a*) *Backbone Domain,* (b) *Access Domain, and* (c) ad hoc *Domain.* IPv6 and cellular network configure the backbone domain. In the subsequent architecture level, the access domain uses third-generation Radio Accesses Networks (RAN) and short-range radio such as Wireless LAN and Bluetooth. Peer-to-peer and ad hoc mesh communication are communication processes in the last layer. The performance of the proposed architecture has been evaluated in a simulated environment. Although this semi-structured ad hoc extends the coverage area, the Quality of Service (QoS) of the architecture is questionable for the dynamic nature of the nodes. A test-bed approach to implementing wireless mesh infrastructure in the context of emergency application has been made in (Dilmaghani and Rao 2008). Communication infrastructure in an emergency application should be quickly deployable at low cost, reliable, robust, easily configurable, and interoperable in a heterogeneous environment with minimum inter-dependencies. Two hierarchical network solutions have been proposed in (Lu et al. 2007) for long-distance high data rate multimedia data transfer in a disaster scenario. This network uses a combination of wireless network technologies, namely, Wi-Fi, WiMAX, and GEO Satellite, for communication. The proposed multi-tier network architecture can support four simultaneous high-quality calls per 2 Mbps channel, which can be extended by using multiple WiMAX base stations. The scalability of the proposed

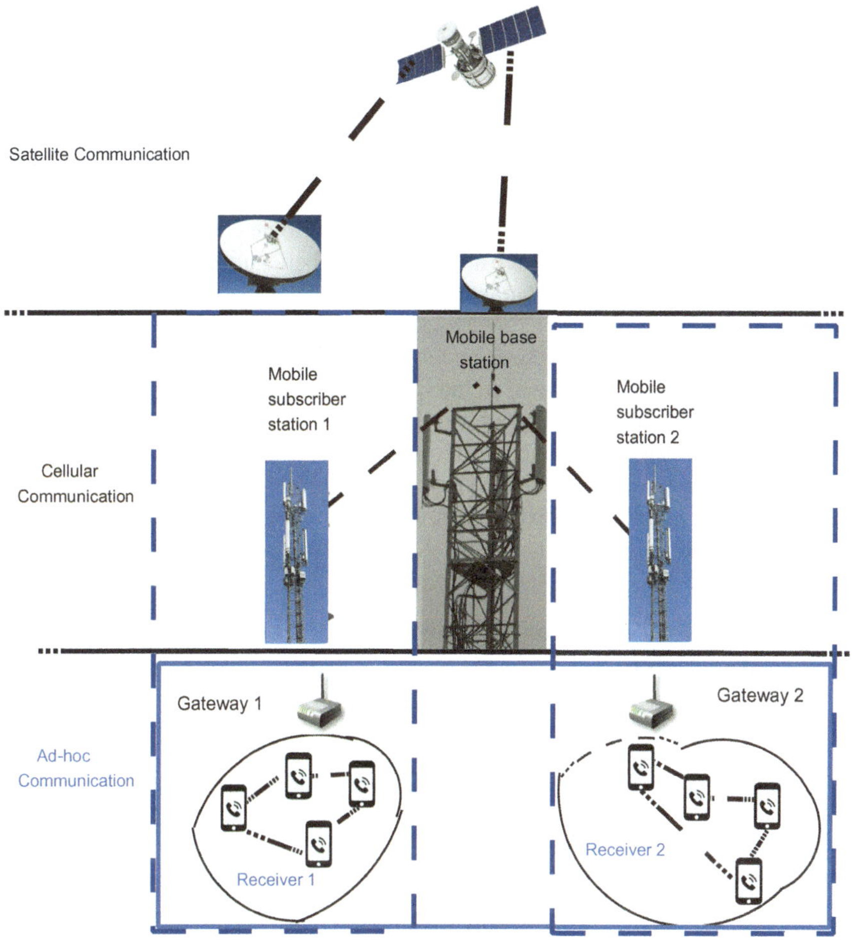

Fig. 10.2 A Sample of Multi-tier hybrid network

architecture has been validated experimentally as well as using simulation. Public safety is paramount. Hence, deploying wireless ad hoc relay devices in real-time using volunteers without pre-planning is unrealistic. A collaborative deployment based on the link quality of the nodes has been proposed in (Bao and Lee 2007) to deploy the mobile nodes. Physical layer metrics such as Signal-to-Noise Ratio (SNR) or Link Layer metrics such as packet loss rate is used to measure the link quality of the nodes. Link quality is considered not reliable when the quality falls below the threshold. In this way, collaborative deployment reduces message delivery latency. After deploying the network, rescuers require a high volume of accurate data for making decisions. Ad hoc, along with wireless sensor networks (WSNs) can significantly enhance situational awareness by automatic updates, monitoring, and reacting to network status changes. Thus extending data communication across the entire disaster zone helps in consolidating situational information to assist in rescuing individuals. This ad hoc based wireless architecture named "DistressNet" has been proposed in (George et al. 2010). Sparsely deployed nodes increase coverage but add a delay in message delivery. To improve the delay, a four-tier hybrid ad hoc network architecture consisting of DTN-enabled mobile user nodes, static Information Drop Boxes, highly mobile Data Mules, and a limited number Long-range Wi-Fi Communication devices have been proposed (Saha et al. 2015). Constraining delay is one of the significant contributions in the above framework. Some effective heuristic algorithms were proposed in the research article to ensure better utilization of the network resources and thereby ensure guaranteed delivery of the users' messages within a fixed delay. A special type of heterogeneous intelligent robotic network (HIRO-NET) is used for real-time disaster rescue operations (Ferranti et al. 2019). It is built on a two-tier wireless mesh network architecture. The bottom-tier exploits Bluetooth Low Energy (BLE) to connect nearby survivors using a self-organized mesh. The upper-tier is responsible for connecting the autonomous vehicles (land/air/water), i.e., UAVs using long-range VHF links. They are used to explore the disaster-stricken area to discover, bridge, and interconnect local mesh networks.

10.5 SurakshIT—A Novel Emergency Network Infrastructure Using Hybrid Communication Interfaces

Given the condition of the conventional digital networks in emergency conditions, there lies the requirement of a cost feasible hybrid communication system that can create a scalable and rapidly deployable networking solution. By addressing these requirements, the SurakshIT system has been proposed. The name SurakshIT comes from the combination of the *Hindi* word "*Suraksha*", which means safety with IT, i.e., information technology. Developed by ForkIT,[15] a DIPP recognized start-up, out of the ICT-based research for rapid disaster communication carried out at NIT Durgapur and IIT Kharagpur funded by Information Technology Research Academy under Ministry of Electronic and Information Technology, Government of India, the SurakshIT system helps the different stakeholders seamlessly connect to reduce the digital gap between them, give a better user experience at the time of disaster by ensuring connectivity, and enhance the safety of its users in the ways that follow. One can provide a multitude of solutions if the Internet is intact, but they would become non-functional if the Internet goes off. Very few works from the literature deal with the above aspect of the problem, and this is our prime focus in building the SurakshIT system.

[15]https//itsforkit.github.io.

10.5.1 Recent Disaster Incidents in Indian Subcontinent & Technical Viability of SurakshIT

In the recent past, the Indian subcontinent witnessed two of the strongest tropical cyclones, viz. *Cyclone Fani (2019)* and *Super Cyclone Amphan (2020)*. The devastation due to these cyclonic storms primarily took place in India, Bangladesh, Bhutan, and Sri Lanka. Both these catastrophes had claimed human lives and extensively wrecked billion dollars of public properties. The severe category four cyclonic storm Fani struck at the Indian states of Odisha and West Bengal and parts of Bangladesh in May 2019. From reports,[16,17] it is evident that such adversity killed around 72 people in India and 17 in Bangladesh. The aftermath of the cyclone had completely disrupted the power supply and telecommunication in the coastal region of Odisha and West Bengal. The districts like Puri, Khurda, and Bhubaneswar were reported as the worst affected regions of Odisha where the cellular communication and power supply were damaged.[18] According to Government officials, it took around one week to normalize the cellular connectivity in these regions.[19] Also, the category five super cyclonic storm "Amphan" made its landfall in coastal regions of India and Bangladesh on May 2020. While countries like Sri Lanka and Bhutan, the cyclone produced heavy rainfall and strong winds, India reported around 128 human casualties,[20,21] The telecommunication and power supplies were severely affected in several districts in West Bengal including Kolkata, East Midnapur, Hooghly, North 24 Parganas, and South 24 Parganas, and Bhadrak district in Odisha. According to the telecommunication industry, in West Bengal alone, 50% of the cell towers were either damaged or stopped functioning due to power cuts which in turn might affect the data and voice services drastically.[22] Such disruption of power and communication services restricted most of the common people from getting situational updates, sharing their current knowledge, and asking for assistance. This even included the metro city Kolkata. In various places in Bengal, the communication services took a couple of

---

[16]https://www.aa.com.tr/en/asia-pacific/india-death-toll-from-cyclone-fani-climbs-to-64/1476487.

[17]https://nenow.in/neighbour/cyclone-fani-leaves-trail-of-destruction-in-bangladesh-17-dead-several-hurt.html.

[18]https://www.hindustantimes.com/india-news/fani-leaves-trail-of-devastation-india-bangladesh-count-losses/story-lKot42RlhZCDzG3D5VKk1H.html.

[19]https://www.hindustantimes.com/india-news/fani-leaves-trail-of-devastation-india-bangladesh-count-losses/story-lKot42RlhZCDzG3D5VKk1H.html.

[20]https://www.dhakatribune.com/bangladesh/2020/05/21/cyclone-amphan-slows-down-moves-towards-rajshahi-region.

[21]https://www.newindianexpress.com/states/odisha/2020/may/22/agony-aftercyclone-amphan-in-odisha-2146551.html.

[22]https://telecom.economictimes.indiatimes.com/news/cyclone-amphan-telcosinfrastructure-providers-rush-to-restore-telecom-network/75867056.

weeks to become regularized.[23] These insights obtained from recent disaster incidents elucidate the susceptibility of conventional telecommunication services in any large-scale disaster. The Government organizations, telecommunication industries, and disaster response stakeholders were pressed in action to restore the communication services for the situation assessment and response in the aftermath of the cyclonic storms. As mentioned in Sect. 10.2, after the cyclonic storm Fani, the telecom operators tried to restore the cellular connectivity through *mobilizing portable towers with power generators and permitting Intra-Circle Roaming (ICR)* to the affected districts and rural affected regions of Odisha, India.[24] Besides, a team of *HAM* radio operators were also involved in damage and need assessment in various affected regions along with the National Disaster Response Force (NDRF) volunteers who had *satellite phones, mobile vehicles among others* with them.[25,26] Similar kinds of strategies were also adhered after the cyclonic storm Amphan. The telecom department had ensured *movable cell towers and ICR* for restoring communication in various affected districts in West Bengal, India.[27] On the other hand, around 42 HAM volunteers were divided into different districts for situation assessment and reporting to NDRF team members.[28] Besides, several web or online applications like *Accuweather, Hurricanezone,* etc,[29] were available for providing periodic updates of Cyclone Amphan to the users through remote sensing.

It is evident from the above studies on the recent disaster incidents that the disaster management stakeholders and policymakers were in action in restoring the communication by utilizing alternative services and applications. However, such services might not be well enough to ensure the resilience of the common people toward disaster mitigation in a challenging network environment. From the study, it is evident that resilient disaster mitigation can be guaranteed through improving the information accessible to the common citizens toward real-time disaster situation assessment.[30] Although there are several multihazard, early warning services are available, viz., *SMS-based services, Radio, TV, Early Warning through Sirens, Online applications among others* through which people can be notified directly about the upcoming disasters and along with their current intensity. However, in disaster aftermath, if the existing communication is critically damaged, people have to rely either on

[23]https://www.rediff.com/news/report/cyclone-amphan-parts-of-kolkata-limp-back-to-normalcy/20200526.htm.

[24]https://www.business-standard.com/article/current-affairs/post-fani-odisha-proposes-disaster-immune-mobile-infra-along-coastal-zones-119052001188_1.html.

[25]https://indianexpress.com/article/cities/kolkata/cyclone-fani-ham-operators-to-help-odisha-communicate-5707844/.

[26]https://zeenews.india.com/india/odisha-braces-for-cyclone-fani-81-ndrf-teams-deployed-iaf-army-navy-on-standby-2200521.html.

[27]https://telecom.economictimes.indiatimes.com/news/cyclone-amphan-telcos-infrastructure-providers-rush-to-restore-telecom-network/75867056.

[28]https://india.mongabay.com/2020/05/west-bengal-faces-the-brunt-of-cyclone-amphan/.

[29]https://www.indiatoday.in/information/story/amphan-cyclone-satellite-view-seethe-apps-and-websites-where-you-can-watch-the-live-streaming-1680056-2020-05-20.

[30]https://www.preventionweb.net/files/44983sendaiframeworksimplifiedchart.pdf.

the *cellular connectivity restoration* for communication establishment or on first responders, carrying *radio transceivers, satellite phones, and other wireless communication devices* for being reported if they are affected by the disaster. Besides, as discussed in Sect. 10.4, such alternate communication services might have other limitations like *substantial mobilization time, security issues, and licensing difficulties.* As a result, the common citizens remain deprived of this communication access and become completely unaware of the current disaster response situation. These issues regarding communication inaccessibility at the local level in disaster aftermath entail the requirement of a resilient disaster response framework; here, *SurakshIT* may serve as one. The proposed SurakshIT framework utilizes (a) portable handheld devices, i.e., *Smartphones and Network storage boxes, i.e., XOBs* (Saha et al. 2015; Paul et al. 2015), (b) applications regarding *data acquisition, processing, and map based information representation* (Paul et al. 2019a, b), (c) UAVs navigation routines (Mondal et al. 2016; Mondal et al. 2018) and mobility of other vehicles like boats, bikes, cars, etc. (Saha et al. 2015; Hazra et al. 2019) and d) short/long-range Wi-Fi connectivity, i.e., *Wi-Fi direct and WiMAX* along with priority-based syncing protocol stack (Paul et al. 2015, 2016) for developing a data-driven disaster response communication for various stakeholders. Moreover, the objective of the present approach is to develop an integrated solution (system) that might be used for communication and information sharing among the various stakeholders of the disaster (common citizens, rescue-relief personnel, local self-help groups, NGO personnel, Government officials, and others) during the golden hours. Such a system can assist the rescue-relief operations to be planned and coordinated correctly based on the causalities and requirements at different affected regions.

Unlike most of the hybrid communication solutions (Sect. 10.4) which are limited to either in a simulated environment or small-scale deployment, here we are involved in the gradual development of an integrated system for post-disaster (geographical) information propagation and processing that would function even in the absence of Internet connectivity. The results and community feedback received from extensive field-tests (Fig. 10.3a–c), demonstrations before the resource persons, and mock trials at disaster-prone sites involving persons having experience in natural disasters and disaster management (Fig. 10.3a) suggest that the developed solution not only has the potential to complement state of-the-art systems but also can become a necessary component of disaster risk reduction protocol in days to come.

10.5.2 SurakshIT Network Architecture

Figure 10.4 portrays a schematic idea used in the hybrid opportunistic network architecture of the SurakshIT system. We have divided the devices into three broad classes: (a) *DTN-enabled Edge Nodes* (DTN) are the edge devices that the users use for data recording and information visualization; (b) *Information Drop Boxes* (IDB) are limited number of special-purpose stand-alone devices placed at strategic locations

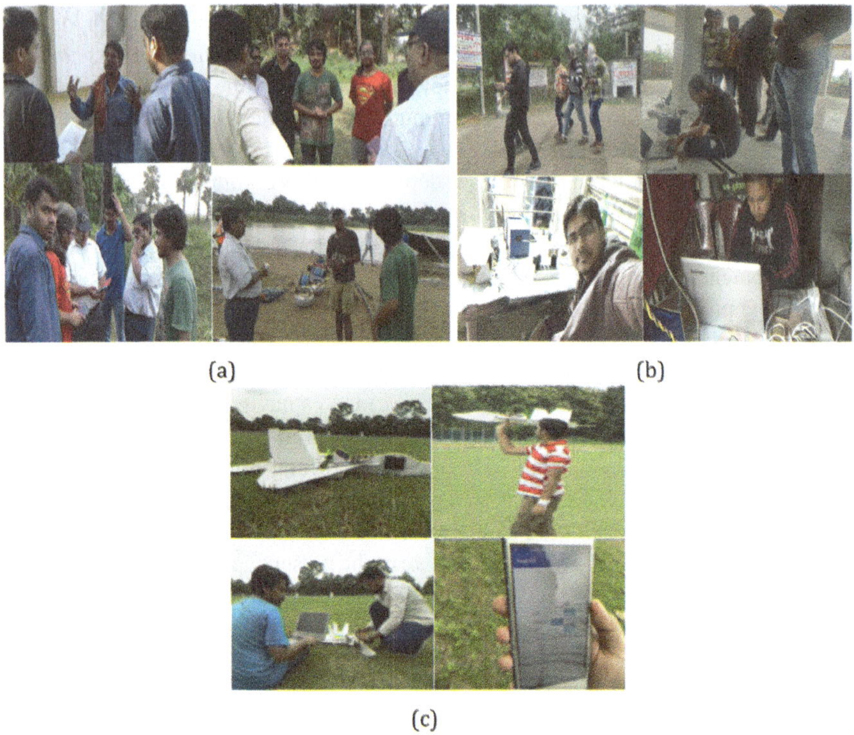

Fig. 10.3 **a** Community Feedback and Product Demonstration to the Government Officials during Disaster Mock Drill at Kandi, West Bengal, India. **b** Deployment of *SurakshIT* Framework at Sundarbans, West Bengal, India. **c** Evaluation of Designed UAV Navigation Plans under *SurakshIT's* Framework at Kalyani University Campus, West Bengal, India

like registered shelters or administrative offices; (c) *Data Mules* (DM) are special-purpose devices (like IDBs) attached to vehicles/boats/UAVs to move data across IDB devices. The outer circle in Fig. 10.4 shows the data movement pattern among the devices in the SurakshIT system when the nodes of different classes are in proximity.

Description of Components in the SurakshIT Architecture DTN Nodes: Smartphones are able to exchange media files with peers in proximity nowadays, and the principle above is the pillar of a bunch of popular smartphone media file sharing applications that operate without the Internet. We have developed a smartphone application that enables a user smartphone to act as a native DTN node exploiting the Internet-less file sharing of the smart devices. A user running SurakshIT application in his/her smartphone can record and exchange data. An intuitive user interface provided by the SurakshIT application helps the users to record data at ease conveniently. The recorded messages are then routed automatically by the application backend via the opportunistic network of the SurakshIT-enabled devices, and the messages are propagated in the network following a *store-carry-forward* principle.

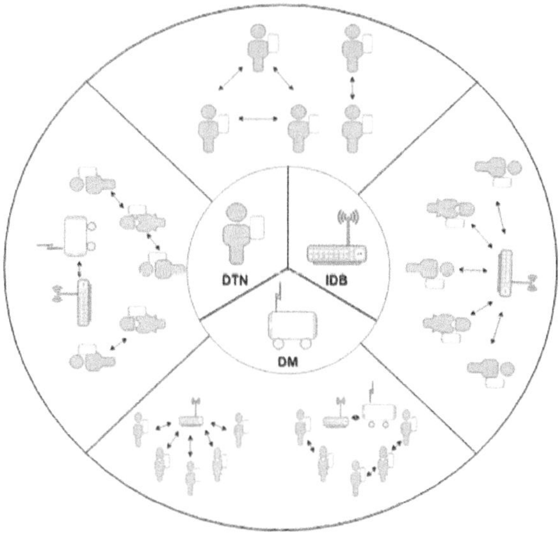

Fig. 10.4 SurakshIT: network architecture

The abovementioned step by step message forwarding continues until the messages end up in their destinations. The users of intermediate non-destination nodes only receive, store, and forward these data to the next node(s) in the hop; they are unable to intercept the messages (*ensures message privacy and security in the network*). However, these intermediate reception and forwarding of messages in SurakshIT are completely seamless; the users of these intermediate nodes are not interrupted in any manner for the same (*provides user convenience and transparency*).

The SurakshIT app features: Role-based user registration using the mobile phone number, multiple ways of situational data collection, namely:

- Capturing Photos
- Recording Videos
- Recording Audio Clips
- Inputting Text Messages (Structured/Unstructured)
- Dropping Device Location Pin

The familiar chat-like interface along with the rich GIS (capturing, storing, checking, and displaying data on map) support with the ability to find other devices with the same app installed and seamless content sharing with them, with a range of about 50–60 m radius further enhances the ability of the system.

Information Drop Boxes and Data Mules: Data propagation in SurakshIT, as mentioned earlier, follows a *Store-Carry-Forward* approach: a device in the network receives a piece of data from a peer, carries with it, and waits for the next opportunity to meet a peer, and relays the piece when it finds such an opportunity. We have developed a customized storage-network box that we have named *XOB x.1*, to strengthen as well as to speed up the data forwarding in the opportunistic peer-to-peer network referred so far. These custom devices are likely to complement the smartphones in the said network. Refer Fig. 10.7a for a reference view of the prototype implementation. These devices can act as Information Drop Boxes (IDB) when placed/pre-installed at strategic locations, and also can act as Data Mules (DM) when they are coupled with vehicles of any kind: ambulances, police cars, emergency utilities vehicle, rescue-relief boats, surveillance UAVs, and rescue-relief helicopters.

The XOB x.1 features:

- Upgradable storage space.
- Removable power pack with backup up to 36 h.
- Seamless working capabilities with mobile devices running SurakshIT Application.
- Comprehensive dashboard for visualization and analysis of collected data.
- Support creation of summary report based on the collected data (compliant with the formats proposed by various Govt. agencies and NGOs).
- Can find and exchange summaries with similar XOB x.1 devices with a range of about 1500–1800 m radius (when used with signal power boosters).

Role of XOB x.1: The XOB x.1 is the mobile server responsible for taking the role of a Master Control Station, Information Drobox, or Data Mule in the decentralized network. Based on the architectural hierarchy, the role is defined as each role has its specific functionalities and weightage in the network. This optimization is required to give the best throughput for the system.

Based on the role that XOB x.1 plays in the SurakshIT network architecture, there lie different predominant features in it.

XOB x.1 as Master Control Station:

- Meant for the top-tier Disaster Managers.
- Provides the global overview taking input from the zonal Information Drop Boxes.
- Generates a global report and crisis map.
- High Storage Capacity as it provides a consolidated view from the zonal devices.
- It has the highest priority in the system.

XOB x.1 as Information Drop Box:

- To be used in the Zonal Level.
- Provides the zonal overview from the crowd-sourced information.
- Generates the zonal report and crisis map.
- Feeds consolidated crowd-sourced data to the nearest Master Control Station.

XOB x.1 as Data Mule:

- Mobile in nature, usually attached to a path-fixed transport vehicle.
- Helpful in data aggregation from several sources covering multiple zones.

- Can consolidate the crowd-sourced data and feed to the nearest Master Control Station (highest priority) and Zonal Information Drop Box.

XOB x.1 has the following additional features, irrespective of its role:

- Work as a data repository.
- Visualize localized crisis map.
- Summarize the collected information to show the need.

10.5.3 SurakshIT Software Stack

Based on the requirements that has been revealed during our extensive literature level and on-the-field survey, we derived the following needs in the current context: (I) need to establish a method for seamless connectivity among the available networking devices to form an opportunistic network on-the-fly, (ii) need to find or develop suitable method(s) for seamless data synchronization across the devices when they are connected via the connectivity protocol built following (I), and (iii) need to devise method(s) for automatically generating crisis maps in the edge devices by aggregating the (shared) data available in their local memories. In a nutshell, We have developed an integrated crisis mapping system that one can use even in the absence of the Internet (Paul et al. 2019a, b, c). The system is built following a "three-tier" software stack (Fig. 10.5): the lowest tier of the stack establishes an opportunistic network that fulfilled the requirement (I); the middle-tier takes care of the seamless syncing of user files across the connected devices in the above opportunistic network, and

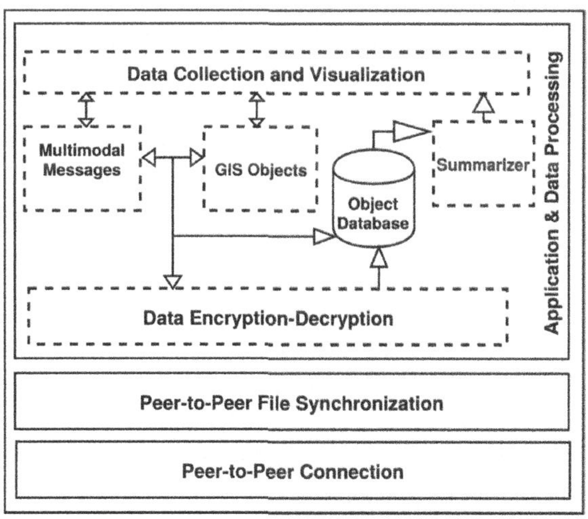

Fig. 10.5 SurakshIT software stack

fulfilled the requirement (ii); the topmost tier is responsible in generating semi-real-time "Local Crisis Map" (LCM) in the edge devices in the network using their local (shared) data, and hence fulfilled the need (iii).

Peer-to-Peer Connection: Our objective in the bottom-most tier is to use a seamless connectivity protocol that would connect the nearby devices seamlessly without requiring any manual intervention. Users would not use the system properly in a tense situation after a disaster unless the system in their devices is intelligent enough to manage the opportunistic connectivity. Portable devices, smartphones, and XOBs are the basic building blocks in SurakshIT; all support Wi-Fi connectivity. We tried various device-to-device connectivity protocols based on Wi-Fi for establishing peer-to-peer connectivity. The most popular protocol in this category is Wi-Fi Direct; almost all portable devices support Wi-Fi Direct now. However, the most severe drawback that we may encounter in using the protocol is energy drainage due to neighborhood scanning; since Wi-Fi scanning is quite power-hungry. In addition, Wi-Fi Direct cannot ensure seamless connection establishment on peer discovery since devices need to share a credential, which requires human intervention. To deal with the situation, we use in SurakshIT a hybrid of Wi-Fi Direct and (near ultrasonic) acoustic communication as a peer-to-peer connection protocol. The latter is used for neighborhood scanning and Wi-Fi Direct credential exchange between neighbor nodes; whereas, the former is used for actual data transfer. The protocol details are available in Paul et al. (2020).

Peer-to-Peer Sync: The purpose of this tier in the software stack is to ensure a seamless delivery of user data over the previously mentioned opportunistic network. In other words, this tier hides the network hiccups from user perception. The user simply sends their messages like they do in a networking application that runs over the Internet. The rest is taken care of by the sync protocol; user experiences only a large delay in his message delivery and response. The details of the protocol may be found in Paul et al. (2019b).

Incident Reporting and Crisis Mapping: The topmost tier provides the user interface; the users can record situational messages using a familiar-looking messaging interface. The user interface provides the users' option to record messages using multimodal data formats: text, image, audio clip, video clip, and GIS shapes (for location-specific information recording). The messages are exchanged between the peer nodes with the help of the lower tier protocols.

The topmost tier performs a couple of additional tasks; generates personalized crisis maps, and provides privacy and security to user data. Since all the messages in SurakshIT are location-tagged, they are treated as GIS objects. The application extracts GIS objects from the messages in the device; aggregates them on demand; portrays them on a map background to present the personalized crisis map.

Another demand of the situation is data privacy and security; many sensitive messages are likely to flow over such an opportunistic network. To restrict unwanted peep through the messages, we implemented a kind of privacy and message security using a customized protocol based on Pretty Good Privacy (PGP). The details of the application may be found in Paul et al. (2020).

10.5.4 Working Principal of SurakshIT System

The working principle of the SurakshIT system is loosely based on the role of bees in cross-pollination. In the process of cross-pollination, the genetic material of different plants is often exchanged with the help of bees as they travel from one flower to another to drink in the nectar. While the bees are more interested in drinking the nectar, the pollen from the flowers stick to them, and it gets transferred to the next plant it travels.

Similarly, the people using the SurakshIT application plays the role of the bees, and the process of data exchange can be compared to cross-pollination. The SurakshIT Application has the capability to

- connect to similar devices in its proximity, and
- can share data seamlessly among them

There have been applications like SHAREit and Xender who have been using the concept of local media file sharing, but the task of SurakshIT is more than just sharing information. The users having the app installed in their smartphones can provide time-critical situational data through a convenient user interface. Here, as we are interested in transmitting information without the Internet, a robust algorithm is required to spread the gathered information to the desired stakeholders. Hence, a dynamic local network is created in the proximity of the mobile device, and the collected information/messages collected from the users are automatically exchanged among the different participants of the network.

Depending on the movement of the mobile devices, the network topology changes, and when introduced in the new network, the mobile is capable of sharing the state of the old network to the new network, and this goes on until the message finally reaches its final destination.

Like bees in cross-pollination, the mobiles carry the information and enrich the network with additional time-critical information, which helps to propagate the messages to the proper destination.

Moreover, as the smartphone's capability is limited by the range, to reduce the latency and deliver more messages in the aforementioned store-carry-forward method, another device termed as XOB x.1 can be strategically placed/pre-installed in the role of IDB. Additionally, XOB x.1 can also be mounted on vehicles going on land like cars or on vehicles going through water like boats or vehicles going through the air like UAVs (Mondal et al. 2018). When mounted on vehicles, it usually performs the role of Data Mules (DM). The SurakshIT system endowed with smartphones, IDBs, and DMs, may be envisioned as a *Digital Postal system*; Information Drop Boxes, like mailboxes, receive the messages (like letters) from the mobile nodes when they visit them and store the messages for a while. Like mail vans, the DMs

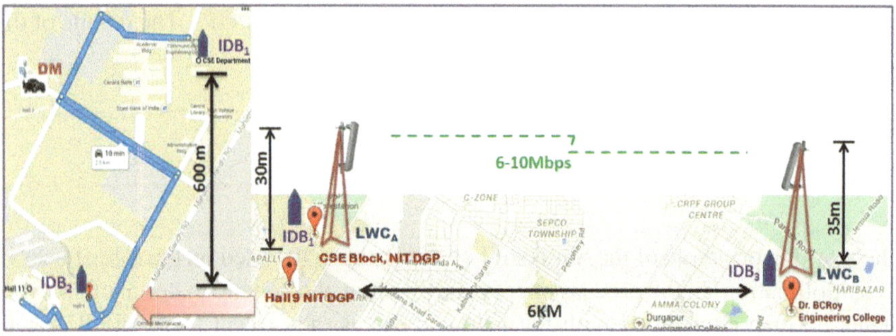

Fig. 10.6 Diagrammatic view of the Campus-scale Testbed. Courtesy: (Paul et al. 2015)

carry the messages from one IDB and forward them to the other IDBs. Hence, this system can also be visualized as a Digital Post Office. The system overview is given here.[31]

10.5.5 Field Trials and Results

We have carried out several field testings of the SurakshIT system at different scales: some of them are campus-scale experiments carried out at test-bed at our institute campus, and the rest are through mock deployment at disaster management drills conducted at disaster-prone sites, some of which are organized by the Government agencies.

Campus-scale Experiments: Fig. 10.6 portrays a Test-bed developed between the campus of the National Institute Technology Durgapur and the campus of Dr. B. C. Engineering College, Durgapur. The test-bed was prepared solely for the purpose of campus-scale testing of the SurakshIT system (Paul et al. 2015). In the test-bed mentioned above, we have used Android smartphones as DTN nodes, custom-built devices as IDB, and DM. The custom-built devices have been a preliminary version of XOB x.1 mentioned above, which has been made of Raspberry Pi[32]/Orange Pi[33] running ARM Linux as the device computing unit, Wi-Fi dongle as the communication interface of the device, and portable power bank as the device power source. In this version of SurakshIT, we have used a pair of long-range Wi-Fi devices (PTP-500[34]) to exchange data between the campuses.

Key Observations: Fig. 10.7c presents some of the observations that we have made in connection with our campus-scale experiments in the aforesaid test-bed. Messages

[31] https://youtu.be/W0kOMsD_UsY.

[32] https://www.raspberrypi.org/.

[33] http://www.orangepi.org/.

[34] https://bit.ly/2Wfcisw.

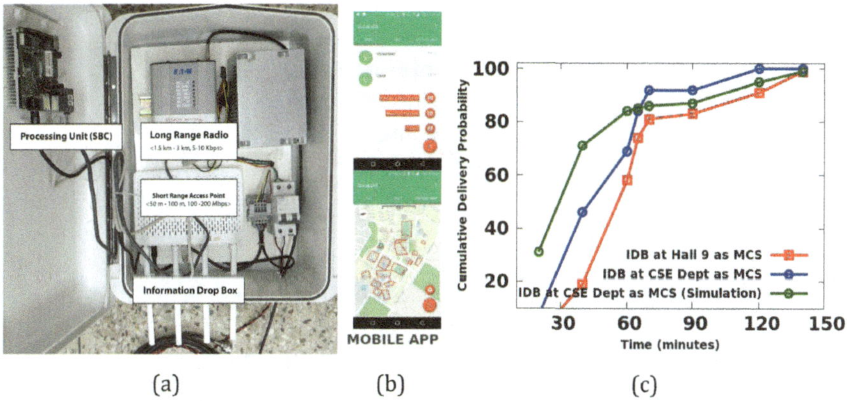

Fig. 10.7 **a** Information drop box: The inside view (left), Screenshot of the SurakshIT Mobile App (right) **b** Campus-scale test results: Observed cumulative delivery probabilities of messages at different IDBs in the test-bed

are recorded using the SurakshIT app by the volunteers present at different parts of the test-bed. The time of creation and time of reaching all the messages generated by the volunteers at different IDBs are recorded from the SurakshIT test log files. The figure above shows how the rate of messages delivery at IDBs changes with time. We have also simulated the scenario using *ONE Simulator*, which shows that the observed message delivery rate conforms with the same in simulation. Details of the above campus-scale experiment may be found in Paul et al. (2015). The working video of the app is available here.[35]

Mock Trials at Disaster-prone Sites: Evaluation of the SurakshIT system via mock deployments spans over four years (2015–2018). During the period, we have tested the system from multiple field deployments, and have made demonstrations to various stakeholders, including disaster relief organizations and Government officials during two different disaster mock-drills organized by the State Government at disaster-prone areas and a mock drill organized by solely by us. During these field tests, we have carried out thorough performance, scalability, and usability testing. We observe that it can efficiently visualize the crisis map without the requirement of any backbone Internet connectivity. We benchmark different performance parameters of the system and find that it is 20% more energy-efficient compared to pure Wi-Fi ad hoc networks and always provides the best-effort service depending on the movement patterns of the end-users.

One of our mock drills was carried out in *Hizole Block*, which is one of the remotest, flood-prone, village block in the district of Murshidabad in West Bengal, India. West Bengal state disaster management authority conducted a mock disaster drill related to *flood and soil erosion* in the above region (refer site plan in Fig. 10.8a) during October 2016. We participated in the drill based on the competent authorities'

[35]https://youtu.be/NfsXt5H_9Xc.

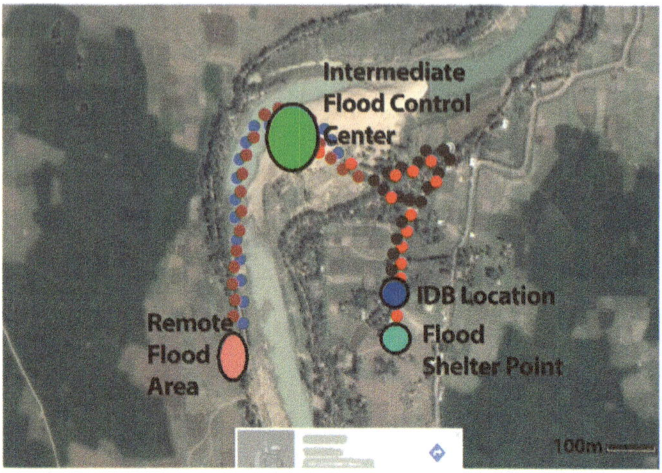

(a)

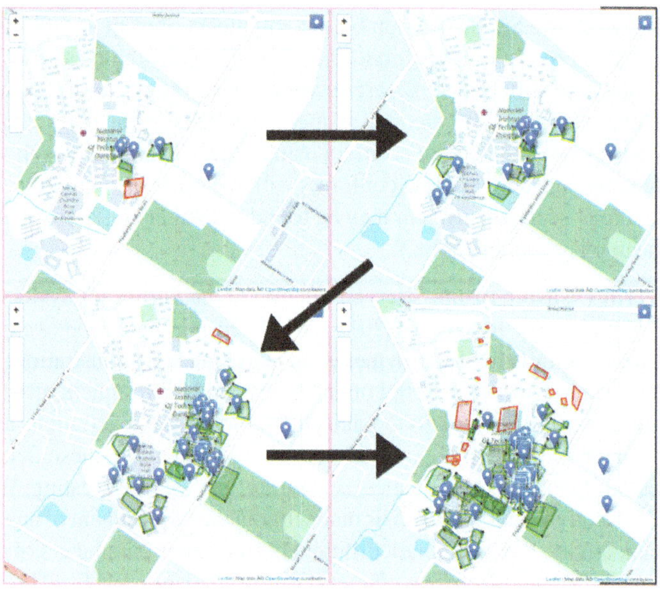

(b)

Fig. 10.8 **a** Site plan of the disaster mock drill at hizole block **b** Crisis map snapshots after periodic merging of GIS objects at an *IDB*—red polygons are without metadata, green ones are with metadata

invitation and deployed the SurakshIT system in the mock site to provide parallel communication support during the drill (Paul et al. 2019b).

The drill began just after the competent authority (Block Development Officer of Hizole) dispatched a mock flood alert signal to all concerned through proper channels. Flood shelter at Ranipur Mouza was selected as the base of mock "rescue-relief" operations. The officials and staff from various participating departments and volunteers from various self-help groups went on with their jobs following the standard operating procedure as they are expected to carry out a real incident.

During this ~3 h drill, the SurakshIT volunteers remain attached to selected "rescue-relief" volunteers, recorded situational messages based on the mock destruction events, and dummy rescue-relief activities using the SurakshIT User Interface; and dispatched for the IDB placed at Ranipur Flood shelter.

Key Observations: Fig. 10.9 plots some interesting performance metrics that may show the performance of the SurakshIT system during the said mock experiment.

SurakshIT follows an importance-based message forwarding paradigm to fully exploit the communication opportunities of the underlying network to exchange essential messages (Paul et al. 2019b). Due to the above, we observe varying reception patterns of messages at IDB in Ranipur Flood Shelter, as shown in Fig. 10.9a, concerning their "content" and their "media extension" type. Inset in the same presents volumetric transfer under an identical environment. Figure 10.9b, on the other hand, reflects the observed cumulative delivery probabilities of different types of messages (based on "media extension" type of the message files) received at

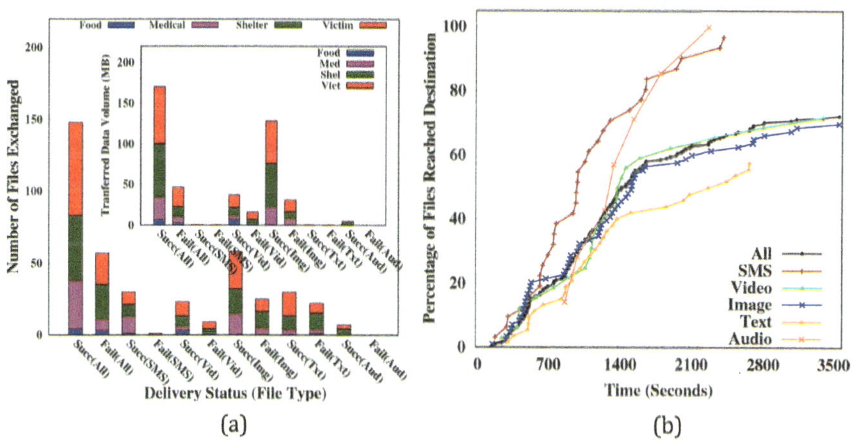

Fig. 10.9 **a** Distribution of the number of messages (outer) and the data volume (inset) reached IDB at Ranipur Flood shelter from the drill site during the mock trial with respect to the message "data contents" and their "media extension types". **b** Observed Distribution of the number of messages of different types from the drill site delivered to the IDB at the Flood shelter with respect to message delivery time

Ranipur Flood Center with respect to their "total message delivery time". The above-observed probabilities let us infer that the SurakshIT system would perform both reliably and efficiently if it is deployed during real disasters.

10.5.6 Remarks

We have an augmented SurakshIT system with an online interface using which it can upload Local Crisis Map snapshots to a server (that maintains a global view for the same) if the Internet connection is available. Such a provision would turn interesting in a scenario where intermittent Internet is available, and the users would like to merge local crisis data obtained via SurakshIT system with the global information from other online sources, such as Twitter, Google, and Facebook; and consequently to generate a more authentic and useful snapshot of the situation. The above is one of our future goals with the SurakshIT. Moreover, we have faced a multitude of challenges in aggregating multimodal crisis data extracting maximum information with minimum computation. Another future direction of research in this end is in designing a fast, energy-efficient, lightweight algorithm for effective summarization of multimodal crisis data, which could be executed on smartphones and custom XOB x.1 devices.

10.6 Conclusion

The devastation of any large-scale natural disaster toward humanity needs to be mitigated. The aftermath of disaster leaves desolation in all types of development sectors, *e.g., Agriculture, Education, Industry, and others* might even disrupt the post-disaster management activities due to the catastrophic failure of conventional digital communication services. For building a resilient disaster risk reduction framework, the substantial reduction of losses in human lives, livelihood, social, and cultural aspects should be initiated.[36] It is evident from several reports that most developing countries are on the same pitch and are committed to building a resilient society for effective disaster risk mitigation.[37,38] In India, the government has provided a special emphasis on disaster mitigation, preparedness, response, and vulnerability reduction. The government is currently involving in capacity building among state-, district-, and block-level disaster management authorities and the first responders for a systematic disaster risk reduction. The establishment of emergency communication for transmission of situational information among these stakeholders is one of the prime instances of such capacity building. The rapid escalation of communication

[36] https://www.undrr.org/implementing-sendai-framework/what-sf.

[37] https://www.ndmindia.nic.in/global-frameworks-for-drr.

[38] https://www.undrr.org/publication/disaster-risk-reduction-sri-lanka.

failure begs the requirement of resilient and rapidly deployable emergency communication services for establishing real-time connectivity in disaster-affected regions for effective situation analysis and policy management. The current chapter elucidates such state–of-the-art emergency communication services and their utility in communication establishment for post-disaster management. Considering the notion of these existing services, we have discussed different types of devices, applications, and network infrastructure, which have been designed to deal with disaster relief situations. Beyond that, we have also specified some popular communication infrastructure built through utilizing the amalgamation of topological structures of existing communication networks to ensure long-range, qualitative, and interoperable end-to-end connectivity in disaster response situations. In Sects. 10.2 and 10.5 various emergency communication services and applications like *Cell on Wheels, Satellite Phones, VSAT, HAM radio, PTT, and many more* have been utilized by NGOs, Government Officials, and First responders in several past disaster cases for rapid situation assessment, relief, and response. But the accessibility of such communication devices for information sharing remains beyond the reach of the everyday citizens and survivors. Considering such a key aspect of community resilience for disaster mitigation, we have presented a case study of a new hybrid communication infrastructure named *SurakshIT*, developed through leveraging the capabilities of handheld portable devices, short/long-range communication interfaces, and applications in order to bridge the gap between ordinary people and other disaster management stakeholders. Through such a data-driven communication framework, different community members of rural and urban regions can seamlessly communicate among themselves and thus contribute to disaster response situation assessment and response in collaboration with each other. The rigorous survey in this chapter would help the readers effectively make out about the post-disaster emergency communication services that have been proposed or deployed in real-time post-disaster scenarios. Besides, we have also discussed our proposed hybrid scalable communication structure along with the modular descriptions, communication interfaces, devices, and applications used to build the network. Such a tailor-made network solution would enable the community to understand the significance of low-cost devices like smartphones, customized UAVs, edge nodes, i.e., XOB in forming a resilient communication environment for post-disaster management.

References

Ali K, Nguyen HX, Vien QT, Shah P (2015) Disaster management communication networks: challenges and architecture design. In: 2015 IEEE International conference on pervasive computing and communication workshops (PerCom workshops). IEEE, pp 537–542

Available (2020) https://econtent.hogrefe.com/doi/full/10.1027/0227-5910/a000679. Accessed 31 July 2020

Bao JQ, Lee WC (2007) Rapid deployment of wireless ad hoc backbone networks for public safety incident management. In: IEEE GLOBECOM 2007 IEEE global telecommunications conference. IEEE, pp 1217–1221

Buyukakkaslar MT, Erturk MA, Aydin MA, Vollero L (2017) Lorawan as an e-health communication technology. In: 2017 IEEE 41st Annual computer software and applications conference (COMPSAC), vol 2. IEEE, pp 310–313

Cheng SM, Huang WR, Cheng RG, Gan CH (2015) Experimental emergency communication systems using usrp and gnu radio platform. In: 2015 11th International conference on heterogeneous networking for quality, reliability, security and robustness (QSHINE). IEEE, pp 75–79

Cyclone Aila (2009) https://earthobservatory.nasa.gov/images/38786/cycloneaila. Accessed 31 July 2020

Devi Pradeep P, Anil Kumar B et al (2015) A survey of emergency communication network architectures. Int J u- e-Service Sci Technol 8(4):61–68

Dilmaghani RB, Rao RR (2008) A wireless mesh infrastructure deployment with application for emergency scenarios. In: 5th International ISCRAM conference

Du J, Zhu W, Xu J, Li Z, Wang H (2012) A compressed harq feedback for device-to-device multicast communications. In: Vehicular Technology Conference (VTC Fall), 2012 IEEE. IEEE, pp 1–5

Earthquake in Nepal (2015) https://www.unfpa.org/emergencies/earthquake-nepal. Accessed 31 July 2020

EL Khaled Z, Mcheick H (2019) Case studies of communications systems during harsh environments: a review of approaches, weaknesses, and limitations to improve quality of service. Int J Distrib Sens Netw 15(2):1550147719829960

Ferranti L, D'Oro S, Bonati L, Demirors E, Cuomo F, Melodia T (2019) Hiro-net: Self-organized robotic mesh networking for internet sharing in disaster scenarios. In: 2019 IEEE 20th international symposium on" a world of wireless, mobile and multimedia networks"(WoWMoM). IEEE, pp 1–9

George SM, Zhou W, Chenji H, Won M, Lee YO, Pazarloglou A, Stoleru R, Barooah P (2010) Distressnet: a wireless ad hoc and sensor network architecture for situation management in disaster response. IEEE Commun Mag 48(3):128–136

Gill GS (2019) When all else fails: amateur radio becomes lifeline of communications during a disaster. Int J Emerg Serv

Ham radio helps combat Cyclone "Aila" (2009) http://www.radioandmusic.com/biz/radio/ham-radio-helps-combat-cyclone-aila. Accessed 31 July 2020

Harvey Shows Progress on Emergency (2017) https://www.wired.com/story/harveyshows-progress-on-emergency-communications-since-katrina/. Accessed 31 July 2020

Hazra K, Shah VK, Bilal M, Silvestri S, Das SK, Nandi S, Saha S (2019) A novel network architecture for resource-constrained post-disaster environments. In: 2019 11th International conference on communication systems & networks (COMSNETS). IEEE, pp 328–335

Heimerl K, Brewer E (2010) The village base station. In Proceedings of the 4th ACM workshop on networked systems for developing regions, pp 1–2

Ho¨chst J, Baumga¨rtner L, Kuntke F, Penning A, Sterz A, Freisleben B (2020) Lora-based device-to-device smartphone communication for crisis scenarios. Technical report, EasyChair

Hossmann T, Legendre F, Carta P, Gunningberg P, Rohner C (2011) Twitter in disaster mode: opportunistic communication and distribution of sensor data in emergencies. In: Proceedings of the 3rd extreme conference on communication: the amazon expedition, ExtremeCom '11. ACM, New York, NY, USA, pp 1:1–1:6

Hurricane Harvey has affected 13 million (2017) https://www.ndtv.com/indiansabroad/hurricane-harvey-2-indian-students-rescued-from-lake-incritical-condition-1743219. Accessed 31 July 2020

Hurricane Maria (2017) https://www.vox.com/2018/9/20/17871330/hurricane-mariapuerto-rico-damage-death-toll-trump. Accessed 31 July 2020

Hurricane Sandy (2012) The deadly storm to impact 60 million. https://www.news18.com/news/india/hurricane-sandy-the-deadly-storm-toimpact-60-million-519146.html. Accessed 31 July 2020

Hurricane Sandy Power Outage Map (2017) https://www.huffpost.com/entry/hurricane-sandy-power-outage-map-infographicn2044411. Accessed 31 July 2020
Iland D, Belding EM (2014) Emergenet: robust, rapidly deployable cellular networks. IEEE Commun Mag 52(12):74–80
Impact of Cyclone AILA (2009) http://www.internationalfloodnetwork.org/aila.htm. Accessed 31 July 2020
Internet Impacts of Hurricanes Harvey, Irma, and Maria (2019). https://bit.ly/2kNYQfm. Accessed 17 Sept 2019
It took 11 months to restore power to Puerto Rico after Hurricane Maria. A similar crisis could happen again. (2018) https://www.vox.com/identities/2018/8/15/17692414/puerto-rico-power-electricity-restored-hurricane-maria. Accessed 31 July 2020
Japan flood (2018) https://www.bbc.com/news/world-asia-44790193. Accessed 31 July 2020
Japan-366 days after the Quake (2011) https://earthquake-report.com. Accessed 31 July 2020
Kabra G, Ramesh A (2015) An empirical investigation of the enablers in humanitarian supply chain management in India. J Adv Manage Res
Kishorbhai VY, Vasantbhai NN (2017) Aon: a survey on emergency communication systems during a catastrophic disaster. Proced Comput Sci 115:838–845
Ku I, Lu Y, Gerla M, Gomes RL, Ongaro F, Cerqueira E (2014) Towards software-defined vanet: architecture and services. In 2014 13th annual Mediterranean ad hoc networking workshop (MED-HOC-NET). IEEE, pp 103–110
Legendre F, Hossmann T, Sutton F, Plattner B (2011) 30 years of wireless ad hoc networking research: what about humanitarian and disaster relief solutions? what are we still missing? In Proceedings of the 1st international conference on wireless technologies for humanitarian relief (ACWR'11), pp 217–217
Lien YN, Chi LC, Shaw YS (2009) A walkie-talkie-like emergency communication system for catastrophic natural disasters. In: 2009 10th International symposium on pervasive systems, algorithms, and networks. IEEE, pp 309–314
Lu W, Seah WK, Peh EW, Ge Y (2007). Communications support for disaster recovery operations using hybrid mobile ad-hoc networks. In: 32nd IEEE conference on local computer networks (LCN 2007). IEEE, pp 763–770
Mecella M, Angelaccio M, Krek A, Catarci T, Buttarazzi B, Dustdar S (2006) Workpad: an adaptive peer-to-peer software infrastructure for supporting collaborative work of human operators in emergency/disaster scenarios. In: International symposium on collaborative technologies and systems (CTS'06). IEEE, pp 173–180
Mehendale Hrushikesh, Paranjpe Ashwin, Vempala Santosh (2011) Lifenet: a flexible ad hoc networking solution for transient environments. ACM SIGCOMM Comput Commun Rev 41(4):446–447
Meissner A, Luckenbach T, Risse T, Kirste T, Kirchner H (2002) Design challenges for an integrated disaster management communication and information system. In The First IEEE Workshop on Disaster Recovery Networks (DIREN 2002), vol 24
Menon VG, Pathrose JP, Priya J (2016) Ensuring reliable communication in disaster recovery operations with reliable routing technique. Mob Inf Syst
Meyer R (2013) Simple messaging and collaboration system for disaster environments. In: 2013 IEEE Global humanitarian technology conference (GHTC). IEEE, pp 382–387
Mondal T, Roy J, Bhattacharya I, Chakraborty S, Saha A, Saha S (2016) Smart navigation and dynamic path planning of a micro-jet in a post disaster scenario. In: Proceedings of the second ACM SIGSPATIAL international workshop on the use of GIS in emergency management, pp 1–8
Mondal T, Bhattacharya I, Pramanik P, Boral N, Roy J, Saha S, Saha S (2018) A multi-criteria evaluation approach in navigation technique for micro-jet for damage & need assessment in disaster response scenarios. Knowl Based Syst 162:220–237. Special Issue on intelligent decision-making and consensus under uncertainty in inconsistent and dynamic environments

Naghian S, Tervonen J (2003) Semi-infrastructured mobile ad-hoc mesh networking. In: 14th IEEE Proceedings on personal, indoor and mobile radio communications, 2003. PIMRC 2003, vol 2. IEEE, pp 1069–1073

Nepal earthquake (2015) The technology helping to save lives. https://www.itproportal.com/2015/05/13/nepal-earthquake-the-technologyhelping-to-save-lives/. Accessed 31 July 2020

Paul PS, Nandi S, Dey SK, De K, Pramanik P, Saha S (2015) Challenges in designing testbed for evaluating delaytolerant hybrid networks. In: 2015 IEEE International conference on pervasive computing and communication workshops (PerCom Workshops). IEEE, pp 280–283

Paul PS, Ghosh BC, De K, Saha S, Nandi S, Chakraborty S (2015) Demo: Psync: a peer-to-peer sync tool for challenged networks. In: Proceedings of the 10th ACM MobiCom workshop on challenged networks, CHANTS '15. ACM, New York, NY, USA, pp 61–62

Paul PS, Ghosh BC, De K, Saha S, Nandi S, Saha S, Bhattacharya I, Chakraborty S (2016) On design and implementation of a scalable and reliable Sync system for delay tolerant challenged networks. In: Communication systems and networks (COMSNETS), 2016 8th international conference on, COMSNETS'16

Paul PS, Mehta N, Das AK, Agarwal S, Saha S, Nandi S (2019a) SurakshIT: A smartphone-based application for 'localized' gis data aggregation in absence of internet. In: Proceedings of the 20th international conference on distributed computing and networking, ICDCN '19. ACM, New York, NY, USA, pp 393–396

Paul PS, Ghosh BC, Datta HS, De K, Basu AP, Pramanik P, Saha S, Chakraborty S, Ganguly N, Nandi S (2019b) CRIMP: here crisis mapping goes offline. J Netw Comput Appl. Elsevier

Paul PS, Mukherjee C, Ghosh BC, Pandit S, Saha S, Nandi S (2019c) On designing a fast-deployable 'localized' gis platform for using 'offline' during post-disaster situation. In Proceedings of the 20th international conference on distributed computing and networking, ICDCN '19. ACM, New York, NY, USA, pp 409–412

Paul PS, Ghosh BC, Ghosh A, Saha S, Nandi S, Chakraborty S (2020) Disaster strikes! internet blackout! what's fate of crisis mapping? In: 22nd International conference on human-computer interaction with mobile devices and services, MobileHCI '20. ACM, Oldenburg, Germany

PDF (2013) https://www.med.or.jp/english/journal/pdf/201302/118126.pdf. Accessed 31 July 2020

Rawat P, Haddad M, Altman E (2015) Towards efficient disaster management: 5 g and device to device communication. In: 2015 2nd International conference on information and communication technologies for disaster management (ICT-DM). IEEE, pp 79–87

Restoring the Internet in Nepal (2016) https://blog.apnic.net/2016/05/25/restoring-internet-nepal-one-year-quake/. Accessed 31 July 2020

Saha S, Nandi S, Paul PS, Shah VK, Roy A, Das SK (2015) Designing delay constrained hybrid ad hoc network infrastructure for post-disaster communication. Ad Hoc Netw 25:406–429

Sakano T, Kotabe S, Komukai T, TKumagai T, Shimizu Y, Takahara A, Ngo T, Fadlullah ZM, Nishiyama H, Kato N (2016) Bringing movable and deployable networks to disaster areas: development and field test of mdru. IEEE Network 30(1):86–91

Sandy Created a Black Hole of Communication (2013) https://www.govtech.com/em/disaster/Sandy-Black-Hole-of-Communication.html. Accessed 31 July 2020

Sciullo L, Fossemo F, Trotta A, Felice MD (2018) Locate: a lora-based mobile emergency management system. In: 2018 IEEE Global Communications Conference (GLOBECOM). IEEE, pp 1–7

Sciullo Luca, Trotta Angelo, Di Felice Marco (2020) Design and performance evaluation of a lora-based mobile emergency management system (locate). Ad Hoc Netw 96:101993

Selim MY, Kamal AE (2018) Post-disaster 4 g/5 g network rehabilitation using drones: SOLVING battery and backhaul issues. In: 2018 IEEE Globecom Workshops (GC Wkshps). IEEE, pp 1–6

Shaw R, Peary B, Ideta A, Takeuchi Y (2012) Emergency communication. Knowledge notes

Shingate A, Borse A, Tiwari S, Jawale A (2015) An electronic solution of amateur radio for life saving in times of natural calamities. In: 2015 Annual IEEE India Conference (INDICON). IEEE, pp 1–6

Slug Causes Power Outage (2019) https://www.news18.com/news/buzz/slug-causespower-outage-delays-dozens-of-trains-with-12000-passengers-in-japan2201345.html. Accessed 31 July 2020

Thomas Anil, Raja Gunasekaran (2019) Finder: A d2d based critical communications framework for disaster management in 5g. Peer-to-Peer Netw Appl 12(4):912–923

Tohoku Earthquake & Tsunami Event Recap Report (2011) http://thoughtleadership.aonbenfield.com/documents/201108abifjapaneqtsunamieventrecap.pdf. Accessed 31 July 2020

Townsend AM, Moss ML (2005) Telecommunications infrastructure in disasters. Preparing cities for crisis communications: new york university centre for catastrophe preparedness and response. http://www.nyu.edu/ccpr/pubs/NYUDisasterCommunications1-Final.pdf. Published April, 1, 2005

Trying to communicate (2017) https://www.theverge.com/2017/9/29/16372048/puerto-rico-hurricane-maria-2017-electricity-water-foodcommunications-phone-internet-recovery. Accessed 31 July 2020

UNISDR (2015) Sendai framework for disaster risk reduction 2015–2030

Utani A, Mizumoto T, Okumura T (2011) How geeks responded to a catastrophic disaster of a high-tech country: rapid development of counter disaster systems for the great east Japan Earthquake of March 2011. In Proceedings of the special workshop on internet and disasters, SWID'11

Zhang B, Wang Y, Wei L, Jin Q, Vasilakos AV (2018) Ble mesh: a practical mesh networking development framework for public safety communications. Tsinghua Sci Technol 23(3):333–346

Zhou Bin, Honglin Hu, Huang Sheng-Qiang, Chen Hsiao-Hwa (2013) Intracluster device-to-device relay algorithm with optimal resource utilization. IEEE Trans Veh Technol 62(5):2315–2326

Part III
Technologies for Decision Support

Chapter 11
Experimental Command and Control Center for Crisis and Disaster Management: A Living-Lab Approach

Jaziar Radianti

Abstract The living-lab is a planned research infrastructure that includes user involvement and the co-design process. This article presents an overview of the innovative experimental control room for crisis management that adopts this living-lab approach in all research co-creation activities. The aims of this paper are threefold: (1) To study possible control room research methods, focus areas, and technologies that can be tailored to the living-lab approach; (2) To illustrate and share experience on the possibilities to tailor an experimental command and control center as a living-lab. (3) To explore the features to fulfill to maximize the benefit of the living-lab for all intended audiences. By using three cases, this paper is able to show the relevance and applicability of the living-lab approach.

Keywords Experimental control room · Living-lab · Use case scenario · Emergency management

11.1 Introduction

Obtaining a comprehensive picture of critical, hazardous events is typically done by activating a specially designed room—the so-called command and control center. It serves as a central point for collecting information from humans and devices, visualizing them, and monitoring the normal operations or crisis situations. Nevertheless, nowadays, the function of this center is more than monitoring information.

A command and control center (C2C) is a physical facility equipped with advanced technologies established for a specific purpose. Usually, C2C is intended for monitoring a process or coordinating multiple sub-organizations or agents, collaborating on tasks and actions, dispatching task force. C2C also serves as a center for providing directions, orders, and decisions. Most control rooms are designed to monitor and increase situational awareness over the situations that need to be followed, ranging

J. Radianti (✉)
Centre for Integrated Emergency Management, Department of Information Systems, University of Agder, Kristiansand, Norway
e-mail: jaziar.radianti@uia.no

M. Sakurai and R. Shaw (eds.), *Emerging Technologies for Disaster Resilience*, Disaster Risk Reduction,
https://doi.org/10.1007/978-981-16-0360-0_11

from production chain in the industries, space center, weather monitoring, transportation and city monitoring, critical infrastructure, the security of network and cyber-attacks, prone-to hazard industries such as nuclear power plants or oil–gas sectors, military, and surveillance to the crisis management. Typically, a control room consists of multiple displays or even wall-sized area and control panels, where operators can collect, visualize, and monitor information received through its facilities in the form of images, videos, or data stream.

There are variations of control room terminologies in the literature such as "*command and control (C2C) center*" (Brehmer 2010), "*operations center*" (Ryan 2013), "*incident command center*" (Jensen and Thompson 2016), or "*situation room*" (Giri et al. 2012). The usage of these terms varies, depending on their purposes or application areas, and especially in the military domain, the terminology variations are broader than C2C, such as *Command, Control & Intelligence—C2I*) (Govindaraj et al. 2013), *Command and Control Information Systems—C2IS* (Hansen et al. 2003), Command, Control & Communications—C3 (Kahne 1983), the most common is *Command, Control, Communications, and Intelligence—C3I* (Russell and Abdelzaher 2018). For emergency management, the term *Emergency Operation* Center (EOC) is used (Chan et al. 2016), while the terminologies NOC and SOC are used in cybersecurity to refer to *Network and Security Operation Center* (Eldardiry and Caldwell 2015).

The typical intention of the control room is to provide a space for organizations to deal with various situations related to their daily business in normal, abnormal, emergency, outage, and startup conditions. In this room, the decision-makers can determine what systems are required to accommodate an event, list the alternative actions to take to cope with unexpected situations. However, in military applications, the purpose can be for "centralized command" and "centralized monitoring of operations." It is about command organizations such as plan, direct, coordinate, and control the resources to accomplish the operation goals.

Inspired by various setups and functions of C2C-like facilities, an experimental command and control room has been set up in Norway, with emergency management as the main focus, and research as the main activities. This innovative room adopts the living-lab approach, i.e., the innovation environment in real-life settings in which user-driven innovation is the co-creation process for new services, products, and societal infrastructures. This room serves as a research facility where different technologies, monitoring systems, and scenarios can be examined, tested, and evaluated by also involving the real emergency management actors in developing various scenarios and innovations.

The aims of this paper are threefold: (1) To study possible control room research methods, focus areas, and technologies that can be tailored to the living-lab approach; (2) To illustrate and share experience on the possibilities to suit an experimental command and control center as a living-lab. (3) To explore the features to fulfill to maximize the benefit of the living-lab for all intended audiences.

This paper is divided into six sections. After the introduction, the literature review on the command and control room is presented. Afterward, the approach and living-lab methods are revealed in Sect. 11.3, while Sect. 11.4 shows the use cases and how such living-lab can contribute to improving the testing related to new technologies. Section 11.5 contains lessons learned and future use of the lab. Section 11.6 concludes this paper.

Note that for now, onward, this room in question is referred to as experimental C2C or C2C.

11.2 Literature Review

This section describes three aspects of command and control room: designs and expected capabilities of the C2C, technologies deployed in the C2C, and methods for evaluation in the C2C.

11.2.1 Design and Capabilities of Command and Control Room

Traditionally, a control room has been seen as a *place* designed for certain *actors* for the *control* of some *process* (Hollnagel and Woods 2005). Koskinen and Norros (2010) argue that today, there is a pressure for change about the main components (in italics) of the traditional control room definition. The authors suggest extending the concept of the control room to be more than just a room space dedicated for monitoring and operating tools. The concept should also consider comprehensive human–system interfaces and places in which the operating personnel accomplishes their work and that is incorporated with cultural norms and social meaning. Thus, the room should fulfill three spatial aspects: physical space, social space, and virtual space. They suggest four points of changes, i.e.,

- *Remodeling of control room structures.* The control room was earlier definitely a stationary and single room space, but the current trend has expanded the possibilities to create mobile or also spatially distributed control spaces.
- *Changes in the allocation of operative tasks.* The concept of an operator has altered. Earlier the operator was always comprehended as a single person. Today the actor is comprehended in the plural, and it typically refers to a team of people or, more recently, also to a joint human–technology system, composing, e.g., of automatic agents that collaborate with human actors.
- *Enlargement of the focus of the process.* The shift occurs primarily in terms of temporal focus. Traditionally, the operators were mainly oriented toward the present situation. Nowadays, there is more and more pressure also to consider both past events and the expected future behavior of the process.
- *Enlargement of the control room focus.* There is also a tendency to enlarge the focus of control from operations to maintenance, design, production planning, and other functions such as threat detections and preventions.

In addition to these four points of control room transformation, there are some future trends of the way the control room is designed (Crowley 2017), among other things are

- *Architecture*. There are different trends of the control room architecture, such as the tendencies to be more centralized, or centralized and distributed regionally, and to be more fully or partially distributed regionally, and the use of single and multiple cloud providers for handling the control room functions.
- *Changes in required capabilities*: Some more advanced capabilities embedded in the control rooms are more demanding, especially those are dedicated to cyber-security. Some functions and capabilities can be improved through technology supports such as network intrusion and prevention, log management and monitoring, risk analysis and assessment capabilities, threat intelligence capabilities, deception capabilities, artificial intelligence, and machine learning capabilities, and other capabilities requiring technologies.
- *Metrics and performance*: The development of the ICT technologies causes the information to flow faster, resulting in higher demands for faster time to respond to events.

11.2.2 Technologies and Command and Control Center

While the most visible infrastructures for C2C are the wall displays, there are enabling technologies that support the operation of a C2C. They include *middleware* (e.g., a system that provides interoperability in a distributed environment); *communication sub-system* (e.g., internet); *information systems* (e.g., command and control information systems, geographical information systems); and *user interface equipment* (such as large displays, table displays) (Hansen et al. 2003).

In the literature, there are many technologies proposed to complement the necessary enabling infrastructures above, especially data carrying devices, data capturing devices, sensing and actuating devices, and general devices that support the communication of these devices with the physical C2C. They are ranging from virtual and augmented reality (VR and AR) technologies, sensors, CCTV, robotic platforms, unmanned aircraft systems (UAS), to wearable and Internet of Things (IoT) devices. These technologies are continuously being tested, deployed, and integrated into the C2C.

Virtual and Augmented Reality: Drøivoldsmo et al. (2003) have already suggested virtual and augmented reality to provide new possibilities to present information to the operators in the control room. AR system is a technology that "supplements the real world with virtual (computer-generated) objects that appear to coexist in the same space as the real world" (Azuma et al. 2001). Typical properties of the AR system are (1) combines real and virtual objects in a real environment; (2) runs interactively, and in real time; and (3) registers (aligns) real and virtual objects with each other. While VR is often described as a hybrid term that refers to an integration of several elements, including computers, worlds and environments, interactivity, immersion, and users, who are usually referred to as participants in a virtual reality experience (Muhanna 2015). There are three main concepts suggested as VR elements, i.e., immersion, interactivity, and presence (Walsh and Pawlowski 2002). In the context of C2C, VR and AR can serve as replacements of systems and areas which are not easily accessed in the real world, which can train the operators to have direct experience to be inside such inaccessible or hazardous environments. The technologieas can also be used to provide the C2C operators the real-world tasks.

Wearable Computers and Devices: Far before today's modern wearable devices are known, Skourup and Reigstad (2002) have suggested wearable computers, compact, self-contained, portable, full-functioning computing devices, which are entirely supported by a user for input, processing, and output of information. The proposed technologies were mobile phones, PDAs, and a wearable computer in a bigger size, which were used by the field operator but would benefit the control room operators in terms of online information, such as direct access to updated readings and observations from the field. Since then, newer technologies have been suggested, such as smart glasses, Go-Pro, customized head-mounted displays to generate images and videos, Microsoft Holo-Lens, embedded sensors for measurements, and location tracking (Chan et al. 2016), wristband (Mora and Divitini 2014). There are more variations of wearable devices that have been suggested in the literature, indicating how important it is to collect data from the field as real time and accurate as possible.

Robotic Platforms: Govindaraj et al. (2013) suggest portable robotic command and control technologies for supporting search and rescue (SAR) operations and acquire the common operational picture through a central mission planning and coordination system. This system supports SAR teams in disaster analysis, narrowing-down search areas, resource management, and coordination. The robotic platforms are available for robot sensor visualizations, fusion, and control algorithms. The robotic platforms can be equipped with a full sensor payload such as stereo camera, laser range finder, GPS, sensors, pan–tilt–zoom camera, and other needed instruments.

CCTV surveillance technology: CCTV is one of the common technologies used for surveillance in public areas and streets to watch events, people, and their behaviors such as anti-social behavior, crime, fire or accidents, or traffic congestion. CCTV surveillance of urban space such as a city center, the public gathering began to appear in the early 1990s (Boersma 2013), and is considered has become an essential part of people's daily life (Hempel and Töpfer 2004), regarded as a multifunctional risk management technology deployed for social control. CCTVs are very likely to be connected to other actors and agencies such as the police, the fire departments, or private security services that receive images in real time into their control rooms.

Sensemaking, Data, and Visual Analytics Technologies: In line with increased the data stream and big data entering the command and control room, the need for technologies that can support sensemaking, data, and visual analytics increases, to help reducing information overload. The need for these technologies is nearly for all types of control rooms, such as emergency management, industrial process, military, security, traffic, urban surveillance, transports, and more. Not only these rooms collect data from sensors, CCTV, and wearable devices but some of them also gather data from social media. Thus, sensemaking technologies can include technology that can harvest, analyze, and making sense of social media information. As pointed by Chan et al. (2016), sensemaking and visual analytics can help to extract essential pieces of information promptly to emergency responders.

Digital Maps and Geographic Information Systems (GIS): In the military and emergency management control room, digital map and GIS is utmost important as they serve as tools to visualize the common operational picture (Karagiannis and Synolakis 2016). It can improve situational awareness (Albina 2019). However, nowadays, businesses, public space surveillance, and most of the government activities that use the control room are very likely would need digital maps for their daily operations for different purposes, such as mapping their infrastructures, resources, location of persons, accidents, events, and more.

11.2.3 Evaluation in Control Room and Training

Articles in the literature that purely reports training models in the control room are rare. Most of the time, the training is often linked to the evaluation context, especially those that are rooted in human factor engineering. When the case has to do with the nuclear control room, there are documents, e.g., NUREG-0711in the US, that specify all necessary steps for evaluating human factors. Therefore, this section is organized based on testing and evaluation approaches implemented in the control room that may or may not be involving training.

Human Factors and Ergonomics: The human factors and ergonomics are examples of control room research focus (dos Santos et al. 2013; Ikuma et al. 2014b; Louka 2015). Gatto et al. (2013) suggest virtual simulations as a tool for ergonomic evaluation, using a nuclear control room case. The environment is a model of the control room that is supposed to realistically mimic of physical layout, personnel, and working environment. The testers should follow a pre-defined script of actions to be executed in responding to an emergency, with the exact time. Video recording is used to evaluate and compare the elapsed time spent during simulations to the reference action times. Ikuma et al. (2014b) also offer a human factor-based assessment framework to evaluate the effects of control room design on the operator performance that takes into account the operator's workload and experience level. Louka (2015) uses a formative usability technique for evaluating virtual mock-up and automated assistance to support human factors. Thus, this work is more about the evaluation of the software that will be able to provide a human factor guideline review.

Interface Evaluation: Several studies in the literature focus on the evaluation of the design interface. (Boring et al. 2014; Hildebrandt and Fernandes 2016; Kim et al. 2012).

Hildebrandt and Fernandes (2016), e.g., employ a micro-task-based questionnaire approach to evaluate the complex user interface (UI) of a power-plant control room. The goal is a compare performance of two experiments on differentiating analog and digital (UI), involving a medium size of testers. Boring et al. (2014) suggest a usability 2X2 matrix, which is widely adopted in human factor engineering, to evaluate the initial design of a control room. It encompasses *formative verification* (design phase through expert review), *summative verification* (after design phase by experts), *formative validation* (design phase by user testing), and *summative validation* (after design phase by user testing). While Kim et al. (2012) introduce the ecological interface design (EID) approach to improve the operator's situational awareness. EID is employed for complex socio-technical and dynamic systems. It is conducted through several steps: preparing test, pre-test, main test, debriefing, and analyzing materials. Note that the design interface evaluation of the control room often found in high-risk industry such as nuclear and power plants, which have to control various machines, processes, and eventually buttons to press.

Usability, task-based, and heuristic testing: Several authors have applied usability methods to evaluate the control room design interface (Gjøsæter and Radianti 2018; Savioja 2014). Gjøsæter and Radianti (2018) use heuristic evaluation to do typical tasks with a product, or simply asked to explore it freely, while their behaviors are observed and recorded to identify design flaws that cause user errors or difficulties. Savioja (2014) uses a model-based system usability evaluation to find out if the operator's attention is attuned in complex work. This work also has provided an extensive overview of various themes and methods raised in the evaluation of control rooms in the previous studies.

Evaluation using eye-tracking: Control room research scholars have combined various testing with the usage of eye-tracker (Ikuma et al. 2014a; Kovesdi et al. 2018; Starke et al. 2017). Modern eye-trackers generally use infrared technology to track pupil coordinates relative to the corneal reflection accurately. These eye-trackers give users greater freedom of movement, allowing them to behave as they usually would in the built environment. Kovesdi et al. (2018) successfully applied the eye-tracking technique for measuring human–machine interaction in terms of visual search efficiency, visual attention, and workload. The authors also measure the usability of the tool itself and conclude that eye-tracking is an acceptable method for operators participating in a simulation study. Using the standard SAGAT method, Ikuma et al. (2014a) are specifically interested in the speed and accuracy of the operators in the process industry, and thus eye-tracker supports to achieve this goal, in addition to the usage of a key-stroke recorder. The authors conclude that eye-tracker is an excellent tool for locating specific areas of an interface that draw the user's attention. Starke et al. (2017) employ eye-tracker devices to observe the workflow of the control room's operators who monitor the live traffic, supplemented with the hierarchical task analysis. From these literature examples, we notice that the use of eye-trackers in the control room is often combined with other methods, both qualitative and quantitative.

Evaluation of Situational awareness, performance, and mental workload: Some studies have focused the control room evaluation specifically on the psychological and cognitive aspects of the control room operators (Corker et al. 1990; Ikuma et al. 2014a, b; Lin et al. 2013; Roberts et al. 2017).

Roberts et al. (2017) employ multiple instruments to evaluate the operator's performance in a submarine control room. These instruments include standardized subjective rating scales (e.g., NASA TLX), physiological measures (e.g., ECG), in-play cognitive capacity assessments (e.g., dual-task paradigm), and SA assessments. The communications between all team members were done using Event Analysis of Systemic Teamwork (EAST) method. Corker et al. (1990) use several techniques that include human performance models, cognitive, visual, auditory, and psychomotor components to observe the impacts of the automation to the tactical command and control operators.

Evaluation of collaborative team communication: Control room scholars have also paid attention to the team interaction in the control room, such as collaborative team communication (Kataria et al. 2015), team learning (van der Haar et al. 2017) collaboration around wall displays (Prouzeau 2016) fleet command and control (Waldenström 2012). Kataria et al. (2015), for instance, examine the communication of control room staff and bridge staff on the ship. Different from other studies that often pick standard usability evaluation, this study uses an interview technique to capture team collaboration and found that lacking advanced warning and updates as barriers for communication. Team leader structuring behavior is a focus in the study of van der Haar et al. (2017). These behaviors cover communications implying goal orientation, clarifying, repeating a question, directed questions, procedural suggestions, summarizing in terms of a decision or command, and time management. This study employed a video-coded examination from overall drills and meetings. Prouzeau (2016) explores the collaboration using advanced, multitouch, fully wall display but emphasizes more on the visualization aspects, and how the users should collaborate on the same large display. The method itself for digging the collaboration is through observation and interview.

It is worth mentioning that in reviewed studies, only a few articles mention the control room evaluation is done in the context of training or realistic full drill (van der Haar et al. 2017). Moreover, there are some similarities that articles using a simulation approach assisted with some technology such as virtual environment (Gatto et al. 2013), or simply, or the testers are exposed to the series of pre-determined, simulated events or provided a set of tasks to do with time limitation. One article shows a test done in a control room simulator (Roberts et al. 2017).

11.2.4 Remarks on Literature Review

This paper examines the design and experiments conducted in the control room that takes into account the living-lab approach. From the review in the previous sections, there are some gaps that can be identified:

- The living-lab concept almost never appears in many experiments in the control room setting. As a result, elements of the living-lab and how is the living-lab approach applied in a case are hard to identify from the reviewed papers.
- The co-creation or co-design process with the target audience or users is often not explicitly elaborated, although some studies try to engage users.
- The literature focuses on emergency management control room is rare. However, regardless of the control room application areas, one of the essential points why this control room exists is to be alerted on potential accidents and incidents. In other words, most of the control rooms actually also deal with emergency management.

11.3 Approach: Living-Lab

11.3.1 Living-Lab Concept and Definition

"Living-lab" is a concept that has been mentioned in various research settings with different emphases, such as those who highlight the importance of co-creation, the importance of the link with the real-world environments, or both. The similarities among authors concerning the meaning of this living-lab are that the lab is not treated as a separate, isolated entity. In essence, a living-lab is "a real-life test and experimentation environment where users and producers co-create innovations (Radianti and Granmo 2015). Pierson and Lievens (2005) describe the living-lab as a "...socio-technical approach ...mainly meant for developing and elaborating sensitizing concepts that draw attention to central characteristics of sociality implicated ICT usage.

In fact, living-lab has been defined in different ways, namely, as *an environment*, *a methodology*, and *a system* (Bergvall-Kareborn 2009). Dell'Era and Landoni (2014) and (Tang and Hämäläinen 2012) clearly refer to the living-lab as a methodology and tools, which lay between the user-centric approach. However, according to Tang and Hämäläinen (2012), the core difference between the living-lab approach and other user-involving approaches is that living-lab is a user-centric innovation approach with real users and in real-life contexts, which provides a real experiment environment and real user experiences. Følstad (2008) proposes living-lab as open innovation platform and testbed applications to users, putting the *environment* as a core. Feurstein et al. (2008), suggest living-lab as a *systemic* innovation approach in which all stakeholders in a product, service, or application participate directly in the development process.

Apart from different perspectives and highlights concerning the definition of living-lab, apparently, there are some fundamental properties that valid in most living-labs.

The key concepts of the living-lab are further elaborated by (Bergvall-Kareborn et al. 2009), i.e., (1) *Continuity*, to ensure the trust-building required for innovation. (2) *Openness*, where the innovation should gather as many perspectives as possible to meet user-driven innovation. (3) *Realism*, to ensure that the innovation focuses on the real users and real-life situations. (4) *Empowerment* of users by motivating and empowering the users to engage in the innovation process. (5) *Spontaneity*, i.e., having the ability to detect, aggregate, and analyze user's spontaneous reactions and ideas. Bergvall-Kareborn et al. (2009) also add a note on openness, where the living-lab practitioners have taken two approaches. On one hand, those who believe that organization should involve as many internal and external stakeholders as possible in the development of innovation. On the other hand, it is essential to limit openness, especially in system development, because it will be too expensive to involve all stakeholders. The overview of the living-lab strands in terms of assumptions and setup can be found further in the work of Alavi et al. (2020). Using business perspective, Mastelic et al. (2015) have also taken into account cost structure, customer segments, and revenue stream to keep the living-lab alive.

This article adopts the so-called Living-Lab triangle suggested by Veeckman et al. (2013) in order to enable one to link the characteristics of the living-lab and their outcomes, as seen in Fig. 11.1. I reused this living-lab triangle to observe

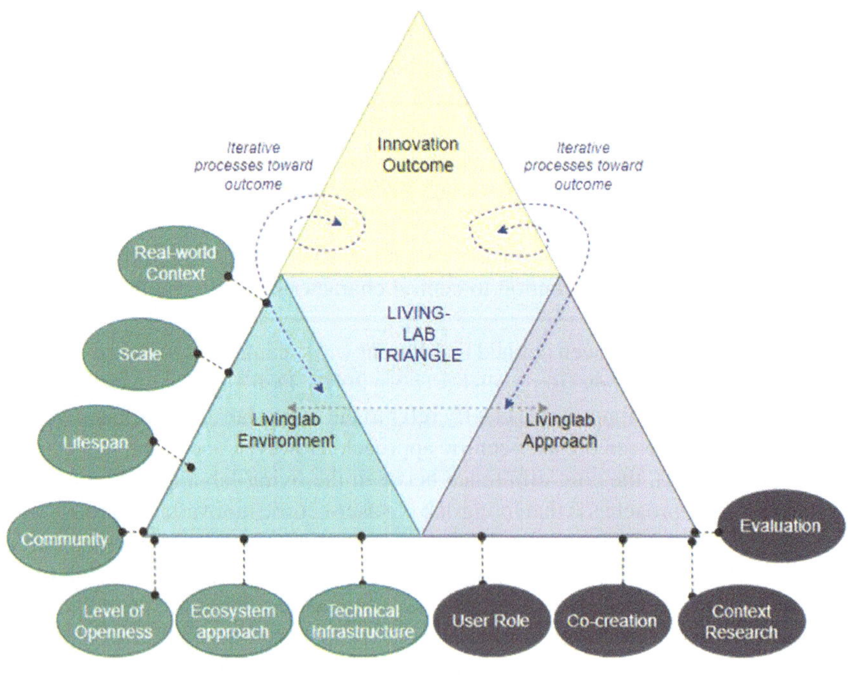

Fig. 11.1 The living-lab triangle (adapted from Veeckman et al. 2013)

if the experimental control room design could fulfill the expected coverage of the living-lab elements in each of the innovation or research activities. There are two main subsystems connected to the innovation outcomes, i.e., *Living-lab Environment* and *Living-lab Approach* represented by two smaller triangles on the bottom part. There are seven elements that emanate from *the Living-lab Environment* (bottom left triangle) (1) **Technical infrastructure** which should be available for the test users. (2) **The ecosystem approach**, where it should give added value to the involved partners. (3) **Level of openness**: the innovation process should be as open as possible. (4) **Community**: it can involve the community of interest or community of practice in the innovation initiatives. (5) **Life span**: it refers to the duration of the living-lab, which can be a short-, medium-, or long-term initiative and is not only based on a single case. (6) **Scale**: It refers to the size of users involved in a project both on a small or big scale. (7) **Real-world context**: It refers to the realism of the living-lab innovation activities, which should be as closer as possible to the users' natural environment. In the context of technologies and professional work, I would like to include the realism of the day-to-day technologies or professional practices in the users' working environment.

The living-lab approach (bottom-right triangle) comprises four elements: (1) **Evaluation**: the users are involved in different phases of innovation, such as test, co-create, and evaluate the results. (2) **Context Research**: Test users should be given the opportunity to shape innovation in the research process through interaction with researchers and developers. (3) **Co-creation**: It means that the approach should be iterative and use methods such as participatory methods. (4) **User Role**: users can take one or more of the following roles in the innovation or activities in the living-lab context, i.e., as an informant, a tester, a contributor, and a co-creator.

With respect to the relationship between user involvement in innovation and living-lab methodologies (Almirall et al. 2012) suggest a mapping, as presented in Fig. 11.2. The mapping is done through a Venn diagram with four subsets, representing the main living-lab methodologies. Almirall et al. (2012) suggest four methodologies: *user-centered* (user is a passive subject of the study), *design-driven* (Designer takes the lead), *participatory* (users are considered equal as partners in a co-creation process), and user-driven (the users actively drive the innovation process). Some elements have intersections, for example, the intersection between *participatory* and *user design* methodologies tend to see the users as co-creators, as an active entity. The subset between *user-driven* and *design-driven* methodologies tends to adopt the *real-life environment* as an experimental setting, as opposed to the subset between participatory and user-centered methodologies the often use *lab-like* environment. The subset between *user-centered* and *design-driven* sometimes puts users as subjects of study, or users are less active.

Living-lab approach has been adopted by scholars given it stresses the importance of individual end-users, customers, community, or even the whole regions to be a part of co-creation processes to achieve more precise results that are in line with the society's goals. In many contexts, the co-creation practices in research and innovations are still facing some issues such as suitable management models, key performance indicators, and tailoring open innovations with, e.g., large companies

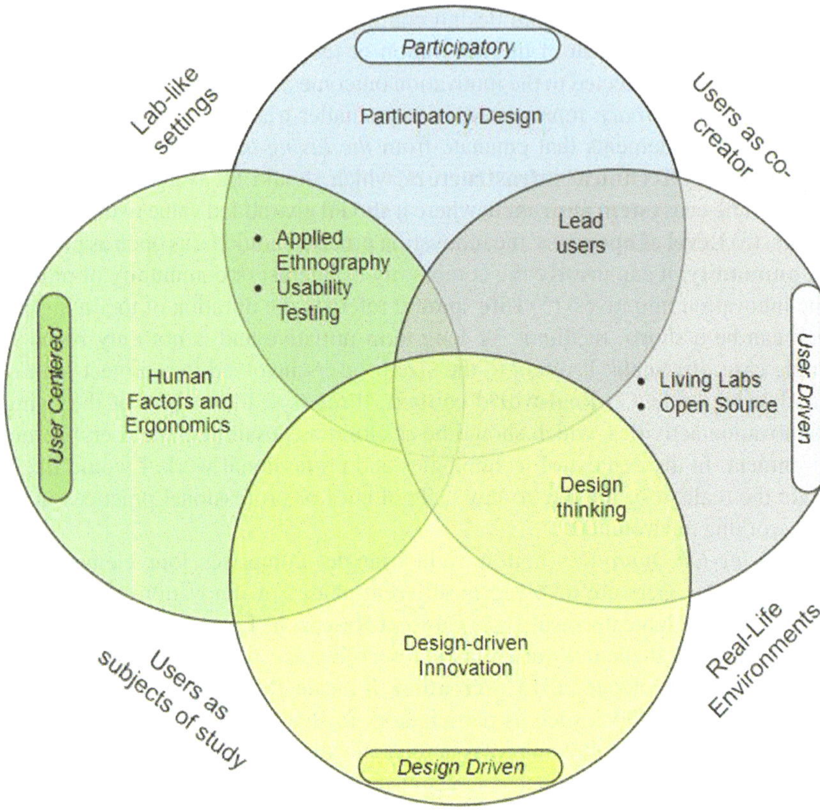

Fig. 11.2 Mapping user-innovation methodologies (Adapted from Almirall et al. 2012)

(Mastelic et al. 2015). Upon a good involvement of different members of communities and a society in general, the approach definitely can bridge the gap, especially with respect to the expectations and requirements of the innovations, or the society's goals to be preserved in any innovation initiatives. It can serve as a mean to teach society members for new innovations by involving them in the testing processes.

11.3.2 Experimental C2C Living-Lab: From Idea to Realization

The experimental C2C was designed as a competence center and a living-lab for accelerating innovation and research in future crisis management technology. This C2C put the Public–Private–People Partnerships (PPPP) as a spirit for user-driven open innovation that can be found at the core of most living-labs today. The essence of PPPP is reflected in the C2C plan to engage academia, research communities, local and national responders, business entities, and voluntary organizations. The lab also planned to support and motivate user-driven technology innovations, experience sharing, knowledge exchange, and stronger cooperation among the stakeholder. This C2C would promote third-party initiatives to share crisis tools and technologies both for collaborative training and testing.

Concerning the living-lab elements suggested by (Veeckman et al. 2013), in terms of *technical infrastructure*, in the experimental C2C context, it refers to all technologies that have been set up and deployed in this experimental C2C. By taking advantage of today's' multimedia technologies, it was possible to design this room as a flexible room for research and training. The flexibility here encompasses flexible display capability to present information, flexible scenarios, and flexible usage of the physical room itself.

With respect to *the flexible wall displays*, in a traditional control room, one operator may control 1–2 PCs. In this experimental C2C architecture, using one digital touchscreen control panel, an operator can control each available PCs (6 PCs) in the room. The operator also can visualize any information sources on any displays in the room easily through "drag and drop" technique. The drag–drop information presentation can be done both on the wall displays and on the desk displays. One operator can control and distribute up to 11 information sources simultaneously. The C2C in question has two wide multi-monitor walls (2×3 and 2×2 monitors) in addition to dual-monitor setups on each workspace (see Fig. 11.3). Any view from the workspace monitors can be mirrored to display on the wide monitors on the wall, either a single one or extended across 2×2 monitors. Any information can be swapped across the wall monitors. These views typically show visualizations simultaneously like charts or graphs, filtered twitter feeds, maps, presentations, or simulations in the form of serious games, sensor readings, or live video.

The *flexibility of selected scenarios* means that the users can choose scenarios to be used in this C2C and then present the information that would be relevant for a particular scene. The scenarios can be fire disasters, humanitarian response, floods, cybersecurity, and other emerging, relevant scenarios. For instance, for a

Fig. 11.3 Experimental C2C setup

fire scenario, one can display the weather forecasting map, twitter feed of crisis management stakeholders, relevant maps, and, if necessary, a video conference.

Regarding the *flexible usage* of the space, it means that the room can be used, e.g., for training or simulating the decision-making process during the crisis, remote monitoring, or experiments for comparing two team performance. The technologies and physical infrastructure can support this type of activity.

In terms of the ***ecosystem approach***, we paid attention to the testing design that we had to have adequate instruments that allow us to understand if people can get benefit from using this experimental C2C lab, regardless of their professional background. As the design of the lab functions was quite flexible, intended to involve multiple relevant stakeholders in many research activities, to a certain degree, the ***level of openness*** was much less granted in all these three case examples. In terms of real-world context, we keep in mind that all activities in this lab should come as close as possible to the real-world context and setting. In this first experiment, we wanted to make sure that the experience of monitoring the information and the use of the technologies are in line with the practices and should be barrier-free.

Concerning ***community***: This C2C living-lab has been developed through a set of discussion with those who have experience at developing such room: individual professionals, companies, and emergency management operation center, and to ensure that the lab and innovation research projects built in this lab would be as realistic as possible to the ***real-world*** practice. Given the lab is designed for a long-term period, the involvement of the community of users and practices will continuously be nurtured. So far, in terms of the number of participants, we only focus on ***small-scale communities***.

Previously, we have conducted testing on this room (Gjøsæter and Radianti 2018), which will be used as one of the cases how can one use this room for research activity and technology testing. The next Sect. 11.4 provides examples of research experiments and results. The description will include the living-lab framework without mention explicitly which one of the element categories, as these elements are summarized in Table 11.1, at the end of Sect. 11.4. In addition, there are elements that are valid for all cases and, therefore, no point to be repeated. In the discussion part, weaknesses and opportunities are evaluated, including living-lab components that relevant and not relevant.

11.4 Use Cases and Results

Three cases of research experiments conducted in the C2C living-lab are selected as a proof of concept on the usefulness of this C2C, and that it possesses the living-lab properties. *First*, Usability and Accessibility Tests of the C2C *(Case A)*; *Second*, Live X monitoring of emergency management exercise *(Case B)*; and *Third*, Testing virtual training tools (*Case C*).

Table 11.1 Summary of the cases with the living-lab approach

Living-lab environment	Case A	Case B	Case C
Technical infrastructure	Infrastructure with basic monitoring and technical testing	Infrastructure with extensive monitoring and in-depth technical testing	A combination of a software prototype running on personal laptops and the usage of monitoring systems at experimental C2C
Ecosystem: Benefit for users	The opportunity for testing the venue and training venue	Understanding the barriers for evaluating situational awareness and common operational pictures	Opportunity to test a training tool for decision-making
Level of openness	Open invitation	Open, in terms of incorporating new stakeholder partners for C2C lab, but not everyone can access this specific experiment	Open invitation
Community	Emergency management stakeholders, students	Emergency management stakeholders	Emergency management stakeholders, students
Real-world context	Yes, built a lab that mimics the real world C2C	Yes, design a way to evaluate situational awareness and common operational picture	Yes, build a software prototype that mimics the decision-making process in C2C and field
Life-span	Long term (no time boundary)	Short term (6 months)	Medium term (2 years)
Scale	Small groups	Small groups	Small groups
Living-lab approach			
Evaluation	Yes, usability and accessibility evaluation	Yes, real-time, SMS-based questionnaire to evaluate situational awareness of multiple stakeholders	Yes, SEGUE testing to detect barriers
Context research	Connection with the researcher	Connection with the researcher	Connection with the researcher
Co-creation	Yes	Yes	Yes
User role	Co-creator; Tester	Contributor, informant, tester	Tester, contributor

11.4.1 Case A: Usability and Accessibility Tests of the C2C

Living-lab environment: In this *Case A*, we tested the complete set of the technical infrastructure of the lab, as described earlier, for the first time. As the focus of this lab is not only to make this space a "physical space" but also to include as many as possible the living-lab components, the testing of the usability and accessibility of the room will be crucial. Thus, the technologies were tested as they are. The testing aimed at investigating whether there were barriers and accessibility issues when using the room, with the focus on mastering the usage of the control panel equipment that will control information distribution on the wall screens and PC input and output controls on the table.

Living-lab approach: The evaluation of *Case A* was achieved through a usability testing method, designed as an experiment. Usability testing is one of the living-lab approaches, which is defined as a technique involving users who interact systematically with a product or system under controlled conditions, to perform a goal-oriented task in an applied scenario (Wichansky 2000). A couple of testers were invited to the C2C, as seen in Fig. 11.4. A combination of open questionnaires and focus group discussions were employed.

The experiment consisted of two main activities: *First*, how to understand the use and change the PCs controlled by the operator desk. *Second*, how the users master the usage of the functionality for presenting multiple information on the wall screens. A script was carefully developed and tested in advance, ensuring the clarity and understandability of the prepared script by walking-through all assigned tasks have corresponded with the features and functionalities of the room. After the experiments, the testers shared their experiences using this flexible C2C, especially when taking control of various PCs, displaying and moving different information to the multiple wall displays. The discussions touched upon several topics such as

Fig. 11.4 Accessibility and usability testing

information overload, the complexity of the user interface, the most challenging task, the easiest task.

Note that the complete overview of the experiment was documented by Gjøsæter and Radianti (2018). In this paper, we emphasize the living-lab application approach to the usability problem and the incorporation of the living-lab elements into the experiment.

The results: The experiment demonstrates several results. First, on the usability testing, where some usability problems were detected. For instance, the confusion regarding sources, screens, and PCs due to flexible control. Second, on the methodology, which was quite promising and is repeatable by adapting it for other similar research contexts, especially for technology testing. Third, on feedback, where the testers suggested better ways of organizing names of the information sources (from the PCs and matrix technologies) and the use of a logical naming convention. Another revealed issue has to do with an ergonomic given the testers had to bend the neck backward to look up at the top wall screens when sitting at the operator desk. The feedback serves as the future C2C improvement. It thus represents another co-creation process at the testing stage by removing the barriers, such as having a better logical naming of information sources.

11.4.2 Case B: Live-X Monitoring of Emergency Management Exercise

Living-lab Environment: Live-X monitoring was an experiment conducted together in collaboration with the regional stakeholders (Fig. 11.5). It was a real exercise concerning the scenario of a wildfire that occurred in two municipalities in the south of Norway (Steen-Tveit et al. 2020). The C2C research team participated in this exercise

Fig. 11.5 Life X monitoring

in connection to the ongoing nationally funded research project, INSITU. The project will explore the process of sharing incidents and threat information for common situational understanding, incorporating sub-topics such as harmonization of crisis terminologies, map symbols, and learning from incidents (Munkvold et al. 2019a, b).

The aim to include the C2C was to strengthen its role as an experimental venue, besides to contribute to INSITU. The C2C team aimed at obtaining a systematic overview of the establishment of the common operational picture (COP). The COP refers to a checklist of the characteristics in a particular situation within a geographical area. It is also described as a display of relevant operational information, such as positions, infrastructure, and different resources (Karagiannis and Synolakis 2016). However, Wolbers and Boersma (2013) point out differences in defining the COP in the literature, which often understood as shared geographical locations combined with a checklist that describes the characteristics of the emergency response operation.

The arrangement of the research experiment in the C2C was as follows: a mock-up of an emergency management sharing tool deployed in the C2C. The tool is the same system used in emergency management systems in the majority of municipalities in Norway. It has features such as log system, sending SMS, updating status, assigning tasks, and monitoring the progress. The tool also equips with a new experimental map sharing system and emergency management symbols. The deployed/tested tool in C2C was connected to key stakeholders who participated in the Live-X. They supposedly would use it to log and monitor incoming information, to share map location and other information expected to be handed out via this platform. The stakeholders had been informed beforehand of the electronic address and the expected information to share through the experimental C2C, which could encompass documents, messages, event logs, screenshots of map locations, pictures, shared locations, or symbols on different resources location or event put on the digital map—whenever it was relevant.

In the exercise, each stakeholder's participant (e.g., police, hospital, fire service, municipality—10 organizations in total) had each organization's specific goals. For the INSITU team, the primary purpose was to observe and analyze whether the discrepancies occurred among multiple agencies concerning the understanding of the shared map, text information, or audio information. The goal was to investigate further if these discrepancies lead to various situation understanding and response delays.

The Living-lab approach: The research team in the experimental C2C engaged emergency management practitioners, monitored the abovementioned list of data, follow the exercise through media, which regularly reported the events from time to time. Besides, we had a researcher in one of the crisis operation centers, and two persons in the Live-X field location, especially in a crisis management meeting at the affected municipality. However, their participation in the field was more like a non-obtrusive observation. However, by mobilizing the research team into several locations, we could coordinate, especially on the time when to send the SMS survey.

In the experimental C2C, the crisis manager sometimes improvised by conducting a real-time interview with media and national agency that was responsible for the exercise, to obtain more information. The INSITU team also sent twice the real-time SMS questionnaires to all involved key emergency service stakeholders both in the field and in the command and control centers (police, health, and fire service). The result of the SMS data collection was documented by Steen-Tveit et al. (2020). At the end of the exercise, a quick debriefing was conducted for evaluating the overall exercise impression. This quick evaluation was done together between researchers and the crisis stakeholder that participated in full time at the lab.

The Results: A set of data from twice a real-time SMS-based questionnaire was successfully collected. However, the information sharing process through the tested digital platform did not fully happen as expected, especially the information sharing through the digital map, or active sending of map screenshots, and the use of symbols. The C2C research team received some documents from the county's crisis manager. However, it was not at all about real-time information on events that happened during the exercise from time to time. The post-Live-X research was implemented for compensating the missing information and validation concerning the development of situational awareness and the common operational picture.

11.4.3 Case C: Testing Virtual Training Tools

Living-lab Environment: The testing of the virtual training tool was a part of a research activity called KriseSIM (Fig. 11.6). The KriseSIM project goals were threefold. *First*, to develop a realistic control room as a venue for experimentation and training in the crisis management area. Second, to collect user requirements and validate the concept of the experimental control room for crisis management training. *Third*, to develop an interactive virtual training tool and support time-critical decision-making in the control room, considering various information. In *Case C*, we talk about the experiment with a co-created VTT tool, which involved the crisis management stakeholders in the requirement gathering and development. The existing C2C lab infrastructure was used together with the developed VTT prototype. The technicalities and the detailed description of the tested technology are reported in the following work (Radianti et al. 2017; Radianti et al. 2017; Skogen and Radianti 2018).

Fig. 11.6 Testing of virtual training tool

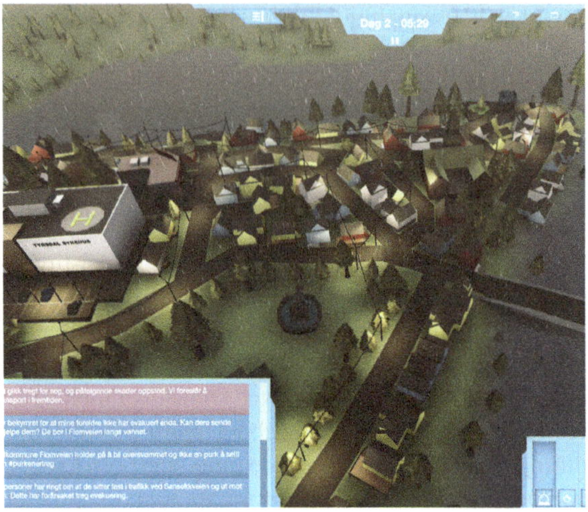

Fig. 11.7 Low fidelity tool with extreme weather scenario

Living-lab approach: In this *Case C*, the method again was testing the developed VTT, which was designed as a serious game, and evaluating the user performance, user awareness, and usability of the tool. Were developed two prototypes, that is, a low fidelity with extreme weather scenario (simpler graphical user interface) and a high fidelity tool (advanced graphical user interface) with a fire scenario.

There were two experiments for these two prototypes were tested. *First experiment:* to test the *first version* of low fidelity tool (See Fig. 11.7) that emphasized the evaluation of the testers' impressions on the look and feel of the developed user interface, and identified potential barriers when interacting with the developed product. The experiment adopted the simplified version of the SeGUE method (Serious Game Usability Evaluator) method (Moreno-Ger et al. 2012). SeGUE's framework suggests two dimensions as the basis for evaluation: the system dimension and the user dimension.

The system dimension covers the functionality, layout, game-flow, content, technical error, and other events that have no categories or are not applicable. The user dimension entails learning, reflecting, satisfied/excited, mildly frustrated, frustrated, confused, annoyed, unable to continue, non-applicable, commenting, and other perceptions not covered by the above-mentioned categories. A questionnaire was used, consisting of evaluation points above, after the playing session. In this experiment, the testers were eight students with multimedia master education, which would have adequate knowledge and skills to evaluate the barriers.

The second experiment, to test the *first complete version* of the low fidelity tool (See Fig. 11.7) and the *first version of the high fidelity tool* (See Fig. 11.8). In the second testing, we also employed game-play of the prototypes and was followed by a questionnaire and discussions. This time the real first responders were a subject of the testing. Overall, the co-design approach for the requirement gathering and testing is documented in a couple of papers (Radianti et al. 2018a, 2018b).

Fig. 11.8 High fidelity tool with fire in the city scenario

The Results: the living-lab infrastructure has been used in combination with a newly co-created technology, and adopted as an approach during the co-design process that contributes to the iterative development of the training tool. The data and discussions of these two experiments conducted during the development phase of the VTT tool were used to feed the next step of the VTT development. For example, the SEGUE method has helped revealing barriers when it comes to the user interface interaction, which has been improved in the prototype version. Tailoring the lab venue and newly created tool to be used by testers, is another lessons learned on the applicability of the C2C as a living-lab.

11.4.4 Summary of the Cases Examples

Recall that the purpose of presenting all these three cases is to understand whether or not the living-lab properties are maintained when conducting innovations in the emergency management research area. The results above demonstrate some details in what way the living-lab elements have been embraced in the technology testing in the experimental C2C. Table 11.1 summarizes features of living-lab that have been used in the three above-mentioned cases.

11.5 Lessons Learned and Future Usage Scenarios

11.5.1 Lessons Learned

The example of the cases shows that this experimental C2C has been a promising and exciting way of conducting research, especially in terms of the possibility of being in a real-life setting. However, after using the lab for design and testing cases, there are several lessons learned derived from using this C2C living-lab:

- Nurturing a relationship with various target users, stakeholders, and practitioners for a longer time is necessary. In our experience, i.e., working with the emergency management domain, the stakeholders are sometimes busy with the actual crisis response. Therefore, the time they are willing to spend with researchers is very valuable. Therefore, planning of each research step is highly recommended, including planning in which stage of research and innovation they need to involve.
- Privacy concerns should be appropriately addressed in all innovations and research in a living-lab. Although openness is one of the key-concept of living-lab, it is not at all about privacy openness. When conducting an experiment, it is essential that the users know how their data will be used. Anonymity should be granted. In this way, the subjects will feel "safe" during the experiments.
- When working together with users, it is crucial to manage their expectations. For example, will the research results in a product? Will this product error-free, ready for a market already, or just a proof-of-concept?
- The technology infrastructure can support the research, but sometimes it needs to be updated, to catch-up with the latest development. In this case, the living-lab environment should consider the time frame when the technology will obsolete, and how to anticipate it.

11.5.2 Future Scenarios

Between 2018 and 2022, several granted research projects have been developed and tailored with the use of this experimental C2C, with a living-lab as a spirit. These projects are INSITU (Sharing incident and threat information for common situational understanding), AUREAS (Augmented Reality Support for Decision Making in Crisis Management), and RISE-SMA (Social Media Analytics for Society and Crisis Communication). It shows that the applicability and relevance of the lab for testing new technology and cooperation with the end-users, practitioners, academia, and research entities.

The ongoing INSITU project (Case A) will further test the tool for information sharing, technologies for supporting harmonization of crisis terminologies, crisis maps and symbols, and learning from incident evaluation, in the lab together with practitioners. The co-design process for all project outputs has been done through the requirement gathering together with the Norwegian stakeholders, were followed up by further development of the tools and technologies, and possibly to apply them in the exercise context with practitioners.

The AUREAS project is about the use of Augmented Reality for crisis decision-making focuses on the potential of AR for enhancing the integration of social media data into decision-making processes. The developed prototype will be evaluated with emergency management professionals at the experimental C2C.

The RISE SMA Project focuses on crisis communication and the societal impact of social media. This includes the communication activities unfolding among ordinary citizens and communicating crucial information to them in a timely and coordinated manner during a crisis. Social media have been highlighted for enabling new forms of citizen engagement that strengthen civic participation at local and national levels. Hence, there is an urgent need for comprehensive concepts as well as methods, platforms, and applications. RISE SMA will provide practical recommendations, and technical solutions need with respect to social media for crisis communication. In this case, the C2C will also be used for testing prototypes developed in this project together with practitioners.

In short, in the near future, there are several technologies developed or tested tailored with the experimental C2C such as desktop-based Virtual environment, VR (Virtual reality) Head Mounted Device, Augmented Reality technology, as well as maps and GIS technologies in general as well as a map for information sharing connected to the abovementioned projects. In addition, there will be new scenarios and settings that can be developed further, such as wildfire scenarios, extreme weather, cybersecurity, remote support, digital volunteer, and any other scenarios that could be relevant for making the living-lab continuously alive.

11.5.3 Impact C2C Research on Societal Security Issues

In societal security and emergency management settings, C2C has also served as a mean to facilitate the communication between citizens and crisis responders, for example, to receive emergency notifications. Even in some cases, the communication processes are mediated through social media monitoring, although in the Norwegian case, this is not yet fully absorbed as standard practices. However, social media has been discussed extensively as a part of alternatives to achieve the common operational picture in the C2C context such as in Australia (Ehnis and Bunker 2020), in the USA (Lovari and Bowen 2020), or Europe (Gizikis et al. 2017).

Social media adoption in the C2C setting is just one of the examples of how the living-lab approach, in combination with experimental C2C, can give impact to improve societal security. The combination of the C2C and living-lab approach expands the possibilities to conduct experiments with various stakeholders and communities on technology innovations and technology adoption to reduce disaster impacts on society. Different groups in society can take advantage of being involved in the co-creation process, in different innovation stages. However, to make the living-lab influence society, decision-makers and influential stakeholders should participate in supporting and promoting the co-creation process initiated under the living-lab umbrella to reach out to the relevant communities. These stakeholders can serve as agents to build and nurture trust with different communities as a key enabler for the co-design process.

11.6 Conclusion

This paper has shown the design and approach of the living-lab related to the experimental control room. The LivingLab is a planned infrastructure that will provide an experimental platform for future crisis management. The illustration of how such experimental command and control room design with some advanced technologies can be treated as a living-lab, and support the research co-creation together with the crisis management stakeholders in different settings. Developing such kind of venue is already an innovation in itself as there are very limited living-lab has been dedicated for this co-creation purpose. Although the purpose of the lab is very specialized, i.e., crisis management, in fact, there are many other application areas other than crisis management that can also make use of this room, such as cybersecurity and safety issues. The use case scenarios can be expanded into a broader area of application such as monitoring of crowd in a specific event, surveillance, social media, humanitarian crisis. In addition, this lab is open for innovation in terms of methods that can be relevant for human-centered design, human–computer interaction, usability and user testing, performance and workload analysis, as well as situational awareness and common operational pictures.

The limitations of this study are (1) The living-lab approach is that the lab should have a strong connection with users and practitioners as enablers for the co-creation process. Therefore, it is important for the living-lab to nurture a long-term relationship with the users beyond the project. (2) The C2C lab experience is still limited to a relatively small community of practices. It is important to be able to connect with broader target audiences, which is quite challenging. (3) Most cases discussed in this paper treated C2C as a physical room, but it is technically possible to design research activities with the C2C as a core, but cover broader geographical areas.

References

Alavi HS, Lalanne D, Rogers Y (2020) The five strands of living lab: a literature study of the evolution of living lab concepts in HCI. ACM Trans Comput Human Interact (TOCHI) 27(2):1–26

Albina AR (2019) Assessing the impact of a GIS for improving novice crisis decision-making

Almirall E, Lee M, Wareham J (2012) Mapping living labs in the landscape of innovation methodologies. Technol Innov Manage Rev 2(9)

Azuma R, Baillot Y, Behringer R, Feiner S, Julier S, MacIntyre B (2001) Recent advances in augmented reality. IEEE Comput Graphics Appl 21(6):34–47

Bergvall-Kareborn B, Hoist M, Stahlbrost A (2009) Concept design with a living lab approach. Paper presented at the 2009 42nd Hawaii International Conference on System Sciences

Boersma K (2013) Liminal surveillance: an ethnographic control room study during A local event. Surveill Soc 11(1/2):106

Boring R, Lew R, Ulrich T, Joe J (2014). Light water reactor sustainability program operator performance metrics for control room modernization: a practical guide for early design evaluation: Idaho National Lab.(INL), Idaho Falls, ID (United States)

Brehmer B (2010) Command and control as design. 15th ICCRTS

Chan E, Anslow C, Seyed T, Maurer F (2016) Envisioning the emergency operations centre of the future. In: Collaboration meets interactive spaces. Springer, pp 349–372
Corker KM, Cramer NL, Henry EH (1990). Methodology for evaluation of automation impacts on tactical command and control (C2) systems: Implementation. BBN Systems And Technologies Corp, Cambridge MA
Crowley C (2017) Future SOC: SANS 2017 Security operations center survey. SANS Institute InfoSec Reading Room
Dell'Era C, Landoni P (2014) Living lab: a methodology between user-centred design and participatory design. Creativity Innov Manage 23(2):137–154
dos Santos IJAL, Farias MS, Ferraz FT, Haddad AN, Hecksher S (2013) Human factors applied to alarm panel modernization of nuclear control room. J Loss Prev Process Ind 26(6):1308–1320
Drøivoldsmo A (2003) New tools and technology for the study of human performance in simulator experiments. (PhD), NTNU, Trondheim
Ehnis C, Bunker D (2020) Repertoires of collaboration: incorporation of social media help requests into the common operating picture. Behav Inf Technol 39(3):343–359. https://doi.org/10.1080/0144929X.2019.1621934
Eldardiry OM, Caldwell BS (2015). Improving information and task coordination in cyber security operation centers. Paper presented at the IIE Annual Conference. Proceedings
Feurstein K, Hesmer A, Hribernik KA. Thoben K, Schumacher J (2008). Living labs: a new development strategy. In: European Living Labs-a new approach for human centric regional innovation, 1–14
Følstad A (2008) Living labs for innovation and development of information and communication technology: a literature review
Gatto LBS, Mól ACA, dos Santos IJL, Jorge CAF, Legey AP (2013) Virtual simulation of a nuclear power plant's control room as a tool for ergonomic evaluation. Prog Nucl Energy 64:8–15
Giri J, Parashar M, Trehern J, Madani V (2012) The situation room: control center analytics for enhanced situational awareness. IEEE Power Energ Mag 10(5):24–39
Gizikis A, O'Brien T, Susaeta IG, Habdank M, Schubert A, Reuter C, Delprato UD (2017) Emergency management in social media generation
Gjøsæter T, Radianti J (2018) Evaluating accessibility and usability of an experimental situational awareness room. Paper presented at the International conference on applied human factors and ergonomics
Govindaraj S, Chintamani K, Gancet J, Letier P, van Lierde B, Nevatia Y, Bedkowski J (2013) The icarus project-command, control and intelligence (c2i). Paper presented at the 2013 IEEE international symposium on safety, security, and rescue robotics (SSRR)
Hansen BJ, Mevassvik OM, Bråthen K (2003) A demonstrator for command and control information systems technology experimentation. Paper presented at the 8th International command and control research and technology symposium
Hempel L, Töpfer E (2004) CCTV in Europe. Final report, 15
Hildebrandt M, Fernandes A (2016). Micro task evaluation of analog vs. digital power plant control room interfaces. Paper presented at the proceedings of the human factors and ergonomics society annual meeting
Hollnagel E, Woods DD (2005) Joint cognitive systems: Foundations of cognitive systems engineering. CRC press
Ikuma LH, Harvey C, Taylor CF, Handal C (2014a) A guide for assessing control room operator performance using speed and accuracy, perceived workload, situation awareness, and eye tracking. J Loss Prev Process Ind 32:454–465
Ikuma LH, Koffskey C, Harvey CM (2014b) A human factors-based assessment framework for evaluating performance in control room interface design. IIE Trans Occup Ergon Hum Factors 2(3–4):194–206
Jensen J, Thompson S (2016) The incident command system: a literature review. Disasters 40(1):158–182

Kahne S (1983) Control migration: a characteristic of C3 systems. IEEE Control Syst Mag 3(1):15–19
Karagiannis GM, Synolakis CE (2016) Collaborative incident planning and the common operational picture. In: Paper presented at the international conference on dynamics of disasters
Kataria A, Holder E, Praetorius G, Baldauf M, Schröder-Hinrichs J-U (2015) Exploring bridge-engine control room collaborative team communication
Kim SK, Suh SM, Jang GS, Hong SK, Park JC (2012) Empirical research on an ecological interface design for improving situation awareness of operators in an advanced control room. Nucl Eng Des 253:226–237
Koskinen H, Norros L (2010) Expanding control room–a new frame for designing spatial affordances of control places: VTT
Kovesdi C, Spielman Z, LeBlanc K, Rice B (2018) Application of eye tracking for measurement and evaluation in human factors studies in control room modernization. Nucl Technol 202(2–3):220–229
Lin CJ, Hsieh T-L, Lin S-F (2013) Development of staffing evaluation principle for advanced main control room and the effect on situation awareness and mental workload. Nucl Eng Des 265:137–144
Louka MN (2015) Using virtual mock-ups and automated assistance to support human factors engineering design evaluation activities for control room layouts
Lovari A, Bowen SA (2020) Social media in disaster communication: a case study of strategies, barriers, and ethical implications. J Publ Aff 20(1):e1967. https://doi.org/10.1002/pa.1967
Mastelic J, Sahakian M, Bonazzi R (2015) How to keep a living lab alive? Info DaF 17(4):12–25
Mora S, Divitini M (2014) Supporting debriefing with sensor data: a reflective approach to crisis training. Paper presented at the international conference on information systems for crisis response and management in mediterranean countries
Moreno-Ger P, Torrente J, Hsieh YG, Lester WT (2012) Usability testing for serious games: making informed design decisions with user data. Adv Hum Comput Interact
Muhanna MA (2015) Virtual reality and the CAVE: taxonomy, interaction challenges and research directions. J King Saud Univ Comput Inf Sci 27(3):344–361
Munkvold BE,Opach T, Pilemalm S, Radianti J, Rød JK, Snaprud M (2019a) Sharing information for common situational understanding in emergency response
Munkvold BE, Radianti J, Rød JK, Opach T, Snaprud M, Pilemalm S, Bunker D (2019b). Sharing incident and threat information for common situational understanding
Pierson J, Lievens B (2005) Configuring living labs for a 'thick'understanding of innovation. Paper presented at the ethnographic praxis in industry conference proceedings
Prouzeau A (2016) Collaboration around wall-displays in command and control contexts
Radianti J, Granmo OC (2015) CIEM emergency management living-lab: concepts and design for research, innovation and knowledge exchange. In: Proc Natl Symp Tech Methodol Secur Crisis Manage (TAMSEC 2015)
Radianti J, Martinez SG, Munkvold BE, Konnestad M (2018a) Co-design of a virtual training tool with emergency management stakeholders for extreme weather response. Paper presented at the international conference of design, user experience, and usability
Radianti J, Martinez SG, Munkvold BE, Konnestad M (2018b) Co-designing a virtual training tool for emergency management. Paper presented at the ISCRAM
Radianti J, Tronslien MN, Moland ME, Kulmus CA, Thomassen KK (2017) A crisis management serious game for responding extreme weather event. Paper presented at the international conference on information systems for crisis response and management in mediterranean countries
Radianti J, Tronslien MN, Thomassen KK, Moland MEO, Kulmus CA (2017b) Serious game design for flooding triggered by extreme weather. Int J Inf Syst Crisis Response Manage (IJISCRAM) 9(3):55–75

Roberts A, Stanton NA, Fay D (2017) The command team experimental test-bed phase two: assessing cognitive load and situation awareness in a submarine control room. In: Advances in human aspects of transportation. Springer, pp 427–437
Russell S, Abdelzaher T (2018) The internet of battlefield things: the next generation of command, control, communications and intelligence (C3I) Decision-making. Paper presented at the MILCOM 2018–2018 IEEE military communications conference (MILCOM)
Ryan M (2013) Planning in the emergency operations center. Technol Forecast Soc Chang 80(9):1725–1731
Savioja P (2014) Evaluating systems usability in complex work-development of a systemic usability concept to benefit control room design. Aalto University
Skogen SE, Radianti J (2018) Architecture of high fidelity simulation tool for crisis management training. Paper presented at the 2018 5th international conference on information and communication technologies for disaster management (ICT-DM)
Skourup C, Reigstad M (2002) Operators in process industry: interaction with wearable computers. Cogn Technol Work 4(4):245–255
Starke SD, Baber C, Cooke NJ, Howes A (2017) Workflows and individual differences during visually guided routine tasks in a road traffic management control room. Appl Ergon 61:79–89
Steen-Tveit K, Radianti J, Munkvold BE (2020) SMS-based real-time data collection for evaluation of situational awareness and common operational picture: lessons learned from a field exercise, Paper presented at the The 17th international conference on information systems for crisis response and management, Virginia Tech in Blacksburg, Virginia (USA)
Tang T, Hämäläinen M (2012) Living lab methods and tools for fostering everyday life innovation. Paper presented at the 2012 18th international ICE conference on engineering, technology and innovation
van der Haar S, Koeslag-Kreunen M, Euwe E, Segers M (2017) Team leader structuring for team effectiveness and team learning in command-and-control teams. Small Group Res 48(2):215–248
Veeckman C, Schuurman D, Leminen S, Westerlund M (2013) Linking living lab characteristics and their outcomes: towards a conceptual framework. Technol Innov Manage Rev *3*(12 december), 6–15
Waldenström C (2012) Using a low-fidelity wargame for training fleet-level command and control in the classroom. Paper presented at the proceedings of the 17th international command and control research and technology symposium
Walsh KR, Pawlowski SD (2002) Virtual reality: a technology in need of IS research. Commun Assoc Inf Syst 8(1):20
Wichansky AM (2000) Usability testing in 2000 and beyond. Ergonomics 43(7):998–1006
Wolbers J, Boersma K (2013) The common operational picture as collective sensemaking. J Contingencies Crisis Manag 21(4):186–199

Chapter 12
Real-Time Mapping System of Shelter Conditions for Safe Evacuation

Makoto Kitsuya and Jun Sasaki

Abstract This chapter introduces a newly developed real-time mapping system for shelter conditions. Local governments in Japan maintain data useful for an evacuation, such as the location of shelters, a list of open shelters, and the shelter capacity. Such data are available on several websites for local residents; however, they are not integrated and are difficult to use during an emergency. We believe that it will be helpful for the purpose of a mass evacuation to integrate and provide such data in a map form on the smartphones of local residents. In this chapter, we describe the concept and design of a real-time mapping system of the shelter conditions. Further, we present a case study of the prototype system for Kamaishi City in Iwate Prefecture, Japan. We conclude that the system will be helpful for local residents to accurately understand the state of the evacuation shelters and reduce the risks of a natural disaster.

Keywords Mapping system · Evacuation support · Shelter condition · Information system

12.1 Introduction

In recent years, various natural disasters have occurred throughout the world. In the case of flood and tsunami disasters caused by typhoons, heavy rains, and earthquakes, residents in disaster-affected areas have some time to evacuate to a shelter after an evacuation alert is received from a governmental office.

A delay in evacuation may result in a significant number of casualties. Weathernews Inc. reported the relationship between evacuation delay and human risk during the 2011 Great East Japan Earthquake and following tsunami disaster (Weathernews Inc 2011). The report shows the evacuation start time of both (a) the survivors and (b) the dead and missing residents after an earthquake. There is a significant difference between (a) and (b): 71% of the survivors evacuated within 120 min; by contrast,

M. Kitsuya (✉) · J. Sasaki
Iwate Prefectural University, Iwate, Japan
e-mail: g231s008@s.iwate-pu.ac.jp

M. Sakurai and R. Shaw (eds.), *Emerging Technologies for Disaster Resilience*, Disaster Risk Reduction,
https://doi.org/10.1007/978-981-16-0360-0_12

for the deceased (confirmed dead or missing), only 22% evacuated within the same time. Therefore, an early evacuation is extremely important for decreasing the risk to human life.

The report also indicated that the people who arrived at the emergency shelters decreased their risk of becoming a casualty. Three-quarters of the survivors evacuated to the emergency shelters; however, in the case of the dead and missing, only one-quarter made it to a shelter. During such an emergency, more people may be saved by providing information on the location of the available shelters and the evacuation conditions of the neighborhood.

Another problem is a change in the destination shelter after an evacuation starts. Such a problem occurred when typhoon Hagibis hit Japan on October 12, 2019. The Meteorological Agency issued an evacuation advisory because a huge rainfall and river flooding had been forecasted. At the time, some shelters in Kanagawa (NHK NEWS WEB 2019a) and Fukushima prefecture (NHK NEWS WEB 2019b) exceeded their capacity and refused to accept additional evacuees. The rejected evacuees were forced to move to another acceptable shelter despite the dangerous conditions. To avoid such a problem, evacuees should know where the optimal shelters with sufficient space are located before starting their evacuation.

12.2 Related Studies

Owing to technical improvements and the popularization of mobile devices and information communication systems, people can now receive up-to-date information easily and quickly from related websites. Once a disaster occurs, an evacuee can access the disaster information published on the websites to decrease the risk of injury.

Many studies have shown that the integration of a geographic information system is effective for a disaster risk reduction. Nakajima et al. (2007) built an evacuation guide system based on GPS-capable cellphones, which provides evacuation route guidance on maps for massive evacuations. Rahman et al. (2012) proposed a location-based early disaster warning and evacuation system using OpenStreetMap (OSM) (OpenStreetMap 2010). They used OSM, a free and rapidly growing open-source map of the world, to share disaster data, such as the type of disaster, the probable disaster-affected area, and the shortest path to a shelter. In addition, Ahn and Han (2011) developed an indoor mobile augmented-reality evacuation system that presents the most optimal and uncrowded exit path even within large-scale buildings with complex paths. The users can check the exit path on a smartphone intuitively, and thus quickly and safely evacuate. Itoi et al. (2017) proposed an offline mobile application for automatic evacuation guidance in an outdoor environment. They developed an automatic evacuation guidance scheme to estimate the state of the evacuees and applied it to the application, which presents a suitable evacuation path. A longitude- and latitude-based travel route recommendation and disaster management system developed by Soman and Divya (2019) is used for two purposes: tourism and disaster reduction. A user can receive travel route recommendations, check into a tourism location on the system, and receive evacuation alerts if any hazards have occurred within the area.

However, the above studies did not mention the sharing of shelter conditions or the evacuation conditions during a natural disaster. In addition, the Japanese government provides different disaster-related information depending on the local level. For example, the city government provides the addresses of the shelters, the prefectural government provides the current number of evacuees and the open/closed statuses of the shelters, and the national government provides early alerts about disasters and is required to declare an evacuation. However, such data are not integrated, and thus it is difficult for general evacuees to use the information during an actual evacuation.

We believe it would be helpful for a safe evacuation to integrate these data onto a smartphone map. With our proposed method, evacuees can check the available shelters and decide where to evacuate by themselves, and thus reach an optimal shelter quickly and safely. Based on this concept, we propose a real-time system for mapping the shelter conditions for a safe evacuation. In this chapter, we describe the concept and design of the newly developed real-time mapping system. Further, we present a case study of the prototype system for Kamaishi City in Iwate Prefecture, Japan. We conclude that the system will be helpful for local residents to have an accurate understanding of the state of the evacuation shelters and contribute to a reduction in disaster risk.

12.3 Proposed System: Concept and Structure

The structure of our proposed system is shown in Fig. 12.1. The system consists of four subsystems: (1) a web crawler, which fetches shelter data from the government website, (2) a database to store the shelter information, (3) a shelter map app for a mobile device, and (4) a web API that connects the above components. The detailed functions of the four subsystems are described in the following.

(1) Web crawler: Data on evacuation shelters are published on government websites. There are two types of data: stable and unstable. Some of these data, such as the name, location, address, and capacity of the shelters, are stable and rarely change, whereas the data on the current condition of the shelters, including the number of evacuees and the open/closed status, are unstable and frequently change. The web crawler fetches these two types of data at different

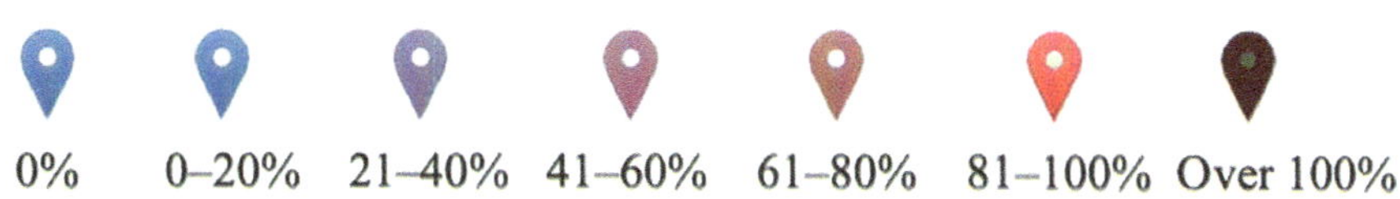

Fig. 12.1 Structure of the proposed system

intervals for each type: at 1-day intervals for stable data under typical conditions and at 1-min intervals for unstable data during an emergency. By fetching data based on this method, the system can provide information in real time.

(2) Database: The database stores evacuation shelter data, such as the name, location, capacity, and the number of evacuees from the web crawler through the web API. If the web API requests to receive data, the database responds.

(3) Shelter Maps App: Our system provides shelter information as a smartphone map. The map includes markers that are placed on the location of the shelters. If the user of our system clicks a marker, the tooltip extends the shelter information such as the name, open/closed status, address, and rate of occupancy. Furthermore, the color of the marker represents the current occupancy rate of the shelter, as shown in Fig. 12.2. When the color of the marker turns red, it indicates that the occupancy has increased. We believe it will be easy to understand for general evacuees. The map and markers will automatically update if the data in the database are affected, and thus users can check the shelter information in real time.

(4) Web API: The web API connects the three subsystems mentioned above. In the relationship among the web crawler, web API, and database, the web crawler fetches the updated data and posts the data to the web API. The database then stores the data posted from the web API. Regarding the relationship among the Shelter Maps App, the web API, and the database, the Shelter Maps App requests map-related resources from the web API, and the web API transfers the request to the database. The database then passes the requested data to the Shelter Maps App through the web API.

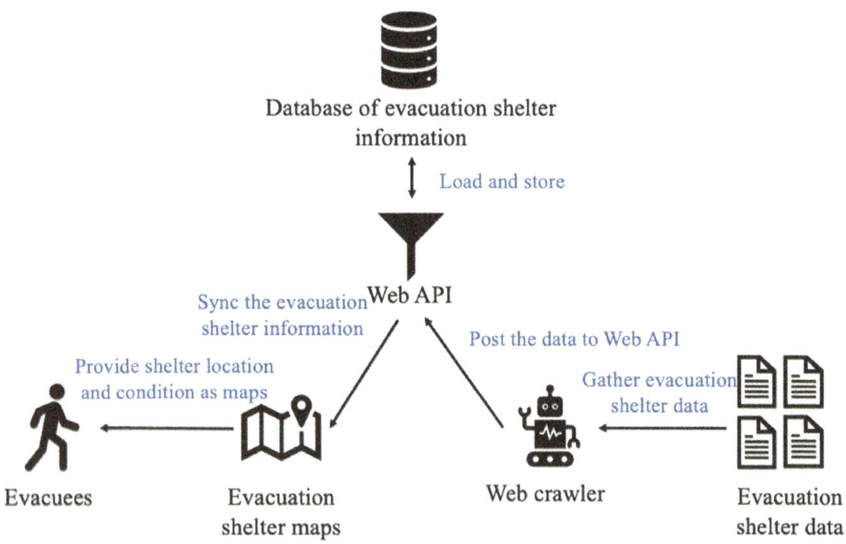

Fig. 12.2 Relationship between color of the marker and the occupancy rate

The proposed system, consisting of the subsystems described above, provides shelter conditions for evacuees in real time. In the next section, we describe the prototype system and its behavior based on a simulation using actual data from a regional disaster.

12.4 Case Study and Prototype System

In this section, we introduce a case study and implementation of the prototype system. For the case study and use of the prototype, we collected data from a past disaster, i.e., typhoon Hagibis in 2019.

12.4.1 Study Area

Kamaishi City, Iwate Prefecture, Japan, was selected as the case study area because the data required for this research were obtainable. Kamaishi is located in northeast Japan (shown in Fig. 12.3), faces the Pacific Ocean on the east, and has a population of 32,000 and a total area of 440 km^2. The city has been damaged by numerous tsunamis: during the Sanriku Earthquake in 1896, Sanriku Earthquake in 1933, and Great East Japan Earthquake in 2011, 4,985, 409, and 1,046 people died or went missing in the city, respectively. Moreover, other disasters such as floods caused by typhoons have occasionally occurred in the city.

Owing to these events, the city manages multiple disaster shelters and publishes its data on a website. We focused on typhoon Hagibis, which hit on October 12, 2019, and collected shelter-related data on the typhoon. The data used for the prototype system were obtained from the following websites:

1. Unstable data including the open/closed status and the current number of evacuees of the shelter are published on the Iwate Disaster Prevention Information Portal by Iwate Prefecture (2015) in HTML format.
2. Some stable data, including the shelter name, address, longitude/latitude, and types of disasters to be dealt with, are published on Designated Emergency Evacuation Site Data by the Geospatial Information Authority of Japan (2017) in CSV format.
3. Other stable data, including the capacity of the shelters, are published by Iwate Prefecture (2020) in PDF format.
4. In addition, data on welfare shelters, i.e., shelters for people who need extra help such as the elderly and disabled people, are published by Kamaishi city (2016) in HTML format.

We developed and used a web scraper to gather data written in Node.js and Nightmare.js (Segment 2010). As a result, we obtained shelter-related data for a total of

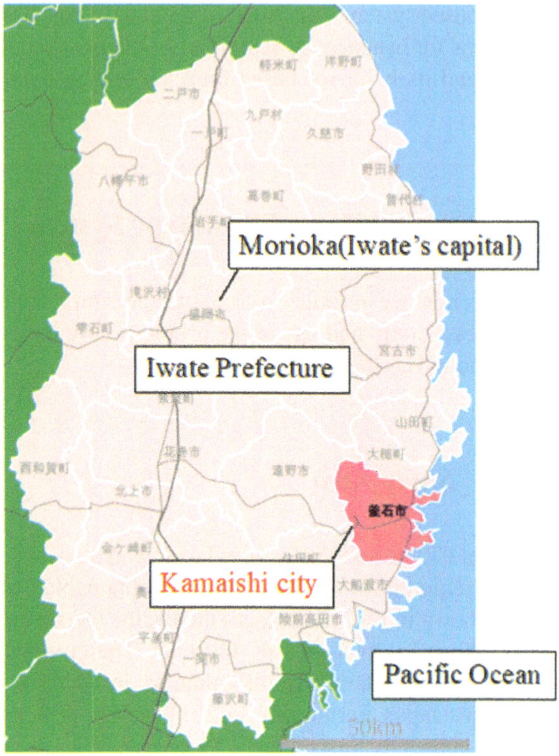

Fig. 12.3 Kamaishi city of Iwate Prefecture in Japan (Lincun 2006)

226 shelters from the start of the disaster on October 12, 2019, to the closing time of the last shelter on October 28, 2019.

12.4.2 Prototype System

We developed the prototype system proposed in Sect. 12.3 and used the collected data in the case study. We used the following programming languages and frameworks to develop the prototype:

1. For flexible software combining the web API and database, the Hasura GraphQL Engine (Hasura Inc 2017) was used.
2. For the Shelter Maps App, Vue.js (Evan You 2020), a reactive front-end framework, and Leaflet (Vladimir Agafonkin 2018), an open-source JavaScript library for mobile-friendly interactive maps, were applied.

We did not develop a web crawler to collect the shelter-related data in real time. In addition, to maintain confidentiality, the capacity of evacuees and the actual evacuee data from the welfare shelters could not be contained in the prototype system data.

Fig. 12.4 Marker indicating a welfare shelter

Instead, we simply set the green markers, shown in Fig. 12.4, to indicate welfare shelters on the map of the prototype system.

An example of a display image of the prototype Shelter Maps App is shown in Fig. 12.5. The positions of the markers show the shelter location based on the latitude and longitude information. The color of the markers presents the number of evacuees per shelter at a particular time. In the lower part of Fig. 12.6, the users can see that two shelters exceeded the capacity limit, allowing them to avoid going to these locations, and instead evacuating to one of the shelters presented by a blue marker.

When a user clicks a marker, the tooltip extends, as shown in Fig. 12.6. The tooltip contains information on the name, address, current number of evacuees, and capacity of the shelter. This function helps users check these current condition data and make a decision regarding where to evacuate.

We confirmed that both the desktop and mobile versions of the Shelter Maps App operate without any problems. However, the system is currently under development and has some missing functions. For example, the Shelter Maps App should show the user's current position and the optimal evacuation path to the safe shelter on the

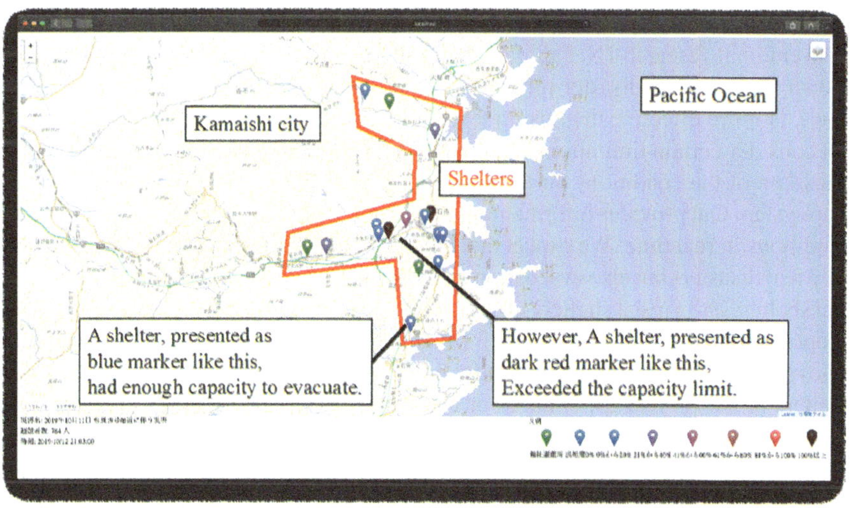

Fig. 12.5 Example of a display image of the prototype Shelter Maps App

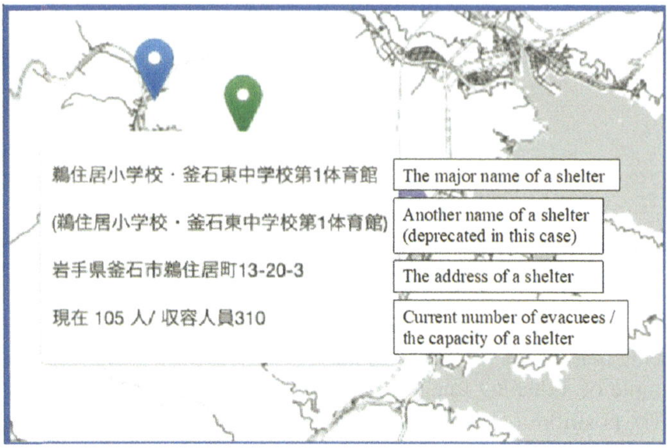

Fig. 12.6 Example of a tooltip

map. The web crawler is not yet used in the prototype system, and thus we should implement, test, and confirm that the system works well during an actual disaster.

We are planning to add these missing functions and update the prototype system. Further, we will introduce the Shelter Maps App to actual regional areas and verify whether the users can actually evacuate safely and quickly to the optimal shelter in the case of a disaster.

12.5 Discussion

Conventional research (Nakajima 2007; Rahman et al. 2012; Itoi et al. 2017) has shown that sharing disaster-related information through visual methods, such as maps, is more effective than using text-based methods. However, these studies did not consider certain limitations, such as the capacity of the shelters and the dynamic transition of the conditions during an actual disaster evacuation. We propose a new map system that provides information on the capacity of the shelters and the changing conditions in real time. We expect that our proposed system will be useful under not only real disasters but also evacuation drills because it can provide conditions on both real shelters and virtual shelters in a simulation. Further, the proposed method can be adopted in other areas that require information on the shelter conditions. For example, a government can create a new shelter construction or assignment plan for current shelters based on real experiences or disaster simulations. However, our proposed system is still in the development stage. To use our developed system effectively, there are two issues that should be resolved: (1) data reusability and (2) data format standardization.

(1) *Data Reusability*

It is necessary to transfer a large amount of data that are difficult to reuse, such as the location and capacity of the shelters, into digital information. Regarding the data that are difficult to reuse, there are some available examples, such as data on the capacity of the shelters, published as PDFs, and data on the open/closed status of the shelters expressed as HTML text. However, the HTML text is currently only surrounded by a <p> tag and has no semantics. In the case of the developed prototype, we parsed the HTML texts and found a designated regular expression, and converted the information into a PDF file manually to be used as data in a database because there is no way to correctly recognize text in a PDF. If the data that are difficult to reuse are converted beforehand into a general format such as CSV or JSON, or as published data on a standard web API, the data will be much easier to obtain using a web crawler.

(2) *Data Sharing and Data Format*

Currently, data sharing between government staff members in evacuation shelters and in government offices is typically conducted using a paper-based method. For example, in Morioka city, Iwate, Japan, the current population of a shelter is sent by Fax, using the format shown in Fig. 12.7. In this case, the city-level government (Morioka city office) receives the Fax and then transcribes it on a spreadsheet tool such as Excel. The spreadsheet is then sent to the prefecture-level government (Iwate Prefecture office) by Fax again. Thus, there is a large time lag when sharing the information, which does not occur in real time. To solve this problem, we believe that digitizing the format for government communication during an emergency will be an effective approach. As a tool for digitalization, web-based and cloud-based spreadsheet tools such as Google Sheet will be suitable in terms of usability and availability. We expect that such a digitized format will increase the speed of data sharing and increase the opportunities of evacuees to obtain the latest information as a result. We also plan to propose an optimal data input/output format using Google Sheet for government organizations in Japan.

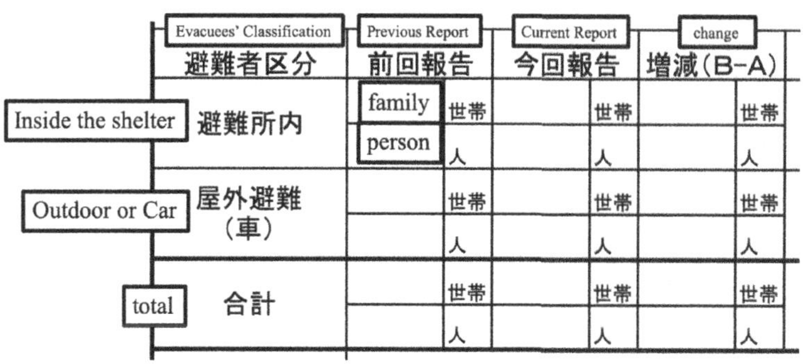

Fig. 12.7 Format used in Morioka city (2018)

12.6 Conclusion

In this study, we described the importance of early evacuation in the case of natural disasters in regional areas. To realize an early evacuation, the evacuees need to know the shelter conditions in real time. Because the shelter information is currently not integrated on government websites, people cannot determine the best shelter for evacuation. To solve this problem, we proposed a real-time mapping system of the shelter conditions for a safe evacuation to reduce disaster risk. We described the system development and presented a case study showing the behavior of the prototype system. Some future issues that remain in the development and testing phases are also described. In the future, by using our developed system, evacuees can easily find and check the information on the shelter conditions on a map, for example, the open/closed status and the number of evacuees per shelter. They can then determine the optimal shelter and evacuate quickly and safely during a regional disaster. When the development of the system is complete, we believe that the risk of a disaster will be reduced in regional areas.

Acknowledgements We would like to thank Editage (www.editage.com) for English language editing.

References

Ahn J, Han R (2011) Rescueme: an indoor mobile augmented-reality evacuation system by personalized pedometry. 2011 IEEE Asia-Pacific services computing conference. IEEE

Evan You (2020) Vue.js. https://vuejs.org

Geospatial Information Authority of Japan (2017) Designated Emergency Evacuation Site Data. https://hinan.gsi.go.jp/hinanjocjp/hinanbasho/koukaidate.html

Hasura Inc (2017) Hasura. https://hasura.io

Itoi J, Sasabe M, Kawahara J, Kasahara S (2017) An offline mobile application for automatic evacuation guiding in outdoor environments. Sci Phone Apps Mob Devices 3(1):1

Iwate Prefecture (2015) Iwate Disaster Prevention Information Portal (2015) https://iwate.secure.force.com/PUB_VF_HinanList

Iwate Prefecture (2020) Evacuation shelters and designated emergency evacuation sites data. https://www.pref.iwate.jp/kurashikankyou/anzenanshin/bosai/kokoroe/1004197.html

Kamaishi city (2016) Welfare shelters data. http://www.city.kamaishi.iwate.jp/kurasu/bosai_saigai/hinanbasho/detail/1190992_2227.html

Lincun (2006) Location Map of Kamaishi-shi Iwate-ken Japan. https://en.wikipedia.org/wiki/File:Kamaishi_city,_Iwate_prefecture_Japan.svg, licensed under CC BY-SA 3.0, modified. Accessed 9 Aug 2006

Morioka city (2018) Shelter Operation Manual: Form. http://www.city.morioka.iwate.jp/_res/projects/default_project/_page_/001/031/502/youshiki_tanki.pdf (in Japanese)

Nakajima Y et al (2007) Disaster evacuation guide: using a massively multiagent server and GPS mobile phones. 2007 International symposium on applications and the internet. IEEE

NHK NEWS WEB (2019b) Some evacuation shelters are full of evacuees and can't be accommodated in Hayama-cho, Kanagawa. https://www3.nhk.or.jp/news/html/20191012/k10012125301000.html. Accessed 12 Oct 2019

NHK NEWS WEB (2019b) 13 evacuation shelters are having trouble accepting people in Iwaki-shi, Fukushima. https://www3.nhk.or.jp/news/html/20191013/k10012127731000.html. Accessed 13 Oct 2019
OpenStreetMap (2010) http://openstreetmap.org
Rahman KM, Alam T, Chowdhury M (2012) Location based early disaster warning and evacuation system on mobile phones using OpenStreetMap. 2012 IEEE Conference on open systems. IEEE
Segment (2010) Nightmare. http://www.nightmarejs.org
Soman A, Divya SB (2019) Longitude and latitude based travel route recommendation and disaster management system. Int J Adv Res Ideas Innov Technol 5(3)
Vladimir Agafonkin (2018) Leaflet. https://leafletjs.com
Weathernews Inc. (2011) The Great East Japan Earthquake: Tsunami Survey (Survey Results). http://weathernews.com/ja/nc/press/2011/pdf/20110908_1.pdf. Accessed 8 Sep 2011

Chapter 13
Decision Support System and New Technologies

Yuichiro Usuda

Abstract This chapter highlights the application of emerging technologies to a decision support system. When a disaster occurs, many agencies and companies start to conduct disaster response for rescue, evacuation, relief supplies, shelter, and so on. For effective disaster response, it is very important to build common situational awareness of the disaster among various organizations. SIP4D (Shared Information Platform for Disaster Management), which we developed, is an interagency cooperative information-sharing system. This system was utilized at every disaster countermeasure headquarters (government and prefectures) in recent disasters in Japan and its effectiveness was well recognized. As a result, "ISUT: Information Support Team" was put into operation from 2019 lead by the Cabinet Office, and SIP4D will continue to be used as a basic distribution network of information for resilience to natural disasters. To expedite yet more effective and dynamic decision support in disaster response, we will pursue technological innovation by evolving SIP4D into CPS4D—Cyber-Physical System for Disaster Resilience—which blends real space and virtual space at an advanced level and leads disaster response through information. A future decision support system will require automatically analyzing disaster dynamics. We must actively continue applying technologies to actual disasters and improving the system by taking in various forms of evidence from the institutions and organizations that are actually engaged in disaster response.

Keywords ICT · GIS · Information sharing · Disaster management · Cyber-Physical system

13.1 Introduction

In light of the lessons learned from disasters such as the Great Hanshin Earthquake in 1995 and the Great East Japan Earthquake in 2011, Japan has continued its efforts in constructing the framework, system, and equipment to accelerate disaster response.

Y. Usuda (✉)
National Research Institute for Earth Science and Disaster Resilience, Tsukuba, Japan
e-mail: usuyu@bosai.go.jp

M. Sakurai and R. Shaw (eds.), *Emerging Technologies for Disaster Resilience*, Disaster Risk Reduction,
https://doi.org/10.1007/978-981-16-0360-0_13

Since the Great East Japan Earthquake in 2011, Japan has experienced several other serious disasters, including the Kumamoto earthquake in 2016 and the heavy rain disaster in northern Kyushu in 2017. The frequency of natural disasters has doubled in the last 30 years, and large-scale wide-area disasters such as a Nankai Trough earthquake or an earthquake directly below the Tokyo metropolitan area are foreseeable. Against this backdrop, a faster response in the event of disasters is strongly desired.

In response, we developed the Shared Information Platform for Disaster Management (SIP4D) to facilitate early situation assessment and quick response in the event of a disaster. This system collects and aggregates information on the state and extent of damage that each organization obtains continuously, processes it into useful on-site information, and then infers and adds information that would otherwise take a long time to obtain. The core disaster information integration technology synchronizes and converts various kinds of information and displays it all on a single map and infers information from insufficient information. Concurrently, we are developing a Cyber-Physical System for Disaster Resilience (CPS4D) as a decision support technology based on disaster dynamics analysis.

Information and communications technologies (ICT) required for sharing, distributing, and utilizing disaster information—such as cloud computing, social media, AI, and geospatial information system (GIS)—are at a mature stage. The important thing is an innovative design and empirical implementation of an information-sharing platform and decision support system for various disaster response organizations.

In this chapter, I introduce SIP4D/CPS4D as a case study to establish decision support systems and new technologies in the event of a disaster. Section 13.2 describes issues in disaster response. In Sect. 13.3, we discuss a common operational picture and system interoperability as solutions to these issues. Section 13.4 gives an overview of SIP4D and details of the disaster information integration technology that constitutes the core of SIP4D and describes challenges in social implementation of the system, with examples of its application in actual disasters. Section 13.5 provides an example of decision-making using SIP4D. Section 13.6 introduces the concept of CPS4D and examples of the latest technological developments as the future of decision-making. Section 13.7 concludes this chapter.

13.2 Issues in Disaster Response

In the event of a disaster, assistance activities must be carried out while the situation changes from hour to hour. In particular, as the damage caused by a disaster increases both in scale and in area, unexpected events will occur frequently, making it difficult to deal with the situation promptly and accurately. Actions for disaster response are implemented simultaneously by many agencies during the time of a disaster. Because of this, it is important to share information not only within but also across agencies, to establish a common understanding of the situation so that individual agencies can properly respond to the disaster based on that understanding.

However, for the early stages of a disaster, there is currently a shortage of information necessary for disaster response. In addition, because disaster information on roads and evacuation shelters—which is indispensable for prompt responses on site—is held individually by various ministries, local governments, private organizations, and other organizations, on-site responders are flooded with information in various types and formats. They must process it all into usable information, making it difficult for them to use in circumstances where time is of the essence.

One cause of the inadequate situation assessment was a shortage of information to be used in decision-making, due to the difficulty in collecting and aggregating information amid the confusion at the site and the shortage of personnel. Another factor was that various types of disaster information, including information from sensors and prediction simulations that were expected to be available to some extent immediately after the occurrence of a disaster, were present only in a piecemeal fashion. It was not available to be applied immediately and effectively to various types of disaster response.

Information-sharing systems based on the GIS are being developed, to enable disaster responders to quickly and accurately understand various situations in a disaster area. However, in the event of a large-scale disaster, the expected information may not be available, due to factors including disruption of local government, causing gaps in information and leading to a period when there is no information to share on the system during the emergency response period of 72 h, the most critical period for disaster mitigation. In addition, the information to be shared may be fragmented, or the timing of sharing and information formats may not be unified, making it difficult for disaster responders to make immediate use of the exact information that they need. Although technologies and systems to support disaster response are being developed, the overall system becomes dysfunctional due to the lack of information immediately after the occurrence of a disaster. The unavailability of site information prevents the provision of prompt and efficient initial response support.

13.3 Common Operational Picture and Systems Interoperability

Since many organizations must act simultaneously in parallel in disaster response initiatives, it is important to construct and share a common operational picture (COP) to grasp the disaster situation, share a common recognition of the overall situation, and for individual organizations to respond appropriately (Fig. 13.1).

However, given that many organizations have already constructed and are operating individual information systems, it is unrealistic to newly construct a separate extensive system that covers all aspects of disaster response. On the other hand, the conventional approach in which two organizations are individually connected

Fig. 13.1 Common operational picture

requires adjustment and development for each connection. It may be effective to have a uniform specification for all disaster prevention information systems or to have a standardized format for all information. However, each disaster prevention information system also has the important goal of offering necessary features and conveniences for their respective users, meaning that it is impractical to apply an identical specification for different systems.

Meanwhile, information exchange through an "interoperable system" may be effective. This involves standardizing only the interface of systems to exchange information between them. By standardizing the interface, which varies for each server, the information provided by separate IT communication systems can be shared by the systems. This scheme makes it possible to mutually circulate the information being handled between the diversified disaster prevention information systems. As a result, the systems are mutually connected to allow users to share a series of information on the network. Traditionally, information was provided by distributed and independent systems among institutions and organizations. Therefore, users could only use the information on a system constructed by the provider. On the other hand, interoperability requires a system that is jointly coordinated among institutions and organizations. Users can use the information provided by various systems by dynamically importing it into his or her own system. Thus, in the future, an environment in which everyone can use all information on their own system is required (Usuda 2008).

13.4 SIP4D: Shared Information Platform for Disaster Management

It was necessary to design a system that connects various information systems and acts as a "pipeline" for the movement of information between these systems. Therefore, we developed an information system that connects existing information systems and serves as the intermediary role of facilitating the flow of information between systems. The system is SIP4D (Fig. 13.2).

13.4.1 Concept of SIP4D

The concept of SIP4D is to mediate between systems and ensure interoperability. Interoperability can be ensured by standardizing the interfaces between systems, but even that is difficult in reality. Each system has its own separate interface.

In response, SIP4D will accept N types of disaster-related information sent out by various information systems and provide information by automatically converting

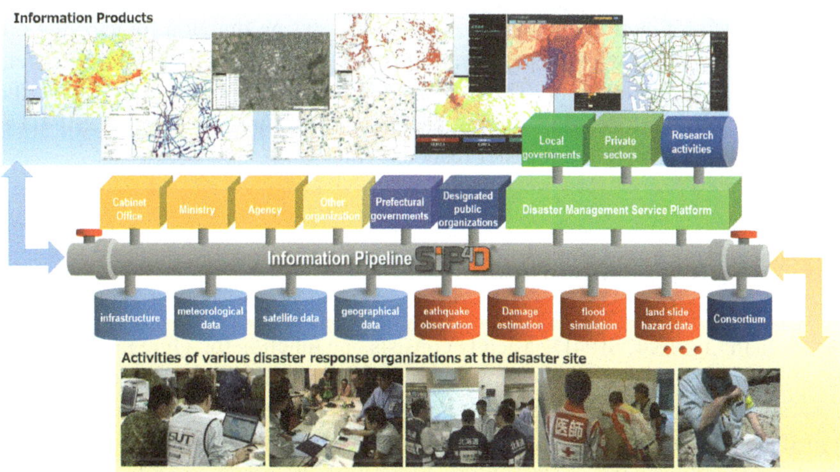

Fig. 13.2 Overview of SIP4D

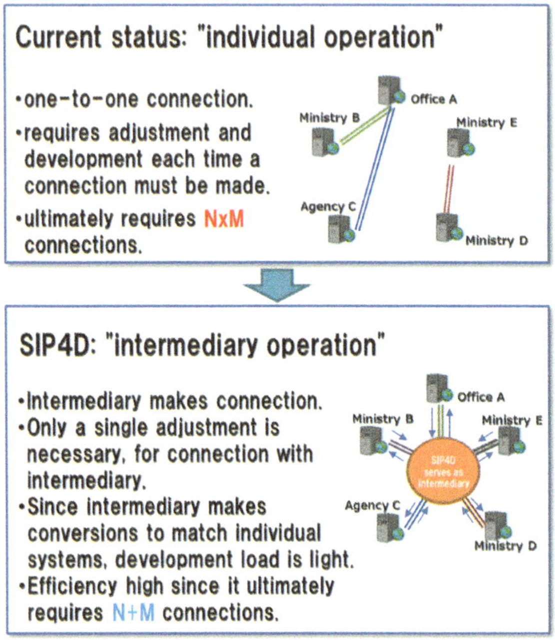

Fig. 13.3 Concept of the intermediary information-sharing system (Usuda et al. 2017a)

it into M types of formats that various information systems tend to use. This will increase the efficiency by changing the combination of information sharing from N x M to N + M. Through this, we aim to efficiently achieve information sharing by reducing the energy required for coordination related to the connection as well as reducing the development load. This requires an information aggregation function for accepting various formats of information and converting them properly, an information provision function, and an information processing function for carrying out integrated processing when necessary, which is why we have developed a system equipped with these functions. The more systems that are connected to SIP4D, the more valuable the information sharing becomes. Therefore, the target of SIP4D is all organizations involved in disaster response (Fig. 13.3).

13.4.2 System Configuration

As shown in Fig. 13.4, SIP4D basically consists of a function for aggregating various forms of information handled by various organizations and systems (data analysis and registration); a function for processing the aggregated information into forms that can immediately be incorporated into the tasks carried out by disaster responders/users (logical integration); and a function for converting the processed information into formats desired by the users (data conversion and distribution).

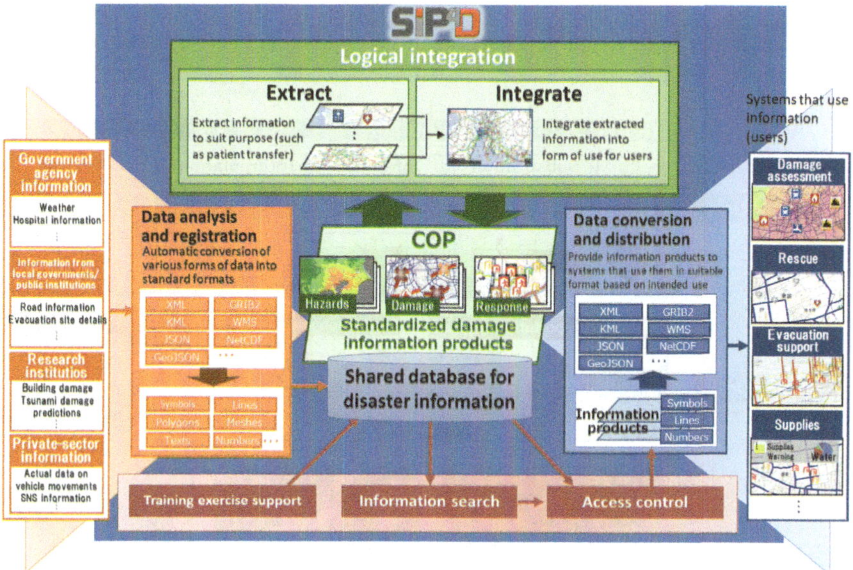

Fig. 13.4 Functional structure of SIP4D (Usuda et al. 2019)

Logical integration is the core technology of SIP4D. This is made possible by technology that integrates various types of disaster-related information coming in at various times, complements anything missing in the information, and processes this into information suitable for the tasks of the disaster responders (Usuda 2017b).

As shown in the example in Fig. 13.5, it integrates fragmentary information—such as road damage information, vehicle movement information, and hospital information—into information that can be utilized immediately for patient transportation, etc. This will then be combined with information on medical institutions and shelters that require patient transportation, as well as roads that can be used for patient transportation. When the information required has not been obtained at this point, the system is able to use any data that has been obtained and make estimations accordingly.

13.5 Challenges in Social Implementation

Technologies or systems that support the whole, such as SIP4D, do not have direct users. Because of this, it is often difficult to appreciate their effectiveness or role. Thus, we employed a strategy under which we would facilitate the momentum of social implementation of SIP4D by offering it in actual disaster response while it was still in its R&D stage and then evaluating its effectiveness and role in the social context.

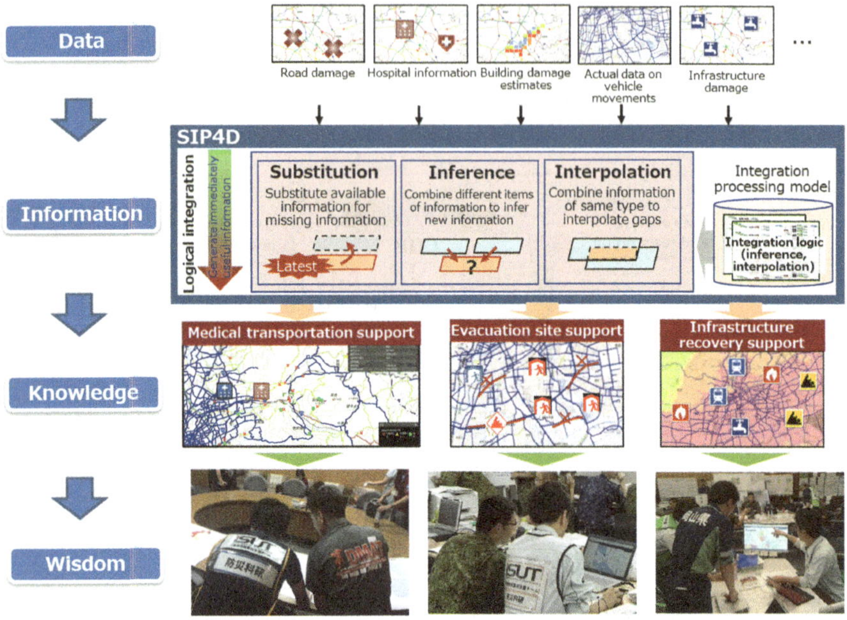

Fig. 13.5 DIKW-Flow and logical integration function of SIP4D

Starting with the September 2015 Kanto and Tohoku heavy rainfall, we have responded to a series of natural disasters that occurred every year. We have dispatched researchers and other personnel to disaster sites and supported information sharing between agencies working in disaster-struck areas. Through these efforts, we have evaluated and tested SIP4D, identified challenges, and used the latter as feedback in the development of the system.

13.5.1 Increased Overall Efficiency of Information Sharing

In April 2016, in response to the Kumamoto earthquake, in which two magnitude 7 shocks were recorded within a short-time frame, we arrived at the Kumamoto Prefectural Office the following day. SIP4D was still at an early prototype stage, but we decided to implement support for information sharing between disaster response agencies. Moreover, because SIP4D is only an information pipeline, there was no way to view or confirm the shared information. Therefore, we built a Web site "NIED-Crisis Response Site (CRS)" that allowed users to view various disaster information shared by SIP4D using a WebGIS application. Figure 13.6 shows the information-sharing flow during this event.

In the aftermath of the Kumamoto earthquake, data on the distribution of the estimated number of totally destroyed buildings (Fig. 13.7) released from the Real-

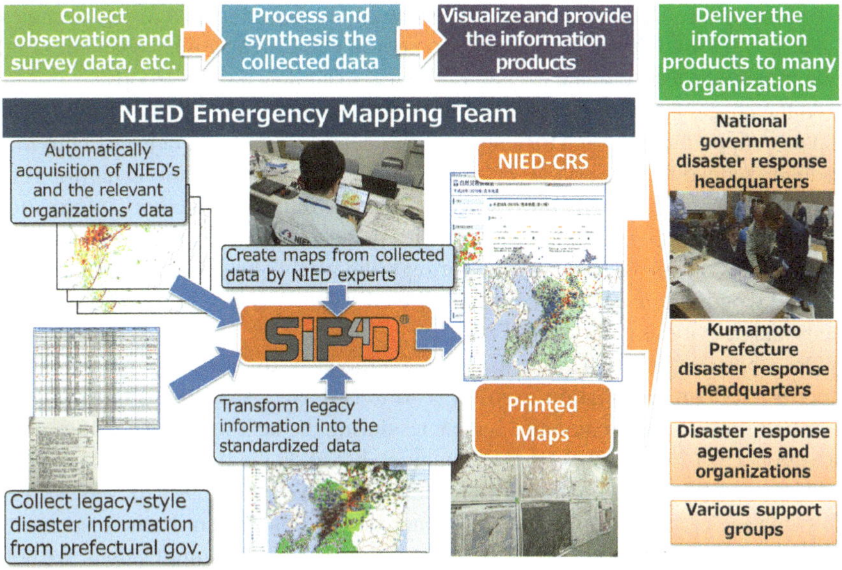

Fig. 13.6 Information-sharing flow after the Kumamoto earthquake

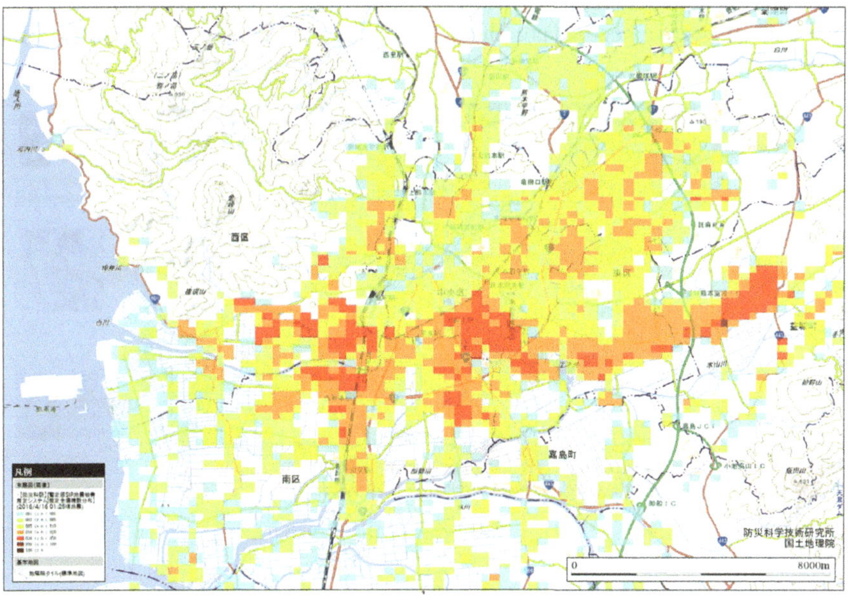

Fig. 13.7 Data on the distribution of the estimated number of totally destroyed buildings (Usuda et al. 2017a)

Time Earthquake Damage Estimation System were shared with relevant agencies. The data were used during the initial response, to make an overall assessment of the scale of damage and to make decisions about dispatching support troops.

At the onset of our support, the notion of a research institution providing disaster response support was foreign to many agencies. However, the significance of this idea gradually gained recognition as we continued to support information sharing. As a result, we were able to verify the overall efficiency through intermediary information sharing; data integration beyond space, time, and jurisdiction; and both the need and effectiveness of information sharing through the establishment and provision of a Specific Common Operational Picture (S-COP) that was directly linked with the needs and activities, as shown in Fig. 13.8.

One objective of SIP4D was to improve efficiency by reducing the number of patterns to obtain information from "$N \times M$ to $N + M$." As many as 631 pieces of information were shared among 11 agencies during the next four and a half months, through August 31. Using a simple calculation based on the figures $N = 631$ and $M = 11$, the combination of patterns was reduced from $N \times M = 6941$ to $N + M=641$. Although the efficiency did not actually increase by this amount in the response to the Kumamoto Earthquakes, as these figures represent the maximum values, we note it as a quantitative index.

To increase overall efficiency, we asked the national government Onsite Disaster Response Headquarters and the divisions of the Kumamoto prefectural government what their respective needs were, then compiled a single data set to cover data for

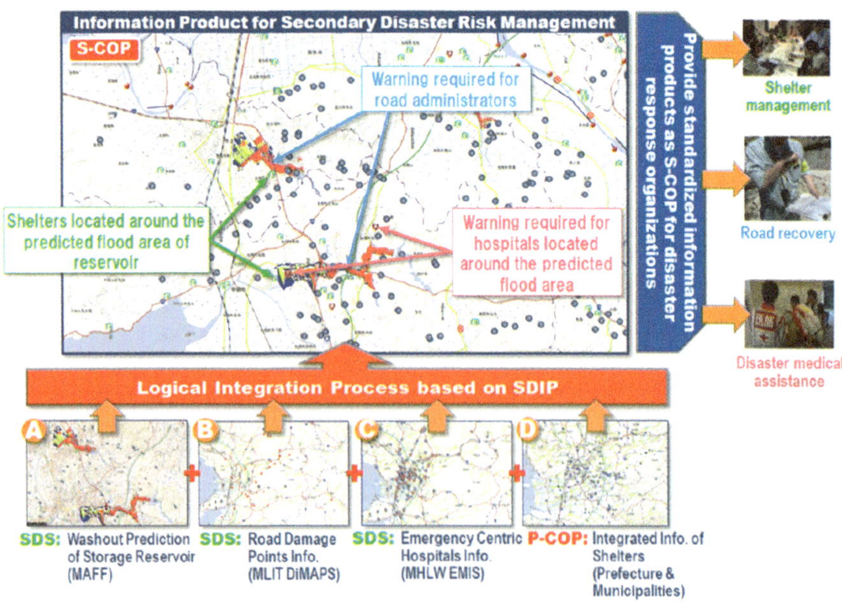

Fig. 13.8 Conceptual image of an information product as a service of S-COP (Hanashima et al. 2017)

Table 13.1 Map information required for each disaster response organization (Ise et al. 2017)

	Body	Utilization scene	Base thematic map	Main data	Display range	Media	Notes
1	Cabinet Office Government field headquarters	Quickly comprehends the damage scale and immediately sends the information to relevant bodies. Information used to comprehend the overall outline is necessary.	-Status of evacuation shelters	-Evacuation shelters	-Entire Kumamoto Prefecture -Kumamoto City -Mashiki Town -Around Aso City	-Sheet of paper A0 -Sheet of paper A3 and the like	-Continually updated
2	Cabinet Office Government field headquarters		-Status of evacuation shelters -Status of road damage	-Evacuation shelters -Road situation	-Entire Kumamoto Prefecture	-Sheet of paper A0	-Displays evacuation shelter status and road situation together for evacuation shelter support
3	MEXT Government field headquarters	Due to its role of taking care of school education, it analyzes and take measures to the effect of management of the evacuation shelter on school education. Detailed information on education facilities is necessary.	-Status of evacuation shelters	-Evacuation shelters (school facilities) -Evacuation shelters (Facilities other than schools) -Spreadsheet of number of evacuees -Transition table of evacuees in Mashiki Town	-Entire Kumamoto Prefecture	-Paper *	-Classifies evacuation shelters into school facilities and facilities other than schools when written -Adds a spreadsheet
4	Kumamoto Pref. Command team	Comprehends the whole picture of damage situation and response situation and make a decision on the overall policy of disaster response. Information used to comprehend the overall outline is necessary.	-Status of road damage	-Road situation	-Entire Kumamoto Prefecture	-Sheet of paper A0	-Continually updated
5	Kumamoto Pref. Command team		-Damage situation	-Evacuation shelters -Road situation -Other damage situations	Entire Kumamoto Prefecture	-Sheet of paper A1	-Continually updated together with the following hazard map
6	Kumamoto Pref. Command team		-Hazard Map	-Sediment disaster emergency inspection result -Sediment disaster dangerous places	-Entire Kumamoto Prefecture	-Sheet of paper A1	-Continually updated together with the above damage situation map -Hazard Map is a reprint of one created before the disaster occurred
7	Kumamoto Pref. Information team	Pieces of information gathered at each team of the disaster management headquarters, the prefectural office are managed in an integral manner. It is necessary to exhaustively organize the information.	-Hypocenter, seismic intensity-distribution (Active fault)	-Active fault diagram	-Entire Kumamoto Prefecture	-Paper *	-Creates a map of static information
8	Kumamoto Pref. Information team		-Status of evacuation shelters -Status of road damage	-Evacuation shelters -Road situation	-Mashiki Town -Minamiaso Village	-Sheet of paper A0	-Similar demand to that of the Cabinet Office but the display range is different
9	DMAT	Conducts medical support activities in affected areas. Information for the headquarters to comprehend the overall outline and information for each team to carry out activities in the field are necessary.	-Medical Relief Situation -Status of road damage	-Health department -Spreadsheet of the number of aid team sent	-Entire Kumamoto Prefecture	-Paper *	-Adds a spreadsheet -Medical Relief Situation was created on the basis of the data of the Health department
10	DMAT		-Status of evacuation shelters -Status of road damage	-Evacuation shelters -Road situation diagram	-Entire Kumamoto Prefecture	-Sheet of paper A0	-Similar demand to that of the Cabinet Office
11	DMAT		-Status of evacuation sheltersNumber of examinees	-The number of evacuees in the Mashiki Town -The number of those received consultation in the Mashiki Town -Bus stop	-Mashiki Town	-Paper *	-Map used for consideration of a replacement bus for the evacuees in the Mashiki Town to go to the hospital -Creates a new map for the number of those received consultation
12	DMAT		-Status of evacuation shelters -Long-Term Care Health Facilities	-Evacuation shelters -Senior care health facilities -Medical institutes	-Around Aso	-Sheet of paper A3	-Creates a new map for Long-Term Care Health Facilities

* For description of only "Paper", there is no record about the size of the sheet of paper.

which there was high across-the-board demand. We printed multiple copies of these data sets and delivered them to the parties requiring them (Table 13.1).

For example, it was found later that the information on evacuation centers was compiled not only by the local governments, which are charged with this task, but also individually by the Self Defense Force, Japan Disaster Medical Assistance Team (DMAT), communication infrastructure companies, nonprofit organizations (NPOs), and volunteer groups, all of whom required this information for their activities. When we presented the unified data set to these organizations, we received feedback that; "it would have been more efficient if we had known this." As the information was effectively used, the validity of information sharing was confirmed.

Furthermore, when we conducted an interview survey of the Kumamoto prefectural government Road Maintenance Division, we were told that they received numerous phone inquiries about road information following the earthquake. The frequency of these inquiries remained high for about a month following the earthquake disaster and often included inquiries about how to reach evacuation centers. Since the Road Maintenance Division did not have information on hand about evacuation centers, they used the information on evacuation centers provided on NIED-CRS to check the locations and any landmarks or signs in the vicinity. As demonstrated here, the organization that possesses the original data receives many inquiries. Therefore, if the information-sharing system is clearly recognized by all parties and if it becomes well known that data can be obtained from this system, it will be possible to increase overall efficiency and reduce the number of inquiries to the data-holding organization, lightening the load on the personnel in charge.

13.5.2 Homogenous Integration Processing

Homogenous integration processing is a matter of integrating and complementing homogenous information collected from multiple information sources and consolidating it into one piece of information. In the event of a disaster, the common situation map showing road conditions can be created by integrating information held by various organizations, such as information on expressways and national roads managed by the national agency, and information on auxiliary national roads and prefectural roads managed by local governments.

From June 28 to July 8, 2018, in a wide area nationwide, damage was caused by factors including concentrated heavy rain associated with typhoon No. 7, and the rainy season front. In particular, concentrated heavy rain from July 6 caused heavy damage in western Japan. SIP4D applied disaster information integration processing to the data collected continuously from various sources. For example, the road information individually collected from and updated by the Regional Development Bureaus of the MLIT and each prefecture were aggregated by homogenous integration processing to provide the road situation as shown in Fig. 13.9.

On September 8, 2019, Typhoon No. 15 hit the Boso Peninsula. This typhoon caused a lot of damage due to fallen trees, which hindered the restoration of power. Even though the power and communication companies tried to restore the area, the roads were blocked by fallen trees, and it was difficult to determine the extent of the

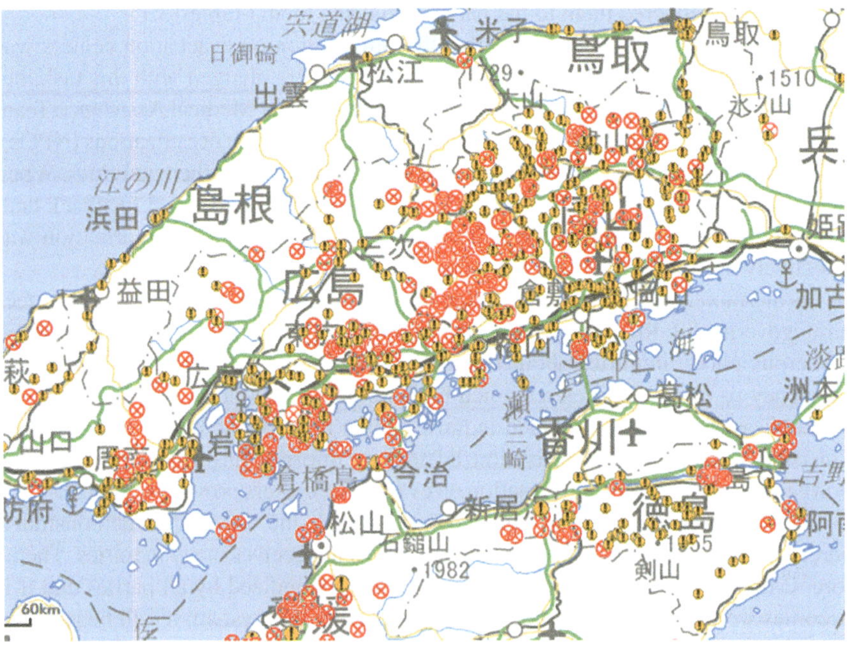

Fig. 13.9 Integrated road situation data

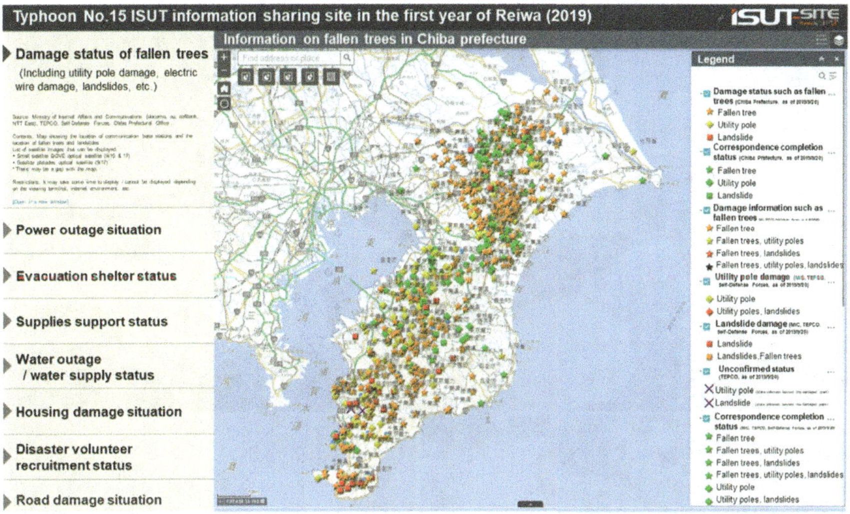

Fig. 13.10 Example of a map supporting collaboration between multiple agencies

damage, let alone the restoration work, for a long time. The Cabinet Office, prefectures, the Self-Defense Forces, the Ministry of Internal Affairs and Communications, the utility companies, and the telecommunications companies all came together to unify their awareness of the situation by using the common form we presented and having each organization input the location of the fallen tree and map it. The maps were shared and used to check the progress of activities and prioritize the removal of fallen trees (Fig. 13.10).

13.5.3 Rules and Teams

Our experience revealed that it was very important that not only was the system (tool) developed but also various frameworks were formed to facilitate information sharing during a disaster, such as rules and teams.

Therefore, a national, local, and private sector 'Disaster Information Hub' establishment team was formed in 2017 by the Cabinet Office to discuss the rules for sharing information during disasters. The Information Support Team (ISUT), a public–private team led by the Cabinet Office to compile and share disaster-related information, was trialed in 2018. ISUT was officially put into operation in fiscal 2019 and was specified in the Basic Disaster Management Plan in May. At disaster sites, as Fig. 13.11 shows, agencies reported and confirmed status and made decisions in meetings attended by multiple agencies while they viewed information provided by SIP4D.

Fig. 13.11 Activities to support information sharing

The experiences mentioned above in actual disaster responses showed that it is important to integrate SIP4D, the rules, and the team to facilitate interagency information sharing during a disaster. Instead of one organization providing all three components, the components should be developed collaboratively by society as a whole, and implemented in society. This is essential if we are to respond effectively to anticipated disasters.

13.6 Example of Decision Support

One of the important roles of information sharing is to facilitate collaboration across organizational boundaries. Heterogeneous integration processing generates information that can be used for operations by combining and integrating heterogeneous pieces of information, including the information generated by the homogenous integration processing already described. For instance, information on roads, hospitals, and shelters can be integrated to provide information that can be used promptly by medical facilities and DMAT for patient transportation.

An example of decision support in a real disaster is presented here: on June 18, 2018, an earthquake struck in northern Osaka Prefecture. The earthquake caused widespread building damage and disrupted the city's gas supply. Therefore, the Self-Defense Forces (SDF) decided to provide water and bathing support. However, since the population is very large, it was necessary to make decisions on how to provide efficient and effective support.

Therefore, ISUT created a map that superimposed two sets of data shared in SIP4D. One was the recovery status data of the gas network released by the private sector, and one was the distribution of shelters released by Osaka prefecture.

The status of gas service restoration and the distribution of evacuation sites are mere "information." But by melding them together, we can use them to surmise that where there are many evacuees with no gas supply, there must be many people who need a bath. As a result, the Self-Defense Forces were able to make the decision to provide bathing support at the site in order to maximize the effectiveness of their support.

Figure 13.12 is the map showing the results of the decision-making. Colored polygons represent information on the gas network restoration area, blue circles represent the distribution of shelters, and green marks represent the locations of the SDF's water supply and bathing support. In this way, SIP4D has created a model that integrates information provided by multiple organizations to help another organization make decisions.

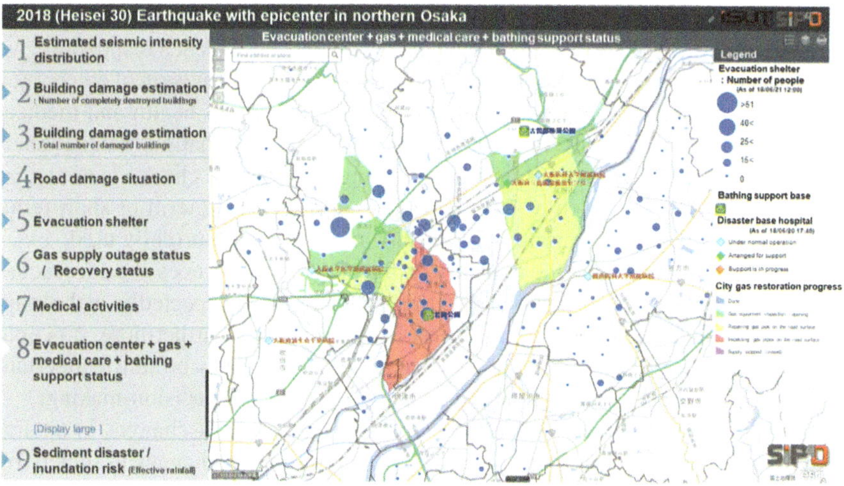

Fig. 13.12 Example of integrating private, government, and field agency information

13.7 CPS4D: Cyber-Physical System for Disaster Resilience

In order to enhance disaster response actions and activities, it is necessary to implement research and develop that goes one step ahead further than merely standardizing situational awareness. In terms of a future direction, it is crucial to create information regarding the next course of action, based on various real-time data.

Under the 5th Science and Technology Basic Plan (formulated by Japan's Ministry of Education, Culture, Sports, Science and Technology), "Super-smart society (Society 5.0)" is indicated as the ideal future society that Japan should aim for. What makes this possible is "CPS: Cyber-Physical System", which unites real space and virtual space at an advanced level. We want to lead this aim in the field of disaster prevention research. Our goal is to generate technological innovation by evolving "SIP4D," which shares information that necessary for disaster response, into "CPS4D: CPS for Disaster Resilience," which leads disaster response with information.

The circumstances of natural disasters change every moment. Similarly, natural disasters (hazard—earthquake, torrential rain, etc.) are phenomena that occur at the intersection of nature and society (people, city environment, economics, etc.). However, unlike the former, there is no observation network to accurately grasp the latter. Furthermore, a lot of the information used for disaster response is static information that cuts off at a certain point and is thus not effective for representing the changing circumstances.

For example, maps that indicate the distribution of shelters and the number of evacuees are often used during the period of disaster response. When responding, we need dynamic information to make better support such as the provision of emergency supplies in the appropriate amount and dispatching experts of health and medical welfare to the disaster areas. For example, the dynamic information includes shelters where evacuees are increasing and decreasing, whether the change is occurring rapidly or slowly, and which of those changes will go on long term or short term. However, this dynamic information is not shown on the maps currently used.

If there is a way to gauge the transition in the number of evacuees at each evacuation site, we can alert the evacuation sites that are changing unexpectedly on the map. This is also conducive to efficient decision-making support. Furthermore, if people utilize their respective mobile phones and smartphones, they may be able to ascertain the transition more accurately in real time and promote quick decision-making.

Thereupon, in addition to the observation and prediction of changes in natural phenomena, we will develop technologies for identifying the changes in society by using various information and communications technologies. In doing so, we will build a system to handle "disaster dynamics" that combines these technologies for grasping changes in both nature and society. We also aim to create technology to support decision-making (Fig. 13.13).

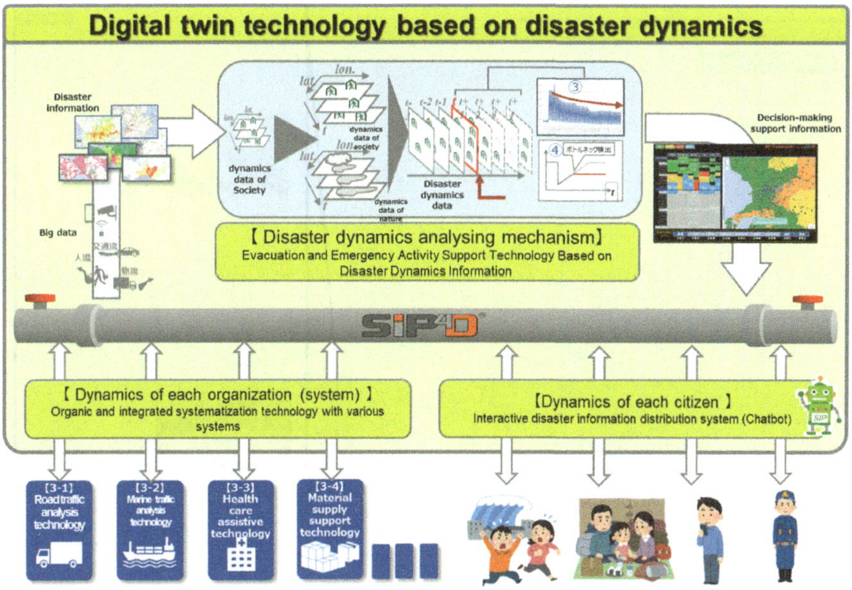

Fig. 13.13 Overview of CPS4D

As an important component of CPS4D, SOCDA (a social-dynamics observation and victims support dialogue agent platform for disaster management) is being developed as a technology to support individual decision-making as well as to understand social changes.

Nowadays, social media (SNS) is an indispensable tool for exchanging information among individuals. With the spread of smartphones and other devices, the number of people using social networking services has been increasing year by year. There is a lot of research on the use of SNS in the event of a disaster in Japan and abroad. If each person has a mobile phone or a smartphone, it will be possible to grasp the transition in real time and more accurately, and to deliver information directly to the person according to his or her situation, thereby increasing the speed of decision-making.

For example, by automatically classifying the large amount of information posted on SNS during a disaster using natural language processing AI, it will be possible to understand the big picture of the disaster situation and the needs of the victims (Fig. 13.14).

These technologies have been transferred to the private sector for social implementation and have also been useful for analysis in actual disasters (Cui et al. 2019).

Therefore, we decided to further develop a technology to observe social dynamics at the time of a disaster and to transmit information conducive to the evacuation of

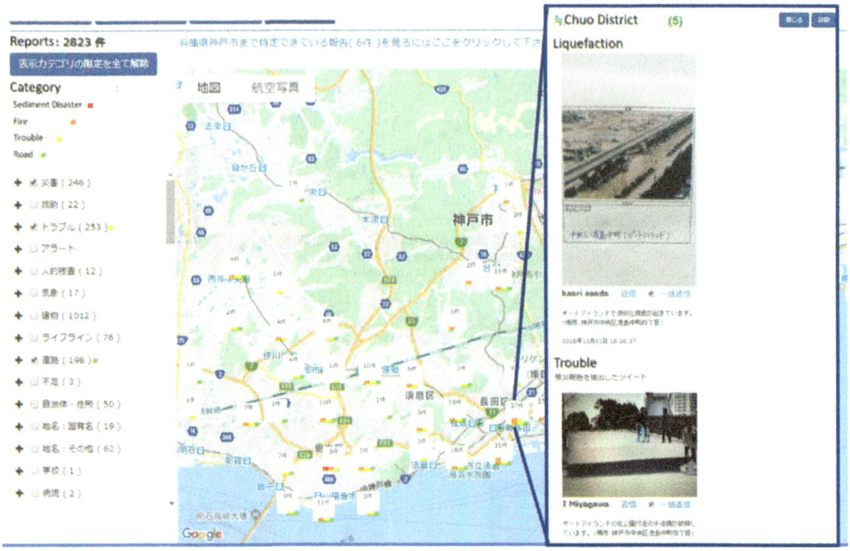

Fig. 13.14 Automatic classification of SNS post information by AI

individuals through a system that interacts with individuals in an autonomous manner, as well as by aggregating information transmitted in one direction such as Twitter.

Specifically, the system extracts a large number of individual situations and specific requests from the dialogue history with the system, generates social dynamic information, and realizes the technology to autonomously and cooperatively select, recommend, and communicate information that contributes to evacuation (Fig. 13.15).

13.8 Conclusion

In this chapter, I introduced SIP4D and CPS4D, which enable information sharing and decision support at the time of disaster, as well as the inherent challenges of implementing these in society. In the future, it will be necessary to incorporate more new technologies and implement them in stages as "social infrastructure" for full-scale operation. It is hoped that the number of organizations and systems working toward such initiatives will increase and contribute to improving the disaster prevention and response capabilities of society as a whole. It is also necessary to make SIP4D more technologically advanced and to link it with other fields (agriculture,

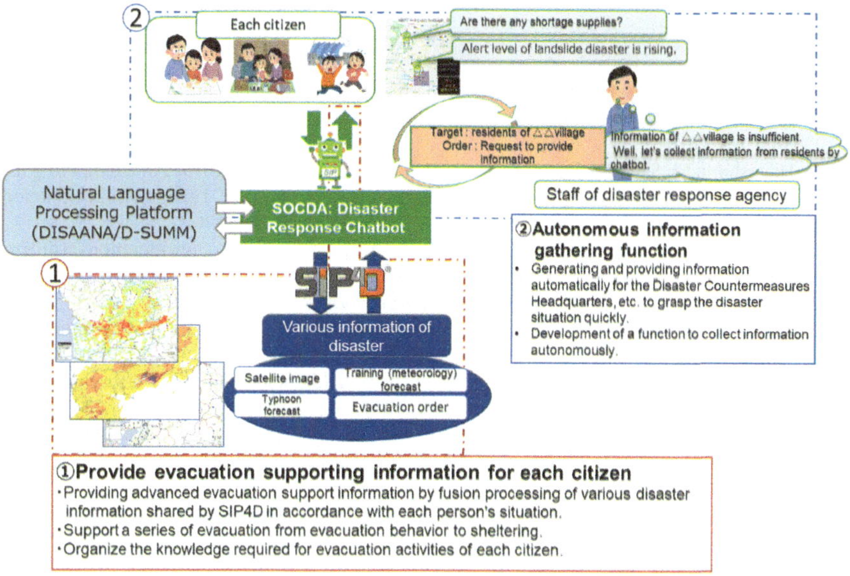

Fig. 13.15 Overview of SOCDA

satellites, national infrastructure, etc.). Furthermore, in order to maximize the effectiveness of information sharing, it is essential to have a mechanism of coordination, technology, and procedures in place, as well as continuous training and practice.

The standard approach to research and development is to separate it from the real world and apply it to the real world only after the results have been obtained. However, social change is so rapid that the methods used in the past are no longer viable. Even in the research and development phase, it is effective to introduce the technology to the field in the event of a disaster and receive feedback to continue the research and development. In order to achieve a disaster-resilient society, it is crucial to build a close and collaborative relationship between research and development and the real world.

References

Hanashima M, Sato R, Usuda Y (2017) The standardized disaster-information products for disaster management: concept and formulation. J Disaster Res 12(5):1015–1027. https://doi.org/10.20965/jdr.2017.p1015

Cui Q, Hanashima M, Sano H, Ikeda M, Handa N, Taguchi H, Usuda Y (2019) An attempt to grasp the disaster situation of "The 2018 Hokkaido Eastern Iburi earthquake" Using SNS information. J Disaster Res 14(9):1170–1184. https://doi.org/10.20965/jdr.2019.p1170

Ise T, Takahashi T, Sato R, Sano H, Isono T, Hanashima M, Usuda Y (2017) Consideration on utilization of information in disaster response site–based on information support for 2016 Kumamoto earthquakes–. J Disaster Res 12(5):1028–1038. https://doi.org/10.20965/jdr.2017.p1028

Usuda Y (2008) Interoperability of information and communication system for disaster prevention and mitigation. Sci Technol Trends Q Rev 28:88–102

Usuda Y, Hanashima M, Sato R, Sano H (2017a) Effects and issues of information sharing system for disaster response. J Disaster Res 12(5):1002–1014. https://doi.org/10.20965/jdr.2017.p1002

Usuda Y, Tanimoto K, Ono I, Matsui T (2017b) Enhancements to resilient functions for preventing and minimizing disasters development of sharing information platform for disaster management. Hitachi Rev 66(7):108–114

Usuda Y, Matsui T, Deguchi H, Hori T, Suzuki S (2019) The shared information platform for disaster management–the research and development regarding technologies for utilization of disaster information–. J Disaster Res 14(2):279–291. https://doi.org/10.20965/jdr.2019.p0279

The manufacturer's authorised representative in the EU is Springer Nature Customer Service Centre GmbH, Europaplatz 3, 69115 Heidelberg, Germany. If you have any concerns regarding our products, please contact ProductSafety@springernature.com

Printed and bound by CPI Group (UK) Ltd, Croydon, CR0 4YY
30/09/2026
02225254-0012